Norfolk Record Society
Volume LXXXVI for 2022

Thomas Rowlandson, 'Doctor Syntax: Rural Sports', c. *1812*

The Literary Papers of the Reverend Jermyn Pratt 1723–1791

Edited by

Ema Vyroubalová and James Robert Wood

General Editor
Anthony Howe

Norfolk Record Society
Volume LXXXVI
2022

This project was supported by funding from the Norfolk and Norwich Archaeological Society

First published in 2022
by the Norfolk Record Society

ISBN 978-0-9957736-5-3

Typeset by Carnegie Book Production, Lancaster
Printed and bound by Short Run Press, Exeter

Contents

Illustrations

Acknowledgements

The editors would like to thank Sarah Pratt and Barbara Church for generously allowing us to undertake fieldwork at Ryston Hall and at Watlington Church respectively. The Norfolk and Norwich Archaeological Society supported the publication of this book with a research grant and the University of East Anglia granted us a publications award which allowed us to include the images in this book. We are grateful to Canon William Burke for inviting us to read Jermyn Pratt's poetry to his congregation and to Kate Moorhead-Kuhn for inviting us to read a selection from *The Zgubbs* at UEA's 'Literature Live' series at Dragon Hall. We thank Richard St Peter for organizing the Zoom premier of *The Grange* and all the actors for their enthusiastic performances. Members on the Eighteenth-Century Questions Facebook page and the wider eighteenth-century studies community were extraordinarily helpful in solving puzzles that had us stumped. We would like to thank Emily Friedman, Rebecca Haidt, Amanda Louise Johnson, David Mazella, Richard Nash, Daniel O'Quinn, Jenny Davidson, and David Goldstein especially for their help on specific points. We give special thanks to Daniel Cook, Andrew Hopper, and Min Wild for their support of this project. We are grateful to the staff at the Norfolk Record Office, Cambridge University Libraries, and the British Library for their help locating documents and answering queries. Anthony Howe has steered this project over its long gestation and provided detailed comments on draft after draft, and checked our transcription. We give special thanks to him for his assistance and patience over the course of this long project. We are very grateful for Rachel Clarke's careful typesetting of a very complicated manuscript and her help on many technical matters. Ema thanks her colleagues in the School of English at Trinity College Dublin and James thanks his colleagues in the School of Literature, Drama, and Creative Writing and the Faculty of Arts and Humanities at the University of East Anglia for their support. Both editors thank their (uncropped) cats Grimalkin and Tikka for their companionship. Any errors are the responsibility of the editors alone.

Abbreviations

AC	*Alumni Cantabrigienses: A Biographical List of All Known Students, Graduates, and Holders of Office at the University of Cambridge, From the Earliest Times to 1900*, ed. John Venn and J. A. Venn, 4 vols. Cambridge: Cambridge University Press, 1924
BCP	Book of Common Prayer, ed. Brian Cummings. Oxford: Oxford University Press, 2013
BEKE	*Biographical List of Boys Educated at King Edward VI. Free Grammar School, Bury St Edmunds: From 1550 to 1900*, ed. Sydenham Henry Augustus Hervey. Bury St Edmunds, Paul & Mathew, 1908
BGC	*Biographical History of Gonville and Caius College, 1349–1897*, ed. John Venn, 2 vols. Cambridge: Cambridge University Press, 1898 (references are by volume and page number)
BLPC	British Library Public Catalogue
CDB	*Clergy of the Church of England Database*
Contest	*The Contest. Or, A Collection of the Most Material Papers in Prose and Verse, Published During the Controverted Election in the County of Norfolk in 1768*. London, 1768
CUL	Cambridge University Library Rare Books and Archives
DLCL	*Digital Loeb Classical Library* (for the Latin originals given by book/epistle/canto, etc. numbers, followed by line/paragraph numbers and for the English translations by page numbers in parentheses)
DOP	George Latimer Apperson, S. J. Curtis, and M. H. Manser, *Dictionary of Proverbs*. London: Wordsworth Editions, 2006
ECCO	*Eighteenth-Century Collections Online*
EEBO	*Early English Books Online*
Gard	*Memoirs of the Life and Writings of R-ch--d G-rd-nr, Esq.* London and Norwich: G. Kearsley and M. Booth, 1782

HT	*HathiTrust Digital Library*
IA	*Internet Archive*
Milton	John Milton, *Paradise Lost,* ed. Alastair Fowler. London: Taylor & Francis, 2011 (references are to book and line number)
NACC	National Archives Currency Converter
NRO	Norfolk Record Office, Norwich
OED	*Oxford English Dictionary Online*
Oxford DCC	*Oxford Dictionary of the Christian Church*
Oxford DNB	*Oxford Dictionary of National Biography* Online
Oxford KJB	*Oxford King James Bible*
Pope	Alexander Pope, *The Poems of Alexander Pope: A Reduced Version of the Twickenham Text*, ed. John Butt. New Haven: Yale University Press, 1966 (references are to line numbers)
Shak	William Shakespeare, *Complete Works*, ed. Jonathan Bate and Eric Rasmussen. Basingstoke: Macmillan, 2007 (references are in the format act.scene.line)
Smart	Christopher Smart, *The Poetical Works of Christopher Smart*, ed. Katrina Williamson et al., 6 vols. Oxford: Oxford University Press, 1980–96 (references are to volume, page and/or line number as indicated)
Spec	Joseph Addison and Richard Steele, *The Spectator*, ed. Donald F. Bond, 6 vols. Oxford: Oxford University Press, 1965 (references are to volume and page number)
Sterne	Laurence Sterne, *Tristram Shandy*, ed. Melvyn New et al., *Florida Edition of the Works of Laurence Sterne,* 9 vols. Gainesville: University Press of Florida, 1978–2014 (references are to volume and page number)
TCDL	Trinity College Dublin Library
UA	University of Aberdeen Library Catalogue
UCL	University College London Library Catalogue
UM	University of Manchester Library Catalogue
VEA	Robert Forby, *The Vocabulary of East Anglia*, 2 vols. London: J. B. Nichols and Son, 1830 (references are to volume and page number)
Woodforde	James Woodforde, *The Diary of a Country Parson*, ed. J. Beresford, 5 vols. Oxford: Clarendon Press, 1924–31 (references are to volume and page number)

A Note on Dates

Dates before 2 September 1752 are Old Style, except that the year is taken to begin on the 1st of January, not the 25th of March.

Jermyn Pratt's Family Tree

(Note that this tree is designed to show relationships between people mentioned in this edition and is not complete.)

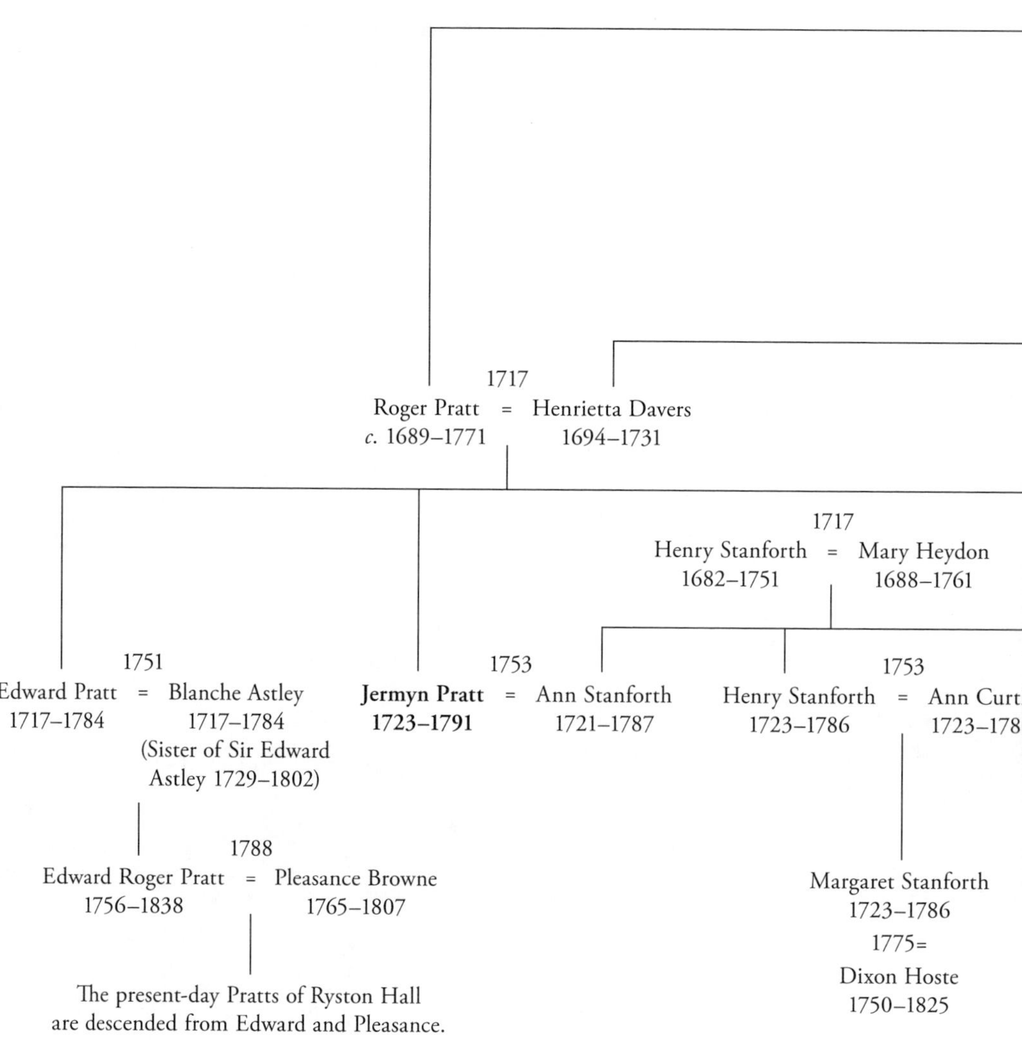

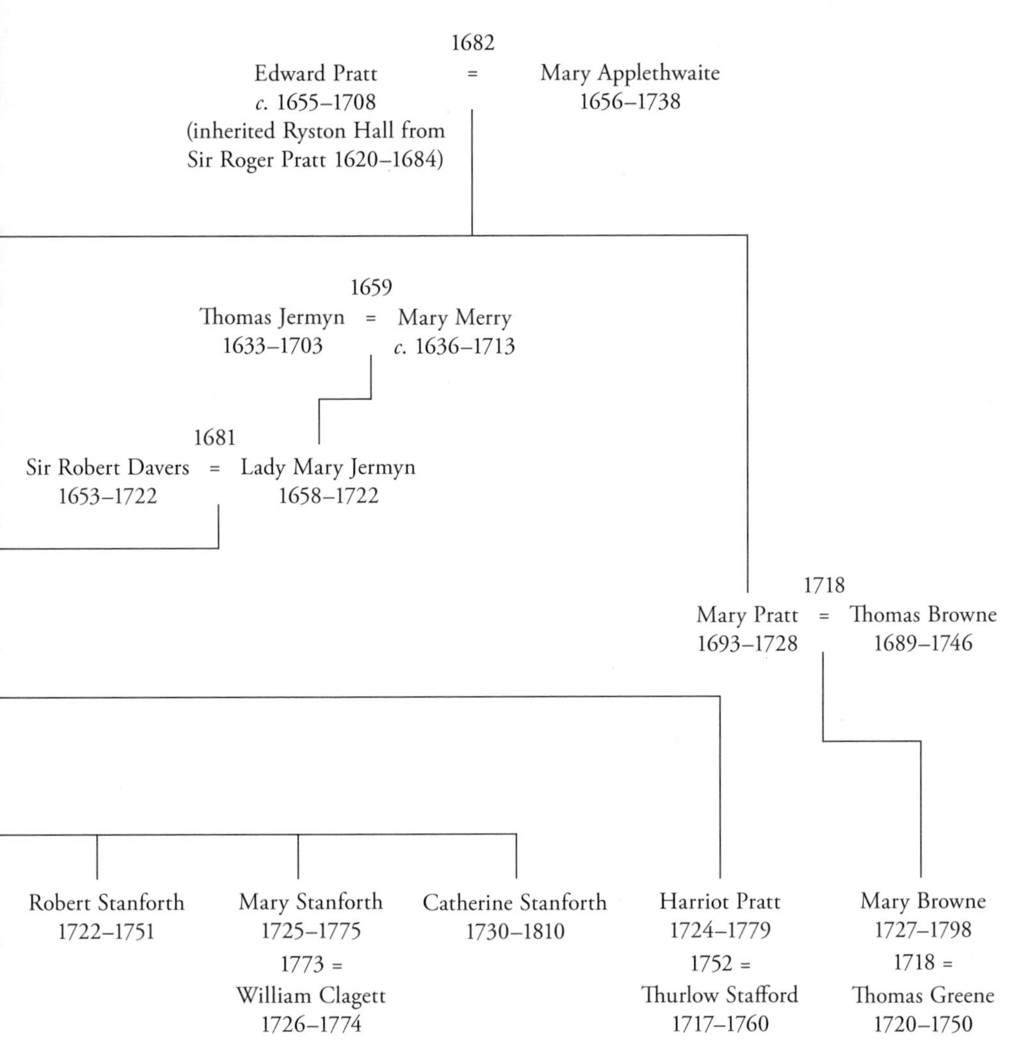
1682
Edward Pratt
c. 1655–1708
(inherited Ryston Hall from
Sir Roger Pratt 1620–1684)
=
Mary Applethwaite
1656–1738
1659
Thomas Jermyn
1633–1703
=
Mary Merry
c. 1636–1713
1681
Sir Robert Davers
1653–1722
=
Lady Mary Jermyn
1658–1722
1718
Mary Pratt
1693–1728
=
Thomas Browne
1689–1746
Robert Stanforth
1722–1751
Mary Stanforth
1725–1775
1773 =
William Clagett
1726–1774
Catherine Stanforth
1730–1810
Harriot Pratt
1724–1779
1752 =
Thurlow Stafford
1717–1760
Mary Browne
1727–1798
1718 =
Thomas Greene
1720–1750

Introduction

If Jermyn Pratt's name is mentioned at all, it is likely because of his association with Christopher Smart, the poet and miscellanist, who is now most famous for his fragmentary religious poem *Jubilate Agno*, written between 1759 and 1763 while Smart was incarcerated in London madhouses, and first printed only in 1939. Smart's lines on his cat from this poem are often excerpted under the title 'My Cat Jeoffry'. After Pratt and Smart befriended each other as students at Cambridge in the early 1740s, Smart became besotted with Harriot Pratt, Pratt's younger sister, and made her the subject of many of his early poems.[1] Years later, after both he and Harriot had married other people,[2] Smart remembered Harriot and Jermyn Pratt in *Jubilate Agno*. The Pratt siblings appear in the section of the poem in which Smart ties letters of the alphabet to words beginning with the same letter, many of which he then in turn associates with people he knows: the line in question reads, '*For T is truth. God be gracious to Jermyn Pratt and to Harriote his Sister.*'[3] Smart also included a tribute to the Pratts and their family seat at Ryston Hall in another part of *Jubilate Agno* that links Smart's acquaintances and their families with plants. Smart chose to give the Pratts the honour of associating them with a diuretic herb, writing 'Let Ruston, house of Ruston rejoice with Fulviana Herba, ab inventore, good to provoke urine. Lord have mercy upon

1 See, for example, 'On Seeing Miss H——— P——T, in an Apothecary's Shop' (*Smart*, vol. 4, pp. 108–9), and the prologue as originally published in the *Gentleman's Magazine* to his lost play *The Grateful Fair, or, A Trip to Cambridge* in 1747 (*Smart*, vol. 4, p. 128), 'Lovely Harriote, A Crambo Song' (*Smart*, vol. 4, pp. 181–2), first published in 1751. Even after they had both married other people, Smart continued to publish poems about Harriot. See, for example, 'Ode to Lady Harriot' (*Smart*, vol. 4, p. 184), first published in 1755.

2 Harriot married Thurlow Stafford on 18 September 1752. See 'Marriage licence bond: Thurlow Stafford and Henrietta Pratt', NRO, ANF 12/15/145. Smart married Anna Maria Carnan around the same time although the exact date is unknown. On Smart's marriage see Chris Mounsey, *Christopher Smart: Clown of God* (Lewisburg: Bucknell University Press, 2001), p. 162.

3 *Smart*, vol. 1, p. 77; Fragment B, l. 531.

Roger Pratt and his family.'[4] Apart from his association with Christopher Smart, Jermyn Pratt is now known only as one of the many clergymen from gentry backgrounds who ministered to the country parishes of eighteenth-century England—and certainly not as an imaginative and idiosyncratic writer in his own right.

In this volume we present an edition of Jermyn Pratt's literary papers, most of which have only been available to read in manuscript until now. Most of the writings that we have assembled in this volume are contained in a single large pasteboard folder in the Norfolk Record Office in Norwich, with the main exceptions of Pratt's letter to William Windham, Senior, enclosing his poem 'Grunnelia or the Sow in the Dumps', and the printed poem *The Inundation or the Life of a Fen-Man* (1771), which we think is very likely by Pratt. The folder had been stored at Ryston Hall until 1965, when it was handed in to the Norfolk Record Office for preservation. Its main purpose seems to have been to act as a cache of Pratt's writings. The unpublished manuscripts in the folder include a play entitled *The Grange* (*c.* 1774), a mock-serious disquisition on invisible and imaginary beings entitled *The Zgubbs* (*c.* 1782), an essay in defence of the Norfolk clergy, satirical and comic poems on various subjects, a collection of prayers, and a catalogue of books in Pratt's library at the time of his death. Together with the manuscript material, the folder includes unbound prints of the anonymously published poems *September: A Rural Poem* (1780), *The Coal-Heavers* (1774), and *Cinderetta* (1768), all of which we believe to be by Pratt.[5] There are also clippings of poems from the local newspapers, including newspaper versions of several poems that also exist in manuscript versions in the folder. Although most of the writings included in the folder are by Pratt, there are several printed and manuscript texts by other authors that have been slipped into the folder as well.[6]

---

4 *Smart*, vol. 1, p. 118; Fragment D, l. 105. Smart took this plant, and many others, from *Natural History*, by Pliny the Elder, who claims 'Et herba Fulviana trita ex vino, et haec nomen inventoris habet, nota tractantibus.' *DLCL*: Pliny, *Natural History*, 26:88 (p. 331) 'The plant of Fulvius, beaten up with wine, is another remedy for stone. It is one of the plants named after the discoverer, and is well known to botanists.'

5 See the headnotes for these texts in this edition for an explanation of authorship.

6 Among these other items are a short piece of epistolary fiction in an unknown hand which a country boy named 'Roger Carter' writes back to his father 'Jonas Carter at Bridgeway' detailing his and his sister's first visit to London. This fictional letter is contained in the manuscripts catalogued as NRO PRA 664/12 and 644/13. At the back of this fictional letter is what appears to be an undated but real letter in a different hand by Jane Blomfield to 'My Dear Kemp', who calls the fictional letter 'a very droll Letter' and makes plans to meet Kemp at the next assembly. (The annotation 'I think it is very natural'

Pratt's writings illuminate a distinctive culture of writing in eighteenth-century Norfolk. The poems *The Inundation or the Life of a Fen-Man* and *September: A Rural Poem* are explicitly located in the Norfolk landscape of fens and hunting grounds. *Cinderetta* is a satire written against one of the candidates for the Norfolk election of 1768 and *The Coal-Heavers* is inspired by an actual riot that took place in King's Lynn in 1773. Pratt's play *The Grange* is set in the Norfolk countryside and incorporates elements of the East Anglian dialect, with words like 'Dodman' (a snail), 'Summertil' (a term applied to a field left fallow over the summer), and 'Tettarvetch' (a plant used for curing pimples) all appearing within a single scene [*f. 9r–f. 9v*].[7] Pratt's interest in the distinctive patterns of local speech is also demonstrated in his promise in the letter inclosing 'Grunnelia or the Sow in the Dumps' to send William Windham, Senior, 'some choice, & familiar words in the Norfolk phraseology' [*f. 1v*]. This letter also attests to a continuing tradition of manuscript circulation in provincial East Anglia, in which poems, plays, and essays circulated within coteries of readers without the mediation of printers and booksellers. In the letter to Windham, Pratt mentions having already sent the poem to the man of letters and MP Soame Jenyns, who 'was pleased to like it' [*f. 1v*].[8] The folder also demonstrates the mutual reciprocity and influence between print and manuscript cultures at the time. The neatness with which most of Pratt's handwritten texts are presented, for example, mimics the orderly appearance of print on the page. Several of the poems in manuscript,

---

appears at the end of the fictional letter in the same hand followed by the initials 'J. B.') Unfortunately, we have not been able to identify this Jane Blomfield. There is also a letter from Sir Charles Cottrell (1615–1701) to Lady Ann Pratt (1643–1706), Sir Roger Pratt's wife, dated 6 December 1684 (catalogued as NRO PRA 664/2) and a sewn printing of The Reverend William Greenwood's *A Poem Written During a Shooting Excursion on the Moors* (Bath: R. Cruttwell, 1787) (catalogued as NRO PRA 664/33). The folder also contains a small manuscript prayer book in Pratt's hand with a marbled cover containing text from The Order for the Visitation of the Sick from the Book of Common Prayer (catalogued as NRO PRA 664/8).

7 For a recent study of the uses of dialect in eighteenth-century literature more generally, see Janet Sorensen, *Strange Vernaculars: How Eighteenth-Century Slang, Cant, Provincial Languages, and Nautical Jargon Became English* (Princeton, NJ: Princeton University Press, 2017).

8 On the continuing vitality of manuscript culture in the late seventeenth and eighteenth centuries, see Margaret J. M. Ezell, *Social Authorship and the Advent of Print* (Baltimore, MD: Johns Hopkins University Press, 1999). On the mingling of manuscript and print in eighteenth-century literary coteries, see Betty A. Schellenberg, *Literary Coteries and the Making of Modern Print Culture: 1740–1790* (Cambridge: Cambridge University Press, 2016).

moreover, are drafts for poems that Pratt later published anonymously in local newspapers, whose printed versions are included in the form of newspaper clippings in the folder. Other texts present only in manuscript versions in the folder appear to have been written with the intention that they would be published, although these pieces seem never to have reached the printer's workshop. This seems to be the case, for example, with Pratt's manuscript *A Modest Address to Lewis* (*c.* 1784) addressed to Lewis Bagot, Bishop of Norwich, which includes the words 'Publishd with his Lordships Permission' written in Pratt's hand on its first page [*tp*]. We have found no evidence that this text was ever printed. If Pratt did seek Bagot's permission to publish this tract, it is not surprising that Bagot turned him down, given that it rather audaciously suggests that he, the Bishop of Norwich, had been too harsh in criticizing the collective failings of the clergy in his diocese, however much Pratt's address is couched in the language of deference.

Other texts in the folder seem to aspire to a level of publicity that they never actually achieved. Pratt's play *The Grange*, for example, whose composition we tentatively date to around 1774, appears to have originally been written in the hope that it be performed at the Theatre Royal in Norwich, built to replace the White Swan Playhouse in 1757 and first named the 'New Theatre near Chapel Field', and then from 1758 'The Grand Concert Hall', before its renaming as the Theatre Royal in 1768 upon receiving its royal licence.[9] As evidence for the intention that the play be performed at this venue, there is the encomium to Norwich as 'this fair City of immortal name' [*f. 28r*, l. 29] in the prologue and the references to 'Box, Gallery, and Pit' [*f. 29r*, l. 30] in the epilogue. The prologue and epilogue conventionally tack back and forth between praising the play and defending its author from anticipated criticism, with the prologue taking special care to forestall the censures of the imaginary critic 'with his pinch of snuff', who would dismiss the play as 'Norwich stuff', with the ladies in the audience enjoined to 'frown' upon the critic and 'save this first poor Bantling of your own' [*f. 27v*, ll. 17–18]. The prologue shows an awareness that a play by a local playwright written specifically for the Norwich Theatre Royal would be a novelty in a provincial theatrical culture that was dominated by plays that had originally premiered in London. One exception in the eighteenth century was a pantomime written especially for the Norwich Theatre Royal entitled *Harlequin from the Rocks; or, A Trip to Norwich* (1782), whose text

9 See Michael and Carole Blackwell, *Norwich Theatre Royal: The First 250 Years* (Norwich: Connaught Books, 2007), pp. 19–20.

has not survived. The reviewer for this production in the *Norfolk Chronicle* took the pantomime as a hopeful sign that more plays written by Norfolk playwrights might be performed at the Theatre Royal, observing that 'The metropolis has long usurped the exclusive right of producing theatrical entertainment; but this instance, among many others, may convince the credulous, that genius is not confined to the London stage; nor judgement to its admirers: That blind partiality which warps the opinion of so many to whatever is produced abroad, will, we doubt not, be removed in favour of home manufacture, where Art and Science has found its way.'[10] *The Grange* appears to have been written with the ambition that it form part of just such a roster of plays of 'home manufacture', the kind of play that the theatre critic for the *Norfolk Chronicle* imagined might one day grace the Norwich stage. *The Grange*'s prologue concludes by expressing the hope that Norfolk playwrights may 'By Gradual Labours find the way to Fame:/ And Norwich plays be heard, in Drury Lane' [*f. 28r*, ll. 37–8]. In the event, however, the play does not appear to have been performed at the Theatre Royal, much less Drury Lane.[11] *The Grange* appears to have remained a manuscript play that was likely read as closet drama or perhaps performed privately in the manner of the planned staging of Elizabeth Inchbald's *Lovers' Vows* (1798) at Sir Thomas Bertram's country house in Jane Austen's novel *Mansfield Park* (1814). In the case of *The Grange*, the fact that the play survives only in manuscript may well be the result of Pratt's failure to convince either the Theatre Royal to stage it or a printer to print it.

The fact that *The Grange* seems never to have been publicly performed or printed would appear to represent the disappointment of Pratt's ambitions for his play. On the other hand, 'Grunnelia or the Sow in the Dumps', Pratt's vulgar travesty of pastoral poetry, shows that scribal publication could also be a deliberate choice. It enabled Pratt to indulge in some crude humour with a friend without involving a printer or bookseller. Scribal publication could help limit the readership to a known circle of sympathetic friends, an understandable desideratum even if the content of a text was not indecent. The letter in the folder from Charles Davy to Pratt includes a poem that translates and extends the medieval lyric 'Sumer

10 'Theatrical Intelligence', *Norfolk Chronicle*, 26 January 1782, p. 2.

11 A search through the advertisements for plays at the New Theatre/Norwich Theatre Royal in the *Norfolk Chronicle* and *Norwich Mercury* failed to produce a performance of *The Grange*. However, we did find an advertisement for a 'PLAY and FARCE' that would be revealed by handbills on the day of performance: Monday 27 December 1773. See *Norwich Mercury*, 18 December 1773, p. 3. What was performed is not clear, but it is just possible that Pratt's *The Grange* was performed on this occasion.

is Icumen in'. Davy modestly writes in the letter enclosing the poem, 'I have learnd wit enough to know that what I am capable of writing is not of sufficient Importance to induce any persons to read what I can put together. I have no Invention left, if even I found any such power: yet I now & then amuse myself during my sleepless & often painful nights, with the Muses, if my silly rhymes will authorise my saying so much, I shall trust a specimen of my poor attempts to your candour' [*f. 1r*]. Davy was himself no stranger to print, being the author of *Conjectural Observations on the Origin and Progress of Alphabetic Writing*, published in London in 1772, as well as *Letters, Addressed Chiefly to a Young Gentleman, upon Subjects of Literature*, published in Bury St Edmunds in 1787. But he seems to have preferred to circulate his own original poetry in letters to friends. Davy's poem 'Onehouse' (1782), written in praise of the parish he served as rector, was only printed years after his death in the *Suffolk Garland* (1818), which reproduces the poem and a fragment of the letter in which it was originally included, although the original manuscript seems to have been lost.[12]

The practice of circulating handwritten poems, then, could be a way of creating intimacy between friends. Two of Pratt's poems, 'To Christopher Anstey' and 'To N. S.', are addressed to friends that Pratt had known from his youth, the former the well-known author of *The New Bath Guide* (1762) and the latter we believe to be Nicholas Styleman of Snettisham in Norfolk.[13] These manuscript poems create a sense of closeness between writer and addressee by invoking memories held in common of school and university days, through their verbal playfulness (as in Pratt's extended metaphor of 'FriendShip' [*f. 1v*, l. 60] as an actual ship in the poem addressed to Styleman), and through the material form in which they are written, which imbues them with the handwritten poem's personal touch. This is not to say that print and manuscript were necessarily opposed to one another in the textual culture in which Pratt participated. As we have seen, Pratt wrote poems to be printed in newspapers and we, with varying degrees of confidence, ascribe the three provincial mock epics in this volume—*The Inundation or the Life of a Fen-Man*, *The Coal-Heavers*, and *September: A Rural Poem*—to him. His literary papers offer plenty of evidence for the entwinement of print and manuscript in eighteenth-century Norfolk.

12 See *The Suffolk Garland: or, A Collection of Poems, Songs, Tales, Ballads, Sonnets, and Elegies* (Ipswich: John Row, 1818), pp. 17–20.

13 For details of the research on which the identification is based, see the headnote to 'To N. S.'

We have chosen to organize the print and manuscript texts in this edition by genre and length: dividing them into drama, longer poems, shorter poems, longer prose writings, and shorter prose writings. Within those categories the texts appear in chronological order—though for many texts we had to use our own conjectures (and material evidence like watermarks) to establish a likely date of composition. In the remainder of this introduction, rather than discussing Pratt's life and his writings separately, we move between the two. The plan of this introduction is loosely chronological: we follow Pratt's progress from his childhood at Ryston Hall, his studies at Edward VI School in Bury St Edmunds and at Cambridge, to his work as a minister in Norfolk parishes, interweaving the story of Pratt's life with his writings. We begin by briefly becoming geographers and topographers—honourable vocations that Sophy Appleyard and Daniel Cub in *The Grange* mistake for insults—and survey the small corner of Norfolk where Pratt was born.

Pratt's Norfolk

Jermyn Pratt lived out most of his days within the triangle whose vertices are marked by the small town of Downham Market, the village of Stoke Ferry (about six miles to the east of Downham Market), and the village of Watlington (about six miles to the north of Downham Market). Starting out from Downham Market, near Pratt's childhood home of Ryston Hall, a traveller could take the road north to the port of King's Lynn, the road south to Ely and Cambridge, and the road east to Norwich. Pratt's Norfolk was a promontory of permanently dry land surrounded by a large region of fen and marshland to the south and west, albeit one that was becoming less and less waterlogged (see Figure 1). A series of projects, starting in the seventeenth century, had begun to drain the fens, a process that Ian D. Rotherham has called 'the greatest single loss of wildlife habitat in Britain and maybe in Europe' and 'an ecological catastrophe almost beyond comprehension'.[14] Despite the changes being wrought on them, the fens continued to support a profusion of birdlife in Pratt's day. In 1787, John Aiken described how 'Wild-geese, grebes, godwits, whimbrels, coots, ruffs

14 Ian D. Rotherham, *The Lost Fens: England's Greatest Ecological Disaster* (Stroud: The History Press, 2013), p. 22. For another recent study of the draining of the fens, see Eric H. Ash, *The Draining of the Fens: Projectors, Popular Politics, and State Building in Early Modern England* (Baltimore: Johns Hopkins University Press, 2017) and for a recent account stressing the fraught nature of the enterprise, see David Alff, *The Wreckage of Intentions: Projects in British Culture, 1660–1730* (Philadelphia: University of Pennsylvania Press, 2017), pp. 90–113.

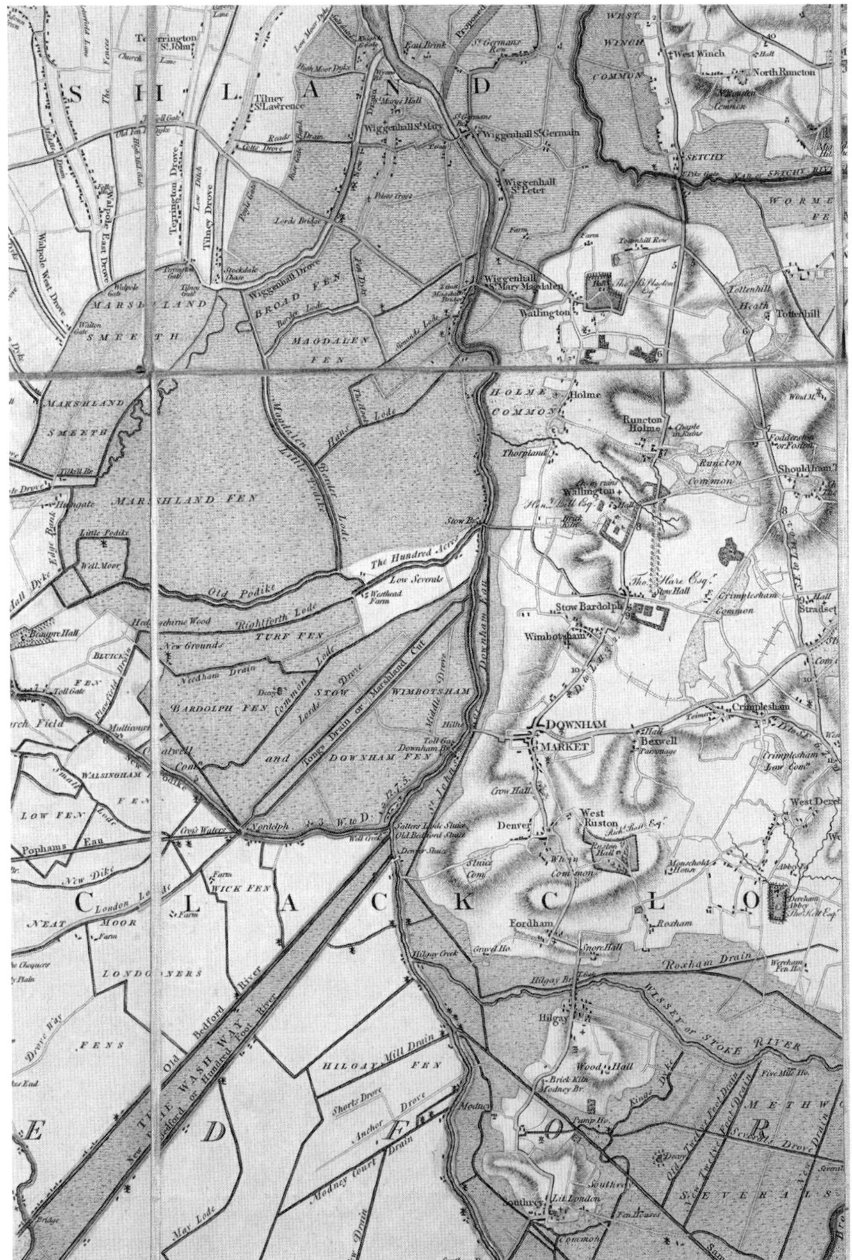

Figure 1 *Pratt's Norfolk, detail from William Faden's 1797 map of Norfolk, courtesy of the NRO*

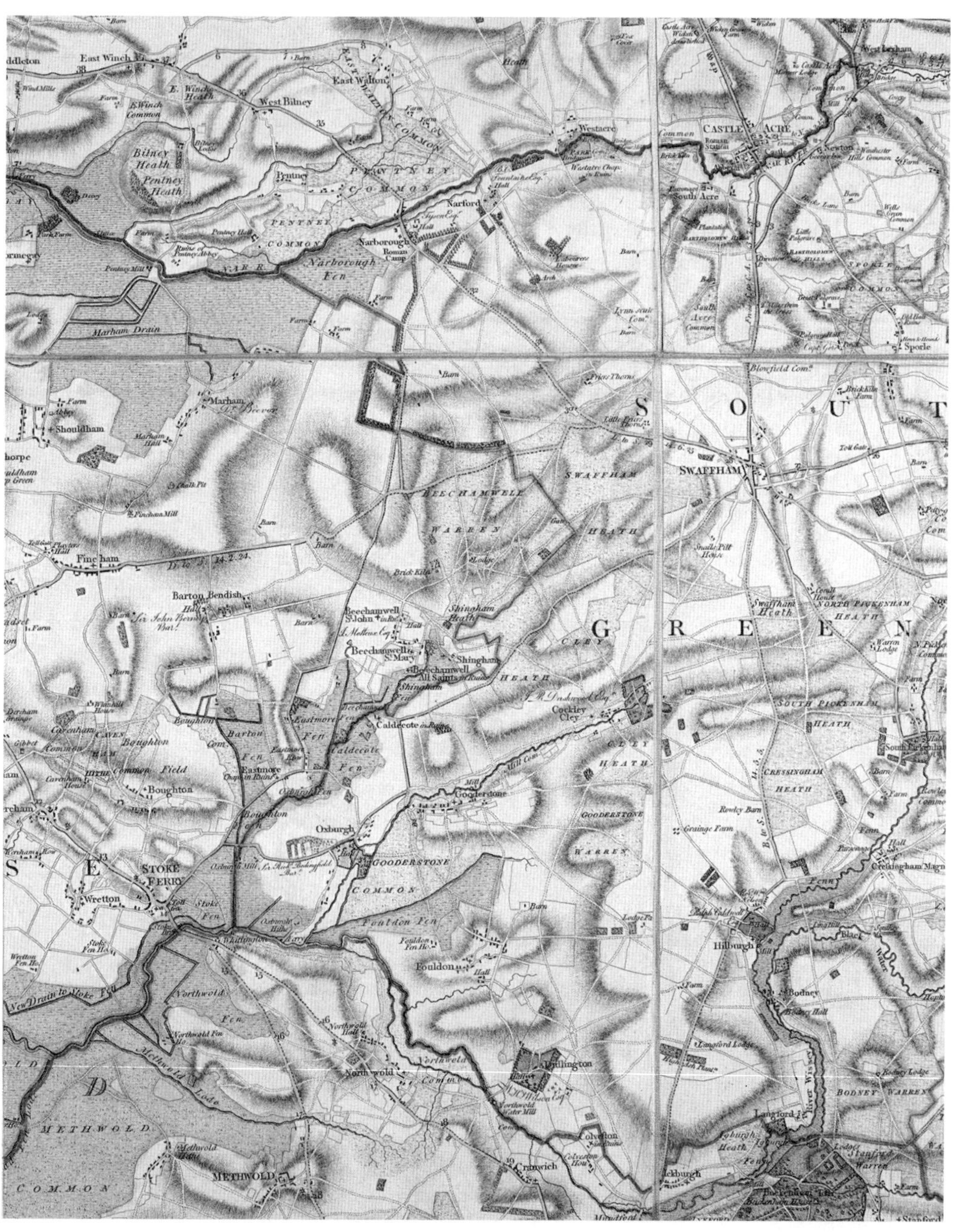
East Winch
West Bilney
East Walton
Westacre
CASTLE ACRE
West Lexham
Newton
Bilney Heath
Pentney Heath
Pentney
PENTNEY COMMON
Narford
Narborough
Narborough Fen
South Acre
Marham Drain
Sporle
Marham
Shouldham
Fincham
SWAFFHAM
SWAFFHAM HEATH
BEECHAMWELL
WARREN
S O U T
Barton Bendish
Beechamwell St. John
Beechamwell St. Mary
Shingham
G R E E N
NORTH PICKENHAM
SOUTH PICKENHAM
CRESSINGHAM HEATH
Cockley Cley
Caldecote
Boughton
Eastmore Fen
Gooderstone
Oxburgh
GOODERSTONE COMMON
GOODERSTONE WARREN
STOKE FERRY
Wretton
S E
Foulden Fen
Foulden
Hilburgh
Bodney
BODNEY WARREN
Northwold
Northwold Fen
Didlington
Langford
Colveston
Cranwich
Ickburgh
METHWOLD
D
METHWOLD
COMMON

and reeves, and a great variety of other species of water-fowl, breed here in amazing numbers, and obtain plentiful food from the fishy pools and streams.'[15] Even as the fenland was increasingly being turned into farmland, wild birds were still able to flourish—and birds in general are a pervasive presence in Pratt's literary papers, from the woodcock of 'The Death of the Woodcock' (1765) to the partridges of *September: A Rural Poem*.

Local landowners like the Pratts, who owned land in the fens that were designated for draining, were required to pay tax on those lands to support the projects from which they stood to benefit. In 1758, for example, Pratt's father Roger Pratt was taxed £56 on his landholdings in Denver and Hilgay to support drainage projects.[16] Pratt himself played a part in the eighteenth-century extension of the turnpike system of roads across Norfolk, providing capital for a turnpike road between Downham Market and Stoke Ferry.[17] The road-building projects undertaken in Norfolk are alluded to in *The Grange*, when Kitty Toy tells how the stagecoach in which she was travelling contained, among other undesirables, 'a Lunatic sent into ye fen to make a turnpike road' [*f. 18v*]—a comment that implies that the project of laying these roads over such unpromising land might be regarded as a form of insanity in itself. The precarious nature of the road leading north from Cambridge to Lynn along the Denver Sluice, just south of Downham Market, was vividly described by the twelve-year old William Manning (1732–1825) in a journal detailing his family's 1744 journey from King's Lynn to Cambridge: 'this road must be very Dangerous in wet weather the Banks (which the greatest Part of the Way are close to the River & perpendicular & but just broad enough for two Horses to pass & in several places but barely enough for a single one to go on) are two or three Yards in heighth so that if a Horse shou'd start or stumble the Rider wou'd be in great danger of being thrown into the River or Ditch so that no wise man will come here more than once to gratify his curiosity.'[18] Travellers on the road between King's Lynn and Cambridge falling into the adjacent waterways must have been a common occurrence. In Pratt's comic essay *The Zgubbs*, one of the many mischiefs attributed to the sprite-like Zgubbs is the pitching of a vicar

15 John Aiken, *England Delineated; or, A Description of Every County in England and Wales* (London: J. Johnson, 1787), pp. 192–3.

16 *The Lot Book of the Commissioners for Draining the Fen Lands lying between the Hundred Foot River and the River Ouse* (Cambridge: J. Archdeacon Printer to the University, 1768), p. 137.

17 See J. F. Fone, 'The Stoke Ferry Turnpike', *Norfolk Archaeology* 38 (1981), pp. 195–202.

18 William Manning, 'Journal of Tours, England, 1744–45', CUL, MS Add. 9457, *f. 21r–f. 21v*.

on his way from Middleton to Cambridge into a 'ten foot drain' [*p. 27*]. The continuing difficulty of travelling on the roads through fenland only exacerbated the isolation of Ryston and its environs from the rest of England.

This sense of isolation could have some benefits. In Pratt's case it helped foster a distinctive body of writings that bear the imprint of the place in which they were written. And his Cambridge friend Christopher Smart reported positively enjoying the sequestered nature of the region in a 1749 letter to the Charles Burney, then the organist for St Margaret's Church in King's Lynn, later famous as a historian of music. At this time, Smart was living in Downham Market and making frequent visits to Ryston Hall to hear 'my Harriote on her spinet & organ at her ancient mansion'. In his present environs, Smart wrote, 'I am as much a stranger as you to what is going on at Vaux Hall, for we are so wrapt up in our own snugness at this part of the kingdom, that we know little what's doing in the rest of the world.'[19] But only a short distance south from the arcadian snugness that Smart found at Ryston Hall, the leagues of inhospitable fenland began.

We believe that Pratt is likely the 'Fen Parson' who is identified as the author on the title page of *The Inundation or the Life of a Fen-Man* (1771).[20] In the preface to this poem, the fen is described as '*a vast plain, intersected with various natural and artificial rivers, defended with high banks, to prevent the over-flowing of the high country floods in their passage to sea. On these banks the inhabitants, for their better security, erect their miserable dwellings, at great distance sometimes from each other, and very remote from their parish churches, to which they rarely resort, unless to a wedding, a christening, or a burying. So that they seem to be cut off from the community, and are deprived of almost every advantage of social life*' [*p. 3*]. The poem itself tells the story of a fen-man who grows rich as a farmer of the fields and pastures that were formerly fenland. He loses nearly everything, however, when a flood spoils his crops and his animals either drown or starve. With his livelihood and home destroyed, the fen-man turns once again to his former life, supporting himself and his family by supplying the wild fowls he shoots on the fen for the London market.

The poem's own footnotes tell us that this narrative is inspired in part by the life of John Leaford, who is described as 'a common labourer in the fen' who worked for the Bedford Level Corporation as a repairer of flood banks, acquired a fortune by farming lands reclaimed from the fens, and

19 Christopher Smart, *The Annotated Letters of Christopher Smart*, ed. Betty Rizzo and Robert Mahony (Carbondale: Southern Illinois University Press, 1991), pp. 42–3.

20 For an explanation of authorship see the headnote to this poem.

built an 'elegant dwelling for a rural squire' in the village of Oxload near Ely (also known as Oxlode), and became a conservator for the corporation. A footnote to the poem claims Leaford was 'perfectly illiterate' [*p. 8*], although the historical John Leaford was the credited author of a short pamphlet setting out a plan for preventing the flooding of the south level of the fens, published in 1740, and was not simply a repairer of banks but the surveyor responsible for the plans for rebuilding the Denver Sluice between 1746 and 1750.[21] The poem's Leaford, however, serves to mark out a zero degree of literacy to which the poet opposes his own familiarity with the Bible and with classical literature, with the poem's prospective readership envisaged as occupying a middle ground between the two. The Preface expresses the hope that the poem will be read by parishioners living in the fens, explaining that '*The idiom of this poem is, in the general, calculated for the meridian of their understanding, some few instances only excepted, where imitations of the most eminent Latin and English authors are introduced for the amusement of the learned*' [*p. 3–p. 4*]. The 'Fen Parson' presents the poem as an extension of his own pastoral work, inviting readers to compare the inundation described in the poem with the biblical flood and drawing attention in the footnotes to allusions to the Bible. More broadly, the travails of the Fen-Man recall the suffering of Job, while the collapse of the mansion he has built on former fenland and his subsequent return to his older, poorer, but more sturdily built house parallels the Parable of Wise and Foolish Builders in Matthew 7:24–7 and Luke 6:46–8.[22] The poem also uses lengthy footnotes that explain the classical references for the benefit of readers living in the region of the fens who had never read the authors of antiquity. One of the guiding ideas of the poem, however, is that uneducated people living in the fens have an insight into classical literature that a scholar residing on dry land could never possess. The Fen-man witnesses with his own eyes, for example, the fantastic descriptions in the first book of Ovid's *Metamorphoses*, like the sight of fish swimming over fields where sheep used to graze [*p. 13*, l. 120]. The fens as a whole recreate the circumstances of Noah's and Deucalion's floods in contemporary life.

Pratt grew up surrounded by the woods, fields, and gardens of Ryston Hall, which had been in the family's possession since the early fifteenth

21 See John Leaford, *Some Observations made of the Frequent Drowned Condition of the South Level of the Fenns, and of the Works made for Draining the Same* (London, 1740) and his entry in Mike Chrimes et al., *A Biographical Dictionary of Civil Engineers in Great Britain and Ireland, Volume 1, 1500–1830* (London: Thomas Telford Ltd., 2002).

22 For a study that traces a distinctive Anglican poetic tradition see H. G. Sampson, *The Anglican Tradition in Eighteenth-Century Verse* (The Hague: Mouton, 1971).

century.[23] Near the house stands one of the two oak trees that have been known as 'Kett's Oak' (the other one being at Wymondham), where rebels in the area were supposed to have met up before joining Robert Kett at Norwich in 1549 to rise in protest against the depredations of the landowning classes. In the late nineteenth century, E. R. Pratt, then the proprietor of Ryston Hall, told the antiquarian Walter Rye the story that the rebels had pinned notes containing a taunting piece of doggerel on the sheep that they had killed and eaten addressed to his sixteenth-century ancestor, reading 'Mr Prat, your sheep are very fat/ And we thank you for that/ We have left you the skins to pay for your wife's pins/ And you must thank us for that.'[24] The anecdote is probably apocryphal, but it nevertheless speaks to the overturning of the hierarchical relationship between landowner and tenant during Kett's Rebellion. In *The Grange* Pratt would depict another situation in which the lord of the manor, Sir Harry Lopwood, is unable to assert his authority over his estate.

Ryston Hall as Pratt knew it was the work of the well-known architect Sir Roger Pratt, who had the house rebuilt according to his own design between 1669 and 1672 (see Plate 1). Nigel Silcox-Crowe describes the form of the new Ryston Hall as 'of unusual appearance, a hybrid of French and English classical styles' that contained two stories of nine bays wide, with a distinctive central projection that held an upper storey of three bays wide. This projection was 'crowned by a large segmental pediment on top of which perched a small cupola, or lantern bell turret, a whimsical addition of Pratt's own choosing'.[25] As part of his designs for Ryston Hall, Pratt specified what trees and flowers were to be planted in the gardens, many of which were sourced from the Whitechapel Nursery established by Captain Leonard Gurle in the 1660s.[26] The gardens remained in the latter half of

---

23 H. Repton and M. Armstrong, *The History and Antiquities of the County of Norfolk* (10 vols., Norwich, 1781), ii, 146. We have drawn information about the Pratt family from John Burke, *A Genealogical and Heraldic History of the Commoners of Great Britain and Ireland* (10 vols., London, 1833), i, 231; Walter Rye, *Norfolk Families* (2 vols., Norwich, 1911), ii, 68; and the pedigree of the Pratt family provided in Reverend G. H. Dashwood and Reverend C. Boutell, 'Notes on the Parish and Church of Wimbotsham', *Norfolk Archaeology*, 2 (1849), p. 142.

24 Walter Rye, *Songs, Stories, and Sayings of Norfolk* (Norwich: A. H. Goose, 1897), p. 19.

25 Nigel Silcox-Crowe, 'Sir Roger Pratt', in Roderick Brown, ed., *The Architectural Outsiders* (London: Waterstone and Company Limited, 1985), p. 17.

26 For Pratt's instructions on the plants and trees to be planted at Ryston Hall, see R. T. Gunther, ed., *The Architecture of Sir Roger Pratt, Charles II's Commissioner for the Rebuilding of London After the Great Fire: Now Printed for the First Time from His Note-books* (Oxford: Oxford University Press, 1928). On Sir Roger Pratt's purchasing of trees and

the eighteenth century, since an advertisement appeared in the *Norwich Mercury* in 1766 for a gardener at Ryston Hall, who 'must raise melons and cucumbers, understand grafting, spreading and nailing of fruit trees etc'.[27] During the last few years of Pratt's life, Ryston Hall was radically remodelled by Sir John Soane, with a whole second level added, and Sir Roger Pratt's 'whimsical turret' taken down.

Pratt's play *The Grange* is set in and around a fictional country house in Norfolk, but its plot nevertheless reflects some of the actual conditions of country estates such as Ryston Hall in the eighteenth century. The prominence given to the fir plantations on Sir Harry Lopwood's estate is an example. Actual Norfolk landowners planted such a number of pines and other trees that the total area of land covered by trees increased over the eighteenth century. Among them were the Pratts of Ryston Hall, whose grounds were described by Humphry Repton and Mostyn John Armstrong in 1781 as 'a park beautifully disposed with lofty timber, and young plantations'.[28] As Gerry Barnes and Tom Williamson explain in their study on the history of Norfolk's woodlands, Norfolk landowners planted forests for profit, to provide cover for game, to beautify their estates, and to create an arboreal legacy to pass on to their heirs. They planted trees not only for their own private benefit, however, but out of a sense of public spirit as well, heeding contemporary warnings of a national dearth of timber for shipbuilding that might potentially threaten Britain's dominance of the seas.[29] In *The Grange*, Sir Harry says that he chooses to stay on his estate and manage his fir plantations rather than removing himself to London 'to throw away my time and my fortunes, in ye fashionable follies of a Town Life' [*f. 2v*]. For Sir Harry, the pleasures of looking after and looking at his plantations are far superior those of 'ye Horse race; or ye Gaming table' [*f. 7r*] and he supposes that his plantations enable him at once to improve his estate and, through his active presence and example, to improve the characters of his tenants.

But *The Grange* also shows just how deluded Sir Harry's fantasies of arboreal and moral improvement are, at least before he has managed to

---

plants from Whitechapel Nursery, see David Brown and Tom Williamson, *Lancelot Brown and the Capability Men: Landscape Revolution in Eighteenth-Century England* (London: Reaktion Books, 2016), p. 80.

27 Cited in E. A. Goodwyn, *Selections from Norwich Newspapers, 1760–1790* (Ipswich: East Anglian Magazine Ltd., [1972]), p. 34.

28 Repton and Armstrong, *The History and Antiquities of the County of Norfolk*, 1:148.

29 Gerry Barnes and Tom Williamson, *Rethinking Ancient Woodland: The Archaeology and History of Woods in Norfolk* (Hatfield: University of Hertfordshire Press, 2015), p. 111.

set things to rights at the end of the play. Sir Harry Lopwood's last name signals his inability to govern his own estates. Tenants were traditionally said to have the right to cut 'lopwood' or under branches from trees on an estate, although the custom had, by the eighteenth century, come to be seen as an infringement on the landowner's property rights.[30] Far from establishing Sir Harry's power over his lands, the plantations and their walks mark the limits of Sir Harry's authority since they offer a place in which the play's two pairs of lovers, Leonard and Fanny, and Sophy and Wilson, may at least partially escape his oversight. And for all the pride he takes in being an active manager of his own manor, Sir Harry has in reality delegated the actual running of his estate and its plantations to his steward Clinch, who, as Gibbet says to Clinch's own face, 'has ruined ye Tenants', 'built a good House; with other mens money', and 'Stolen ye timbers; & ruind y^{r} master' [*f. 6r*].[31] Meanwhile, Clinch's sycophant Nettle busies himself in threatening the aged tenant Appleyard with a lawsuit for taking small pieces of clay from Lopwood's estate to make bungholes for bottles—and encouraging the other villagers to lodge spurious lawsuits against one another. Although Clinch and Nettle certainly are malign influences on the rural society depicted in *The Grange*, the play suggests that the rot goes deeper than these characters alone. As the honest servant Williams remarks, 'ye Boy would be man; ye man would be Master, ye Tenant would be ye Landlord, ye Landlord would be ye Esqr, ye Esqr would be ye Knight; ye Knight would be ye Nobleman; ye Nobleman would be ye King; and ye King (God bless him) can be no better' [*f. 9v*]. Larger forces appear to be destabilizing the traditional social hierarchy in the thoroughly commercialized rural community depicted in *The Grange*.

The corruption of manners and morals under commercialisation is seen not only in Clinch's venality and Nettle's pettifogging but also in Sophy's taste for expensive foreign cloths and clothes, as well as Kitty Toy's aggressive marketing of the cloths that she claims are expensive imports

30 For a discussion of how customary rights to the use of woodland became points of contention between tenants and landowners, see James P. Bowen, '"The Struggle for the Commons": Commons, Custom and Cottages in Shropshire during the Sixteenth and Seventeenth Centuries', in *Custom and Commercialisation in English Rural Society: Revisiting Tawney and Postan*, ed. J. P. Bowen and A. T. Brown (Hatfield: University of Hertfordshire Press, 2016), pp. 96–117.

31 For a study of actual stewards in East Anglia, see Jonathan Theobald, 'Estate Stewards in Woodland High Suffolk 1690–1820', in Christopher Harper-Bill, Carole Rawcliffe, and Richard George Wilson, eds., *East Anglia's History: Studies in Honour of Norman Scarfe* (Woodbridge: The Boydell Press, 2002), pp. 243–58.

from Italy and India. Chloe Wigston Smith observes that the coveting of calico cloth, much in evidence in *The Grange*, 'was viewed not merely as poor taste, but as a form of consumer behavior in which women threatened the nation, politically and economically, by purchasing imported goods'.[32] A parallel emerges between the prologue's depiction of foreign theatrical imports damaging the domestic theatrical industry and *The Grange*'s depiction of foreign fashions corrupting the morals of English women who ought to be making do with local woollens. Both the prologue and the play itself suggest that the nation benefits most from those who help the local cultural and mercantile economies to flourish. Just as Pratt anticipates serving the Norfolk stage, and potentially the theatrical culture of the country as a whole, by writing *The Grange*, so too does Sir Harry see himself as contributing to both the local and national economies through overseeing his plantations, rather than spending his time in London. But Sir Harry's enterprise also gives Clinch the opportunity to turn his estate to his own private gain—at least before he is unmasked after he accidentally drops his pocketbook containing evidence of his corruption in the very plantations that he has been profiteering from. Sir Harry's turning of the plantations to profit is the basis on which his virtue rests, but the play shows how larger commercialising forces threaten to lay waste to his estate.

As a playwright, Pratt would have drawn on his observations of his father Roger Pratt's management of Ryston Hall. Roger Pratt came into the possession of the estate after the death of his own father, Edward Pratt, in 1708.[33] In 1715, he married Henrietta Davers, the daughter of a family whose wealth had been founded on their ownership of 600 acres of plantations in Barbados and hundreds of enslaved human beings.[34] (Kitty Toy's assumed identity in *The Grange* as a rich Barbadian heiress would probably have been read by Pratt's personal circle as a reference to the Barbadian connection of Henrietta's father, Robert Davers.) Pratt's father was a prominent member of the governing elite in Norfolk. He served in 1727 as the High Sheriff of Norfolk and his name frequently appears in the list of justices sitting at the local assizes over the eighteenth century.

32 Chloe Wigston Smith, *Women Work and Clothes in the Eighteenth-Century Novel* (Cambridge: Cambridge University Press, 2013), p. 114.

33 'Parish Records of Ryston with Roxham', NRO, PD 464/1.

34 See Richard Maguire, *Africans in East Anglia, 1467–1833* (Martlesham: The Boydell Press, 2021), p. 109. After the Davers family relocated from Barbados to Rougham in Suffolk in the late seventeenth century, a young black woman named Rosanna lived in their household in conditions that Maguire describes as 'near slavery'; ibid., p. 109.

Roger Pratt was also involved in charitable pursuits. His name appears on the list of governors and guardians of the Foundling Hospital in Lamb's Conduit Fields in London, founded by Thomas Coram in 1739 to shelter children deserted by their parents.[35] He also took an interest in new methods for improving crop yields. A letter from Roger Pratt to the Hertfordshire agricultural writer William Ellis was printed in Ellis's *The New Art of Brewing and Improving Malt Liquors to the Greatest Advantage* (1761).[36] In it, Roger Pratt attested to the effectiveness of Ellis's method of steeping barley seed before sowing it. Pratt's father played a part, then, however small, in the general interest in the experimentation with new farming methods across Norfolk that earned the county a reputation as a leading centre of the eighteenth-century agricultural revolution.[37]

The parish register for the small parish of Ryston records that a 'German Pratt' was born to Roger and Henrietta Pratt and baptized on 7 July 1723, 'German' presumably being a phonetic rendering of 'Jermyn'.[38] Jermyn Pratt's rather unusual given name was the last name of his great-grandfather Thomas Jermyn, 2nd Baron Jermyn, to whom he was related through his maternal grandmother.[39] The Pratts followed the common practice at the time for gentry families to draw attention to their relationship to their highborn ancestors by giving these ancestors' last names as first names to their children.[40] Despite the aristocratic ancestry announced by his name, as a second son, Pratt needed to enter one of the vocations. He was to choose the church.[41] With this profession ahead of him, Jermyn Pratt followed his

35 *A List of Governors and Guardians of the Hospital for the Maintenance and Education of Exposed Young Children* (London, 1768), p. 28.

36 William Ellis, *The New Art of Brewing and Improving Malt Liquors to the Greatest Advantage* (London: M. Cooper, 1761), pp. 13–14.

37 See Naomi Riches, *The Agricultural Revolution in Norfolk*, 2nd ed. (London: Cass, 1967).

38 The register also records another son to the Pratts named 'German', who was baptized on 16 February 1721, although this son lived a little less than a year and was buried on 2 February 1722. See 'Parish Records of Ryston with Roxham', NRO, PD 464/1.

39 Lady Mary Davers was Thomas Jermyn's eldest daughter and one of her father's co-heiresses along with her three surviving sisters. See John Bernard Burke, *A Genealogical History of the Dormant: Abeyant, Forfeited, and Extinct Peerages of the British Empire* (Harrison, 1866); Augustine Page, *A Supplement to the Suffolk Traveller or Topographical and Genealogical Collections, Concerning that County* (Ipswich and London, 1844), p. 789.

40 George Redmonds discusses this phenomenon in *Christian Names in Local and Family History* (Toronto: Dundurn Press, 2004), p. 130.

41 For a study of the predicament of younger sons in the later Georgian period, and an account of the various professions open to them, see Rory Muir, *Gentlemen of Uncertain Fortune: Younger Sons in Jane Austen's England* (New Haven: Yale University Press, 2019).

elder brother Edward to King Edward VI School in Bury St Edmunds in October 1731.[42]

Edward VI School and Cambridge

The master of Edward VI School was the Cambridge-educated teacher Arthur Kynnesman. On being appointed master in 1714, Kynnesman increased the number of pupils to 150 and brought the Westminster curriculum with him to Bury St Edmunds, using it to teach Greek and Latin there.[43] As we have already mentioned, one of Pratt's schoolmates was the future author of the *New Bath Guide*, Christopher Anstey, who was admitted in 1733.[44] In 'To Christopher Anstey', Pratt recalls 'The slow, dull work, of Grammar School:/ Where, yok'd betimes, to Classic Team;/ We Drag'd up Hill, our Loaded Theme', urged on by 'Kin'smans Grins' and 'vile Grimaces' [*f. 1r*, ll. 2–5]. The dramatist Richard Cumberland, who attended King Edward VI School between 1738 and 1744, remembered in his memoirs that Kynnesman was 'an excellent master, a very sufficient scholar, and had all the professional requisites of voice, air and aspect, that marked him out at first sight as a personage decidedly made on purpose—*habere imperium in pueros* [to have dominion over the boys]'.[45] 'To Christopher Anstey' depicts the strictness and rigor of grammar schools like Kynnesman's. But it also recalls the school exercises in writing poetry in English and the learned languages of Latin and Greek that were commonly set at grammar schools, in which the writing of witty poems was especially encouraged.[46] The poem creates comic effects through unexpected juxtapositions—for example, placing 'Old Peg' between Xanthus and Bucephalus, the steeds, respectively, of Achilles and Alexander the Great [*f. 1r*, l. 24]. As well as writing poetry, Pratt would have had the opportunity to perform in the Latin and English plays that were staged there every year. In the year that Pratt arrived at Edward VI School, for example, the boys performed George Ruggle's

42 *BEKE*, 312–13.

43 'Kynnesman, Arthur': *Oxford DNB*.

44 *BEKE*, 9.

45 Richard Cumberland, *Memoirs of Richard Cumberland: Containing an Account of his Life and Writings* (Cornhill: David West, John West, and O. C. Greenleaf, 1806), p. 15.

46 For an account of the exercises in the writing of playful poetic forms like anagrams and acrostics in Westminster School, whose curriculum Kynnesman brought to Bury St Edmunds, see Aaron Santesso, 'Poetry and the Public School', *Eighteenth-Century Life*, 32 (2008), pp. 57–80.

Plate 1 *Painting of Ryston Hall by an Unknown Artist,* c. *1680*

Plate 2 *Portrait of Sir Roger Pratt by an Unknown Artist, 1670, courtesy of Ryston Hall, photograph by Mark Parker*

Plate 3 *Portrait of Roger Pratt by an Unknown Artist,* c. *1710, courtesy of Ryston Hall, photograph by Mark Parker*

Plate 4 *Portrait of Edward Pratt*, c. *1750*,
courtesy of Ryston Hall, photograph by Mark Parker

Plate 5 *Portrait of a Girl we believe to be Harriot Pratt, by an Unknown Artist,* c. *1734, courtesy of Ryston Hall, photograph by Mark Parker*

Plate 6 *Christopher Anstey and his Daughter by William Hoare*, c. *1775*,
© *National Portrait Gallery, London*

Plate 7 *Portrait of Christopher Smart by an Unknown Artist,* c. *1745, courtesy of Pembroke Hall, University of Cambridge*

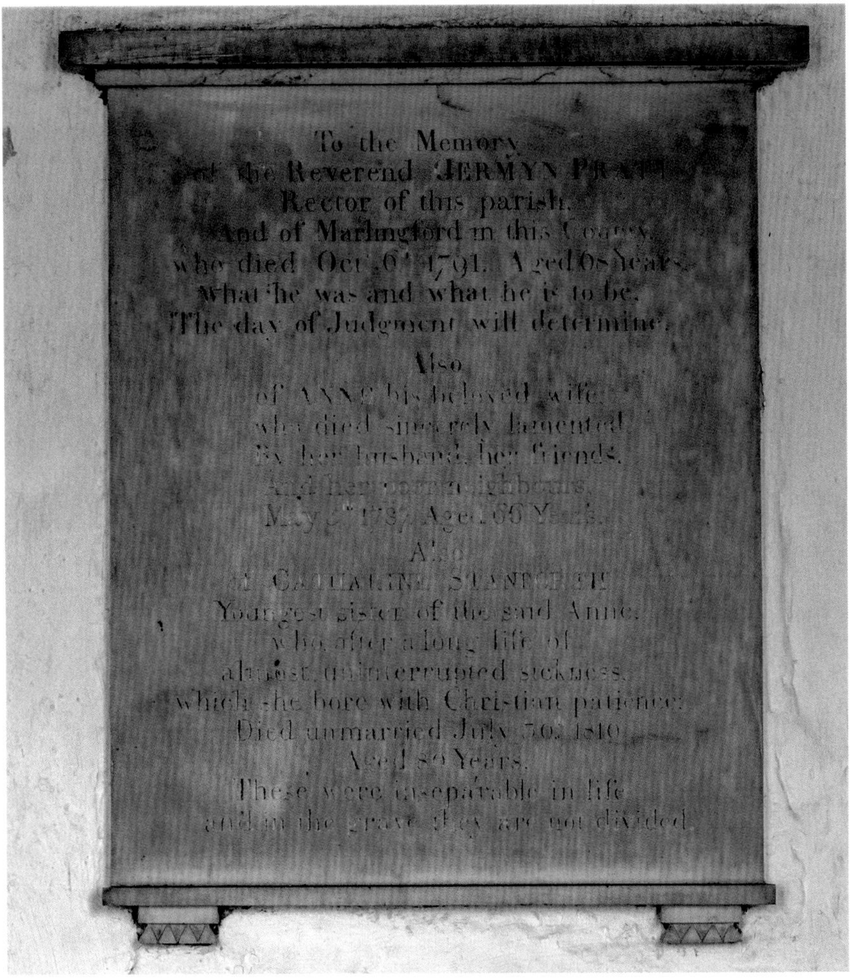

Plate 8 *Monumental Inscription for Ann Pratt, Jermyn Pratt, and Catherine Stanforth at Watlington Church, photo by Mark Parker*

Plate 9 *Flagstones for Catherine Stanforth, Ann Pratt, and Jermyn Pratt, photo by Mark Parker*

Latin satire on the common law *Ignoramus* (1615) and George Farquhar's comedy *The Constant Couple or a Trip to the Jubilee* (1700).[47]

After completing his education at King Edward VI School, Pratt arrived at Cambridge in 1741 at the age of 17 and entered Gonville and Caius College (Figure 2). His elder brother Edward had studied for his Bachelor of Arts at this college from 1736 to 1740 and was now a fellow at the college, a position he would hold until 1751.[48] At Gonville and Caius, Pratt would have almost certainly met Charles Davy, who had already been a student at Cambridge for two years when Pratt arrived there, and who would become Pratt's lifelong friend. Christopher Anstey, Pratt's schoolmate from King Edward VI School, came to Cambridge the year after Pratt arrived, and enrolled in King's College. Pratt was admitted to Gonville and Caius as a pensioner, occupying the middle position in the Cambridge student hierarchy, beneath the fellow-commoners, who paid double fees while enjoying special privileges, but above the sizars, such as Pratt's friend Christopher Smart, who performed menial work in exchange for reduced fees and often acted as servants to the fellow-commoners.[49] In the year he arrived at Cambridge, Pratt received a financial windfall in the form of £100, paid by George Snagg, a tenant of Chesterton just north of Cambridge, claimed as part of a customary duty on land that had been given to Pratt by his father.[50] Like Sir Harry Lopwood in *The Grange*, Roger Pratt appears to have paid for his son's university fees by selling wood cut from his plantations: the entry in Gonville and Caius's legal account book for 3 March 1741 reads 'Seal'd wth our common Seal a Letter of Attorney [to] Roger Pratt Esquire for the sale of Timber.'[51] Pratt was tutored, like Edward before him, by the Reverend Thomas Eglinton, who was also from Norfolk, hailing from the village of Bawdeswell, and having himself studied at Gonville and Caius.[52] The college had long disproportionately drawn its fellows from East Anglia and trained most of Norfolk's clergymen, including Edmund Nelson, the father of Admiral Lord Nelson,

47 R. W. Elliott, *The Story of King Edward VI School Bury St Edmunds* (Bury St Edmunds: Foundation Governors of the School, 1963), p. 80.

48 *AC*, 1.3.391.

49 See Christopher Wordsworth, *Social Life at the Universities in the Eighteenth Century* (Cambridge: Cambridge University Press, 2009), p. 107; reprint of first edition from 1874.

50 See 'Copy of Release of Heriots from Copyhold Lands of Jermyn Pratt held of the Manors of Crowlands, Lyles and Sames in Cottenham, for £100', PRA 346, 379X3.

51 Cambridge University Libraries, Gonville and Caius College, Pandectae, 1658–1821, GOV/02/01/02.

52 The information on Eglinton is drawn from his entry in *AC*. On Gonville and Caius College in the eighteenth century, see Christopher Nugent Lawrence Brooke, *A History of Gonville and Caius College* (Woodbridge: Boydell Press, 1985), pp. 159–87.

Figure 2 *Gonville and Caius College* c. *1680*,
from The Architectural History of the University of Cambridge (1886),
Courtesy of the University of East Anglia

who was ordained as the curate of Sporle in 1745.[53] The links between the college and the Anglican episcopate in Norfolk were especially close at this time, with Sir Thomas Gooch serving as Master of Gonville and Caius and, by the time Pratt entered the college, also serving as Bishop of Norwich.[54] The early eighteenth-century church was thoroughly entwined with the party system and its networks of patronage and preferment and Gooch, despite his former allegiance to the Tories, was active in his support of the Whig party by the time Pratt arrived at Cambridge.[55]

Pratt refers to the texts he studied at Cambridge in his writings. A footnote to *September*, for example, includes an anecdote that 'A tutor at Cambridge visiting his pupil, found his LOCKE open for a week together at the same page on Simple Ideas. "Child, says he, thou hast a strange affection for Simple Ideas," and he was right; for his pupil never went any where without them afterwards' [*p. 2*]. Newton's name is joined to Locke's in the poem as the two authors whom Cambridge students neglect in order to indulge their passion for hunting. In his poem 'To N. S.' Pratt remembers the break at 1 o'clock 'When Rohoust, Puffendorf, & Rowning/ Gave way to Love & Nancy Downing' [*f. 1r*, ll. 11–12]. Jacques Rohault, and Samuel von Pufendorf were seventeenth-century authors of books on physics and jurisprudence respectively and their names appear on the reading list in a recommended course covering the four years of undergraduate study that was created in 1707 by a fellow of Clare College, Robert Green.[56] The mathematician and physicist John Rowning's *Compendious System of Natural Philosophy* (1735) was also part of the roster of texts that Pratt studied at Cambridge. The prominence of mathematicians and physicists in Pratt's remembrances of his studies at Cambridge reflects the heavily mathematical bent of the curriculum.[57] But Pratt would have also continued his studies

53 On Gonville and Caius's connection to the Anglican Church in East Anglia, see Victor Morgan, *A History of the University of Cambridge Volume II: 1546–1750* (Cambridge: Cambridge University Press, 2004). On Edmund Nelson's education at Gonville and Caius and his subsequent career in the church, see *BGC*, 2:50.

54 'Gooch, Sir Thomas, Second Baronet': *Oxford DNB*.

55 Gooch wrote to the Duke of Newcastle in 1733, for instance, that 'he had already, and would again declare his firm resolution of supporting Mr Pelham and Mr Butler's interest at the next election'; qtd. in Norman Sykes, *Church and State in England in the 18th Century* (Cambridge: Cambridge University Press, 1934), p. 83.

56 Christopher Wordsworth, *Scholae Academicae: Some Account of the Studies at the English Universities in the Eighteenth Century* (Cambridge: Cambridge University Press, 1877), pp. 338–42.

57 For mathematical studies at Cambridge, see John Gascoigne, *Cambridge in the Age of the Enlightenment* (Cambridge: Cambridge University Press, 1989), pp. 270–99.

in the literature of ancient Greece and Rome that mark so many of the poems in the folder: the list of the books in his library shows that he had an extensive collection of Greek and Roman authors in both the original languages and in English translation at the time of his death.

Pratt also imbibed the latitudinarian theology that was especially associated with Cambridge, which sought to eschew needless disputes over points of religious doctrine by emphasizing the rationality of Christianity and its efficacy as a guide to personal ethics and the good life.[58] Many of latitudinarianism's major figures from the latter half of the seventeenth century to the eighteenth century were Cambridge scholars. At the time of his death Pratt had many of their books in his library, including twelve volumes of John Tillotson's collected sermons (first published as a complete set in 1695), Simon Patrick's *The Witnesses to Christianity* (1675) and *The Christian Sacrifice* (1671), as well as *The Principles of Moral and Political Philosophy* (1785) by the contemporary latitudinarian William Paley. Pratt's comic essay *The Zgubbs* is a defence of latitudinarian principles, although it begins as a sendup of pneumatology: the science of the immaterial world of spirits. A prominent example of the kind of metaphysical speculation that Pratt was satirizing was his friend Soame Jenyns's *A Free Inquiry Into the Nature and Origin of Evil* (1756), which suggested that much of the evil in the world is wreaked by invisible spirits who take a sadistic joy in tormenting human beings. The essay pretends to undertake a learned defence of the hypothesis that immaterial beings known as 'Zgubbs' are to blame for such mishaps as coins rolling away into odd places, animals rubbing against newly painted fences, and sermons falling out of cassocks on the day they are to be read. After its absurd first half, the essay turns serious and begins to take on the cadences of a sermon. *The Zgubbs* ends by reproaching those theologians 'Who by being over nice and scrupulous in ye preserving of mint & Cummin, and over resolute not to part with a single advantage; who by passing over ye Weightier considerations of morality & by writing upon Subjects which they never understood, and by disputing for things of Little or no Importance, have unfortunately left behind them a wide and unbounded field, for cavil and Disputation' [*p. 28*]. A stubborn belief in the existence of Zgubbs, the essay suggests, may be relatively harmless, but a similarly inflexible insistence on theological points that are just as unproveable might threaten the integrity of the established church. Pratt recommends tolerance and good humour as the best antidotes to dissention on religious matters. Against dogmatism and intolerance, *The Zgubbs* advocates

58 On the latitudinarian tradition at Cambridge, see ibid., pp. 40–51.

humility in the face of the mysteries of religion, and an awareness of one's own eccentricities, as well as the eccentricities of others.[59]

The evidence we have of Pratt's friendships suggests that he was attracted to eccentrics like Christopher Smart, who reportedly exasperated his tutor Leonard Addison with his habitual drunkenness and general extravagance.[60] Two other characters that Pratt likely befriended at Cambridge were Nicholas Styleman and Richard Gardiner. We believe Styleman is the person addressed in Pratt's poem 'To N. S.' At the time when he was a student at Cambridge, Styleman was the heir to the estate of Snettisham Old Hall on the north Norfolk coast. In a poem published during the 1768 general election, when Styleman, Gardiner, and Pratt were campaigning on behalf of the anti-ministerial candidates Sir Edward Astley and Wenman Coke, Styleman was described in a poem written by an author on the side of the incumbents they were challenging as 'that bellowing Wild Man/ With his Thanks, and his Gibe, and his Jeer'.[61] Later in life, Styleman was vividly described by François de La Rochefoucauld, a young Frenchman who spent a year touring East Anglia along with his brother Alexandre and their tutor Maximilien de Lazowski in 1784, by which time Styleman had retired as lord of the manor in favour of his nephew. Rochefoucauld recorded in his journal that 'his ideas are very unusual' and 'He is well-educated but not like anyone else: everything he knows takes on an original quality, without losing anything, becoming singular.' Lazowski, for his part, compared Styleman to Squire Western in Henry Fielding's novel *Tom Jones* (1749), commenting that 'after two hours with him you think Fielding must have copied him'.[62]

---

59 For a reading of *Tristram Shandy* (1759–67), which *The Zgubbs* pastiches, as similarly embracing a tolerant and liberal strand in latitudinarian thought, see Carol Stewart, *The Eighteenth-Century Novel and the Secularization of Ethics* (Farnham: Ashgate, 2010), pp. 131–63.

60 See Arthur Sherbo, *Christopher Smart: Scholar of the University* (East Lansing, MI: Michigan State University Press, 1967), p. 25. Although Smart later gained a reputation for madness, in part because of his habit of praying in the street, Chris Mounsey cautions in his biography of Smart that 'there is no evidence to demonstrate conclusively that he was mad.' *Christopher Smart*, p. 146.

61 *Contest*, 76.

62 François de La Rochefoucauld, *A Frenchman's Year in Suffolk*, ed. and trans. Norman Scarfe (Woodbridge: Boydell and Brewer, 1988), p. 182. Lazowski describes Nicholas Styleman as holding apparently incompatible political sympathies, being both an 'ardent Jacobite' and a 'Whig' who was 'ready to die for the Republic'—which the editor Norman Scarfe takes to mean the revolutionary settlement of 1688. It seems likely to us that this account reflects the limitations of Lazowski's grasp of British politics.

During his time at Cambridge, Pratt would have probably also encountered Richard Gardiner, a man who was memorably described by the Norfolk historian R. W. Ketton-Cremer as 'a busybody, a sponger and a cad'.[63] Gardiner was the son of Sir Robert Walpole's chaplain, the Reverend John Gardiner, although in the early 1740s, when Gardiner was serving in the British army and navy on the continent, he would claim to be illegitimate son of Sir Robert himself in an attempt to gain a promotion. After being released from prison after his ship was intercepted by a French privateer in 1747, Gardiner was ordained as a deacon, but soon abandoned holy orders and resumed his career as an army officer, to which he added a literary career in hack writing, including writing a scandalous roman à clef entitled *The History of Pudica a Lady of N-rf-lk* (1754) under the pseudonym 'William Honeycombe', aimed at a Norfolk woman whom Gardiner had been unsuccessfully trying to court, her family, and her other suitors.[64] A copy of this book with a key to the personages in an unknown hand is in the Pratt family papers in the Norfolk Record Office.[65]

During the 1768 general election, Pratt assisted Gardiner as a propagandist for the candidacies of Wenman Coke and Sir Edward Astley for the county seat of Norfolk. Pratt also assisted Gardiner in holding a special performance of George Colman the Elder and David Garrick's play *The Clandestine Marriage* (1766) on 22 March 1779, performed by local 'gentlemen' in King's Lynn for the benefit of the families of impressed soldiers at the height of the American Revolutionary War. Pratt wrote a prologue and Gardiner an epilogue especially for the performance. Both men may also have acted in the play, which is a comic farce that hinges on the other characters' ignorance of the illicit union between Fanny and Lovewell that the play's title refers to. Gardiner also penned a letter to the *Norfolk Chronicle* defending Pratt's poem *September* against the criticisms of the poem in the *Critical Review*.[66] The existence of a literary conversation between Pratt and Gardiner is suggested by the fact that both used a phrase from Horace's first satire, 'Ridentem Dicere Verum Quid Vetat' ('What stops me from telling truth with a smile?'), as an epigraph: Gardiner used it for the epigraph of *A Letter to John Shadwell, Esq* (1754), who had apparently protested about being represented as a suitor of Pudica

63 R. W. Ketton-Cremer, *Norfolk Portraits* (London: Faber and Faber, 1944), p. 110.

64 See Gardiner's entries in the *Oxford DNB* and *AC*.

65 For the Pratt family copy of *Pudica* in the NRO, PRA 661, 382X8.

66 For the original review, see *The Critical Review: or, Annals of Literature*, November 1780, pp. 394–6. For the letter in defence of the poem, see *Norfolk Chronicle*, 27 January 1781, 5. Rpt. in *Gard*, 209–12.

(Mary Sotherton) in Gardiner's *A History of Pudica*. Pratt, in imitation of Gardiner, chose the phrase as the epigraph for *The Zgubbs*.[67] Pratt also borrowed the other epigraph from *A Letter to John Shadwell, Esq*, 'Hit him again, Chicken', using it as the epigraph for his squib on the 1768 Norfolk election 'Mr. Anti-Puff' [*p. 3*].

Two poems cut from the *Norwich Mercury* and the *Norfolk Chronicle* in the folder of papers that contains most of Pratt's writings suggest that Pratt took an interest in Gardiner's posthumous reputation. The first poem printed in the *Norwich Mercury* lists the various misfortunes attendant on Gardiner's death, including a mind 'distracted with corroding Care' and a family who 'bear imperious Sway,/ O'er Him they ought to cherish and obey', and concludes 'Where one Man meets with these Ills combin'd,/ The Grave's the only Refuge such a Wretch can find.'[68] The second poem, published in the *Norfolk Chronicle* a week after Gardiner's supposed epitaph was printed, compares Gardiner to the heroic Hector who, after his death, was stabbed by Greek warriors who no longer had to face him in actual combat. 'The Dead are Sacred—let Revilings cease,' concludes the poem, 'And Gardiner's Shade, with Hector's, rest in Peace.'[69] In the same issue of the *Norfolk Chronicle*, a 'character' of Gardiner, which was claimed to be 'acknowledged to be a just one' by Gardiner himself, attempted to provide a more equitable view of the satirist, describing him as, 'A man who has much wit, but too little discretion; one who has talents sufficient to adorn the best subjects, and to give some consequence even to the worst; but who has (except in a few cases) been so unfortunate in his choice of subjects, that our smiles are frequently mixed with pain, and our admiration with disgust.'[70] Pratt's writings often mix learning with the kind of scurrilousness that characterize the writings of Richard Gardiner. Much like the writings of the Anglican satirists Jonathan Swift and Laurence Sterne, whose influence Pratt explicitly acknowledges in *The Zgubbs*, Pratt's writings are full of clashes and juxtapositions of the high and the low.

---

67 The motto is also quoted at the beginning of *The Memoirs of Richard Gardiner* (*Gard*, 1). This book appears to have been put together by acquaintances of Gardiner's, since the prologue ends with the coy observation that 'memoirs are of the plural—and so are WE!' (*Gard*, iv). Pratt may have contributed to this project. In any case, he had a copy of the book in his library at the time of his death.

68 *Norwich Mercury*, 6 October 1781, p. 3; rpt. in *Gard*, 236.

69 *Norfolk Chronicle*, 13 October 1781, p. 2; rpt. in *Gard*, 236–7.

70 ibid, p. 2.

Priesthood

After graduating from Cambridge with a Bachelor of Arts, Pratt was ordained deacon on 25 December 1746 and exchanged his academic dress for the clerical robes in which he appeared in a portrait that once hung at Ryston Hall, now lost, where he was depicted as a man with 'full dark grey eyes', and wearing a 'short white wig' and a 'Black gown and white bands'.[71] Soon after his ordination as deacon, Pratt was appointed as the perpetual curate of the consolidated parishes of Wereham and Wretton, just to the east of Stoke Ferry, which were in the gift of his father and lay five miles to the west of Downham Market.[72] In Wereham Pratt acquired the farm that he would later bequeath to his nephew, Edward Roger Pratt, in his last will and testament.[73] As W. M. Jacob points out, the country priest 'had to be an astute man of agricultural business if he was not to lose through his ignorance of what should be paid, for it was unlikely that parishioners would prompt him to ask for higher payments'.[74] With tithes still frequently received 'in kind' rather than in the form of money in the eighteenth century, many country clergy like Pratt had to involve themselves in the collection, storing, and selling of animals, grain, and produce, many becoming farmers themselves as well as men of the cloth.[75]

Pratt was ordained priest on 11 March 1749. Two years later, Pratt was awarded the rectorship of Marlingford, a village about six miles to the west of Norwich on 26 January 1751. The rectory was sworn of the total value of £31 6d a year and augmented under Queen Anne's Bounty by another £50 per annum.[76] Pratt's patron for the Marlingford rectory was

---

71 The portrait is estimated to have been painted between 1750 and 1760. See Frederick Duleep Singh, *Portraits in Norfolk Houses*, ed. Edmund Farrier (2 vols., Norwich: Jarrold and Sons, Limited, 1928), ii, p. 259. Unfortunately, the present whereabouts of this portrait are unknown: a search of Ryston Hall failed to turn up any portrait answering this description.

72 See *BGC*, 2:50. Roger Pratt leased the curacies to Jermyn for life in 1758. See NRO, PRA 328-329, 378X9.

73 'Last Will and Testament of the Reverend Jermyn Pratt'. PRO PROB 11/1213.

74 William M. Jacob, 'Clergy and Society in Norfolk 1707–1806', unpublished PhD thesis, University of Exeter, 1982, p. 123. For another study of tithes in Norfolk, see Peter William Whitfield, 'Change and Continuity in the Rural Church: Norfolk 1760–1840', unpublished PhD thesis, University of St Andrews, 1977, pp. 131–53.

75 See Peter Virgin, *The Church in an Age of Negligence: Ecclesiastical Structure and Problems of Church Reform 1700–1840* (Cambridge: James Clarke & Co., 1989), p. 38.

76 John Bacon, *Liber Regis*, p. 678. Caution needs to be exercised at taking these figures at face value as actual values of livings fluctuated according to agricultural yields and the

Figure 3 *Wereham Church, engraving by Robert Ladbrooke,* c. *1821–43.*

Figure 4 *Wretton Church, engraving by Robert Ladbrooke,* c. *1821–43.*

Figure 5 *Marlingford Church, engraving by Robert Ladbrooke,* c. *1821–43.*

Figure 6 *Watlington Church, engraving by Robert Ladbrooke,* c. *1821–43.*

the local lord of the manor Thomas Greene, who was linked to the Pratts of Ryston Hall through his marriage to Mary Browne, the daughter of Mary Browne (née Pratt), Jermyn's paternal aunt.[77] Although Pratt was the incumbent, he did not serve Marlingford in person: the distance between Marlingford and Wereham and Wretton (approximately 30 miles) would have made it impossible for him to serve all the parishes in his charge. A list of clergy drawn up some time between 1752 and 1765 shows that Pratt had a curate (one Christopher Tuck at the time when the list was drawn up) officiate at Marlingford, while he continued to serve Wereham and Wretton as perpetual curate.[78] Non-residence (not residing in the parish that one served) and pluralism (the holding of two or more livings at once) were very common amongst the clergy in the eighteenth century, although there was an expectation that they reside in or near to the parish or parishes they directly served, and that they employ curates to act in their stead in any parishes they could not reach in person.[79] Although the issue of non-residence and pluralism is never directly broached in Pratt's *Modest Address to Lewis*, the focus being on the intractability of the countryfolk and the difficulty of policing their behaviour in isolated parishes, Pratt's own pluralism helps account for the defensive tone of the piece.

Soon after his presentation to the rectory of Marlingford, Pratt married Ann Stanforth on 3 July 1753, with his lifelong friend Charles Davy and Ann's sister Catherine Stanforth acting as witnesses. Pratt received a dowry of £300 as part of the marriage agreement.[80] The Stanforths came from the village of Salthouse on the north Norfolk coast and belonged to a prominent family of Salthouse maltsters and merchants. Ann's father, Henry Stanforth, had died two years before in 1751 and was buried in the

parishioners' willingness to pay tithes. See W. M. Jacob, *Lay People and Religion in the Early Eighteenth Century* (Cambridge: Cambridge University Press, 1996), pp. 35–40.

77 *Norwich Mercury*, 2 February 1751, p. 3. On Jermyn Pratt's relation to Thomas Green see the pedigree for the Browne family in George Alfred Carthew, *The Hundred of Launditch and Deanery of Brisley in the County of Norfolk* (Norwich: Miller and Leavins, 1877), pp. 464–5.

78 'List of Clergy', DN/VSM 9/1. We know that the list was made after 1752, when Pratt was made rector of Marlingford, and before 1765, since Horatio Fawcett, who ceased to be rector of Watlington in 1765, is still listed as its rector in 1765: *CDB*.

79 For a study of non-residence and pluralism and the various arrangements clergy made to provide services to the parishes in their charge see W. M. Jacob, 'A Practice of a Very Hurtful Tendency', in Derek Baker, ed., *The Church in Town and Countryside* (Oxford: Basil Blackwell, 1979), pp. 316–26.

80 'Marriage articles of Revd Jermyn Pratt of Downham Market, clerk, and Anne eldest daughter of Mary Stanforth of Salthouse, widow', NRO PRA 519-520, 381X7.

church of St Nicholas in Salthouse.[81] The Stanforths had acquired land around Salthouse in the early eighteenth century and were able to send a son, Robert Stanforth, to Cambridge.[82] Pratt may have met Ann through her brother Robert, who attended Gonville and Caius College from 1745 to 1749. Robert had also embarked on a career in the church, becoming the curate of Wiveton, near Salthouse, on 11 March 1750. His career was, however, cut short by his death the following year at the age of 24.[83]

In 1759 Jermyn Pratt and his brother Edward served in the newly formed Western Regiment of the Norfolk Militia which, with the Eastern Regiment of the Norfolk Militia, was the first new militia to be embodied after the passage of the Militia Acts of 1757 and 1758. The passage of these Acts through Parliament had been led by the Norfolk soldier and politician George Townshend, who subsequently became the colonel of the West Norfolk Militia, with Sir Armine Wodehouse, his fellow MP for the county of Norfolk, serving as colonel of the East Norfolk Militia. Under the 1758 Militia Act, militias were made up of men between the ages of eighteen and fifty, who were selected by ballot from lists drawn up by each parish in the kingdom. They were intended to act as a bulwark against the threat of foreign invasion during the Seven Years' War (1756–63). In a wider sense, Matthew McCormack observes, the new militias were 'a central component of a political worldview in which national pre-eminence was predicated upon the citizenry's masculine virtues of independence, vigilance, patriotism, and martial valour'.[84] By joining the militia, Jermyn and Edward Pratt could claim to be serving their country. At the same time, they were solidifying their connections to influential figures in Norfolk.

81 W. N. Dew, *The Monumental Inscriptions in the Hundred of Holt*, ed. W. Rye (Norwich, 1885), p. 117.

82 Henry Stanforth is described as a maltster in the entry for Robert Stanforth, in the *Biographical History of Gonville and Caius College 1349–1897* (*BGC*, 2:56). A detailed picture of the business of malting can be found in Mary Hardy's diary, who lived twenty miles inland from Salthouse in Coltishall. See *The Diary of Mary Hardy 1773–1809*, ed. Margaret Bird (4 vols., Kingston upon Thames: Burnham Press, 2013) and idem, *The Remaining Diary of Mary Hardy*, ed. Margaret Bird (Kingston upon Thames: Burnham Press, 2013).

83 Dew, *Monumental Inscriptions*, p. 118. It is possible that Robert's death was the occasion for Christopher Smart's ode 'On the Sudden Death of a Clergyman', dated 1751, the year of Robert's death, and first published in the *Poems, on Several Occasions* of 1752, to which Robert, along with Pratt, was a subscriber.

84 See Matthew McCormack, *Embodying the Militia in Georgian England* (Oxford: Oxford University Press, 2015), p. 14. For how the new militias were created see J. R. Western, *The English Militia in the Eighteenth Century: The Story of a Political Issue 1660–1802* (London: Routledge & Kegan Paul, 1965), pp. 127–61.

Edward Pratt was made a captain in the West Norfolk Militia and given command of a company that numbered about 40 men at any one time. Although as a militia regiment the company saw no actual fighting, it was hit especially hard by the outbreaks of smallpox that spread easily in the environment of the camp. Between 21 June 1759 and 23 May 1760, Edward Pratt lost nine of his men to the disease—more than any other captain.[85] A 'Pratt'—almost certainly our Jermyn Pratt—is listed as one of the three chaplains serving in the Western Regiment of the Norfolk Militia in George Walpole's return as Lord Lieutenant of Norfolk dated 9 June 1759.[86] Together with his brother, Pratt would probably have travelled with the Norfolk Militia in their march in the summer of 1760 to Portsmouth, pausing to assemble before King George II at Kensington on their way there on 17 July.[87] The familiarity of the letter and its accompanying vulgar poem 'Grunnelia or the Sow in the Dumps' that Pratt sent to William Windham of Felbrigg Hall in February 1760 may be partially explained by the fact that Windham was serving as lieutenant-colonel of the same regiment of the Norfolk Militia in which Pratt was serving as a chaplain.[88] Windham himself published *A Plan of Discipline Composed for the Use of the Militia of the County of Norfolk* (1759), a guide that promised to impart 'so much military knowledge, as is sufficient to enable a gentleman to go through the common course of duty, and be what is called a good battalion officer'.[89] As we shall see, however, in the late 1760s both Jermyn and Edward Pratt were attempting to distance themselves from the Norfolk Militia.

Pratt's sister Harriot married Thurlow Stafford in 1752, but their marriage was shortlived. In 1760, when Pratt sent his letter to Windham with his naughty poem about the lascivious sow Grunnelia, she was staying with the Windhams at Felbrigg Hall and mourning her husband's recent death. After his brother-in-law's passing, Pratt began collecting and recording the

85 See 'Return of the N° of men that Has had the Small pox and the No dead May 23 1760', NRO MS 265, 3A3.

86 See Colonel Sir Charles Harvey, ed., *The History of the 4th Battalion Norfolk Regiment (Late East Norfolk Militia)* (Jarrold & Sons: London, 1899), p. 27. There are no other Pratts listed in the *Clergy Database* for the Diocese of Norwich so we can be nearly certain Jermyn was the chaplain listed here.

87 For the Norfolk Militia's movements around the country see ibid., pp. 30–42.

88 By February 1760, however, Pratt was at home at Stoke Ferry and Windham was at Felbrigg Hall, rather than with the recruits of the Norfolk Militia, who were then quartered in Cirencester.

89 [William Windham], *A Plan of Discipline, Composed for the Use of the Militia of the County of Norfolk* (London: J. Shuckburgh, 1759), p. xxxiv.

rent that was owed to his sister on the lands formerly owned by her husband in Denver, the parish adjoining Ryston to the west. Half-yearly records in Pratt's hand appear in an account book in the Norfolk Record Office from 1761 until Harriot's death in 1779, after which the entries stop.[90] In 1765, Pratt was presented to the benefice of Watlington (between King's Lynn and Downham Market) by the local landowner John Davis, presumably because his predecessor as rector, Henry Robinson, had become too infirm to perform his duties. Although the living itself was only sworn of a clear yearly value of £14 16s 8d, it was accorded a large augmentation of £80 under Queen Anne's Bounty.[91] On this appointment, Watlington became the parish that Pratt served in person, employing a curate to minister at Wretton and Wereham. His hand appears in the parish register from 1768 and he affirms in his visitation return for 1777 'I keep a strict & regular residence at Watlington.'[92] (This may not be entirely true, however, since at the time of his death Pratt kept a house in Downham Market.) Whilst at Watlington, he officiated over the wedding between his and Ann's niece Margaret and the Reverend Dixon Hoste, the Rector of Tittleshall, in the church at Salthouse in 1775.[93] Pratt must have been close to the Hostes and their family, since he directed his executors to lay out the profits arising from his estate, after his debts had been settled, in the form of legacies to the Hostes' children.[94] The Pratts would remain childless themselves, although the presence of Nicholas Rowe's English translation of Claude Quillet's didactic poem *Callipædia; or, An Art how to have Handsome Children* (originally published in Latin in 1655 and in English translation in 1710) in Pratt's library suggests that the couple may at one time have intended

90 See 'Tenant receipt and expenditure accounts of Jermyn Pratt for estates in Denver, Roydon, Fordham etc.', NRO BUL 8/10, 614X8, 1739–79.

91 Bacon, *Liber Regis*, p. 671. Notice of Pratt's preferment to Watlington was given in the 'Ecclesiastical Preferments', *The London Magazine, or, Gentleman's Monthly Intelligencer* 36 (1767), p. 147.

92 'Visitation Questions: Fincham 1777', NRO DN/VIS 27a/8.

93 See 'Parish Records of Salthouse: Marriages, 1755–1812; banns, 1780–1958', NRO, PD 23/2.

94 A suit was subsequently filed on behalf of the children born after the eldest surviving child had attained the age of 16, claiming that they ought to benefit from the bequest just as their elder siblings had, with the judge Edward Thurlow, Lord Thurlow ruling in favour of the younger children on 19 March 1798. See Charles Sumner, ed., *Reports of Cases Argued and Determined in the High Court of Chancery, from the Year MDCCLXXXIX to MMDCCCXVII* (20 vols., Boston: Charles C. Little and James Brown, 1844), 3:1730–3. The case subsequently became important for the development of case law around perpetuities and the case is still mentioned in legal textbooks. See, for example, Philip H. Petit, *Equity and the Law of Trusts*, 12th ed. (Oxford: Oxford University Press, 2012), p. 470.

to have them.[95] At some point in the couple's lives, Catherine Stanforth, Ann's unmarried sister, seems to have come to live with them. The epitaph for Catherine in Watlington Church, carved into the same plaque on the north side of the church as Jermyn's and Ann's, describes her as having lived 'a long life of almost uninterrupted sickness', although she did survive the couple, dying in 1810 at the age of 80. According to the epitaph, the three were very close: 'These were inseparable in life/ and in the grave they are not divided' (see Plate 8).

An impression of the rhythms of Pratt's life as a country priest can be gleaned from a fragment of a diary that appears at the end of the manuscript version of his poem 'The Sunday Visit' (1781). By this time Pratt was serving as the rector of Watlington Church and a short series of diary entries at the end of the poem records that he buried three people between Wednesday 21 February and Sunday 4 March 1781. The yearly round as a working parish priest would have seen Pratt officiate over christenings and marriages, in addition to holding regular services every Sunday. In his visitation return of 1777, Pratt wrote that 'Public Service is duly performed twice; every Lords Day, & one Sermon preachd; I Catechise the children generally during the time of Lent, the Sacrament of ye Lords Supper is administered thrice at least every year; the number of Communicants, from Sixteen to twenty four.'[96] Pratt owned a large collection of sermons in his library, from which he might have drawn inspiration for his own sermons or, when inspiration flagged, perhaps pilfered from. Pratt also owned a copy of Thomas Sheridan's *Lectures on Elocution* (1752) in which Sheridan discusses the importance of gestures of emphasis, which Sheridan noted 'is no where so strongly perceived as in the general manner of reading the Church Service; which is often so ill performed, that not only the beauty, and spirit of the service, but the very meaning is obscured, concealed, or wholly perverted'.[97] In the content of their sermons as well as their delivery of them, Pratt and other clergymen were charged with making the scripture intelligible to the laity. In his charge written during his visitation of 1763, Philip Yonge, the Bishop of Norwich, advised that 'controversial Sermons are in general to be avoided as having tendency rather to perplex the understanding than inform the conscience', but he also stressed that the parishioners should be well versed

95 John Armstrong in *The Art of Preserving Health* objected to the poem on the grounds of indecency. See his *The Art of Preserving Health: Eighteenth-Century Sensibility in Practice*, ed. Adam Budd (Farnham: Ashgate, 2011), p. 214.

96 'Visitation Questions: Fincham 1777', NRO DN/VIS 27a/8.

97 Thomas Sheridan, *A Course of Lectures on Elocution: Together with Two Dissertations on Language* (London: W. Strahan, 1769), p. 59.

in the scripture, especially 'the various meanings of those words, which have become somewhat like technical, in school divinity especially, and have been the subject of so much misrepresentation' and be able to see extracts from the Bible 'as parts of one coherent and regular discourse'.[98] Aside from serving as preachers and spiritual guides, clergymen were responsible for maintaining the church buildings and highways in the parish and administering poor relief in their role as chairs of the vestry meetings that were held at the church.[99] Clergymen were also called on to serve as doctors and comforters and spiritual guides to parishioners on their deathbeds. In the manuscript prayerbook that is included in the Pratt folder, Pratt copied down two prayers from The Order for the Visitation of the Sick from the Book of Common Prayer, probably so he would have a lightweight copy of the prayers to take with him when he was called to minister to the sick and the dying.[100] This duty brought together the clergyman's double role as minister to the bodies as well as the souls of his flock.[101]

The priest was also expected to exhort his parishioners to lead exemplary Christian lives and hold them to account when they failed to do so. Clergymen were meant to impress upon their parishioners the sinful nature of sexual offences such as fornication and bastardry. In his *Modest Address to Lewis* Pratt proposes harsh measures for punishing women who have children out of wedlock, suggesting that they be made to wear a badge with a 'W' (for 'Whore') on it 'at large for two or three sundays together in ye Parish church where ye Bastard was born' and that they be jailed or fined 'in case of Obstinacy and disobedience' [*p. 28*]. Pratt's plan, had it ever been put into effect, would have gone against the current, since evidence from ecclesiastical church records points to a marked decrease in prosecutions for fornication and bastardy across England, including in Norwich, from the mid-eighteenth century.[102] The clergy increasingly had to rely on persuasion rather than punishment in upholding sexual mores. In Pratt's play *The Grange*, the story of Sophy Appleyard seems intended to show the

98 Philip Yonge, *The Charge of the Reverend Father in God, Philip, Bishop of Norwich, Delivered to the Clergy of his Diocese, at his Primary Visitation, A.D. 1763* (Norwich: William Chase, 1763).

99 See W. M. Jacob, *Lay People and Religion*, pp. 9–11.

100 See NRO PRA 664/8.

101 Lewis Bagot, the Bishop of Norwich, took care to note this role in *A Sermon Preached at the Cathedral Church in Norwich, On Thursday August 21, 1783. On Occasion of the Anniversary Meeting of the Governors of the Norfolk and Norwich Hospital* (Norwich: 1783), pp. 5–6, 8.

102 See R. B. Outhwaite, *The Rise and Fall of the Ecclesiastical Courts, 1500–1860* (Cambridge: Cambridge University Press, 2006), pp. 10–11, 83–4.

consequences of premarital sex for eighteenth-century women: after many assignations with Captain Wilson in the plantations, Sophy is left pregnant and without legal remedy, while her lover is imprisoned.

Sabbath-breaking was another sin that was often animadverted upon by the clergy. A sermon against Sabbath-breaking, published by an anonymous clergyman in Cambridge in 1733, lamented that, 'The Sabbath, instead of being observed as a Day of Rest and Devotion, we too often see a Day of Noise and Tumult,' with parishioners choosing to frequent pubs rather than churches and children frolicking in the streets instead of receiving religious instruction.[103] In his answers given as part of the 1784 visitation, Pratt reported that there were no parishioners in Watlington who 'totaly absent themselves' from Sunday service, although he did add that there were 'too many very remiss with respect to the Sunday duties'. Pratt warned readers of the *Norwich Mercury* against Sabbath-breaking in his poem 'The Sunday Visit in a Letter from Brother William to Brother Gregory', in which the decision of a family to skip church in favour of paying a social visit is punished when a series of mishaps strike them on their return home. The idea that God could enact immediate vengeance for Sabbath-breaking was widespread. The young Parson Woodforde, before his presentment to the Norfolk living of Weston Longville, recorded an incident in which he broke a razor on its strop as a warning not to shave or do any other kind of work on the Sabbath.[104] A much greater misfortune was reported in the *Norfolk Chronicle* to have befallen a young man who went into the sea on the Sabbath to bring ashore a large fish that had injured itself against a large rock and 'fell a lifeless corpse, his body floating on the water'.[105]

Pratt expressed his pessimism about his own ability to improve his parishioners' penchant for Sabbath-breaking, or their morals more generally. In his handwritten responses to the questions issued to Norfolk clergymen as part of the 1777 visitation, Pratt admitted that 'ye Labours of ye Clergy can do but Little in these times, for ye preservation of morality, & good Order.' He expressed his scepticism that one priest could do much to prevent parishioners taking the Lord's name in vain or breaking the Sabbath, writing that a substantial improvement in morals would only be possible if there were 'more Magistrates for ye due execution of ye Laws; or invest ye Parochial Clergy with power to put in force such Laws, as respect only ye morals of

103 *A Dissuasive from Sabbath-Breaking Deliver'd in a Sermon on April the 22nd* (Cambridge, 1733), p. 6.

104 *Woodforde*, 1:85.

105 *Norfolk Chronicle*, 1 December 1787, p. 3.

our people, such I mean; as profane swearing & cursing, Sabbath breaking & ye like; for which Individuals cannot be punished in many places without punishing ye Parishioners in a greater degree by the advancement of Rates.'[106] In his unpublished *A Modest Address to Lewis*, written when he had, by his own count, spent 'very near to forty years' in the church' [*p. 5*] Pratt also complained of the incorrigible sinfulness of his flock. *A Modest Address to Lewis* was written to defend both himself and his fellow clergymen from the Bishop of Norwich Lewis Bagot's *A Charge Delivered to the Clergy at the Primary Visitation of Lewis, Lord Bishop of Norfolk* (1784),[107] in which Bagot upbraided the Norfolk clergy for failing to fulfil their pastoral responsibilities to their congregations by not living in the parishes they were supposed to be serving. Pratt must have felt himself to be among the clergy whom Bagot was criticizing.

In his effort to play up the hardships afflicting him in the early part of his career in *A Modest Address*, Pratt appears to have counted the consolidated curacies of Wereham and Wretton as two curacies and to have counted the rectorship of Watlington as a third in referring to 'ye hard Duty of my triple curacies' [*p. 1*]. As we have seen, Pratt soon acquired the rectory of Marlingford after being appointed as perpetual curate of Wereham and Wretton, although he continued to serve his curacies in person until acquiring the rectorship of Watlington. But the impoverished and harried curate of no independent means, forced to serve multiple parishes to scratch out a meagre living, was a familiar type in the literature of the time. In Jonathan Swift's 'On a Curate's Complaint of Hard Duty' the fictional curate recounts walking three miles to one church, riding four to another, marrying three couples, baptizing two babies, and delivering three sermons, exclaiming at the end of the poem 'All this perform'd by Robert Hewit/ What mortal else could e'er go through it!'[108] Pratt's own comic essay *The Zgubbs* describes a curate named 'Mr Twist', who 'served a triple curacy for a very small Stipend (ye great Tithes were <u>all</u> in ye Bishop) and by ye great fatigue from his duty was supposed to be in what is commonly calld a Galloping consumption' [*p. 18*]. Pratt offers some advice for impecunious curates in his manuscript poem 'The Jay A Fable', which warns curates

106 See 'Visitation Questions: Fincham 1777', NRO DN/VIS 27a/8. Pratt made the same point in his return for the 1784 visitation. See 'Visitation Questions: Fincham 1784', NRO DN/VIS 30/3.

107 *A Charge Delivered to the Clergy at the Primary Visitation of Lewis, Lord Bishop of Norfolk 1784* (Norwich: Printed by W. Chase and Co., 1784).

108 Jonathan Swift, *The Complete Poems*, ed. Pat Rodgers (Harmondsworth: Penguin Classics, 1983), p. 545, ll. 16–17.

against marrying women solely for their riches in order to escape their impoverished condition:

> Would you ye priests Lead Happy Lives.
> Take not for wealth these Jays for wives
> Let Merit Lead you to preferment:
> A Jay at best is but Interment. [*f. 1v*, ll. 83–6]

Of course, the road to preferment was much more easily trodden by well-connected men from relatively wealthy backgrounds like Pratt, who did not have to contemplate such recourses as marrying a 'Jay' in order escape from poverty.

Clergymen like Pratt formed part of the social world of the landed gentry and they shared in their pleasures and diversions. Pratt's long poem *September: A Rural Poem*, deliberately published at the beginning of the partridge shooting season on 1 September 1780 opens as a mock epic satirizing the mania for hunting that united country squires and priests (the 'gifted sons/ Of mitred Aaron' [*p.* 5, ll. 90–1]). Pratt takes aim at childish sportsmen who neglect their wives and their country (which was embroiled in the American Revolutionary War) for the diversion of shooting birds, the laying of man traps to discourage poaching, and the over-zealous prosecution of the game laws.[109] The poem includes several descriptions of the suffering of the birds shot by hunters, who 'rob Creation to enrich a pye' [*p. 9*, l. 158]. Pratt's name appears on a list of people who had paid the Norfolk game duty however,[110] and the poem does not oppose hunting per se, but rather emphasises the need to keep the passions of shooting more or less within the bounds of decorousness, as when in a footnote Pratt notes that 'Fiery young sportsmen will sometimes, we are informed, crush the head of a partridge in the mouth, to shorten the time of its dying: we wish this to proceed from an act of tenderness only, and not for the sake of expedition' [*p. 10*]. The poem often wanders from a strict focus on shooting, however, finding room for satirical reflections, for example, on the elections that take place every seven years, when, as Pratt writes in another footnote, 'It is wonderful to consider, how smooth, and how very much in season great men are, on the approach of an election year; occasioned, it is said

109 Advertisements that man traps have been placed on estates to deter poachers were common in the period. Pratt's nephew Edward Roger Pratt placed an advertisement in the *Norfolk Chronicle* in 1789 that 'MAN-TRAPS' and 'SPRING-GUNS' would be placed on his lands. See *Norfolk Chronicle*, 29 August 1789, p. 3.

110 See 'Norfolk Game Duty', *Norfolk Chronicle*, 3 October 1789, p. 1.

by a certain *political rouge*, which clarifies the face, and gives a delightful simmering to the whole countenance, keeping all the muscles and dimples for a time, at least, in excellent preservation' [*p. 18*]. Pratt had had occasion to experience this political rouge for himself, especially in the contested election of 1768. We turn in the next section to Pratt's engagement with politics, both local and national.

Politics

Many of Pratt's writings address the two great political disputes that marked the two decades between 1764 and 1784: the debate over the prerogatives of the king and the ministry in the wake of the Wilkes affair and the controversy over British government's handling of the American Revolutionary War. Pratt's first political satires were written as part of the flurry of political squibs that circulated in Norfolk during the 1768 general election, in which the seats of Norwich, King's Lynn, and the county of Norfolk were all contested in campaigns that became acrimonious and generated a large volume of fractious election literature.[111] The ostensible issue over which the contest was fought can be traced back to the 1763 arrest of the radical MP John Wilkes, after the publication of the famous number 45 of the *North Briton* on 23 April 1763.[112] The warrant on which Wilkes was arrested did not name any persons, referring only to 'the authors, printers and publishers' of the *North Briton*. After voting that number 45 of the *North Briton* was libellous, the House of Commons debated the legality of general warrants themselves and voted on 17 February 1764 narrowly in

111 The literature that circulated about the Norfolk campaign is collected in *The Contest*. For the King's Lynn election literature see *The Lynn Magazine: or A Collection of Papers, Published during the Contest in that Town* (?Lynn, 1768). The Norwich election literature is collected in *Miscellaneous Pieces in Prose and Verse: Relative to the Contested Elections for Members of Parliament in the County of Norfolk and City and County of Norwich* (Norwich: S. White, 1768). For the context of the Norfolk 1768 election see Kathleen Wilson, *The Sense of the People: Politics, Culture and Imperialism in England, 1715–1785* (Cambridge: Cambridge University Press, 1998), John A. Phillips, *Electoral Behavior in Unreformed England: Plumpers, Splitters, and Straights* (Princeton: Princeton University Press, 1982), Nicholas Rogers, *Whigs and Cities: Popular Politics in the Age of Walpole and Pitt* (Oxford: Oxford University Press, 1989), P. J. Corfield, *Towns, Trade, Religion, and Radicalism: The Norwich Perspective on English History* (Norwich: Centre of East Anglian Studies, 1980), and Brian David Hayes, 'Politics in Norfolk, 1750–1832', unpublished PhD thesis, University of Cambridge, 1958, pp. 162–89.

112 In this number, Wilkes denounced George Grenville's King's Speech made in praise of the Peace of Paris that ended the Seven Years' War.

favour of the ministry's position that general warrants were legal.[113] The incumbent MPs for Norfolk Sir Armine Wodehouse and Thomas De Grey were identified by their opponents Sir Edward Astley and Wenman Coke as supporters of 'General Warrants'.[114] Both Wodehouse and De Grey also served in the Norfolk Militia: Wodehouse as colonel of the East Norfolk Militia and De Grey as the lieutenant colonel of the West Norfolk Militia. The militia itself became an election issue in the Norfolk campaign, with supporters of Coke and Astley reportedly drinking a toast to 'No Militia Power in Elections'.[115]

Richard Gardiner was the prime propagandist on behalf of the anti-ministerial challengers in the 1768 election in King's Lynn and for the Norfolk election from his residence in Swaffham, 15 miles to the east of Watlington. Pratt assisted him in his efforts to elect Astley and Coke. In Gardiner's poem 'Clackclose Triumphant', written after Sir Edward Astley was elected MP for Norfolk, Jermyn Pratt, along with his father Roger Pratt and his brother Edward Pratt, are identified as joining 'the patriot train' in favour of Astley and Coke:

> See *Riston*'s old Sire join the patriot train,
> And forget for a while, diseases and pain!
> His two gallant sons the first summons attend,
> And with vigor support their relation and friend ...[116]

Pratt may well have sincerely sympathized with Wilkes and the radical tradition he represented. He had a copy in his library of Henry St. John, First Viscount Bolingbroke's *On the Idea of a Patriot King* (1749), a key influence on the radical patriot tradition of the 1760s and beyond (Octavo, no. 78).[117] Despite the framing of the 1768 contest for Norfolk as one between supporters and opponents of 'General Warrants', however, private interests

---

113 'John Wilkes (1725–1797)': *Oxford DNB*.

114 Sir Armine Wodehouse was accused of voting in favour of general warrants. While Thomas De Grey was not an MP at the time that the vote on the legality of general warrants was held, he was accused of supporting their legality in two separate speeches. See *Contest*, 11–12. An advertisement printed in the *Norwich Mercury* on 1 November 1767, however, issued in Wodehouse's and De Grey's names, denied the charge that either of them voted for general warrants, claiming that the question of their legality had never been moved in the House of Commons; see ibid., pp. 34–5.

115 *Contest*, 56.

116 *Gard*, 145.

117 See David Armitage, 'A Patriot for Whom?: The Afterlives of Bolingbroke's Patriot King', *Journal of British Studies*, 36.4 (1997), pp. 397–418.

were powerful shapers of loyalties to the candidates.[118] The Pratts had a clear personal rationale for supporting Astley's campaign. They were linked to the Astley family through marriage: Pratt's brother Edward had married Blanche Astley, Sir Edward Astley's sister, on 31 December 1751.[119] In *September: A Rural Poem*, Pratt interpolates an encomium to Astley, who was elected in the 1768 contest and was still in 1780 one of the two MPs for Norfolk, in which Astley is distinguished from those politicians who only affect to love liberty at election time:

> O! how unlike to this is his good name,
> Whose virtues are as public as his fame;
> His country's idol, and the good man's praise,
> And uncorrupted in the worst of days:
> Statesmen and Peers, if this be worth approv'd,
> Know A——y lives, thus honour'd and belov'd. [*p. 19*, ll. 377–82]

Pratt's connection with Astley is a good example of the difficulty of separating out ideological principles from personal allegiances in eighteenth-century politics.

Pratt sought to aid Astley's election by penning a scurrilous poem on his opponent Thomas De Grey in the final stages of the 1768 Norfolk election. *Cinderetta* follows Gardiner's example in giving De Grey the name of 'Hurlo Thrumbo', after the braggadocious warrior in Samuel Johnson of Cheshire's play *Hurlothrumbo* (1729). The poem is obviously modelled on Pratt's poem 'Grunnelia or the Sow in the Dumps' about a lovesick sow pining for her lover, translating the earlier poem's travesty of pastoral poetry into political satire. The poem opens on the kitchen maid Cinderetta languishing in the absence of De Grey, who neglects her for the Norfolk Militia and Parliament. The dirty house in which she cooks and cleans serves as an extended metaphor for the corruption of the House of Commons. Like the riotous labourers in *The Coal-Heavers*, Cinderetta belongs to a gallery of lowborn characters in Pratt's writings who are brought into uncomfortable proximity with genteel society.[120]

---

118 Brian David Hayes in a PhD thesis influenced by Sir Lewis Namier's approach to the politics of the mid eighteenth century goes as far to suggest that Thomas De Grey's private correspondence, which hardly mentions 'General Warrants' at all, 'gives no support to any conclusion but that the gentry's choice of party in 1768 had little or no reference to any but distinctively private motives', see Hayes, 'Politics in Norfolk, 1750–1832', p. 36.

119 Parish Records of Melton Constable, NRO PD 656/2.

120 For a study of the contemptuous humour directed at the lowborn in eighteenth-century literature and culture see Simon Dickie, *Cruelty and Laughter: Forgotten Comic*

Pratt also sparred with his fellow clergyman the Reverend Robert Potter, who supported De Grey and Wodehouse, in the pages of the *Norwich Mercury*. The literary spat between Pratt and Potter began when Pratt published a satirical mock news article that reported that the two colonels De Grey and Wodehouse had marched to Downham Market to recruit voters to their cause but 'it so unluckily happened, that not one single Recruit appeared, either at the Drum's-Head or at their Quarters', whereas the 'The Sons of FREEDOM, to the Number of Ninety-four' had enlisted with Astley and Coke 'under the Banner of LIBERTY' [*p. 3*].[121] The following week, a short letter probably penned by Potter under the name of 'Mr. Anti-Puff' appeared in answer to Pratt's article.[122] The letter charged that the mock news article published the previous week had misrepresented the canvassing at Downham Market. It added that even if there had been more supporters of Astley and Coke at Downham than their opponents, the hundred of Clackclose as a whole was solidly in favour of De Grey and Wodehouse [*p. 3*]. Pratt then responded with a short poem entitled 'Mr. Anti-Puff' that asked rhetorically 'WHO first began to puff and crack and boast/ From Yarmouth-Wells—and down along the Coast?' [*p. 3*, ll. 1–2]—and queried which of the two pairs of candidates had supported general warrants—ironically contrasting 'HOLKHAM's rich Heir' (Coke) with 'sweet Sir ARM[INE]' and 'Imperious AST[LE]Y' with 'the meek De G[RE]Y' [*p. 3*, ll. 3–4]. (Of course, Pratt intended the reader to mentally reverse the epithets given to the respective pairs of candidates.)

This little squib of Pratt's provoked a further squib ('To Mr. Ranti-Puff') that was probably written by Robert Potter, which we have reproduced in the appendix. The poem highlights the hypocrisy of Jermyn and Edward Pratt attacking De Grey and Wodehouse for being colonels in the Norfolk Militia when they themselves had served in the Norfolk Militia as, respectively, a captain and a chaplain. Its pointed epitaph is 'The Man who lives in a House of Glass, should not be the first, to throw Stones' [*p. 3*]. The squib ridicules Jermyn and Edward Pratt and the other supporters of Astley and Coke at Downham Market, well known for its butter market, having them level the absurd charge against De Grey and Wodehouse that they mean to 'take away our butter' [*p. 3*, l. 15].[123] The squib's caricature of Pratt is

Literature and the Unsentimental Eighteenth Century (Chicago: The University of Chicago Press, 2011), pp. 111–55.

121 For the whole mock news article see Two Squibs on the 1768 Norfolk Election in Shorter Poems.

122 For the response see Two Replies to Pratt's Two Squibs on the Norfolk Election in Appendix 1.

123 Downham Market was famous for its butter market that was held near a stone bridge

one of the few independent pieces of evidence we have for what he was like in person: it may well have drawn on Potter's own personal observation of Pratt's mannerisms, especially since Pratt and Potter were contemporaneous students at Cambridge and the writer of the squib claims he was himself a witness to the canvassing at Downham Market. Potter mocks Pratt's pretentions to learning and wit, having the denizens of Downham Market chant 'Now J[ermy]n P[ratt] we look to you,/ For you are both witty and wise:/ In this distress what shall we do,/ To save both ourselves and our pies?' [*p. 3*, ll. 40]. It also dwells on Pratt's affectedly diffident manner:

> His modest eyes first cast upon the ground,
> Then rais'd his head, and leering look'd around:
> He cough'd, he spit, and after much deep studying,
> At length thus spoke the reverend Jack Pudding. [*p. 3*, ll. 43–6]

The poem ends with 'the learned clerk … feeding of his hounds' [*p. 3*, l. 66], hinting that Pratt's real interests lie more with hunting than either learning or religion. The whole exchange suggests that the increasingly divisive politics of the late 1760s led Pratt to align himself with Astley and Coke and to pit himself against other prominent Norfolk figures, particularly those who commanded the militia that he once served.

The poem *The Coal-Heavers*, published anonymously in 1774, is a heavily fictionalised retelling of a violent riot that occurred in King's Lynn in 1773. On 9 October 1773, ten men and two women were arraigned on charges of gathering at the ship *Good Intent*, owned by Richard Tindall and, with the aid of 'Sticks Stones and other offensive Weapons', preventing Tindall and labourers from working. When justice Charles Hazlewood arrested John Cross, one of the rioters, three other rioters were reported to have beaten Hazlewood, along with a homeowner, Thomas Ghent, to the extent to that both of their lives were 'greatly despaired of'. The motive that was imputed to the rioters was 'to raise enhance and increase the price and wages of Work and labour'. Of the twelve people accused of rioting and assault, Samuel Fane was imprisoned for seven months, John Austin, Daniel Knapp, and Daniel Yates for six months, Thomas Austin and Thomas Moore for three months, Elizabeth Jarrett for one month, and Clement Swinger and George Hall for ten days. Ann Coker was released but required to pay a surety for her good behaviour and, although Ralph Long was in fact acquitted of all charges, he

across the Ouze. See *The Universal British Directory of Trade, Commerce, and Manufacture* (4 vols., London: The British Directory Office, 1790–2), ii, pp. 782–3.

was also made to pay a surety because, while being held in prison on charges of assault, he had threatened the justices that he would exact his revenge on them for imprisoning him. As part of its verdict, the court imposed a curfew on victuallers in King's Lynn in order to discourage further riots in the future.[124] This incident resembled an earlier outbreak of violence involving coal heavers. George Rudé describes how on 23 May 1768, in a year in which worker disputes spread across the kingdom, East London coal heavers 'boarded the *Thomas And Mary*, lying in Shadwell Dock, and threatened to murder any sailor who continued to load; on the next day, sailors coming ashore from another collier, the *Free Love*, were attacked with bludgeons and cutlasses, two were wounded and a young sailor, John Beatty, was stabbed to death.'[125] The striking coal heavers on the East London docks had earlier celebrated the temporary release of Wilkes from prison on 20 April 1768 with cries of 'Wilkes and Liberty, and coal-heavers for ever!'[126] The echo of the Shadwell Dock incident at King's Lynn posed the question of how 'respectable' supporters of liberty like Pratt could distinguish themselves from the plebian radicals who had also adopted Wilkes as a figurehead.[127]

The Coal-Heavers uses the resources of mock epic to diminish the incident at King's Lynn—although its writing may have been prompted by the awareness that the cry of 'Wilkes and Liberty!' had opened a Pandora's box, with invocations of 'liberty' not confineable to the language of elite politics alone. The leader of the rioters is associated with Entellus, the Sicilian hero who fights Dares in a boxing match in Virgil's *The Aeneid*. The riot itself in the poem is imputed to a demon sent by the jealous Olympic gods to make trouble in King's Lynn, whose leading citizens 'dare to live, and act like Jove' [*p.* 4, l. 26]. The coal heavers are stirred up by the demon who temporarily inhabits the body of the landlord of the Three Pigeons tavern, the place 'Where for good Cheer, the loud Coal-heavers meet' [*p.* 5, l. 80], and urges them to fight for better wages so that they

124 John Cross was also found guilty but there is no record of his sentence. For arraignment and the verdict see King's Lynn, Court Record of 9 October 1773, KL/C20/3. The dispute is briefly described in John M. Barney, 'The Merchants and Maritime Trade of King's Lynn in the Eighteenth Century', unpublished PhD thesis, University of East Anglia, 1977, p. 186.

125 George Rudé, *Wilkes and Liberty: A Social Study of 1763 to 1774* (Oxford: Oxford University Press, 1962), p. 98.

126 ibid., p. 47.

127 Adrian Randall discusses how Wilkes 'managed in the years from 1763 to 1771 to redefine the relationship between the patrician politicians and the plebs' in *Riotous Assemblies: Popular Protest in Hanoverian England* (Oxford: Oxford University Press, 2006), pp. 195, 199.

can afford better drink. The poem culminates in a brawl pitting the coal heavers against gods who have taken the shape of King's Lynn's mayor and various dignitaries and dandies. Pratt draws attention to how the rioters' work makes them racially ambiguous, making it difficult to know if 'Negro *Daniel*' [*p. 7*, l. 121] or 'Black George' [*p.* 7, l. 125] are white European men turned black from hauling coal or black men of African origins working as coal heavers.[128] In any case, the repeated identification of the coal heavers as black marks their difference from the prosperous citizens they fight. But the poem is also animated by the transgression of social boundaries, as when the climactic battle results in the 'mingled Blood of Watermen and Beaux' [*p. 3*, l. 10].

In the late 1770s and early 1780s, Pratt was preoccupied with the American Revolutionary War. The leading questions in the manuscript entitled 'Constitutional Queries', which we believe dates to early 1778, show that Pratt had little enthusiasm for the war itself or faith in the competence of the ministry managing it. But the central implication of the queries is that there is no use in agitating against the war, for to do so would 'Unsettle ye minds of his Majestys Lower Subjects, who neither are, or can be capable of forming a proper Judgment, of ye true & real State of these Kingdoms' [*f. 1r*]. As we have seen, Pratt contributed 'An Occasional Prologue' to a performance of *The Clandestine Marriage*, which is ostensibly written in support of the war, though the main motivation for the performance and the Prologue itself was to raise funds for the 'Wives, Widows, and Families of Impress'd Men'.

> Far from these peaceful Scenes, by Nature brave,
> Our Sons of Neptune, mount the boist'rous Wave:
> For Britains Weal, the Dang'rous Torrent stem,
> They play their parts for us, and We for them:
> Without their Aid, the blessings of our Isle,
> Wou'd soon drop off, and Love forget to smile;
> If thro' their Valour, we with comfort live,
> Returns are claims! 'tis gratitude to give. [Print Version, ll. 13–20][129]

Writing as a living witness of the period in his history of King's Lynn, William Richards noted that 'The effect of the war with America … was

128 Richard Maguire observes that slave ships visited King's Lynn and that people of African origins and descent, whether nominally free or enslaved, laboured on them in *Africans in East Anglia*, pp. 134–6.

129 We quote from the print version; for the manuscript draft see the Appendix 3.

severely felt at Lynn. Our trade was much cramped, many of our ships were captured, our sailors were reduced mostly to old men and lads, by the guardians of the constitution, and the demonstrators of the unalienableness of our rights, the reality of our freedom, the *press gangs*.'[130]

Pratt's poem 'Political Duck-Hunting' (1779) allowed him to vent his frustrations at the conduct of the war, for which as a clergyman he was obliged to support in his fast day sermons. (The fact that a short entry recording the fast day of 21 February 1781 at the bottom of the manuscript version of 'A Sunday Visit' suggests that Pratt in this poem may have been displacing his own reluctance to observe the fast day onto his parishioners' reluctance to observe the Sabbath.) 'Political Duck-Hunting' uses a hunting dog's unsuccessful pursuit of a duck to allegorize the engagement of the British and French navies at the inconclusive Battle of Ushant (27 July 1778) during the American Revolutionary War. However, the Battle of Ushant itself was old news when 'Political Duck-Hunting' was published in the *Norwich Mercury* on 18 September 1779. The poem uses the Battle of Ushant as a synecdoche for the American Revolutionary War as a whole, which appeared to be dragging on with no end in sight. The poem may also be an oblique comment on the political fallout of the battle which, like the war, could be seen as a great deal of fuss with 'nothing doing' [*p. 4*, l. 30]. Augustus Keppel, the commander of the English navy at the time of the battle, was court marshalled on charges that he had fled the French fleet when he should have engaged it. The court martial was at the instigation of Sir Hugh Palliser, in what was widely seen as a partisan attack on the anti-ministerial Keppel, between January and February 1779. After Keppel was exonerated, mass demonstrations broke out in support of Keppel across England and Palliser's house in Pall Mall was pillaged. The *Ipswich Journal* reported that on 15 February the bells at Beccles in Suffolk had rung for 3 hours and 23 minutes 'being the greatest performance ever done on those bells' and that there had been 'illuminations and fireworks at Norwich, Cambridge, Chelmsford, and Sudbury, on account of Admiral Keppel's acquittal'.[131] Palliser would himself be court-martialed in April 1779, although Keppel declined to have him prosecuted.[132] 'Political Duck-Hunting', then, is less about the Battle of Ushant itself as the

130 William Richards, *The History of Lynn* (King's Lynn: W. G. Whittingham, 1812), p. 956.

131 *Ipswich Journal*, 20 February 1779, p. 3.

132 For a detailed account of the Keppel-Palliser affair and the popular reaction to it, see Nicholas Rogers, *Crowds, Culture, and Politics in Georgian Britain* (Oxford: Clarendon Press, 1988), pp. 122–51.

experience of military and political paralysis in the age of the American Revolutionary War.

Pratt lived to see the loss of the American colonies and the advent of the French Revolution. Although there is no record of what he made of the latter event, he did have a copy of Edmund Burke's *Reflections on the Revolution in France* (1790) in his library at the time of his death. Pratt survived Ann Pratt, who died in the spring of 1787, by four years. In *September: A Rural Poem*, Pratt included a section in praise of married life, with an apostrophe to an idealised wife that might also be read as an apostrophe to Ann in particular:

> With thee conversing, each returning day
> Springs with fresh joy, and sheds a brighter ray:
> When fev'rish heats, or anxious thoughts molest,
> Thy arm sustains and holds me to thy breast:
> Not winter's spite or low'ring clouds displease,
> If thou art there, my soul, my heart's at ease. [*p. 36*, ll. 723–8]

Ann's obituary in the *Norfolk Chronicle* described her as 'a person of exemplary piety and unparalleled goodness in her the neighbouring poor have lost a constant benefactress; her husband, friends, and acquaintance, a most valuable woman, deservedly respected through life, and now universally regretted'.[133] Her epitaph in Watlington Church records that 'She stretched out her hands to the poor,/ And in her tongue was the law of kindness' (see Plate 8). She was buried by John Allen, the vicar of Stanhoe, on 9 May 1787.[134] Pratt died on 6 October 1791 and was buried at Watlington on 16 October 1791.[135] In his will, he left the farm and the lands he had acquired in Wereham and Wretton to his nephew Edward Roger Pratt, which were later sold at auction. He gave bequests of money to several people, including £50 to his friend the Reverend Charles Davy, with the remainder of his personal wealth given as legacies, as we saw earlier, to the children of Dixon and Margaret Hoste. An advertisement in the *Bury and Norwich Post* of an auction of his property held in 1792 suggests that Pratt enjoyed a comfortable life: it includes 'a neat chariot and harness complete, a pair of black coach horses' and 'a neat one-horse chaise and plated harness'.[136] Another auction

133 *Norfolk Chronicle*, 12 May 1787, p. 2.

134 NRO 1517, 1OE1.

135 A short obituary appeared in the *Gentleman's Magazine* in 'Obituary of considerable Persons; with Biographical Anecdotes', *The Gentleman's Magazine* 70 (Nov. 1791).

136 *Bury and Norwich Post*, 23 November 1791, p. 3.

advertisement shows that Pratt owned a home 'pleasantly situated in the parish of Downham-market, a short distance from the town' that comprised 'three parlours, several good chambers, kitchen, and convenient offices, with a stable and coach-house, walled garden planted with choice fruit-trees' as well as farmlands in Downham Market, Wereham, and Wretton amounting to 17 acres.[137]

A fleeting impression of Pratt's sanguine personality is given in the 1791 letter written by Charles Davy to Pratt, which begins with the arresting first sentence 'I am very sorry to hear you can laugh but on one side of your mouth' [*f. 1v*]. Davy's letter suggests that Pratt had some kind of stroke in his last years, which paralyzed one side of his face, as Davy writes 'I was entirely a stranger to your having met with any affliction to interrupt your chearfulness since the loss of your good wife, my dear Friend, and impute what may have happend to you since to your excessive sorrow upon this account' [*f. 1v*]. Davy had himself been struck by what he described in the 'Advertisement' to his *Letters, Addressed Chiefly to a Young Gentleman* as an 'apoplectic stroke' that had taken him 'from the most perfect state of health and cheerfulness amidst his friends, to a paralytic permanent debility; a debility which hath not only fixed him to his chair, but brought on spasms so exquisitely painful, and frequently so unremitted, as scarcely to allow a single hour's repose to him for many days and nights together'.[138] The shaky handwriting in the letter is material evidence of the effects of Davy's 'apoplectic stroke'. As a counterpoint to the letter's preoccupation with the dilapidations of old age and the prospect of death, Davy's original adaptation of the medieval lyric 'Sumer is Icumen in' celebrates renewal of life in the countryside at the advent of summer. The collection of Pratt's own writings in the folder provides a similarly vivid sense of rural life, with its wild and domestic animals, its labours and diversions, and its cruelties and pleasures. The monumental inscription on the north wall of Watlington Church gives a rather noncommittal epitaph to Pratt: 'What he was and what he is to be, the day of judgement will determine' (see Plate 8). What is to be made of his literary papers, we leave our readers to determine.

137 *Norfolk Chronicle*, 10 March 1792, p. 3.

138 Charles Davy, *Letters, Addressed Chiefly to a Young Gentleman* (Bury St Edmunds, 1787), p. iv.

Editorial Conventions

^ ^	word(s) (or part of word) inserted by author
^^ ^^	author's insertion within an insertion; any unusual placements of insertions are indicated by footnotes
<word>	deleted by author etc.
<illeg.>	illegible word or illegible word deleted by author
[word]	word or single letter supplied by editors
[*sic*]	used sparingly to confirm word as that written
ad.	advertisement
f.	folium or physical sheet (used to identify beginnings of pages of texts with no page numbers)
l. and ll.	line and lines (for poetic texts)
p.	page (used to identify pages of texts with page numbers)
r	recto (used to identify pages of texts with no page numbers)
tp	title page
v	verso (used to identify pages of texts with no page numbers)

Silent Corrections and Omissions

Words divided over two folia were united before the break, words divided over two lines by hyphens were united, catchwords and printer's characters in printed texts are omitted, and all instances of the long 's' ('ſ') silently changed to 's'. In *The Grange* we have italicized all stage directions. We expanded, standardized and used all-capitals for all speech prefixes (e.g. 'Clin.' is changed to 'CLINCH') and introduced spaces between acts, scenes, and the entrances and exits of characters to make the play script easier to navigate visually. Where we have made emendations we have recorded them in the footnotes.

Capitalization

In *The Grange* we have capitalized the first line of every speech, and the first word of each stage direction. For poetic texts in manuscripts we have capitalized the first word of every line. Otherwise, we have done our best to capture the capitalization indicated in the original manuscript. In cases of letters like 'c' it was sometimes difficult to decide whether the word is supposed to start with a capital letter or not. (Inevitably, print imposes a binary choice between a lower and upper-case letter that can be more of a continuum in manuscript writing and this is also the case with Pratt's manuscripts.) The letter 'a' presented special difficulties for transcription. Very occasionally, Pratt uses an 'A' to indicate capital 'A'—but more usually uses a large lower case 'a' to indicate capital 'A'. We reproduced both large 'a' and 'A' alike as upper-case 'A'.

Contractions

With the exception of speech prefixes in *The Grange* (see above), we reproduced all contractions and abbreviations in the manuscripts as written, e.g. 'y^{e}', 'y^{s}', 'y^{t}', '&', and 'rec^{d}'. Pratt is not consistent in his use of contractions. Although he usually writes 'y^{e}' for 'the' in manuscript, it is not uncommon for him to write 'the'. When the uncontracted version of the word appears in our transcription this indicates that the word appears as indicated in the original manuscript.

In the manuscripts, Pratt is very inconsistent in the way he handles the ending 'ed' in verbs that end in 'ed' in the past tense. Sometimes Pratt writes 'ed', sometimes he uses an apostrophe to indicate the ellipsis of 'e', and sometimes he simply leaves 'e' out before the final 'd' of a word. There are also cases in which Pratt writes *both* an apostrophe and an 'e' at the end of the word, resulting in words like 'receiv'ed', perhaps in order to indicate that the 'ed' is pronounced. In all these cases, we have attempted to reproduce the appearance of the word in the original manuscript and to avoid regularizing Pratt's practice.

Footnotes

If a text has its own footnotes then we reproduce these at the bottom of the page on which they originate as identified by the references in brackets (e.g. [*f. 3r*] or [*p. 5*]). In the case of footnotes that in the original text are spread over two pages we keep the whole footnote on the page on which it originates. All the footnotes using symbols are Pratt's and all the footnotes using numbers or letters of the alphabet are our own.

Line Numbers

For simplicity, we have added our own line numbers to poems whether the original text has line numbers or not. The line numbers we have given do not necessarily correspond to those in the original text and we count cancelled and uncancelled lines alike. We always number every tenth line.

Punctuation

Like Laurence Sterne, Pratt liked to use different sizes of dashes and we have attempted to reproduce this feature of his style. Short dashes used as punctuation (rather than hyphens) are reproduced as em dashes (—), medium dashes are reproduced as double em dashes (——), long dashes in the manuscript are reproduced as quadruple em dashes (————) and very long dashes as double-quadruple em dashes (————————). Both in the print versions of Pratt's manuscripts and in the manuscripts, series of dashes with spaces in between are sometimes found (— — — —) and we reproduced these as written or printed in our edition. We have exercised restraint on reproducing long dashes in the original manuscript, since especially in *The Grange* Pratt often uses a long dash simply to reach the end of the page. We reproduce long dashes only when they seem to us to be intended for their own sake.

Pratt has a tendency to put two punctuation marks on top of one another—for example, putting a dash straight through a colon without making it clear which is to be put first. He also sometimes in *A Modest Address to Lewis* appears to make the top dot of a colon do double duty as the dot of an explanation mark. In such cases, we put the colon or semicolon before the dash and the explanation mark before the colon. He also sometimes uses two hyphens that resemble an equals sign ('=') instead of a single hyphen: we have reproduced these as single hyphens. We place the quotation marks directly next to the sentence they surround, or line of poetry they begin, without leaving a gap, even if a gap is there in the original text. In the case of printed texts we reproduce italicized punctuation marks or unitalicized punctuation marks as they appear in the original text.

Titles

We supply short titles or, in the case of several poems that are untitled, a title based on the first line of the poem in bold at the beginning. If the poem exists in two or more versions, our title specifies which version we are transcribing. Our transcription follows directly after the title we supplied, including the full title Pratt himself gave to the text, if any.

Headnotes

Each document is preceded by a headnote, consisting of four components: archival reference; date of composition (and where applicable) publication; authorship; physical description; and sometimes an additional explanatory note.

Dramatic Writings

So – And I to ye Greenman, that Hangs up at ye
alehouse Door – or to ye case of a base viol –
Cub – She is as fiery as ye Spitting plant in S[t] Harrys
Garden – A man would no sooner touch her, but she would fly at ye Eyes of Him –
So – A Fellow without a capacity ——
Cub – A woman without a Sweetheart ——
So – A forked carrot, not worth ye Scraping ——
Cub – A Dried Eel Skin for a School Boys Top ——
Fran – Bravo, it goes on admirably Well (Aside)
Cub – A bent nunifer, not worth ye Stooping for
So – Pig at Second Hand ——
Cub – A dough cake spoiled in ye baking ——
So – meer barley water, and Nothing better ——
Cub – (Embarrasd) I believe I must give it up (Aside
Fran – (Whispering Cub) Never mind her, Cousin, tell
her she is a Geographer.
Cub – You are a Geographer Madam
So – So So, What you are come to your Latin at
Last, are you.?
Cub – a Flimsey Geographer –
Fran – (Going to Sophy) never give it up Miss Sophy:
Tell him, he is a fumbling Topographer –
So – A fumbling Topographer –
Cub A flimsey Geographer –
So – A fumbling Topographer.
Cub. A flimsey Geographer –
Fran – Come, Come, Let there be an End to this
Quarrel – He is only a Tyranical creature Sophy, Who wont Suffer a Dog to bark
at him; rather too Philosofical you find, Ha, ha, ha! – One would think these
simpletons were members of ye Feathers Tavern Society: As they are quarrelling
about words they do not Understand – (Aside)
So – To be calld; Ge, o, gra, pher at Last
by such a thing as this – I who have drank negus with ye Chairman himself
at ye Quarter Sessions; – I Who have danced – (Crying all ye time)
Fran – These Little Altercations in courtship

Figure 7 *Page from* The Grange [*f. 20v*]

The Grange

NRO PRA 664/7

Date: The most likely time of composition is 1773–74; the earliest possible date is 1771 since Fanny makes a topical reference to the Feathers Tavern Association, which first met on 17 July 1771 [*f. 20v*]. The action of the play itself takes place in the autumn of 1774 [*f. 7r*], which suggests the play may have been written with a view to a performance then. If this conjecture is correct, this would suggest a date of composition earlier in 1774 or late 1773. The play would have been written by 1779, since Pratt drafted 'An Occasional Prologue to *The Clandestine Marriage*' on the back of the booklet holding *The Grange* and a polished version of this Prologue was printed in the *Norfolk Chronicle* on 19 February 1779, p. 3.

Authorship: The manuscript of the play is in Pratt's hand and is included in the Pratt folder. The play can confidently be attributed to him.

Physical Description: Manuscript play written in ink in a sewn paper booklet with a marbled cover, measuring 20.5 cm by 32 cm.

[*f. 1r*]

The Grange

—A comedy. Est quodam prodire tenus, si non Datur Ultra.[1]

Hor.

[*f. 1v*]

Dramatis Personæ

Men.

SIR HARRY LOPWOOD; Lord of the Manor
LEONARD, Son to S^{r}. Harry
APPLEYARD Tenant to S^{r}. Harry (very Infirm)
HUMPHRY son to Appleyard, a reformed Libertine
MEADOWS, Tenant to S^{r}. Harry; a Gambler.
CLINCH, Steward to Sir Harry, (occasionaly Deaf)
WILSON, ye Lying Ensign, companion to S^{r}. Harry
WILLIAMS, Servant to Appleyard:
DANIEL CUB, a Country Bumkin, in Love with Miss Meadows
NETTLE, an Ignorant Pettifogger, Creature to Clinch—
HUGO BUZ, a Parish Clerk
GIBBET, Boy in the family.

Women.

SOPHY, Daughter to Appleyard
FANNY, Sister to Meadows.
KITTY TOY, a milliner kept by Meadows
BRIDGET, maid to Appleyard

1 *DLCL*: Horace, *Epistles I*, 1:32 (p. 253) 'It is worthwhile to take some steps forward, though we may not go still further.' The context in the original epistle is Horace explaining to his patron Maecenas that he is giving up writing poetry in his old age in favour of studying philosophy, which he only imperfectly understands. Nevertheless, Horace says it is worth taking a few hesitant steps in philosophy, even if there are limits to how far he can go in it. Fanny echoes the motto in the play when she says 'surely there can be no presumption in us, to Look up to Heaven; tho we cannot reach it' [*f. 7r*].

[*f.* 27*v*]

Prologue[2]

Poets of Late in these our Rhiming Days;
With French materials, build their Brittish plays:[3]
Yet has our Stage no Law, to punish those
Who Strole abroad to pilfer forreign Prose:
Plays Like Brew'd Wines, ye worst Effects produce:
When Forreign Lees are mixd, with Brittish Juice——
Thus Drones Dramatic Leave their Labours Here;
To rob the Hives of Bee's Poetic There——
To night our Author, Humbly bids me Say;
Ladies and Beaux, Protect this Infant Play:—
He Country thing ne'er Breathd in Drurys Air:
Nor knows a Wish, beyond His Elbow Chair.
No borrow'd Scenes are here; no pilferd Art;
His Wish to please; his Aim to mend ye Heart,
Yet should some Critic, with his Pinch of Snuff;
Condemn our Piece; and call it Norwich Stuff:[4]
Ladies on such with indignation frown
And save this first poor Bantling,[5] of your Own.
Some future Bard, to Grace our Stage may rise
Fird with ye Beauties, of those Heavenly Eyes:

---

2 Both the Prologue and the Epilogue appear at the end of the sewn manuscript containing *The Grange*. We have placed the Prologue before the first act in our edition.

3 A conventional complaint. The prologue to Richard Cumberland's play *The Brothers* (1769) censures 'The recreant Bard' who 'Gleans the vile refuse of the Gallic Stage'. One of the poems that appeared in the print version of Thomas Baker's *Tunbridge Walks; or the Yeoman of Kent* (1703) addressed to its author expresses the desire to see more 'Humour and Wit on th' *English* Theatre,/ Unborrow'd from the French: For to our Shame,/ Comedy of late from *Gallia* came'. On English borrowings from French comic theatre, see Willard Austin Kinne, *Revivals and Importations of French Comedies in England, 1749–1800* (AMS Press, 1967).

4 The primary meaning is in the sense of 'stuff' as a worthless piece of writing: *OED*. There is also a pun on 'Norwich stuff' as cloth made in Norwich: *OED*. Pamela in Samuel Richardson's *Pamela in her Exalted Condition* sends yards of '*Norwich* stuff, for Gowns for Cloths and Coats for Girls' to needy housekeepers in London. See Samuel Richardson, *Pamela in her Exalted Condition*, ed. Albert J. Rivero (Cambridge: Cambridge University Press, 2011), p. 337.

5 A bastard child: *OED*.

Some future Genius; may with truth report—
The Queen of Love here reigns, & keeps her court.
Long has our Stage with borrow'd Lustre Shone
Like ye Pale moon; with Glories not her Own:
No Ray Poetic warms our Northern Air
Nor comic muse to Charm ye Attentive Ear;

[*f. 28r*]

Yet when such Beauty Wakes ye sounding Lyre;
Each generous Bard should catch ye sacred Fire:
And this fair City of immortal name;
As first in Beauty, be ye first in Fame:—
Thebes in Old Times, as ancient Bards relate;
From small beginnings rose a mighty State,[6]
The Theban Chiefs to Gradual Honors rose;
And Sparta wept to find such men were foes:[7]
So may our Stage; by every Studious Art
Willing to please, inform, and mend ye Heart
By Gradual Labours find the way to Fame:
And Norwich plays be heard, in Drury Lane.

6 According to Greek mythology, Thebes was founded by Cadmus, who was guided by a special cow to the site. Cadmus was then told by Athena to plant the teeth from a slain dragon in the soil and the soldiers who magically thus sprang from the ground helped him construct the fort of the new city. The classical authors writing about this story include Hyginius, Pseudo-Apollodorus, and Ovid. The intended parallel is between the inconspicuous origin of Thebes and the play's humble beginnings in Norfolk.

7 Thebes won the Theban-Spartan War (379–371 BC).

[*f.* 2*r*]

Act 1.st

Scene, y^{e} *Seat of y*^{e} *Lopwoods in a Village—*

Enter Sir Harry; and Leonard:

LEONARD—It would have been kind in you Sr Harry to have continued me in college; where I was happy in ye most agreeable society and in ye way of every Advantage y^{t} could be had; to Improve my Education—

Sweet Social Hours; and you ye Happy Seats:!
Where Silver Camus[8] winds his watery way
Through meads more blest, than Edens flowery Plains
Farewell, a Long Farewell—

SIR HARRY—Poetical I perceive—probably Leonard another thousand or so, might have made you a Philosopher, and me a beggar; for whilst you have been measuring Sun, Moon, & Planets, I have been measuring my Timbers Here; to Support your extravagance——

LEONARD—I should be sorry Sir, any Indiscretion of mine should subject you to ye Smallest inconveniency; and am Afraid there is other mismanagement beside mine; more Justly to be complained of——

SIR HARRY—Yes, yes, this is ye common cant of you young fellows—you carry with you at first, a Little modesty to College, which is commonly Left behind with your bed-makers;[9] and when you return to the country again; ye first proof of your Improvements; is to let ye Old Fellow know it is time for him to retire; to make way for a son; of so much worth & Erudition—(*Bowing*)

LEONARD—It is not usual with you S^{r}, to be thus Satyrical, you would not give misery to an Insect—No Sir, He who is blest with a father, who remembers he himself was young; & whose Heart Like yours is open to ye tenderest impressions; must be more than monster; could he even Entertain a wish, to be deprived of him——

SIR HARRY—Fine Gentlemen must make fine speeches—but it is easier to say smooth things, than to do good ones——

LEONARD—To be free with you Sir; I should think myself blest with your friendship, & happy in your family, if was there not so near a connection between us;—but your Generous unsuspecting temper; Lays

8 The river Cam, which flows through Cambridge.

9 Servants, often older women, tasked with making the students' beds and tidying their rooms: *OED*.

you open to a thousand inconveniences—your House is as public as an Inn;[10] your Steward is purchasing to ye very Pales[11] around you with your own money; your Tenants are rude & Insolent; you have a familiar[12] in your family, who has been Disownd by His own regiment——In short Sir, there is not that Decency, and good behaviour that ought to be paid to ye character, of Sir Harry Lopwood——

[*f. 2v*]

SIR HARRY—Will you do me ye Favour Sir, to Let me know; whose Seat, and whose Plantations[13] these are, I may possibly be mistaken—?

LEONARD—If I have given you Offence Sir, I heartily ask your pardon; but I cannot see you injured, without complaining.——

SIR HARRY:—Would you have me Like ye rest of ye world, not to know ye names of my own Tenants; to pay no Tradesmens bills, to find fault with ye Damps & ye fogs of ye Country air; & so run away to Town, as soon as ye Audit Day[14] is over; to throw away my time and my fortunes, in ye fashionable follies of a Town Life——

LEONARD—No, Sir Harry—

SIR HARRY—No Sir Harry,—it is ye way of ye World[15] and I know it—I do wish with you indeed; that we had that Subordinate behaviour that is so much wanted: but it is easier to find out where we are wrong; than to prescribe rules to have it otherwise—we must give them examples; Leonard——

LEONARD—From my Heart Sir, I both applaud & reverence your noble Hospitality;—and when I see these cottages around you; It Looks as if ye Hand of Heaven had planted you here for their protection—but you Sir, with

SIR HARRY—Hold, Hold; not a Syllable more I beseech you—Self Sufficiency is an Obstacle to merit—my own praise is ye Last thing I would Hear; flattery is not ye food for men in years;—Give it Miss Meadows

---

10 In John Vanbrugh's play *The Country House* (1698), adapted from Florent Carton Dancourt's play *La Maison de Campagne* (1688), the lord of the manor decides to turn his country house into an inn so as to avoid having to give free hospitality to guests and in Oliver Goldsmith's play *She Stoops to Conquer* (1771) the plot hinges on two young men from London, Marlow and Hastings, mistaking Hardcastle's country house for an inn.

11 Wooden fences enclosing fields or stakes from which such fences can be formed: *OED*.

12 A friend, especially a close one: *OED*.

13 Plots of lands artificially planted with trees, often intended for harvesting: *OED*.

14 A day designated for the settling of accounts between tenants and landlords: *OED*.

15 A common phrase but it also recalls William Congreve's comedy *The Way of the World* (1700), which, like *The Grange*, is centered around a marriage plot.

when you walk y[e] Plantations with her;—And Give to me the Duty you ought;—and I shall then be satisfied with it——*Exit Sir Harry*——

LEONARD—*Solus*——I fear I have Offended Him——what pity it is, such unaffected benevolence as this, should be so Abused;—there is not a fault in this excellent man; but an extensiveness of soul to Divide itself away to make others Happy—I fear he suspects my Attachment to Fanny Meadows; O, Fanny! why was so fair a blossom produced from so poor a stem!——My preeminence of Birth will make me miserable—Now must I to my Solitary walk, to avoid the noise and confusion of the family——

Thy strains soft Waller,[16] must my Hours Improve;
And Lead me through, the Dangerous Paths, of Love. *Exit.*

——Scene, the Grange in y[e] same Village——

Enter Clinch, Appleyard; and Nettle——

CLINCH——You must break him up[17] M[r]. Nettle;—Sir Harry will have his Rents;—you shall saddle him besides with an Action[18] or two;——I must rub up[19] his memory I find——*Aside*——

[*f. 3r*]

NETTLE—With all my Heart Sir, just as you please to have it—Curror Lex,[20] that's my notion of business—Ha, ha, ha!——

APPLEYARD—Without knowing for what, M[r] Nettle?——

NETTLE—That is nothing to me Sir, I won't Disoblige Esq[r]. Clinch for a Writ, or two—I know my Obligations, M[r] Appleyard——

APPLEYARD—Bless me how I Loose my breath——mercy on us, that so many should use that Breath in vain; that may be so much wanted

16 The poet Edmund Waller (1606–1687). In her poem 'To Mr. Pope', Judith Cowper (1702–1781) praised Alexander Pope's poetry as combining 'Soft Waller's ease' with 'Milton's vigour'. Cowper's poem is reproduced in Alexander Pope, *The Poems of Alexander Pope, Esq*, 5th ed. (3 vols., Bernard Lintot: London, 1727), i, 27.

17 To disturb or vex: *OED*.

18 A lawsuit: *OED*.

19 To refresh someone's memory or remind them: *OED*.

20 A garbling of the legal phrase 'Si curat lex' (if the law is concerned). 'Si curat lex' is also the subtitle of the *Lecture on Heads* (1764), George Alexander Stevens' popular comic monologue for the stage. See *George Alexander Stevens and the Lecture on Heads*, ed. Gerald Kahan (Athens: University of Georgia Press, 1984), p. 72. Stage lawyers often speak in legal cant as, for instance, Traverse does in *The Clandestine Marriage* (1766).

CLINCH—Death and ye Devil, what have I to do with any mans breath—If you are not able to move a Joint; what a Pox has the Steward to do with it—you Loose your memory, William——

APPLEYARD—What can be ye meaning of this sudden change?—(*Aside*)

CLINCH—Don't be troublesome fellow—none of your canting, and whining with me Sir——He who knows not how to keep his friends, should be made sensible of the want of them—

APPLEYARD—I am all astonishment—*Aside*—

CLINCH—M^{r}. Nettle

NETTLE—Sir.

CLINCH—Take my Deposition in Writing—

NETTLE—It shall be done Sir; (*Pulls out Pen*; *Ink*; *& Paper*)

CLINCH—Write after me, Mr Nettle—zouns,[21] dont stamp upon my feet; Sir—That he ye said William Appleyard; Did—

NETTLE—(*Winking on Clinch*)—You have not mention'd ye word said, as yet—

CLINCH—Leave out said If you please, and, go on——Did cut down; and Destroy, Divers young Timbers—write Divers with a great D; M^{r}. Nettle—

NETTLE—(*Writing*; *& repeating*) Did cut down & Destroy—

APPLEYARD—Never upon my word Sir, you do me wrong, indeed you do—

NETTLE—(*Winking on Appleyard*) You must not know better than ye Steward; Mr Appleyard—

CLINCH—Pray go on; Mr Nettle—Also, Has Digd up, & carried away from ye Lords waste;[22] Divers Large quantities of fine Old clay;[23] reserving, and applying ye same, for his own use————

NETTLE—(*Still writing*) Also, has Digd up, & carried away from the Lords Waste————

[*f. 3v*]

APPLEYARD—It is as false as possible—

CLINCH—Bless me M^{r}. Appleyard, D^id^ I not catch your own Servant with it—?

APPLEYARD—Nothing more than for ye bungs[24] of ye Vessels

---

21 A contraction for 'Christ's wounds' and hence a milder oath: *OED*.

22 A tract of uncultivated land: *OED*.

23 Clay could be used as material for bricks, pottery, and other products.

24 Plugs or stoppers for casks and bottles: *OED*.

CLINCH—Go on Mr. Nettle—That certain wood was cut, and carried away from a certain place; call'd ye Little Plantation; & yt one pair of Good, & substantial crutches, were made of ye same, for ye Use, & by ye Direction of him ye said William Appleyard—

NETTLE— (*Winking on Clinch*) Suppose I should write two Crutches—they might not be perhaps exactly of the same Length—

CLINCH—Let it be so Mr. Nettle;—Also, that one Jeremy Rug; or Bug, his Servant; Did feloniously break down & carry away from a certain furlong,[25] calld Hogs-Pond furlong; one Large & Substantial oaken bough; on ye twenty ninth Day of May Last; setting up ye same at ye Grange Farm, now in ye Use and Occupation of Him; ye said William Appleyard

NETTLE—O, ho, is it so old Gentleman; we shall slice you for this, I warrant you—felony by ye fourth of George,[26] (*Winking on Clinch*) we shall Chip you for this my Master—Curror Lex say I; thats my notion for ever, Ha, ha, ha!—

APPLEYARD—I fancy, I understand Him—*Aside*—Did you receive Mr. Clinch ye Little present I sent you, by Humphry?——

CLINCH—Present Mr Appleyard, (*Smiling*) speak a Little Louder friend William; I should be glad to understand you, (*Advancing nearer*) present Did you Say—

APPLEYARD—Nothing more than ye usual compliment—I have every Day fresh Instances of my sons dishonesty—(*Aside*)

CLINCH—Not a man upon earth is more ready to serve you and my friends than[27] I am; I Look upon a Steward to be ye sweet Oil of Society; to Soften ye Severity of ye Landlord, and encourage the industry of ye Tenant—What Say you, Master Nettle————?

NETTLE—The Greatest blessing on ys side Heaven—

CLINCH—I am always Glad to Oblige you William—and If a Little more covenant[28] wood Should be wanted; what say you Master Nettle; must be merciful where we can——?

NETTLE—True Sir; but If there is scarce a faggot upon ye farm; it may be rather inconvenient to Oblige him——

25 An unenclosed field: *OED*.

26 Acts of Parliament were identified by their ordinal number in the year of the monarch's reign in which they were passed. Nettle does not provide a number or identify which King George he is referring to.

27 Pratt wrote 'then' in the original manuscript.

28 i.e. covenanted wood, wood owed by the tenant to the landowner by deed or contract: *OED*.

[*f.* 4*r*]

CLINCH—You must rub out; Mr Nettle—

NETTLE—Just as you please Sir—Nax, aut nullum[29] it is ye same thing to Nettle—Curror Lex, thats my notion of things,—Ha, ha, ha!

CLINCH—Come, Come, we are all good friends again, you have some excellent cyder William of your own making, old & generous Like yourself—My Physician would have me drink it; but it is so hard, so very hard to get it like yours; What say you Master Nettle; will you wet your Whistle?

NETTLE—With all my heart Sir—(*Whispering Appleyard*) I must be paid for this

APPLEYARD—I understand this Cyder prescription; If there is one Villain on Earth, worse than the rest, it is this detestable Steward——(*Exeunt omnes*)

Scene Grange Continued
Enter Wilson, & Sophy:

SOPHY—Then you have been in ye wars captain;—O Lud!—I do Love to hear of Sieges and battles; of cannons and Trumpets; of Guns and Gunpowder; most prodigiously——

WILSON—A soldiers Life madam; would be insupportable was it not for ye smiles of the Ladies——(*Bowing*)——

SOPHY—O law S^{r}.—you are so exceedingly Obliging (*Curtseys*)

WILSON—You must know madam at ye battle of Minden[30] I had ye misfortune to Loose this Hand; (*Holds his Hand up*)

SOPHY—Mercy on us; Why it appears to me Sir, to be as sound and well, as ye Other—

WILSON—Please to observe me Madam—in ye time of ye Action, I was confined to my tent by a nervous fever,[31] <& so> Lieutenant Bayonet served

---

29 Clinch seems to be attempting to quote the maxim '*aut Caesar aut nullus*', meaning 'either Caesar or nothing'—or 'all or nothing'.

30 The Battle of Minden was fought on 1 August 1759, near the town of Minden in North Rhine-Westphalia between the Anglo-German army on one side and France on the other as part of the Seven Years' War.

31 John Pringle (1707–1782), Physician-General to the British army (1744–48), distinguished between malignant fevers from low or nervous fevers, which 'do not depend upon any putrid cause'. He also claimed that nervous fevers were 'incident to such chiefly as are of a weak or lax habit'. See his *Observations on the Diseases of the Army in Camp and Garrison* (A. Millar: London, 1752), pp. 356, 358.

in my place; and a brisk young Dog he was, & so Lost his Hand—now, had I been well, & had I been in ye action: ^and had I been in his place^ I should have Lost my Hand and so I look upon it as my misfortune; and not His——————————

——SOPHY—What a Heavenly Creature is this—*Aside*—

WILSON—Another time Madam, we were fourteen nights under Arms; nothing but ye cold Earth for our beds; ye Enemy made an attack in ye night when we did not expect it; & so I immediatly Jumpt out of bed; and alarmd ye regiment—

SOPHY—Hey Day;! I thought you had been on ye cold Ground, and not in your tent, Sir?——

[*f. 4v*]

WILSON—Not absolutely on ye Ground Madam—for you must know when we Suspect an Action at hand; we commonly pitch our tents as near to ye Ground as we can; to prevent ye Enemys seeing us at a distance

SOPHY—I understand you Sir—you was not wounded I hope—

WILSON—A few Scratches madam; a Disagreable chain shot[32] carried away part of my thigh; but Little Bob Syringe our Surgeon; (a clever Dog with a needle,) stitchd up ye wound in a Hurry; & so it closed——

SOPHY—(*Looking Wishfully at his Thigh*)——Pray Heaven all may be well there[33]—(*Aside*)—Was you ever concernd in a Duel Sir; I Love a duel Dearly; there is something so Cavaliere in ye Pulling off your Hats and then ye Shute one another so Genteely; that I admire a Duel——

WILSON—The last Madam was with Captain Nog of ye Welch Fuziliers:[34] ye Quarrel was about a freckle in a Ladys Ear; Nog gave me ye Lye[35] (which I hate most damnably;) & so ye Challenge came on—

---

32 A round of chain shot consisted of two iron balls or half-balls held together by a chain: *OED*. Chain shot was generally used in naval warfare, however, a fact that helps cast doubt over the veracity of Wilsons's story, in case any more was needed.

33 Sophy's concern that Wilson's thigh injury may have made him impotent resembles the Widow Wadman's interest in Uncle Toby's groin injury for the same reason in *Tristram Shandy* (*Sterne*, 2:792–3, and passim).

34 A prestigious infantry regiment of the British Army, which fought in the Battle of Minden, mentioned earlier in the scene. See Christopher Chant, *The Handbook of British Regiments* (Oxon: Routledge Revivals, 2013), pp. 167–9.

35 In *Spectator* 99, Mr. Spectator observes 'The great Violation of the Point of Honour from Man to Man is giving the Lie. One may tell another he Whores, Drinks, Blasphemes, and it may pass unresented, but to say he Lies, tho' but in Jest, is an Affront that nothing but Blood can expiate' (*Spec,* 2:74).

SOPHY—Go on, Go on Sir; I Long to hear ye End of it——

WILSON—We took our Distance—Nog fired first & ye Ball came thump on my Left rib Here (*Pointing to ye place*) & rather alarmd me

SOPHY—I shall dye at ye very thoughts of it—and did it not go thro your body, Sir—?

WILSON—You shall hear, Miss Sophy—We Soldiers carry with us generally a good deal of cash; and I had Quilted a pritty Large sum in ye inside of my waistcoat— (Portugal coin[36] you may Imagine—) & so ye Ball grazed against ye metal and saved Jeremiah; much at your Service—

SOPHY—How, Heaven protects, ye Varteous![37]——(*Aside*)

WILSON—My Dear Girl, we are Loosing time very fast; meet me again in ye Plantations; and then you shall hear of my Escapes my Marches and my Attacks; & you shall hear of our bush-fighting[38] amongst ye Indians; and you shall know, (*Taking her in his Arms*) a great deal more, you Gipsey——

SOPHY—O; I shall Like it mightily—!

WILSON—I am certain you will—

SOPHY—We must be in the thicket, then

WILSON—You will Learn it ye better there—

SOPHY—Just at Sun Set

WILSON—With all my Heart————

[*f.* 5*r*]

Grange Continued—

Enter Gibbet, and Bridget,—both out of Breath—(Gibbet lame)—

BRIDGET—My good young Lady; run out of ye back door as fast as you can:—Here are an Ocean of folks come to ye Grange doubled Horses & Single:[39] there is ye Baker & wife; with Little Jemmy before them; ye black[40]

36 Portuguese gold coinage, called 'escudo', which entered circulation in 1711 and circulated for the rest of the eighteenth century: *OED*. 'Escudo' also means 'shield' in Portuguese, which adds to the joke that Wilson's money 'shielded' him from harm.

37 Recalling Shamela's frequent references to her 'vartue' in *Shamela* (1741), Henry Fielding's parody of Samuel Richardson's *Pamela* (1740). Fielding had first used the phrase in his play *Rape upon Rape* (1730).

38 Guerilla-style fighting conducted in a wooded terrain: *OED*.

39 i.e. a number of carriages have arrived, some drawn by two horses ('double') and some by one horse only ('single').

40 i.e. in the sense of having dark-hair and a dark complexion: *OED*.

curate of frogs Abbey;[41] ye Hair Dresser from Town; & my Lords own Gentleman———

SOPHY—How unfortunate is all this———and what have you done with ye company?—

BRIDGET—Jerry Ma'am—by my Direction, Has carried them into ye Orchard to see a flight of Bees; and there they are Gaping Like a parcel of crack'd Plumbs, in a Rainy Season[42]———

SOPHY—And what's ye matter with you, Gibbet—?

GIBBET—Matter, enough for me Madam—running away with ye foul basket of Linnen; I fell over ye Little Horse and ye Devil Has kickd me to pieces—

BRIDGET—Jerry madam Heard Mr Minister say yt he would look over ye cold pigeon pye first; and then eat his Porringer[43] of cream, when ye Tea was over———

SOPHY—Dear captain Wilson advise me, what am I to do to Dismiss them; it will spoil our asseration[44] positively————

WILSON—Suppose madam, as your father is in exceeding bad health; you should send word; yt you cannot possibly Leave his chamber.—

BRIDGET—O Sir, that wont do by a Deal—Miss Sophy will have her company, in spite of my Masters Illness—Marcy on us do you think young Ladies will turn Nurses, & loose their Diversions, to take care of their Parents, truly—?

GIBBET—Suppose madam we should Say; our Dog Jowler has run away with ye loaf; or yt ye Tinker has got ye teakettle, to mend a Hole in it?———

SOPHY—Be quiet Jackanapes—Dear Captain Wilson assist me now, and I will Love you forever————

WILSON—I will Endeavour to Assist you Madam—

SOPHY—As How Dear Sir, do it Immediatly———

WILSON—Step out of ye back door into the Plantations & wait my coming—you Bridget Secure ye fore door; and you [*f. 5v*] Gibbet run you to Jerry; to Lead out their horses————

SOPHY—Dear Creature, Proceed—

WILSON—Then will I go & tell ye company; that as you was Supping with neighbour Gosling; you was unfortunately choaked with ye Drum

---

41 An actual abbey in the village of Coveney, near Ely in Cambridgeshire. The abbey had been converted into a farm after the dissolution of the monasteries.

42 A fluctuating amount of rainfall during the ripening season can cause stone fruits like plums to crack.

43 A small deep dish for liquid foods such as soup or porridge: *OED*.

44 A malapropism for 'assignation'.

Stick of a Turkey; and so was put to bed there and not able to come home; & that I came to ye Grange for ye maid, & ye bottle of Hartshorn[45]—

SOPHY—A very good thought indeed—but suppose they should call at ye widows,[46] and Discover the Plot——

WILSON—Leave that to my management—and so you Sophy to ye Plantations—you Bridget Secure the Doors—you Gibbet to Jerry to get their Horses; and I'll to ye Orchard and Disperse the company—*Exeunt Wilson, Sophy, and Bridget*—

GIBBET *Solus*:—And you Gibbet run you to Jerry Ha, ha, ha!—a pritty fellow this captain as they call him; to think I could run with a Lame Leg truly—my young mistress seems to Like him mightily—but she is of a ticklish sort, I warrant her:—If every body says ye truth; he understood running a Little better when he was in ye Army—Run Gibbet with a pox to him, & so I will; and as fast as I can too————*Exit*—

Scene Grange Continued—
Enter Clinch

[CLINCH]—Zouns I thought I should Have had a Little nap, After my Cyder—but Here has been such a Hurricane in ye family that there is no Sleeping—Here; you Bridget; Jerry, Gibbet; where are you all—fine doings in the family forsooth————

Enter Gibbet

[GIBBET]—Here Sir, what did you please to want—

CLINCH—Who is it Looks after your master Sirrah?

GIBBET—He who goes behind Him Sir, except it is a blind person[47]——

CLINCH—(*Seeming not to Understand*) Speak a Little Louder Child—Nat is a good Apothecary, & does a Deal of Business—

GIBBET—I shall Laugh out, in his face—

CLINCH—They say you came from ye Charity School[48] Lately; and that you have a bright understanding; Sirrah—

---

45 Aqueous ammonia solution, traditionally used as smelling salts, made from the horns and hoofs of red deer and sometimes other animals: *OED*.

46 i.e. the 'neighbor Gosling' mentioned in Wilson's lines above.

47 i.e. nobody looks after Appleyard.

48 Charity schools educated poor children free of charge and were often linked to religious organizations. Norwich had one of the oldest charity schools in England, the Norwich School for Poor Boys, founded in 1617.

GIBBET—Certainly Sir, for I wear nails[49] in my Shoes

CLINCH—Speak a Little Louder, Sirrah; and pray [*f. 6r*] what do they say of their Steward here—? come you are a Stranger in ye family.

GIBBET—I must Have a Little fun with y^s Deaf old fellow—they say he is a fine Old Rogue; and has ruined ye Tenants———

CLINCH—O, ye Dog I shall break every bone in his skin—(*Aside*) —Speak truth at all times; it can never be contradicted———

GIBBET—That you have built a good House; with other mens money

CLINCH—Never be afraid of the truth; it will never deceive you—

GIBBET—That you have Stolen ye timbers; & ruind y^r master

CLINCH—Speak it at all times;—How I Long to Pommel y^s Rascal—(*aside*)—

(*A voice without*) Gibbet,

GIBBET—*within*—Coming, And so Sir when you go down to Beelzebub, I wish you a pleasant Journey—*exit Gibbet*—

CLINCH *Solus*—An Arch wag this; and Little thought that I understood Him—I Look upon this world as one wide Ocean; and its inhabitants a set of sharks of Different Dimensions, ye one preying upon ye other—it Has been my rule of Life not to be over nice in my Dealings———the world will have it Isaac is a Jew;[50] & what is Isaac ye worse for ye worlds Prattle ^a good name^ provides no meat for ye Stomach—now & then I hear a Little too much of myself by this my Occasional Deafness, but what is Isaac ye worse for ye worlds opinion—nature has Given to Animals teeth & claws & to us Sagacity and Forecast: it is a strait world to Live in: must Elbow & twist a Little; or, down we go and fools walk over us——————————

Conscience avaunt, thou busy trifling thing:
A Heart thus Steeld; defies thy feeble Sting
Let Graceless Zealots, of their morals boast———
Give me that conscience, that will make ye most.

End of the First Act.

---

49 i.e. hobnails, nails worn in the soles of shoes. Gibbet is humorously taking 'understanding' literally.

50 The familiar antisemitic stereotype of the greedy and grasping Jew hangs over Clinch's character as it does over Shylock in Shakespeare's *The Merchant of Venice*. Note, however, that Clinch never says that he *is* a Jew: his exact religious and ethnic identity is left ambiguous.

[*f.* 6*v*]

Act Second.
Scene ye Plantations————

Enter Leonard, and Fanny Meadows——

LEONARD—The softness of the Air, and ye Harmony of the Birds, have tempted you and ye butterflies abroad, Miss Meadows

FANNY—The pleasures of the Season Sir; Afford but Little satisfaction to one; who is truly wretched————

LEONARD—When nature is pouring its benefits about us, it is an argument of Ingratitude not to be pleased with them——

FANNY—It is Easier to give advice, than to give conduct, Mr Lopwood—

LEONARD—The education my Father has given to this young creature, was admirably bestowd—I find ye Gifts of Heaven are impartial, and y^t it is Education alone that makes men or monsters—*Aside*—What is it that thus Distresses thee; my Fanny——————

FANNY—My Brother Sir—you are no Stranger to his way of Life, and ye Distrest circumstances we are now under—my Father was Guardian to our relation Cub;—He dying in ye young mans minority his Affairs came into my Brothers Hands; How far his ungovernable temper for Gaming has Led him to Injure this young Creature; I am still a Stranger to it—

LEONARD—It is a misfortune Madam to be Allied to men of infamy, but it is worse to be connected with their Vices—but are you sure there is nothing more than compassion; y^t makes you so partial to His Interest?————

FANNY—You cannot Suppose it surely—our Long fixed and mutual Affections Mr Lopwood; must be proof enough to you of my unalterable Attachment, to your person—

LEONARD—O, Fanny—! forgive a Heart that is too easily alarmed; a Love Like mine must have its fears and Apprehension & my fathers resolution to marry you to this young man, plants Daggers in my bosom—

FANNY—How much is she to be pitied; who has both Love and Virtue—*Aside*—Your Father knows me to be poor & friendless ye very creature of his Mercy; and his goodness of Heart makes him so resolute to marry me to this young man; that His fortunes may place me above want and infamy——He Loves me as an Orphan; but would Despise me as a Daughter——————

LEONARD—O, Fanny,—merit Like yours [*f.* 7*r*] putts down distinctions—ye Qualities of ye mind are those, which make all rational equality; ye rest is Dirt and rubbish, & meer Chimerical Advantages—

FANNY—Distinctions of Birth are at ye Will of Heaven; it is ours to be humble and satisfied with it——but surely there can be no presumption in us, to Look up to Heaven; tho we cannot reach it————

LEONARD—By ye great Powers of Heaven; I would not give up my interest in your Affections; to be ye Emperor of the world; O, Fanny, our years and infant Amusements have been ye same; reciprocal Attraction has long bewitched us both: it has blossomd and opend by Degrees and time has so Effectually improved it, as never to be Effaced————

(*Humphry and Meadows, cross ye Stage Arm, in Arm*)

MEADOWS—If Jerry Had kept his seat; ye mare would have won—She has ye fault of her Dam; runs off too hastily——

HUMPHRY—I beg you would excuse me Charles, indeed I am engaged; I am not in Spirits;—prithee Let go my Arm——

MEADOWS—Come Along, you shall see her in her new clothes;—Six to four she wins ye Saddle;[51] and I say Done—

FANNY—My unfortunate Brother as I live—I do not think they observd us—

LEONARD—These young fellows by imitating the vices of their betters; are too often ye ruin of themselves and families—S'death my Father coming by ye side of ye Wood; and I did not Observe him sooner—

Enter Sir Harry, Clinch following——

SIR HARRY—Sir Anthony[52] Planted those firs the year he married—How preferable are such amusements as these; to ye Horse race; or ye Gaming table—

CLINCH—Fine improvements upon my word Sir;

SIR HARRY—My son in close conference with Miss Meadows; I have Long suspected this Attachment——*Aside*——

FANNY—I am growing to ye Earth; & shall not have ye power of moving—*Aside*—

LEONARD—(*Going up to Sir Harry*)—Miss Meadows Sir, was passing thro ye plantations; to ye village, and so I was; just, as How; (*Confused*) Enquiring, as I may Say—

---

51 A saddle was sometimes given as the prize to the winning rider in a horse race.

52 A previous lord of the manor, presumably Sir Harry's father.

SIR HARRY—No matter what—no apology is necessary—I thought at a Distance; ye were seemingly, very friendly——

[*f.* 7*v*]

LEONARD—If my invention does not Assist me now; I must be Discoverd—*Aside*—*Goes up to Miss Meadows*——The Distinctions Heaven has made Madam; must be submitted too—but he who is proud of being Licentious; is a monster that ought to be muzzled—*Angrily*—

FANNY—(*Embarras'd*) Who Sir, what monster Mr Lopwood, you are not angry with me, surely—?

SIR HARRY——A sly rogue this—*Aside*——

LEONARD—Vice is Detestable in ye Greatest of men; but when Little people stretch out themselves, to be as vicious as their betters; their follies are more Hurtful to Society——

FANNY—(*Still alarmed*)—What society are you speaking of, Sir—I cannot bear to see him thus Disorderd——*Aside*—

SIR HARRY—An excellent young Hypocrite—*Aside*—

LEONARD—Tell it from me Madam, your Brothers conduct is infamous; & if my interest with my father will not remove him Hence ye laws shall do it—He shall not trample upon Authority, I assure you—

FANNY—Would to heaven I may understand him properly—*Aside*—I will endeavour to see him immediatly Sir, and tell him your resolutions—My Heart is at my mouth already—*Aside*—*Exit*—

LEONARD—It is probable Sir; you and your Steward may Have some particular business Here;—I will step into ye walks for a Little Airing, as ye weather is thus agreable——

SIR HARRY—Do so If you please; and hearken me Sir—please to remember that Distance and Decency, which ought to be paid to ye character of Sir Harry Lopwood, Ha; ha, ha—you understand me Leonard—

LEONARD—I fear I am Discoverd—*Aside*—*Exit Leonard*—

SIR HARRY—You first Lived Whipper-in[53] in ye family Isaac?

CLINCH—My Heart Sir, is ever mindful of y^r^ favors—

SIR HARRY—And now in ye Decline of Life, you are handsomely provided for—

CLINCH—If your Honor chooses now and then, to make a Little Addition to ye Wages of a good Old Servant, who has any thing to do with it?——

53 A 'whipper' or a 'whipper-in' was an assistant to a huntsman: *OED*.

SIR HARRY—This fellow was always Occasionaly Deaf—*Aside*——

CLINCH—Had I been as other men are of a rapacious temper, & could I have preyd upon y[e] vitals of my fellow Creatures; I might have done a Little better; but I am too soft and Milky for a Hardned World—[*f.* 8*r*]—must be merciful when we can————

SIR HARRY—My design of fixing my son Here is now determined—Do you make up y[e] Tenants accounts; my Sun is near its setting; & may his Shine out, without a cloud to Shadow it————

CLINCH—Good your Honor, have a Little compassion upon your poor Old Steward—Nature has been over Liberal to me with her soft Impressions; let Alexander Nettle make y[e] Seizures, attorneys are iron Instruments; meer Hammers: & Hatchets to chop & to pull asunder—He has no more feeling, than a blacksmiths Anvil————

SIR HARRY—An excellent old Hypocrite this—*Aside*—I think I hear our Dinner Bell at a Distance—I must in for Dressing—do you attend for instructions————*Exit Sir Harry*————

Clinch Solus—

Now let me Look into my pocket Ledger—(*Pulls out a book*) it has been my rule of Life to keep at Least this worlds Accounts even—Let me see (*Reads*) Sept[r]. 14th. 1774,—Worth this day twelve o'clock, three thousand pounds, twelve Shillings, and sixpence—Good—Where is y[e] word Emoluments—Here (*Turning over y[e] Leaves*) Page the tenth—Sold to Mess[rs]. Plane & Chissel 400 timbers; they giving me twenty pounds for y[e] preference to a better bidder—(Good)—Them Agreed with Josiah Mud for y[e] clay pit Farm; He allowing me one Hundred pounds, for my good will, & Good Services towards Him—Good—for passing, & allowing of Tradesmens bills at one shilling in y[e] Pound 17. ^L^ and three pence—Good—*Shuts y[e] book*—it is a strait World to Live in, must Elbow & twist a Little; or down we go; & fools walk over us

————*Exit Clinch*——

Scene A Room, at an Inn—
Enter Meadows and Kitty Toy.

MEADOWS—Then you wont come into temper positively?—

KITTY—You have almost broke my heart—you are a Brute of a man; M[r] Meadows.

MEADOWS—Why child If I had married you; it might have been

ye case perhaps—you would have made me an animal with a sprouting forehead[54]—

KITTY—To use all your Art and all your cunning to seduce an innocent Creature; & then to be ye first to upbraid her with it—

MEADOWS——To be free with you Kitty; I was thinking your Ladyship had Seduced me—for If you had not turnd up those Dear [*f. 8v*] Little delicious Eyes so often; & so Ogled & prickd with your needle; I might not have complimented you with ye favors I have————

KITTY—Complimented me Monster—favors do you call them—I shall burst into pieces positively—

MEADOWS—Ha, ha, ha! there is no Occasion for it my Dear you have done it already more than once—

KITTY—How much is our sex to be Pittied—If a woman has ye Government of her passions, you will swear her to be coy and Prudish; & should she be consenting to your Wishes; you have ye Ingratitude to reproach her for it—you are monsters M^r^. Meadows—

MEADOWS—And you ladies are a sort of Light Vessels y^t^ are comonly Shipwreckd by a Hurricane of your own making and when that is ye case what matters who goes aboard for Pillage————Ha, ha, ha

KITTY—I have nothing but my contempt Left for you[—]And y^t^ you are Heartily welcome to—Ungrateful Creature—

MEADOWS—And is that all you have to offer me?

KITTY—Mercy on me; If I had but my Dear Virtue again; there should not be a man in ye kingdom——

MEADOWS—Who would not be welcome to it, Ha, ha, ha come Kitty we have no time for fooleries now. I am a beggar and you know it, we have two children a Starving—Do you please to be advised madam?——

KITTY—As how Mr Meadows?——

MEADOWS—Please to hear me then—That old Dotard Clinch, will have ye Sugar-candy of matrimony to rub his Gums with—I have made him believe you had a rich old Uncle a planter abroad, who has left you handsome fortunes; and that I would be his rival——

KITTY—And What of all this—

[MEADOWS[55]]—Do you provide yourself a box of your trinkets, as waiting upon Sophy Appleyard: I will put ye old Churl in your way & he

54 A reference to being cuckolded, a misfortune which was supposed to make the cuckhold's forehead sprout horns.

55 At this point a new paragraph and a direction for Meadows to speak would be expected but Pratt seems to have slipped here and forgotten to specify that Meadows is speaking.

may make you an offer; it is better to creep under an Old Hedge than to be without one———*Going*

KITTY—(*Following, & holding his Sleeve*) Will you promise me then, to love me as much as Ever———

MEADOWS—Most Assuredly—(*Still going*)

KITTY—(*Following*) And do you promise me Charles, you are not angry with me?

[*f. 9r*]

MEADOWS[56]—Not in ye Least—(*Going*)

KITTY—But are you sure; I cannot endure to part in anger—

MEADOWS—Ha, ha, ha! I understand you Hussey——(*Kisses her*) now If you had y^t same dear Little Virtue again you would give it me with all your heart—you will meet at ye Old place——

KITTY—Bless me Charles, you would not be so naughty again surely—

MEADOWS—At Mother Moysts[57]

KITTY—For Heaven sake dont be so Sinful—

MEADOWS—O, woman, woman! How full of frailty art thou![58] Harkee me Kitty—you and I have vices enough already; without adding that of Hypocrisy to ye number of them———*Exeunt*———

Scene ye Grange—

GIBBET *Solus*—Dear Heart, what a sad thing it is to be every ones boy as I am;—tho ye family of ye Gibbets are as High as the best of them:—Father was under Butler; to a great member of Parliament—& Uncle Joe should have been coachman to a Nobleman in ye North; only He had no Horses, & Sister Pru was twice Askd out at church to a Lords Postilion—No sooner am I out of my Crib but away Goes Gibbet to clean the Stables;—then comes our Alice wadling Like a Lame Gosling; and where is our Devil of a Boy squeaks she:—then go I for ye cows, ahoa, ahoa, ahoa; for a mile together: then am I House Boy, Yard Boy, Hog Boy, Harrow boy,

56 In the manuscript, an 'A' appears immediately before the speech prefix. Its purpose seems to be to cover over a faintly visible 'K' that begins a speech prefix that Pratt made in error for Kitty Toy that he subsequently cancelled.

57 Pratt writes 'Moysts' but anyone in an audience would, of course, have heard 'Moist's', with an obvious sexual suggestion.

58 An echo of Hamlet's famous line 'frailty, thy name is woman!' (*Shak*, 1.2.146) in the soliloquy in which Hamlet complains about Gertrude's recent marriage to Polonius.

and every bodys boy for ye rest of ye Day—Whilst I have nothing under my management; but two wild kittins; and an Ill temperd Squirril; thats ready to scratch my Eyes out——

Enter Appleyard and Williams

APPLEYARD—*To Gibbet*—Do you bid my son & Daughter, to come here; immediatly—

GIBBET—It shall be done Sir——*Exit Gibbet*——

APPLEYARD—You have been Long in ye family, Gilbert—

WILLIAMS—Man and Boy Sir near thirty years—but I begin to want a Summertil[59] master; everything is ye worse for ye Wear; but a poor mans saying is worth but Little[60]——————

[*f. 9v*]

APPLEYARD—How industrious have these young people been to ruin themselves & me; I could have wished it from any other Quarter[—]a feather from ones own wing is doubly hurtful——

WILLIAMS—My poor young maister has a Little too much of ye tettarvetch[61] in him; but no soil without its Weeds you know—come come, he will yoke in time: Dodman would not touch[62] at first; but now he is as good as ye best—

APPLEYARD—Were his failings but common ones I could bear them with patience, Gilbert, but that those hands which were designd for industry; should be employd at ye Gaming Table is a Shocking consideration—O my wife, but let me not Hurt her memory; Had she been blest with this mans Sobriety, we had been Happy indeed—*Aside*—

59 'Summer-till' or 'summer-tilth' is an East-Anglian regional term to describe either the practice of letting a field lie fallow over the summer or ploughing previously fallow land in the summer: *OED*.

60 Williams' catchphrase echoes Ecclesiastes 9:16: 'So I said, "Wisdom is better than strength." But the poor man's wisdom is despised, and his words are no longer heeded.'

61 We have not found 'tettervetch' directly attested anywhere. But a 'vetch' is a type of plant used as fodder for animals and a 'tetter' (or 'tetter' or 'tittir') is a small pimple (see the entry for 'titter' in *VEA*). So a 'tettarvetch' would be a type of vetch that would have been supposed to cure tetters on the model of 'tetter-berry', and 'tetter-wort'. See R. C. A. Prior, *On the Popular Names of British Plants* (London: Williams and Norgate, 1863), pp. 224–5.

62 'Dodman' is a regional East-Anglian term for a snail: *VEA*. 'Dodman' seems to be the name of a beast here, probably a bull. The word 'touch' is used in the sense applied to farm animals—to appear to be sound and well-muscled to the touch: *OED*.

WILLIAMS—Odds my Life[63] Sir, every thing is out of ye way at present—ye Boy would be man; ye man would be Master, ye Tenant would be ye Landlord, ye Landlord would be ye Esqr, ye Esqr would be ye Knight; ye Knight would be ye Nobleman; ye Nobleman would be ye King; and ye King (God bless him) can be no better——

APPLEYARD—You Say, He has parted from his Hunter;[64]

WILLIAMS—Sold and gone, Sir—

APPLEYARD—Very Seldom with; Mr Meadows——?

WILLIAMS—Very Seldom—

APPLEYARD—Has Lost His spirits

WILLIAMS—No more Life in him; than there is in a dryd Herring——

APPLEYARD—My Heart is Lighter Gilbert; there is room for amendment in him—Harkee me; I hear them in their usual Disputes[—] Leave us to ourselves, Gilbert—

WILLIAMS—My poor Old Master my Heart is ready to burst for him,—but a poor mans Saying is worth but Little——

Exit Williams—

Enter Sophy and Humphry, Disputing——

SOPHY—To be so snubd; & so teazed,—by golds[65] I will never bear it—

HUMPHRY—You are ridiculous, Sister

SOPHY—Never to be oblig'd, in ones own family—

HUMPHRY—Never Satisfied in it——

SOPHY——Always contradicted

[*f. 10r*]

HUMPHRY—Always deserving of it—

SOPHY—Dear Brother you will turn savage soon, and live in ye wods [*sic*]—

HUMPHRY—Conditionaly perhaps I might; that you would return to your senses; and Stay in ye family—

63 A mild oath substituting 'Odds' for 'God's': *OED*.

64 A horse or a dog used for hunting: *OED*. As Charles Meadows and Humphry Appleyard discuss horse-racing earlier in the play, the reference is most likely to a horse.

65 A mild oath with 'Golds' substituting for 'God's'. We have not found 'by golds' attested elsewhere.

APPLEYARD—Come, come, let there be an end to your disputes—ye world will do this business for you—Come nearer Children, we are ruined Humphry;

HUMPHRY—Ruined Sir—?

APPLEYARD—Yes Ruind I say—that shining stone in thy bosom does not become thee Humphry—by endeavouring to be somewhat more than you ought to be; you make yourself awkward & contemptible————

HUMPHRY—I could excuse your remarks, Sir—

SOPHY—Mercy on us, this Snubd nose Methodist[66] Teacher, has spoiled his temper——*Aside*—

APPLEYARD—Dont be offended Humphry—I would not willingly suspect your want of honesty: but your Indiscretions, neglect of business, & hours of Dissipation, Has made me Suspicious of you—

HUMPHRY—By Heaven He Suspects my want of Honesty and with too much reason.—I Look into myself with trembling——*Aside*—

SOPHY—Law par[67] you are grown so whimsical of Late that I expect to be Locked up soon in ye clock case; and not Sufferd to Stir my own Length——

APPLEYARD—I remember a nobleman who Hunted y^{s} way (your mother was a favourite with him) He it was who gave you a fine name Sophy; and you have Given yourself fine Airs; upon ye occasion——

SOPHY—O, Par I remember Lord Dimple when I was a Little one; He would set me on his knee, rub my Cheek with his beard; chuck me under ye chin; & cry—Egad, she will be as Handsome as her Mother

HUMPHRY—That Noblemans civility as it was calld was ye ruin of my mothers Happiness——*Aside*——

APPLEYARD—An old man Humphry has Little to Loose—I can bear my poverty with patience—but reflection will bring you to yourself: & shew you How wanting you have been to me: and How wanting others will be to you in ye Hour of Affliction—*Exit Appleyard*—

SOPHY—What a comical old Pa, this is—

HUMPHRY—It dont become you to Say so—

66 In the eighteenth and nineteenth centuries, this could refer to someone adhering to a strict interpretation of Christianity but not necessary belonging to the Methodist movement: *OED*.

67 i.e. 'Pa'.

[*f. 10v*]

SOPHY—I thought you was angry with him.
HUMPHRY—Always with your impertinence

Enter Gibbet—

GIBBET—Cards for you Miss Sophy—*gives one*—and this madam (*Gives another*) Joshua waits for answers——

SOPHY—(*Reading out*) Arabella Bellybonds[68] compliments, to Miss Sophy Appleyard; begs ye favor of her, to meet Dolly Trot, & the three Miss Jabbers, to play a Pool of Quddrille;[69] & to spend ye Evening

HUMPHRY—Bless me, you Have so much business upon your hands, (*Snatches ye card from her*) that I must assist you, Sister—(*Reads Loud*)—Letitia Romp Gallery's[70] compliments to Miss See-fire Appleyard; begs ye fever of her (very kind-indeed) to take a cast in her Char,riot to ye new Play; & eat a bit of mu,ton at ye Heath Farm Haff[71] after two[—]Ha, ha, ha! Good Spelling & Inditing truly—mercy on us, what is become of all ye Ursulas and ye Abigails[72]—

SOPHY—Give it me monster—*Snatches ye card from Him*—I wish you & my Ill-temperd squirrel were chaind up together on ye kitchen window—bid Joshua wait for answers—

GIBBET—Yes ma'am,

Exit Gibbet—

Enter Bridget (*in a Hurry*)—

BRIDGET—Madam Churn in her Chariot, now at ye Gate maam; Polly Nog, madam Deborah Gosling, & Master Jackey with her

68 A variant spelling of 'Bellibone', meaning an attractive young woman: *OED*.

69 Quadrille, a card game: *OED*.

70 A 'gallery' is an enclosed space for the spectators in a theatre and a 'romp' is a jaunt or a playful young person, especially a girl or a woman: *OED*.

71 i.e. half.

72 Ursula' and 'Abigail' were names associated with maidservants. In *Spectator* 45, Addison has Mr. Spectator write 'I remember the time when some of our well-bred Country Women kept their Valet de Chambre, because forsooth, a Man was much more handy about them than one of their own Sex. I my self have seen one of these Male Abigails tripping about the Room with a Looking-Glass in his hand, and combing his Lady's Hair a whole Morning together' (*Spec,* 1:192).

HUMPHRY—Kitty Churn in her Chariot, Ha, ha, ha, I never see y^{t} thing of an Equipage,[73] but it reminds me of a Xstmas[74] Hamper so stuffd & cramd that it is ready to burst into pieces—

SOPHY—Dear thing—She has ye best mamma in ye Universe; never contradicted her but once in all her Life; and that was when ye Dear Little Girl would drink her Tea in ye Pig Sty—what was I going to say to you Bridget—

BRIDGET—I fancy you wanted y^{r} cardinal[75] Ma'am[—]Rabin[76] begs ye favor of you to Lend them ye Diamond Horse; He thinks one of ye Jades will Slip Her foal—

SOPHY—No accident I hope—

BRIDGET—None madam, they have been over but ^twice^ once against ye church wall; and once fast in ye Watercourse[77]——

(*A Hoarse voice without*) Put the cold pigeon pye, and ye basket of Apples, into ye Side Pocket, Gibbet—

[*f. 11r*]

(*A voice within*) Coming—

HUMPHRY——Ridiculous—*Aside*—

SOPHY—Remember your Linin Bridget—(*In a Hurry*)

BRIDGET—Yes Maam, (*Curtseys*)

SOPHY—The double Ruffles[78] and Tucker;[79]

BRIDGET—Yes Maam—

---

73 A carriage with horses.

74 Christmas.

75 A woman's cloak, made of red cloth: *OED*.

76 'Robin', spelled 'Rabin' to indicate how Bridget would pronounce his name. Presumably Robin is another servant of Appleyard's responsible for the horses.

77 'To over' is a regional expression meaning 'to leap over': *OED*. However, Bridget appears to mean that the pregnant mares have mated with (or been covered by) stallions, with the possible consequence that the mares will abort their foals. A guide for farriers that was frequently reprinted in the eighteenth century claimed 'If your Mare hath been covered, and the Colt knit in her, if another Horse covers her, he burns her'—i.e. makes her contract glanders, a deadly inflammatory disease in horses. See E. R. *The Experienced Farrier* (London: Rich. Northcott, 1678), p. 4.

78 A strip of lace or other material, gathered along one edge to make an ornamental frill, esp. for the wrist, breast, or neck of a garment; (also) a piece of material gathered as decoration of something else: *OED*.

79 Lace worn by women around the bodice or neck: *OED*.

SOPHY—The two pair of Sleeves & ye Trawley Cap[80]—*In a Hurry*—

BRIDGET—Yes maam—

SOPHY—The short Saque[81] and ye Dresden Apron[82]:——

BRIDGET—Lud madam; ye Ladies are calling you—

SOPHY—Away, Away, Bridget, to ye gate in a moment coming my dear Little souls; as fast as possible————*Exeunt Sophy and Bridget*——

HUMPHRY—This chariot requires as much victualing as a man of war[83]—What with cold chickens; collard Pig; Sliced Ham; and Potted beef;[84] it is as Savoury as a cooks Shop—

Enter Meadows

[MEADOWS]—Just as usual I find all spleen, and melancholy: I verily believe you will Hang in your Garters soon and then will come out a woeful black Ballad[85] with you at ye top: Intitled ye Farmers fall for ye loss of his Margery; Ha! ha! ha!—

HUMPHRY—You are very Witty Sir.

MEADOWS—Zounds I have known ye time, when you & I have outrode our Landlord; Led home ye Doctor; and out whored the Jury; at ye Quarter Sessions[86]—

HUMPHRY—He y^t^ is not easy here; can be Easy nowhere (*Striking his Bosom*)—

MEADOWS—A pritty expression truly—He that is not Easy here, can be

80 Alternate spelling of 'trolley': *OED*. While we cannot find 'trolley' or 'trawley' attested anywhere, it is presumably a style of cap made from 'trolley cloth', a type of textile typically used to line a trolley.

81 Alternate spelling of 'sack', a loose gown worn by women: *OED*.

82 'Dresden' initially referred to items made of Dresden porcelain (e.g. a Dresden doll) but the attribute also came to be used more broadly to describe anything visually resembling delicate porcelain: *OED*. Here the apron is presumably made of delicate frilly fabric reminiscent of porcelain.

83 A large warship.

84 Collard is short for 'collared' and refers to a way of preparing pork and other kinds of meat in the sixteenth to eighteenth centuries, which consisted of rolling and tying up the meat into a collar-like shape and then braising the resulting roll in wine and herbs and spices. All the dishes mentioned here are dishes that can be easily packed and eaten cold.

85 Ballad sheets typically featured a woodcut at the top illustrating the incident of which they told.

86 County courts that met four times a year and included a jury to deal with cases that could not be resolved by justices of the peace alone: *OED*.

Easy nowhere—What I suppose you and Bridget have had ingenuity enough to make a Little one[87] & so you are in wants of a Bondsman[88]————

HUMPHRY—(*Sullen*) No.

MEADOWS—Or, Have you paid money again for riding over y[e] Hunchd back Curate, & Dislocating y[e] poor Devils collar-bone Ha, ha! ha!

HUMPHRY—No—

MEADOWS—Come, Come, I find you are growing a Good young man very fast—It shall have a new Bible soon to clap under its arm; and Diddle after its Grandmother to Hear a funeral Sermon. ha, ha, h[a]

HUMPHRY——My Father Charles——

[*f. 11v*]

MEADOWS—And what of Him, no money I suppose to part from; it is y[e] common cant with these Old fellows; to Lye heartily to save their Pockets—

HUMPHRY—O, Charles, I have ruind his peace of mind and destroyd my Happiness—

MEADOWS—Pshaw, Pshaw,—I have no Stomach for your morality at present—I am to pay a Little money to Old Hocus;[89] for a Little Affair with Kilderkins Daughter[90]—you remember y[e] trifle y[t] is due to me necessity Obliges me to mention it; youl excuse the freedom——

HUMPHRY—He wants no memory, who is indebted to you Sir—but an application to my Father, would be inhuman—

MEADOWS—There is no Occasion for it—

HUMPHRY—How then, I beseech you?

MEADOWS—You was a person once, of some invention do you remember, y[e] Little Walnut tree Scrutore,[91] in your Fathers chamber.

HUMPHRY—Walnut tree Scrutore; & What of that—?

MEADOWS—A few weeks ago when I was with him—y[e] Old fellow put forty of his fat sheep there—fine yellow Rogues I assure you, Humphry—Suppose you should turn Shepherd, and give them a Little Airing—?

---

87 i.e. a child.

88 i.e. someone to stand as bondsman or surety on Humphry's behalf so that he can arrange marriage with Bridget: *OED*.

89 A cheat or a fraud: *OED*. The reference appears to be to Nettle.

90 Both 'Kilderkin' and his daughter are off-stage characters and the reference to an 'affair' implies Meadows has committed some kind of sexual transgression against the daughter.

91 A small writing desk: *OED*.

HUMPHRY—Is it possible you are Serious—?

MEADOWS—Nothing more than a Hint or so; I ask as you please to Use it—(I find I have gone too far—) *Aside*—this I perceive is Intruding too much upon your retirement; & so your Servant—*Exit Meadows.*

HUMPHRY *Solus*——I never found myself so wretched before: this Villain Meadows has undone me—How cautious should a young man be in ye choice of his companions——When I think of ye poor returns I have made to this best of parents; my Heart is ready to burst asunder—Could I recall yesterday back again; How Gladly would I resign my follies & bid Adieu to my profligate companions—

End of the Second Act.

[*f. 12r*]

Act ye third
Scene—ye seat of ye Lopwoods:

Enter Sir Harry, Leonard; and Fanny Meadows,

SIR HARRY—You know my Sentiments of placing you here. ye father who resigns up his fortunes, when he is call'd upon to resign up himself, acts niggardly with his son, & Lays him under ye poorest of Obligations——

LEONARD—You was always kind and Affectionate Sir—

SIR HARRY—Determined to leave ye village I was desirous of seeing you together; as I have something of Importance to communicate—this young woman was Educated at my Expence & you know it Leonard—

FANNY—My obligations to you Sir Harry, are ever fresh in my memory—you are all Goodness, and Generosity——

SIR HARRY—Now it is in your power in some Measure to make her happy—A young woman Left to ye world is as a ship without a Pilot, every minute exposed to Danger—

LEONARD—In what way Sir can it be in my power to make Miss Meadows Happy?—

SIR HARRY—It may be in your power I said—and if you Fanny, have not already placed your Affections Elsewhere; it is in your power to be happy too——

FANNY—My Affections Sir?

SIR HARRY—Your Affections I say—and as I have your interest much at Heart; I shall expect your compliance to what I have to offer you—

FANNY—My obligations to you Sir Harry, are of such ^a^ nature; that they Lay me under y[e] necessity of Obeying you——be still my Heart nor betray my weakness by too Easy a compliance—*Aside*—

SIR HARRY—The peculiar Happiness that arises in a well Educated mind; is in nothing, so Agreably Gratified M[r] Lopwood; as when it engages itself in y[e] cause of Virtue————

LEONARD—You Sir who feel, and know what it is, are the better able to recommend it——

SIR HARRY——A ready compliance in youth to be well advised; is a presumptive proof with me; of a Well disposed mind——

LEONARD—Your commands Sir are always reasonable—

SIR HARRY——Your relation Cub—Why do you Start so, Miss Meadows? has but a moderate capacity[92] poor youth; & I acknowledge it but then by your management of him; he may make you a civil Husband—

[*f. 12v*]

FANNY—I shall drop into y[e] Earth; my Hopes & expectations are all blasted—*Aside*—

LEONARD—Farewell to every minute of my Happiness—*Aside*—

SIR HARRY—A good natured man decently manag'd may make a better Husband than him; who so values himself upon his own good Qualities, as to overlook what is valuable in a woman—

FANNY—What would I give to be rid of my present feelings—(*Aside*)

LEONARD—You would not be so cruel Sir, as to Oblige Miss Meadows?—

SIR HARRY—I was not speaking to you M[r] Lopwood—as to Cubs worldly concerns, there is a Sufficiency to make you happy: five Hundred Acres of Good Land; are worth your Notice——

LEONARD—It may be Sir, the Lady Has engaged her affections, Elsewhere—

SIR HARRY—Dont interrupt me Sir; I was not speaking to you—my Long intimacy with your Father makes me thus desirous to Serve you: If y[e] marriage takes place immediatly y[e] Settlement shall be made under my inspection—

LEONARD—The Natural Liberty we are born too abhors y[e] Tyranny of compulsion—we have a right, S[r]——

SIR HARRY—Not to be troublesome, M[r] Lopwood—

92 In the sense of mental capacity, intelligence: *OED*.

LEONARD—May I Sir be,

SIR HARRY——I beg you to be silent—indeed you are troublesome—Prithee keep your reflections to yourself:——I thought my commands were always reasonable————

FANNY—Oh;—*Fainting*[—]*Leonard*[93] *catches her in his arms*)

LEONARD—For Heavens sake Sir Assist me.

SIR HARRY—(*Unmoved*)—You need not be alarmd—no manner of Harm in these fits; your mother had much of these Vapours—

LEONARD—Sure no mixture of human mold can yield so sweet a fragrance—(*Aside*)—

SIR HARRY—(*Negligently*)—Dont press her so close in your arms, she will soon recover—a Glass of cinnamon water will do the business——

LEONARD—You seem Sir to have Lost your feelings—

SIR HARRY—Common faintings and nothing more[—]dont Grasp her hand so fast—Give me leave madam; to Lead you to [*f. 13r*] my house-keeper—

FANNY— (*Recovering*) I will not Disobey him; but I cannot Love him as a Husband—

SIR HARRY—Give me ye favor of your hand madam (*Leads her to ye end of ye Stage*)—who waits within, Let Howard take y^s young Lady to her Storeroom[94] & Give her some comfortable cordial—(*Returns to Leonard*[95] *deeply Musing*)—The sooner we get 'em married ye better Mr Lopwood—they will be advised by you in ye management of their family—

LEONARD—(*Absent*—) Sir

SIR HARRY—I do not doubt of your endeavours to make them Happy—

LEONARD—(*Musing*) My Endeavours Sir?

SIR HARRY—The young man has a handsome fortune; and under your Eye they will act with caution—As to parts[96] our faculties are not of our own making—

LEONARD—I have not seen your Steward to day; Sir—

SIR HARRY—Pshaw you are Absent man—come there is a family writing for us to Look over; there is a map of ye Estates in my Study; we will Step in, & examine it—It is evident their affections are mutual—*Aside*—

Exeunt Sir Harry: and Leonard:——

93 'Mr Lopwood' in the original text.

94 i.e. a room used for storing food and other household supplies.

95 'M^r. Lopwood' in the original text.

96 Particular abilities or talents: *OED*.

Seat of ye Lopwoods. Continued
Enter Wilson Solus—

[WILSON—]This young Hotspur[97] of ours, will sour his fathers temper; and ruin the Jollity of the family—What with his whimsical college notions; and new regulations, it will be impossible to endure ye coxcomb——Lead me hence by ye nose did he say—Zouns I could have swallowed him as Easily as I could a Pistachia Nut; but my Gratitude to his father kept me patient——I wont be led hence by ye nose young Gentleman—Sir Harry is of a disposition not Easily Suspicious, & my intimacy with him, will give me an Opportunity to do ye young mans business——I do not mightily Like this Intrigue of mine with Sophy Appleyard; ye Girl is raw, awkward, & exceedingly Silly too—this is ye common misfortune in country Villages, where provisions of this sort are so Hard to be met with—However If our Ammunition bread[98] be but sweet and wholesome; we must not find fault with ye coarseness of it—

Enter Sir Harry—

SIR HARRY——You have ye key of ye Book case Wilson, I lent it you to look over the Globes————

[*f. 13v*]

WILSON—I ask your pardon Sir for detaining it so Long—*gives a key*—

SIR HARRY—You seem melancholy Jerry of Late

WILSON—Very much so, Sir—

SIR HARRY—This is more than usual, Surely——?

WILSON—A Friend in Distress Sir, is the heaviest of Afflictions—ye best creature too that ever existed——

SIR HARRY—Is it in my power to be Serviceable to you—

WILSON—Dear Sir you have such softness of soul; that it would rack you beyond measure to know it—Pray Sir drop ye subject—O, That I could Assist him!——

SIR HARRY—You make me ye more inquisitive—I hate to see a face in ye family that is not a happy one——

---

97 The nickname of Henry Percy (1364–1403), who took part in a rebellion against Henry IV and is depicted as a rash young man in Shakespeare's *Henry IV, Part 1.*

98 Bread included in rations given to soldiers.

WILLIAMS—Could I be assured of Secresy indeed—but pray Sir, say no more about it—Let me have my misery to myself—Let us change y[e] subject—O, that it was in my power to support Him—

SIR HARRY—You have my word for Secresy——

WILSON—M[r] Lopwood Sir; my excellent good Friend—

SIR HARRY—And what of Him—

WILSON—Nothing more Sir than ruined, to all intents and purposes—I had a Letter from Cambridge yesterday; (mercy on me it is not in my Pocket) He has a woman & child there both a Starving; there are two Writs[99] out against him besides:—He must be in Jail immediatly If not prevented——

SIR HARRY—My son did you Say: M[r] Lopwood ruined; I must be miserable If he is so—?

WILSON—I see you are Affected Sir——would to Heaven I had never mentioned it—

SIR HARRY—O, Wilson; I have had my follies as well as my Boy;—y[e] most rigid Virtue must make Allowances for y[e] giddiness of youth; & a parent must be y[e] Last to censure him——

WILSON—Pray Sir be composed—O that I had kept my uneasiness to my self—

SIR HARRY—Softly; I have a thought y[t] strikes me—I will be with you in a minute—

Exit Sir Harry————

WILSON—If this Stratagem of mine does not take place; adieu to all my Hopes and expectations—If money can be had from S. Harry; it will enable me to Leave the kingdom—I [*f. 14r*] wont be Led by y[e] nose, young Gentleman—

Reenters Sir Harry with a casket of Diamonds——

[SIR HARRY]—This Little Casket contains some Jewels of my Wifes

WILSON—I find I have worked upon his Affections——(*Aside*)——

SIR HARRY—She took delight fully well in these on our Bridal Day—(*Patting y[e] casket*)—Dear me how weak my Eyes are; that y[e] saltwater runs down so plentifully—

WILSON—A sweet Lady I have heard, Sir—

---

99 A written order: *OED*. In this case it is for the arrest of the person named for outstanding debt.

SIR HARRY—I repose a confidence in you—carry this with my Letter to Filligrew ye Jeweller: it is not far to ye city; His father sold them to me—(you may ride my Strawberry)—when you receive ye Cash from him my Letter mentions; proceed you to Cambridge & pay his Debts—remember ye poor woman, & Infant——

WILSON—Dear Guardian Angels—(*Kissing ye Casket*) Help me in my revenge and direct my Measures—

Exit Wilson—

SIR HARRY—*Solus*—These indiscretions of youth are so common in ye world; as to make mine no particular misfortune & therefore I must share with my Neighbours, this Letter which was dropt in my Study is of a more Alarming nature——Let me read it again—

Reads a Letter—S^{r}—The particular freedoms of Mr Lopwood with my Sister is no Secret with me: If you please to be a witness to his Dishonor: remember to be at ye Dark walk in ye Plantation at ye Hour mentioned below, & you will then be convinced, of his Honor and generosity, to a Deserted and Friendless orphan—Charles Meadows—This must be Attended too—How poor and worthless are ye Supposed advantages of a College Education; when it suffers men to be thus brutal and intemperate——

Scene ye Grange
Enter Nettle Sophy following him——

NETTLE—The inventory must be taken, and that immediatly—(*Looking round*)——

SOPHY—O, M^{r}. Nettle I am so Happy to see you at the Grange—I love every thing you do, and every thing you Say; and every thing you think—

NETTLE—Very Happy indeed If you knew ye occasion (*Aside*)

SOPHY—You Gentlemen of ye Law are so mild; and so Merciful, & have so much feeling; that your very words are healing

[*f. 14v*]

——NETTLE—You are very obliging madam—*Bowing*

SOPHY—O Sir I have such a tale to tell you; but I am so confused already—my Heart beats at my mouth y^{s} Minute—Lud I wish it was over—marcy on me what flustrations am I under: but you shall know it Sir If I dye in ye telling it—I am; I am; with Child Mr Nettle—

NETTLE—Then youl have a son or Daughter, Miss Sophy—Ha, ha, ha—

SOPHY—Dear Sir you are so penetrating; there is no Escaping your Observations—Now I should be Glad to know If I cant execute ye Law upon him—

NETTLE—Prosecute ye law you mean—but we have not all ye Gift of understanding—Did he promise you marriage Madam—

SOPHY—No Sir:

NETTLE—Was you under any particular engagement—?

SOPHY—Under nothing in ye world but his own self I assure you—

NETTLE—You cant recover in this case—thats certain—(*Shakes his Head*)

SOPHY—Do you think then; that I shall dye in childbed, M^r^. Nettle—*Crying*—

NETTLE—Come, come, Let us know ye story—

SOPHY—We were in S^r^. Harrys Plantations: and so he was to Shew me ye manner of Bush-fighting abroad; and so I was to Lay down as an Indian—Now said he Here stand I as a Kings Officer to take you prisoner—& then all at once he came Gulsh[100] upon ye Ground; and brought all my misery—

NETTLE—A pretty Invention truly

SOPHY—Remember to keep it a secret Sir—I have only mentioned it to six or seven of my most intimate friends—we have an Auction at ye Parsonage over ye way; & so Ill Step over for a minute

(*Exit Sophy*)————

NETTLE—Bush-fighting—a pritty engagement truly—I believe Miss Sophy has been in ye wars before now;—Hey! day! Whats ye matter now———

—*Enter Gibbet* (*With a Hankerchief over his eye Buz following*)

GIBBET—Come along neighbour Buz, we will have Law, If it is to be had in England——

BUZ—Aye, aye, Let us ave it; it is a good thing for poor folks, that's certain——

100 An onomatopoeic term for a heavy fall: *OED*.

[*f. 15r*]

GIBBET—Please you Mr Lawyer I should be Glad to know, if you have not a Little law for a poor Boys Eye——

NETTLE—(*Looking wishfully at Him*) Y^{e} right-eye I perceive

GIBBET—I hope Sir there is Law for that as well as ye other——

NETTLE—Yes, yes, we shall make it do I believe; but How Happend this quarrel

GIBBET—You must know Sir, our Alice & I; had a few words—

NETTLE—Aye, aye, Go on Child; thats commonly ye case where there are Quarrels

GIBBET—And so she takes her Patin[101] & closes my Eye for me

NETTLE—No matter for that my Lad; for ye Law is open tho ye eye be shut—ha, ha, ha!—

GIBBET—Then she took a Large cup full of dirty water and throws it all over my face and clothes——

NETTLE—I wish it had been Otherwise—(*Shaking his head*—)dirty water, you said—

GIBBET—And so did I Sir; for it smelt plaguedly strong of ye cabbage Water—

BUZ—(*Twiching his Elbow*)—Take care ow you swear cousin Gibbet; for it mig^ht^ be colliflower water, perhaps—

NETTLE—The Law you must know young man,—Hum,—Does not Oblige a Servant, to keep Dirty water in ye family; for it would be a proof of Sluttishness: now had it been clean water, ye Action would have Laid—

GIBBET—(*Bowing*) Thank you kindly S^{r} for your good Advice

NETTLE—And what would you have, Master Hugo—?

BUZ—Please you Mr Nettle, I should be Glad to be eard a Little——

NETTLE—And so would your Father Hugo, for he Lost his in ye Pillory—(*Aside*)—

BUZ—Mother Died without will; and so she Left beind er, a fat Og, and a Obby;[102]—

NETTLE—Proceed—

BUZ—Brother Ian, becase e, is older, Ian I says; e as a right to ye Og, and ye Obby—

101 A shoe with a thick sole: *OED*.

102 i.e. 'behind', 'her', 'hog', and 'hobby' (small horse or pony). Buz drops initial 'h' (e.g. saying 'e' for 'he').

NETTLE—Go, on—pray Speak a Little faster—

BUZ—Now as I am as good a man as Ian; I should Like to ave, a touch at ye Law with im, provided I can ave it there and there abouts

NETTLE—And what became of ye Hog, Pray:

BUZ—Og, e died of ye murrain[103]—

NET—Very well, and what became of ye Hobby

BUZ—Obby, was Lent to our Alters man[104] to go for the midwife. and so Obby do you see—e died on ye Journey——

NETTLE—How are you insured then?——

[*f.* *15v*]

BUZ—Not at all, not at all Mr Nettle; but as I am a statesman[105] as well as Ian; I should Like a Little Law as well as e—

NETTLE—Leave me Gentlemen—ye Affairs of Europe must be Settled—

BUZ—(*Going*) A fine man this, Cousin Gibbet—

GIBBET—*to Buz*—A Sweetful Scholard I warrant Him

(*Exeunt Gibbet & Buz*)

NETTLE—*Solus*—Must give it up; it is too much to be supported—Lord Chancellor and Alexander Nettle can have no rest—If my opinion could be split into a thousand pieces; I could not have a Shred for myself—Well—When a man sets his hand to ye plough he must not Look forward. Hold I am wrong; must not Look backward; thats right;[106] and so Little Alexander cheer up my Lad; curror Lex thats my notion; Ha, ha, ha! and the world is before me——

Exit Nettle——

---

103 Term for a number of infectious diseases affecting farm animals: *OED*.

104 i.e. 'Alderman', the local justice of peace: *OED*.

105 Presumably a malapropism for 'a gentleman'.

106 Nettle is (mis)quoting Christ: 'No man having put his hand to the plough, and looking back, is fit for the kingdom of God' (*Oxford KJB*, Luke 9:62).

Scene ye Grange
Enter Wilson and Bridget—

WILSON—Your young Lady is seldom at home Mrs Bridget?—

BRIDGET—Seldom indeed Sir; Miss Sophy is a woman of Spirit—She is now at M^r. Ministers Auction; to morrow she is to be at a fidlers consort;[107] then at a Ball; and then to the excisemans wedding————

WILSON—The business of ye family must be easily managed surely—

BRIDGET—My young Lady Sir, Leaves every thing of that sort to us Servants; and when our betters; put a conficance[108] in Us; we are always exceedingly grateful———

WILSON—To be sure, Mrs Bridget—it is impossible to doubt your Servants to be wanting in Gratitude and due Acknowledgements (*Bowing*)

BRIDGET—You are exceedingly kind, Captain Wilson—(*Curtseys*)

WILSON—I thought Miss Sophy had been fond of her evening walks and ye Amusements of y^r family—I must sift her a Little (*Aside*)

BRIDGET—O, those Walks, those walks,—I wish you had never mentioned them—for when young Ladies Love walking so Late & so frequently: there is commonly something in ye Damps and night air; y^t does not agree with them—

WILSON—I wish she dont suspect our intimacy (*Aside*) Miss Appleyard Has very good Health I hope?

BRIDGET—As to that Sir; it is neither here, or there for that;—but you know most of ye matter—As for my part I never knew her so Pale before: ye very Staymaker[109] Laugh'd when he took her measure—

WILSON—I would not have you wonder Mrs Bridget [*f. 16r*] at my Long intimacy in ye family—I expect shortly to be made a Captain of Horse; If a friend of mine does not deceive me—and then Miss Sophy may command a Phaeton[110] and your Humble Servant———

BRIDGET———Captain of Horse truly—O, ye Lying Impudent Rascal—*Aside*—

WILSON—Let this remain a Secret with you———there is no belief in mankind—it is a damnable Lying world we Live in—friends are treacherous; & promises of Little worth———

107 A group of musicians playing the fiddle and other string instruments: *OED*.

108 i.e. 'confidence' deliberately mispronounced.

109 Someone who makes the kind of women's undergarment called a stay (a stiffened bodice): *OED*.

110 A horse-driven carriage with four wheels for one or two passengers: *OED*.

Enter Sophy as from ye Auction—

SOPHY—O Bridget, Bridget,—I have been so unfortunate today—your Servant Captain Wilson—(*Curtseys to him*) by going so Late to this Auction—ye room was filld—and so I axd a Gentleman what was then up; and he said a fine Painting of ^one^ Rubbens in a Large Gilt frame; & so I bid up; and bought it——

BRIDGET—Dear ma'am you wont be able to put it up in your chamber—but when you are, ye Lady of a Captain of Horse, Madam—

WILSON—*To Bridget*—I beg you to be silent (*Aside*)[111]

SOPHY—No, it must be kept below stairs—for what do you think it was—a Smoke Jack[112] as I Live and a kitchen Range——He, He, He!—

WILSON—The Gentleman had a mind to be Witty, madam——

SOPHY—O, but this is not all I assure you—for as I stood at a distance; a fat old Lady said in a red cloke in a sort of a whisper—that she would have ye mahogany Chest of Drawers; and so in order to Spite her; I bid again and Had it——and what do you think it turnd out at Last—a Little nasty Disagreable Pudding cart,[113] and a Pair of Harrows—He, he, he—

BRIDGET—O, madam! ye Captains Phaeton will suit you better

WILSON—Wont you be silent Madam—(*Aside to Bridget*[)]—you are very unfortunate Miss Sophy—Do me ye favor Mrs Bridget to Lay up this trifle for me—Gives money—and If you please, immediatly——

BRIDGET—I understand you Sir, (*Curtseys*)—I would have overturnd his Phaeton, If he had not thought of it——*Aside*——

Exit

WILSON—Our frequent meetings in ye Plantations and Elsewhere my Sophy have been Long observed I find—in order to be more private, I have contrivd this Stratagem—you and Miss Meadows are nearly of ye same height and size;—She has a remarkable pritty Habit, that was Lady Lopwood's: as you are intimate with her, borrow it and wear it at our next meeting—I will provide you with a mask If wanted: Loose no time; about it immediatly; and when you have it, we will fix ye time of our Meeting

SOPHY——With all my Heart—

Exeunt Wilson & Sophy

111 Presumably an aside to Bridget, not the audience.

112 A mechanical device for rotating a roasting spit through the power of wind in the chimney: *OED*.

113 A cart for carrying rubbish or offal: *OED*.

Scene Grange Cont^{d}
—Enter Meadows, & Humphry Williams following————

[*f.* *16v*]

WILLIAMS—Odds my Life, prithee be friends, there are enough in ye world to quarrel, without you two: He who sleeps in Whole bones sleeps comfortably; but a poor mans Saying is worth but Little————

HUMPHRY—Had it been from a common Acquaintance I could have born it patiently; but from you Mr Meadows; it is beyond my patience—

MEADOWS—You are too warm and peremptory—you wont be pacified—

HUMPHRY—Pacified do you call it—to be arrested for a debt made up at ye Gaming table: but you knew your Advantages and Have Used them—

MEADOWS—Will you have temper or not; I am not in ye Humour to quarrel with you——

WILLIAMS—Dear Heart, prithee be comforted my good young maister Indeed I could advise—

HUMPHRY—Indeed you sha'nt—*Angrily*——

WILLIAMS—You sha'nt be ruined indeed you sha'nt—

HUMPHRY—Peace with your babbling, blockhead—

WILLIAMS—Do but Leave things to me, S^{r}.—

HUMPHRY—I won't hear a Syllable further

WILLIAMS——I have indeed,

HUMPHRY—More freedom than you ought to have (*Strikes Him*) and take that for your Pains—

WILLIAMS——Aye, Aye, it is mighty well—but I have paid ye Debt and ye Charges for you—and If I have done wrong in this I will e'en go, and get my money again—

MEADOWS—You are too violent with him Mr Appleyard—Harkee me Master Gilbert—can you call yesterday back again, or pull ye man from ye moon think you—?

WILLIAMS—I pull ye man from ye moon—no, no, he is above poor folkes I warrant him—

MEADOWS—Do that first—and then endeavour to get your money;—you will find it as practicable; I Assure you—

WILLIAMS—Was it for me to see, my poor young maister carried to prison truly—I, who Have carried him before me so often, upon poor Old Diamond—when he used to Say so prittily as we rode to water: Doc a long Dimon,—No, No, my Heart would never suffer it—*Weeping*——

MEADOWS——Poor Fellow, his gratitude Hurts me more than this mans inhumanity—Leave us Gilbert—

WILLIAMS—It shall be as you choose to Have it Sir, but a poor mans saying, is worth but Little——

Exit—

[*f. 17r*]

HUMPHRY—The kind instructions you Gave me; and y[e] pains you have taken to make a Gambler, has very well repaid you M[r] Meadows: you kept dexterity enough in your hand to ruin me at pleasure——

MEADOWS—Still uneasy I find—you knew my necessities, & y[e] Shatterd condition of my circumstances——

HUMPHRY—Necessities Sir—?, no Necessity could Justify your conduct—

MEADOWS—You knew my pressing Occasion for y[e] money and as your Father is confined to his Chamber; I thought it was in your power to procure it——

HUMPHRY—Merciful Heavens would you have me force y[e] key from his Pillow & rob y[e] House again? down conscience & don't distract me

MEADOWS—Pshaw you are Peevish, Humphry——

HUMPHRY—My Obligations to you Sir, are very particular[—]you seduced me first from these happy fields to Houses of Debauchery——

MEADOWS—Prithee deal more friendly with me—

HUMPHRY—You introduced me when a Boy to women of infamy; wretches who perswaded me to rob a Parent to suppor[t] their follies and my own——

MEADOWS—Will you never have done with y[s] nonsense

HUMPHRY—You Alienated my Fathers Affections from me, made me a monster in Society; & a wretch who is truly miserable

MEADOWS—Hold, Hold, I will bear it no Longer—my Affairs being Shatterd as well as yours: poverty, Children, & a thousand things besides; I have engaged with Wilson to serve his Majesty abroad—

——HUMPHRY—It is not in your power I believe to serve a more amiable monarch—you are resolvd then—?

MEADOWS—Absolutely so—

HUMPHRY—Immediatly?

MEADOWS—Immediatly—We have Had some happy Hours together Humphry; and therefore let us part as Friends—you was once a Master of some good nature;—If you have any remains of it, be merciful with your censures;——I am miserable, as well as you——

HUMPHRY—Happy Hours did you call them; O, Charles they were Hours of madness, that must be Accounted for—they were hours y^t carried poison with them; tho undiscernable by Us in ye Heat of Youth and Hours of Gaiety—

MEADOWS—Will you Attend me for an Hour—it is the last favour I shall ask—probably we shall meet no more——

——HUMPHRY—If this be ye case; I have an hour at y^r Service:

Exeunt Humphry & Meadows

The End of the Third Act——

[*f. 17v*]

Act the 4.th
——Scene the Grange——

CUB——*Solus*——Surely of all heavy things; that of Love is the heaviest——I carry more weight about me than would Load a Camel—I feel as hollow as a fish that has just Slipt its spawn, & look as melancholy as a mill without her sails—cousin Meadows Desired me to meet him; and ye Steward Here——but he is as Hard to be found as a Queen Anne's Farthing[114]————

Enter Clinch and Meadows—

MEADOWS—Very much out of Luck Sir; the best of my cocks had ye roop[115] and Lost their battles; Jenny ran through her girths and was double distancd[116]—a little out of ye Elbows[117] Sir at present—

---

114 Copper coinage featuring the queen, which began to be minted in 1713 but the production of which was halted by Queen Anne's death in 1714. While none of the coins were officially released, some illicitly or accidentally entered circulation and their scarcity generated false rumors about their high value. See A. Prior, *The English Illustrated Magazine*, vol. 30, no. 196, 8 November 1903, pp. 193–5.

115 Hoarseness: *OED*.

116 The horse was disqualified from two subsequent races, presumably for going too slowly in the first race.

117 'Out at the elbows' literally refers to a garment worn so much that it has holes at the elbows but in a figurative sense it can also refer to the condition of being poor: *OED*.

CLINCH—Zounds man what have I to do with your cocks, your mare, and your double Distances;—I won't Lend you a Farthing—

MEADOWS—Pray Sir have a Little Patience——a fine Gentleman if you had but a Little temper;——This S^{r}—[(]*introducing Cub*) is my cousin Daniel Cub now at Age—He can cut out a fighting cock[118]; crack a Hunting Whip, and turn up Jack at all fours[119] to Admiration————

CUB—You was Always comical Cousin Meadows, (*Whispers Meadows*) What shall I say to Him now? —

MEADOWS—Anything you Like never mind what

CUB—(*To Clinch*) Any thing you Like never mind what (*Bowing*)

CLINCH—This is no better than meer Curd of Asses milk[120] (*Aside*)

CUB——O, Cousin; What a sad thing it is to be a Man in Love when nobody pittys him—And yet when they see a Pig in a String;[121] a Horse in a Pound,[122] or a Dog with his clog,[123] every one pities the poor animal——

CLINCH——Perseverance young man is ye best weapon to conquer ye fair with—Women are frequently best pleased when they appear to be most out of Humour——

CUB—When I see her I tremble; When she Looks at me I blush; and when she frowns, I am all flutter and confusion—Ah! woe is me for I wish it Otherwise——

MEADOWS—You must know Sir, my Law Affair with Old Hocus,[124] goes on very fast; now Sir If I had your advice and you would be pleased to Lend me two Hundred Guineas, (*Speaks Loud*) I would play the Devil with Him——

118 Reference to the practice of mutilating a rooster's crown and feathers in order to prepare the bird for cock fighting. See 'Supplement. Fighting Cocks, and Cock Fighting' in *Sportsman's Dictionary* (2 vols., London: C. Hitch, 1735), ii, n.p.

119 Reference to winning points in the trick-taking card game of All Fours.

120 Clinch seems to be echoing Alexander Pope's line from *Epistle to Dr Arbuthnot* (1735), 'Paris that mere white curd of ass's milk' (*Pope*, 306) in the second edition of the poem published the same year Pope changed 'Paris' to 'Sporus', targeting Pope's nemesis John Hervey.

121 A pig with its feet tied together (usually to facilitate handling during transport or slaughter).

122 An enclosure for keeping straying or confiscated farm animals: *OED*.

123 A heavy block of wood tied to the dog's neck or leg to keep it from escaping: *OED*.

124 Probably Nettle, see note 89 above, p. 82 in our edition.

[*f. 18r*]

CLINCH—Won't Lend you a single Farthing

MEADOWS—I would as soon have you on my side Sir as a Kings Serjeant[125]——will you be pleas'd to Advance ye money Sir?——(*Very Loud*)

CLINCH——In some things perhaps, in particular cases Mr Meadows—Death and ye Devil what makes you so teazing——

CUB—O, Charles, your Sister Has a heart as hard as marble—ye other day she was coming a Long ye passage of your House and so I drew myself-up close to ye Napkin-press; thus, (*Mimicks it*) and as she passd I touched her Gown & said: Rosebud, Rosebud,—If you will but marry me, you will make me ye Happiest of Mortals——

MEADOWS—And what said she to all this—

CUB—Marry Plain English, said she with a smile—now I dare swear thats; our washing womans Daughter[126]——

MEADOWS——My Cousin Sir, Has some fine Old Pastures, that Join to ye Lands you purchasd of Jemmy Spendal: and as he is going to Marry my sister Fanny:—If you please to advance ye two Hundred Guineas,—you shall have it a pennyworth[127]——*Loud*——

CLINCH—Freehold did you say—

MEADOWS—Every Acre.

CLINCH—Old Pas-ture

MEADOWS—All in a Hedge[128] Sir,

CLINCH—Your Father and I have drank many a bottle Charles; Will was a good companion——

MEADOWS—*Whispering Cub*—This Gentleman cousin is a Sollicitor at Law as well as S^r^. Harrys Steward————

CUB—Yes, yes, that is ye same as a Head borough[129] no doubt——

MEADOWS—Please S^r^. to have ye conveyance ready & we will call it

125 A king's (or queen's) serjeant was a lawyer whose task it was to defend the interests of the crown in courts of law, although in practice the role quickly became more of an honorary one: *OED*.

126 Sophy tells Cub should marry plain English, meaning that he should not speak so formally. But Cub takes Sophy literally and takes the retort to mean he should marry the 'Plain English' washing woman's daughter employed by the Cubs.

127 As a bargain, cheaply: *OED*.

128 Surrounded by a hedge to mark and protect its boundary: *OED*.

129 An officer in the parish with the function comparable to that of a petty constable: *OED*.

for ye money—come cousin; we will Look up my Sister; you shall tickle her as you would a Chub[130]—come courage my Lad; faint Heart neer won fair Lady——

Exeunt Meadows and Cub——

CLINCH—*Solus*—Puppy, Have it a pennyworth—did he think then that Isaac was still a Chicken——He that can Palm an Imposition upon Isaac Clinch; shall be welcome to the advantages of it————

Enter [*Kitty*] *Toy*[131] (*with a Box under her Arm*)

KITTY——I beg pardon for my Intrusion Sir; [*f. 18v*] I thought Miss Appleyard had been in ye family——these fashions Sir are all fabricated upon ye Italian principle[132]—

CLINCH—This is certainly ye rich Milliner[133] Meadows mentioned; whose uncle died at Barbadoes, and left her a handsome fortune—(*Aside*)——

KITTY—We had a full Stage from Town y^s^ week three of us Milliners, a superannuated Alderman; a Puking Child with a swelld belly; & a Lunatic sent into ye fen to make a turnpike road[134]——

CLINCH—Very good company indeed——(Pray speak a Little Louder) —

——KITTY—Anything in my way Sir that can be useful (*Ogles & Curtseys*)——

CLINCH—I have saved a Little money you must know—and as I begin to go into years; (not Old I assure you) No, No,—I should like to have something that is comfortable to my Bosom——

KITTY—Dear Sir, you shall have it immediatly—(*Opening her box*) — Here is ye sweetest Jaganot;[135] that will make you ye warmest cravats you ever wore—

---

130 A chub is a type of fish from the carp family: *OED*. Tickling a fish's belly, causing it to go into a kind of trance, is a fishing technique.

131 For the entirety of this scene, the speech prefixes refer to Kitty Toy as 'Toy'. We have revised these to 'Kitty' to preserve the continuity with the earlier scenes where she appears.

132 Italy (together with France) was a major source of both fashion trends and imports in eighteenth-century England. See Peter McNeill, *Pretty Gentlemen: Macaroni Men and the Eighteenth-Century Fashion World* (New Haven: Yale University Press, 2018).

133 Seller of luxury fashion accessories such as hats and gloves: *OED*.

134 A major road on which toll is collected: *OED*.

135 Alternate spelling of 'jaconet', a cotton cloth originally imported from India: *OED*.

CLINCH—Pshaw, Pshaw, Let the box alone—finding myself a Little inclining to years; I should like to Change——*Smiling*

KITTY—Your Linnen no doubt Sir—pray Sir let me recommend to you Callico[136] night Shirts—there is a Twisterer[137] in ye city who always uses them——

CLINCH—Dear me, you wont understand it—[(]Let ye box alone)——I am in wants then of a bedfellow——

KITTY—Bless me Sir, it is as dangerous for an old man to meddle with a young woman; as it is to rumage an old building; for he no sooner touches her but she falls to piecis by some means or other;

CLINCH——Incomparable creature—thus Let me fold thee in my arms—(*Advancing*) O, thou hast put mountain fire into my soul, & recalld ye Days of my youth——(*Snatches a kiss*)——Bodokins[138] the Jade is as luscious as a Beuret Pear,[139] in November——(*Aside*)——

KITTY—Pho, what a kiss was that—Worse in ye mouth; than Pig, radish, or rocombole[140] at Second Hand[141]—ye toad is as insipid as a bay Leaf in a Custard——(*Aside*)——

CLINCH—Once more Let me reach those Lips—Here Let me riot in your beauty—(*Advancing*) Here let me;—(*Advancing too fast he tumbles down*)

KITTY—O Lud! O Lud! my Dear Good Sir; you must have bruised your forehead;—(*Lifts him up*)—O, you Old Dotard, what a sweet cuckold will I make you—(*Holding her fingers over his head, as Horns*)

CLINCH—The Jade Little thinks y^t^ I understand her; but I'll keep me a double horse, and always take her with me—*Aside*—

KITTY—Fie upon you Esqr Clinch; you are [*f. 19r*] much too amorous; Indeed you make me blush:—Had I indeed a friend who could secure my fortunes abroad—I could then; (*Sighing, & Looking wishfully at Him*)—know where to bestow my Heart; and my fortunes——

CLINCH—I have no time to Loose: and must be careful of Meadows; these Planters abroad are mostly rich—(*Aside*)——Do me the favor madam to Look over my Little building: & you may command both me and my services——O, my back, my back, How very troublesome——

---

136 Calico, cloth made of cotton (named after Calicut in India): *OED*.

137 A twister or spinner of threads: *OED*.

138 A variant spelling of 'bodikins' or 'bodkins', a mild oath meaning 'God's body': *OED*.

139 Beurré pear variety, noted for its mellow buttery taste: *OED*.

140 Variant spelling of 'rocambole', an edible plant resembling leek and garlic, noted for its piquancy: *OED*.

141 Food chewed in someone else's mouth or, even more rudely, digested and excreted: *OED*.

KITTY—I shall think myself Sir; both safe and Happy under your friendly protection——

Exeunt Kitty and Clinch——

Grange Scene Continued—
Enter Bridget—

[BRIDGET]—I would Lay my Maidenhead to anything; this master of Horse of ours, with his thousand Lies; will ruin ye family[;] my old master Dying; my young master mad: my young Lady in a hopeful condition, & I without a Sweetheart——

Enter Williams, beating Gibbet—

GIBBET—Pray Sir, Dear Sir, Master Williams; you will break every bone in my skin Sir,—

WILLIAMS—Liberty Jackanapes another word and Ill hang you upon ye first timber I meet with—

GIBBET—I thank you for that Sir—but I have no mind to Lay under such strong obligations—but Esq Clinch has taken pritty good care of ye timbers I warrant him—

WILLIAMS—What have you to do with Liberty Booby?—

GIBBET—Beat ye French; pull down ye Spaniards; & mend ye constitution of Old England.[142]

WILLIAMS—Mend ye Holes in your Stockings Sirrah—Away to ye cattle this minute; (*Beating him again*) but a poor mans saying is worth but little—

^GIBBET—I am already gone Sir—^

Exeunt Gibbet and Williams

Enter Fanny, and Sophy—

SOPHY—Somebody is at ye door; Bridget—If M^r. Cub calls at ye Grange Shew him into ye Parlour——

BRIDGET—Yes ma'am, I shall be in ye Way—*Exit—*

---

142 c.f. Joseph Addison's observation in *The Freeholder* that 'There is scarce a Fresh-man in either University, who is not able to mend the Constitution in several Particulars.' Joseph Addison, *The Freeholder*, ed. James Laheny (Oxford: Oxford University Press, 1979), p. 264.

FANNY——It is ridiculous in you my Dear; to be thus disordered for trifles—when ye weightier concerns of your family never reach you.

SOPHY—My Dear Madam; she never brings a fashionable thing to ye Grange nowadays; till they are first pawed over by ye two Miss Nogs and ye iron-mongers crooked Niece——

FANNY—We have nothing to do with ye fashionable world; and when we have it is but awkward imitation at best; our betters Look upon us as ye puppets of a Day; Dressd up for ye excitement of public Laughter——

[*f. 19v*]

SOPHY—As to that madam, Mr Minister said in ye Vestry: yt Dolly Trot in her double Taffata,[143] was ye best Dressd Girl in ye Parish—

FANNY—Dear Girl have done with your fooleries—our Happiness does not depend upon ye Hanging of a Gowns Sleeve—nor in ye trinkets we wear—She who is cloathd with an Humble Spirit; may Have a mind richer than hers who is distinguishd for a woman of Quality——I find Sir Harry is going to resign his Seat & Estates to his son immediatly——

SOPHY—O, Madam I should Dye to have it so—he is such a Tyrannical, and meer Philosotical Bookworm——

FANNY—Are you in your Senses, Madam?——I am told Mr Lopwood was as welcome to ye Village; as ye flowers in May—

SOPHY—Believe as you please Madam—He wont suffer a Dog to Look at Him—He shot poor Little Pug at his own door——the Butchers boy told it ye Labourer; ye Labourer told it to ye maid; & ye maid told it to me———

FANNY—You are misinformd Madam;—he is too Studious for such trifling amusements—they mistook him certainly for ye Young Esqr with ye White Hat; Who kills women & Partridges by dozens—

Enter Cub

[CUB]—This poor Heart of mine is ready to burst my ribs—When I walk, I know not where; when I think I know not How; and when I hear ye singing of ye nightingale it makes me melancholy—Ah woe is me; for I wish it Otherwise——*Aside*——

FANNY—(*To Sophy*) I could never pardon those unmerciful creatures of our sex; who as children do, ^their^ kittens, keep their Lovers to torment them——

143 Taffeta, an expensive fabric made usually of silk: *OED*.

SOPHY—A meer whim madam;—If I had a Hundred Lovers; I would stick ye toads on a Pins Point, & roast im[144] over a Candle; as we did our raisins—

FANNY—You was Always a Whimsical Creature; when I have cryd to see a ^poor^ mouse in a trap; you have been roasting it for your diversion——you may come nearer Cousin Daniel——I cannot Love Him; or use him cruelly—(*Aside*)

CUB—Yes ma'am I am coming very fast—(*Goes near Her*) you look Charmingly well Miss Meadows——a fine White and red on your cheek madam—Ah, woe is me for I wish it otherwise—

FANNY—Moderately in Health Sir—pray come a little nearer me; you shan't be ravishd—you seem to have Lost your Spirits

Cub—When I was in a Holiday Humour; I was as well as ye best of them—I have carried your Bible to church [*f. 20r*] before now; and took a pinch of your snuff in ye time of ye Sermon;—but now Ah woe is me for I find it otherwise——

SOPHY—You should take yourself to ye club Sir; two, or three times in a Week: Eat a beef Steak y^t^ is well sholletted[145]—then drink two bottles of Port, and a Quart of Porter; and it would put you into excellent spirits—

CUB—You are before me, both night and Day; I see you in my Sleep; follow you in my Dream; and when you seem to Smile, or Pat my Hand; then I wish I had never woke——

FANNY—How inoffensive is this good Creature; I pity his feelings by my own (*Aside*)

CUB—Every thing you say is Pritty; every thing you do is pritty; and where you are not, there is nothing pritty——

FANNY—I cannot endure to see him Miserable—(*Aside*)

CUB—My own Dog seems to be Ashamed of me—for when I call him Fanny instead of Tray;[146] ye poor thing Looks at me as much as to Say How strangely Alterd——Ah woe is me, for I wish it otherwise——

144 Sophy uses 'im' rather than 'em', perhaps reflecting how she pronounces '[th]em' or, alternatively, idiomatically using a shortened form of 'him' in place of 'them'.

145 Probably in the sense of cooked with a good quantity of shallots. We have not been able to locate any other instance of 'well shalloted' but the *OED* records the earliest instance of 'onioned' in a comparable sense in Tobias Smollett's 1755 translation of *Don Quixote*, 'they treated him with an hachis of beef well onioned'. We thank David Goldstein for this reference.

146 Tray appears to be Pratt's favourite name for a dog as he also uses it in *Cinderetta*, 'The Jay a Fable', and 'Political Duck-Hunting'.

FANNY—I must stop his conversation for I cannot bear it—(*Aside*)—I hope you dont design to be rude, Sir?——

CUB——There; now it is all over with me—*Aside*—Not I madam in ye Least—I have nothing more to Say; I am satisfied and ask your pardon—

FANNY—And what are Sir Harrys resolutions, Cousin

CUB—That we shall be married immediatly——

FANNY—Proceed

CUB—That Mr Lopwood shall be at ye Wedding

Fanny—Very Well

CUB—That five Hundred Acres of Land are worth your Notice—

FANNY—Go, on—

CUB—And that Mr Lopwood has promised to Give me

FANNY—What Sir; (*Hurried*) Speak it immediatly—

CUB—A black Greyhound Dog to keep in ye family—

FANNY—How easily is a woman Alarmd that is realy in Love—now for a Scheme to punish Miss Sophys Impertinence—I was thinking cousin as we are too nearly related for marriage—suppose you should turn your Affections to Sophy Appleyard—

CUB—I would as soon be married, to ye Dried cocodile in the Apothecarys Shop——[*f. 20v*]

SOPHY—And I to ye Greenman, that Hangs up at ye alehouse Door—or to ye case of a base viol—

CUB—She is as fiery as ye spitting plant[147] in Sr Harrys Garden—A man would no sooner touch her, but she would fly at ye Eyes of Him—

SOPHY—A Fellow without a capacity——

CUB—A woman without a Sweetheart——

SOPHY—A forked carrot, not worth ye scraping——

CUB—A Dried Eel Skin for a School Boys Top——

FANNY—Bravo—it goes on admirably well—(*Aside*)

CUB—A bent minifer,[148] not worth ye Stooping for

SOPHY—Pig, at Second Hand[149]——

CUB—A dough cake spoiled in ye baking——

SOPHY—Meer barley water, and Nothing better—

CUB—(*Embarrasd*) I believe I must give it up—(*Aside*)

---

147 Probably *Anneslea fragrans*, an originally Asian plant, whose flowers shoot out blobs of pollen when touched.

148 Variant spelling of miniver, a stoat: *OED*.

149 See note 141 above.

FANNY—(*Whispering Cub*) Never mind her, Cousin, tell her she is a Geographer.

CUB—You are a Geographer madam

SOPHY—So, So, What you are come to your Latin at Last, are you?

CUB—A Flimsey Geographer—

FANNY—(*Going to Sophy*) Never give it up Miss Sophy: Tell him, he is a fumbling Topographer[150]——

SOPHY—A fumbling Topographer——

CUB—A flimsey Geographer——

SOPHY—A fumbling Topographer.

CUB—A flimsey Geographer—

FANNY—Come, Come, Let there be an End to this Quarrel—He is only a Tyranical creature Sophy, who wont Suffer a Dog to bark at him; rather too Phi̲loso̲tical you find, Ha, ha, ha!—One would think these simpletons were members of ye Feathers Tavern Society:[151] As they are quarrelling about words they do not Understand—(*Aside*)

SOPHY—To be calld; Ge, o, gra, pher at Last by such a thing as this—I who have drank negus[152] with ye Chairman himself at ye Quarter Sessions;[153]—I who have danced—(*Crying all ye time*)

FANNY—These Little Altercations in courtship [*f. 21r*] are very common—come do me ye favor to Step Home with me for a Dish of Tea & everything shall be forgot——

SOPHY—I must beg to be excused madam—my poor Aunt Deborah is ill with a Quinsey;[154] and I have promised to call upon her—now my Dear Wilson; for a Happy meeting (*Aside*)——

Exeunt Cub; *Fanny*; *and Sophy*——

150 The 'Geographer' and 'Topographer' insults are perhaps intended to recall the Reverend Francis Blomefield (1705–1752) and his *An Essay Towards a Topographical History of the County of Norfolk* (1739–75).

151 The Feathers Tavern Association, a group of clergy named after the Feathers Tavern in Cheapside, where it originally met, petitioned for the rewriting of the Book of Common Prayer in keeping with latitudinarian principles. The group was active in the 1770s and demanded in particular the abolition of the requirement to subscribe to the Thirty-nine Articles: *Oxford DNB*.

152 Hot beverage consisting of port, sugar, lemon, and spice: *OED*.

153 Court convened before justices of peace: *OED*.

154 An inflamed or abscessed throat: *OED*.

Scene ye Plantations—

SIR HARRY *Solus*—This is ye time ye letter mentions—And this I believe is ye private walk; Let me examine it (*Looking at his Watch*)—

Enter Leonard——(Walking accidentaly; at a Distance)

[SIR HARRY—]Just at ye time too—How punctual to his meetings, but I shall prevent it at present—

(*Sophy, crosses ye stage in a Riding Habit*)——

[SIR HARRY—]By Heaven it is ye same, ye very Habit that was my Wifes: I gave it her with my own Hands—who would wish to be a Father——

LEONARD—My Father I perceive (*Aside*)

SIR HARRY—(*Going to Him*) You are very punctual to your time Mr Lopwood

LEONARD—These rural scenes are most pleasing to me Sir, as they prepare ye mind; for the most serious Impressions——

SIR HARRY—Are you then that mean & unworthy person that have endeavourd so much to Destroy a character; that had nothing but its Virtue to Support it—?

LEONARD—What reason can you possibly have Sir, for such unmerited Suspicions?

SIR HARRY—It is ^a^ poor and unmanly triumph to Endeavour to prevail over ye Affections, of a weak & unsuspecting young woman—& common as it is in ye world; it is as unmanly as it is Vicious——they Have passions to Struggle with as well as we[155]——

LEONARD—You fill me with confusion Sir—

SIR HARRY—I am no Stranger to your Attachment to Fanny Meadows: your Appointments, Assignations, & pitiful Deceptions Have been Long discoverd——Are these ye Advantages from Education; fie upon it: I blush for your Ingratitude——

LEONARD—Surely ye reproaches for Disobedience are registerd within; I can hold no Longer——(*Aside*)—*Kneels*—

SIR HARRY—I never see him miserable; but I find myself ye greater sufferer—*Aside*—

155 Pratt originally wrote 'ourselves' but then erased 'ourselves' and substituted 'we'.

LEONARD—That I love Miss Meadows with a soft & bewitching tenderness my own Heart Witnesses against me——

SIR HARRY—The image of his Mother rises in [*f. 21v*] my mind and pleads in his behalf already—*Aside*—

LEONARD—Oh there is in her such purity of soul and sanctity of manners as makes ambition worthless—Heaven as If ashamed of its niggardly Affection to her fortune has inrichd her mind with more than natural Accomplishments—

SIR HARRY—Rise Sir—(*Lifts him up*)—where there is a Heart Susceptible as yours; reproaches are ye Less necessary——O, who would suspect ye villain should Lye conceald; in so open and Sweet a countenance——

LEONARD—It is ye will of Heaven Sir that directs our Actions and forms our connections for us—

SIR HARRY—Heaven has nothing to do with unworthy actions—And Honor is a dress that sets well on him who wears it tenderly; but it sets awkward upon him; who is not ye Owner of it——so young and so able a Dissembler——(*Aside*)

LEONARD—You are mysterious Sir——

SIR HARRY—Wilson tho partial to your Interest can explain things better—

LEONARD—I detest ye Villain; but he is now so fast in prison as not Likely to be further troublesome to yr family——

SIR HARRY—In Prison—it is then too Late to save him

LEONARD—It is in very good time; Sir——

SIR HARRY—Most unfortunate, at ye very time I wanted Him most—

LEONARD—It could not possibly be more fortunate;

SIR HARRY—Had he satisfied ye Creditors; and made ye poor woman Happy—

LEONARD—The Creditor Will be Satisfied——

SIR HARRY—Pshaw, it is you I am speaking of—

LEONARD—Probably Sir this Letter which was sent to me with your returnd Horse; may explain things better to you——

LEONARD—*Reads out*—A person in ye Dress of an Officer, with a Letter from your Father and a small Casket of Jewels; was unfortunately Arrested as he Left my door; & desiring to speak with me at ye Tavern; he requested ye favor of Letting you know; that had he received ye Cash which was to have been paid ye next morning; he had agreed with one Meadows to Leave ye Kingdom—that in order to revenge a blow from you he dropt a Letter in your Fathers Study Signd Charles Meadows, Accusing you with an intimacy with his Sister; and to Give this an air of probability he perswaded

Miss Appleyard to borrow her Habit; and to be at ye place Appointed; He has also confessd that the Story he made of your Debts & ye woman you kept at Cambridge; was invented to get money from your [*f. 22r*] Father and ruin you in his good opinion—I thought proper to communicate that as Recd from his own mouth—I am S^{r}. y^{r} obe^{t} Hum^{e}. Ser^{t} and Old School-fellow George Filligrew—

SIR HARRY—Mercy on Us—A man cannot set his foot out of door, but he must meet with villainy——Clinch by Droping his pocket book in ye Plantations, has discoverd ye many villainies of his Stewardship—

LEONARD—It is no news to me Sir—but he was married this morning to Kitty Toy ye celebrated Man Milliner;[156] you need not wish him a greater Punishment——

SIR HARRY—I hope such instances are not common in ye World——We are to have a wedding at ye Grange tomorrow; remember you to be present—I feel my Spirits recruit[157] a Little and hope, you will be cautious not to Lower them—

Exit Sir Harry

LEONARD—Good and Amiable man: How ready is he to think well of a world that has ever abused His Goodness—we shall have a wedding tomorrow—it wrings my Heart to pieces—but I must Submit to his will—nor add Affliction to a Life wearing away too fast; in ye services of his fellow Creatures

————Exit————

End of the Fourth Act

[*f. 22v*]

Act: Vth:

Scene ye Plantations—

Enter Leonard and Fanny—

LEONARD—The pleasing hopes, & expectations of meeting you here; have been fortunately gratified; y^{s} morning

156 i.e. a milliner who makes clothes for men.

157 To recover one's strength: *OED*.

FANNY—Under ye same anxiety of mind with yourself; it is as fortunate to me Sir——

LEONARD——I never knew my Father, so Absolutely before—

FANNY—Would I could have my miseries to myself, and I could bear them patiently; but to give pain to you Mr Lopwood, makes me doubly miserable————

LEONARD—Oh, Fanny; my Father is now Acquainted with our reciprocal endearments that began in Childhood; and what induces him to be thus peremptorily Severe to marry you to a person your Heart disowns; is beyond my power of Discovery—

FANNY—My Father dying when I was an Infant, yours adopted me for his Child, & Used me as tenderly as his own—by my Life I love him as ye best of parents; & would not disobey him for a kingdom—but as he knows me to be poor and Friendless; He is endeavouring by this marriage; to remove me from you————

LEONARD—You do him wrong, indeed you do;—no mercenary Views can reach a Heart Like his——but who he should thus press you to marry one, who has nothing but his fortune to recommend him; is a Deviation from his Character, that does not become Him————

FANNY—He pittys me as an Orphan; but will not Love me as a Daughter—

LEONARD—The many Obstacles my Father has thrown in my way adds fuel to my Passion—ye fire of Love Like that of nature grows Stronger by resistance—O, Fanny my Duty should keep me patient; but Love has a superior claim and must be Listned too——

FANNY—Sweet soul; be careful of Disobedience[—]there is a secret curse that will Attend it, & blast your expectations——

LEONARD—This Afternoon we are all to meet at ye Grange—merciful Heavens, how shall I undergo it—you are to Attend Miss Appleyard; till then, thou best of Angels, Farewell, and Heaven protect you————

FANNY—Would to Heaven ye Day was finished——

Exeunt Leonard, and Fanny————

[*f.* *23r*]

Scene ye Grange
Enter Nettle, Gibbet, and Hugo Buz

GIBBET—And I pray Neighbours; what is this sad misfortune—

BUZ—Nothing but a Dead man killd right out of Hand Master Gibbet—Mr Nettle says ye Jury must set upon his Widows servant or he cant be buried; so, you must know I am afraid I shall loose my fees—

GIBBET—Set upon a Dead man; thats rather cowardly neighbour Hugo—

NETTLE (*To Buz*)—I told you Hugo; that ye law says omnnum quos morebit ad mortom;[158] is forfeited to ye Lord; and that Sir Harry would claim ye waggon and Horses——

BUZ—Very true, very true, so you did Mr Nettle but then I said; as ye fore orse,[159] was a mare; Sir Arry could not Ave all ye Orses—

GIBBET—Good Lord! Poor John Hopkins—He who used to ring ye Tenor[160]——?

BUZ—The very same—Opkin, son of umphry and Annah, his Wife—a good Pipe for a Psalm too[161]——As to yr Mr Nettle you Gemmum[162] of ye Law would Starve us parish clerks to Death——I ave not buried a Gentleman like corpse above a Quarter;—then there is your fine inocurating Scheme[163] that has saved ten thousand——O, my maisters (*Shaking his head*) that good Doctor Snatchall was but alive again——

NETTLE—Gentlemen, we have no time to Loose ye jury must be Impanneld, and ye body removed: please to follow me directly—

GIBBET—Aye, aye, Neighbours; Lets flannel ye Jury

BUZ—Ay, Aye Lets flannel ye Jury—

Exeunt Omnes—

---

158 Garbled Latin but the sense is something like 'the possessions of those who die are forfeited to the Lord'.

159 Pratt slipped and initially wrote 'Horse' in the manuscript before remembering that Buz drops his 'h's and erased the 'H'.

160 The largest bells in a set of bells in a church or cathedral: *OED*.

161 To have a good voice for singing in church.

162 i.e. gentlemen.

163 i.e. inoculating.

Enter Humphry; Williams, and Sophy;

SOPHY—You have no mercy upon yourself Brother; you neither eat, drink, or sleep as usual; you must have a Ghost at your Elbow surely: Lud, I think I see ye eyes of it; with a beard as Long as my Apron string——

HUMPHRY—(*Striking his bosom*)—Here is that which neither sleeps, or Slumbereth: A guilty and troublesome conscience——

WILLIAMS—Dear Good Master be a Little Chearly; when things are at ye worst, they commonly mend folks say; but a poor mans saying is worth but Little——

HUMPHRY—O, Sophy ye false indulgence of our parents: and ye vanity to be above ourselves;—Has Lowerd us to y^{s} poor [*f. 23v*] condition—

——SOPHY—Mercy on us, one would think you had robd a church, and run away with ye Plate of it—you are Ever Groaning at Home Like an old Jack[164]; that is in wants of Oiling—

——[HUMPHRY]—[165] No Sophy; not yet so wicked—but it was my early misfortune to be kept away from it—and when I reflect upon the Injury I have done to ye best of parents, and this faithful Creature: I have too much upon my Spirits Sister—

SOPHY—What a profligate set of Nerves must y^{s} monster have, I shall be infected with his maggots[166]—(*Aside*)—As for my part Brother, I never go out to meet Misfortunes: Hang sorrow is a maxim with me—I shall never put myself in ye way of it I assure you——

[HUMPHRY]—There is no occasion for it at present; it is ready at your hands—Unthinking Woman—

SOPHY—Company are to be Here by Sr Harrys order—& so wishing you good Mr Humphry Hippo better Spirits; and a bottle of Hartisher[167] tied to your button—I remain,—no, I dont,—but I go away your most obedient—

Exit Sophy—

---

164 'Jack' in the sense of a mechanical device used for lifting heavy objects: *OED*.

165 In the manuscript this speech prefix and the one that follows Sophy's next line both read 'Leo' but these are clearly erroneous and should read 'Hum' instead. We have corrected both speech prefixes to read 'HUMPHRY' accordingly.

166 On maggots as a metaphor for strange ideas see Kate Tunstall, 'The Embodied Mind and the Entomological Imaginary', in Mary Helen McMurran and Alison Conway, eds, *Mind, Body, Motion, Matter: Eighteenth-Century British and French Literary Perspectives* (Toronto: University of Toronto Press, 2016), p. 207.

167 Ammonia solution made from powdered hart antlers and used as smelling salts: *OED*.

HUMPHRY—Impenetrable Creature——

WILLIAMS—Aye, there she goes; with Just as much prudence as might be Cramd; into a Hazel Nut————

Enter Sir Harry; Leonard, Clinch following

SIR HARRY—I did not think there had been so ungrateful, and so mean a Monster;

LEONARD—You have been so Long imposed upon Sir Harry; but ye mask is now dropt off; and you see him as he is, a mean and mercenary Hypocrite——

CLINCH—There must be something more than I know of; to have Occasiond this sudden change in my good Old Master (*Aside*)

SIR HARRY—Your family I suppose Mr Appleyard can Join ye rest of ye Tenants & Neighbours Here, in Heaping execrations upon ye Head of Him—

HUMPHREY—I confess myself at a Loss Sir, to know your meaning—What can Mr Clinch have done S^{r}, to have thus offended you—?

SIR HARRY—Villainy; and no thing better——

CLINCH—Indeed your Honor has been a Little too hard with me of Late;—I may have been a Little too tenacious for your Honors rights—but who is he that can be perfect in a world like this

SIR HARRY—My Rights, thou Hypocrite [*f. 24r*] No Sir, you are of too soft and milky a disposition: Had I been formd Like other men; & could have preyd upon ye Vitals of my fellow Creatures (*Mimicks Him*) I might Have been worth a Little money—excellent Dissembler——

WILLIAMS—Poor Gentleman; quite Chap fallen[168] indeed it is all over with him; Wheels up as I live——

SIR HARRY—(*To Clinch*) Do you know this Pocket-Book (*Shews it Him*)

CLINCH—Mercy on me, ye same that I Lost in the plantations—I am ruined and undone for ever——(*Aside*)——

SIR HARRY—In this you stand a confest Villain, under your own hand writing; ye other tales of your Dishonesty and meanness are such, as are Even a Disparagement to Manhood—

CLINCH—The world Sir is, very;

SIR HARRY—Out with it, Deceitful as well as you Are:

LEONARD—Give me Leave Sir to add one Instance more of his abundant modesty: I applied to him when in College for a Hundred

168 Crest-fallen, in low spirits: *OED*.

pounds: this Letter of his required, a payment of two Hundred pounds at your death; with ye next turn of ye Vicarage;[169] at his own disposal——

SIR HARRY—These are ye Leeches, who take ye Advantages of youth; as Hurtful to society as sword, or famine—you shall Disgorge your Ill-gotten treasure——*Loud*—

CLINCH—Dear Heart what makes me tremble so—(*Aside*) Immediatly do you say Sir?

SIR HARRY—Immediatly—and you shall enable this hones[t] fellow, (*Pointing to* Williams) to have better bread, & he shall have my assistance with it—

HUMPHRY—I have not felt such a minutes Happiness for some time (*Aside*)—

CLINCH—I will avoid ye Law; and Submit to your mercy; I will avoid,

Enter Mrs Clinch[170] (*Much out of temper*) —

MRS CLINCH—And pray Sir is it me you would avoid—Sir Harry, I ask your pardon—(*Curtseys*)—And you young Esquire (*Curtseys again*)—— Is a woman of my condition to be thus abused—(*To Clinch*) that could have married a Tallow-Chandlers Nephew in an honest corporation,[171] you Sir—

CLINCH—Worse, and Worse, my Bride too; O that I should Listen to y^{t} Villain Meadows—Curse on his Barbadoes Planter—(*Aside*)

SIR HARRY—I dare swear M^{rs}. Clinch, If you was not a person, of a mild, and obliging temper, it would be impossible to Live with Him————

MRS CLINCH——O, Sir he is ye most Sniveling Driveling, whimpering puppy, that ever Lived——there is no more [*f. 24v*] Life in him than there is in a dryd weazel:——

LEONARD—But your Happinss of temper M^{rs}. Clinch will make all things Easy——A good temper madam is a valuable blessing—

MRS CLINCH—Temper do you call it Sir——a woman must have ye temper of ye Devil to deal with him—to be brought Home as a Bride to naked walls—to have every place bolted; and Lockd, and made fast against me: to see nothing but a Brood Goose[172] in ye chimneys corner; and a poor cropt[173] kitten; that is almost famishd——

---

169 i.e. when the next vicar comes in after the current one retires or dies.

170 i.e. Kitty Toy, now newly married to Clinch.

171 In the sense of a 'trade-guild': *OED*.

172 i.e. a goose kept for hatching eggs.

173 The ears of pet cats were sometimes cropped to prevent them from going outside and

CLINCH—Tum, Tum;[174] I will gow home with thee my chicken—

MRS CLINCH—(*Mimicking Him*) Tum, Tum; I will gow Home with thee: and so you shall, you Dotard——Home I say (*Shoving him*)—this very minute—*Still Shoving Him*——Away with you—or Ill Isaac your noddle for you——

Exeunt Mr & Mrs Clinch——

WILLIAMS—Poor Esq[r] Clinch—He was always fond of Lumping penny-worths; and egad he has it now—Wheels up as I Live—

SIR HARRY—I have observed in you M[r]. Appleyard a very different behaviour from what it Used to be——you seem to have Lost that Giddiness of temper which did not become you——

HUMPHRY—I have Lost much more Sir; myself, my Father, and everything that was valuable——

LEONARD—Meadows declared before he left y[e] Village that y[e] Injury He had done this young man, by an Early Seduction; sat heavier upon his Spirits, than his own Misfortunes————

SIR HARRY—I have heard much of it from Wilson—and it is too often y[e] case; that a good Disposition is ruined; before it is Sufficiently formd to resist temptations——

——LEONARD—It is not improperly Applied, to M[r] Appleyard

SIR HARRY—You must know then; that I have interested myself in your behalf—my son will make you Steward Here, in the room of Clinch; an inexorable Heart that cannot overlook y[e] follies of Youth Has frequently too many Defects of its own to Hinder it—Let Gratitude bind you to Him with Chains of iron——

HUMPHRY—I am all distress and confusion—*Aside*—my future conduct alone must answer for me——

WILLIAMS—Odds my Life I shall burst with Joy—this is too much for Gilbert—must cry, & cannot Help it—(*Weeps*)—but a poor mans saying is worth but Little—

SIR HARRY—Poor fellow, his tears are becoming him—He too shall have his reward—A good Heart feels frequently more than is necessary[—] take him aside Humphry and Give him some refreshment—He who [*f. 25r*] eases an Aching Heart; does more than Him, who conquers a City——

---

hunting. The unprotected ears became extremely sensitive and vulnerable to the elements and so such cats often preferred to stay indoors.

174 Imitating the sound of a string instrument.

WILLIAMS—O Gemini Sars;![175]—this puts me in mind of an old dream that I had on Valentines night: as How, I had four mares all big with foal; and y[t] I drank Nog[176] with y[e] Minister, at my Childs Christning——

SIR HARRY—You must give me Leave M[r]. Appleyard; to see you & your father together——we will follow you immediatly—

LEONARD—Surely, such men as these are sent on Earth to be y[e] Deputies of Heaven—*Aside*—attend me Gilbert—

Exeunt Humphry & Williams—

SIR HARRY—(*Pulling out His Watch*)—I find Miss Meadows and her Lover are not punctual to their time—We will Step in for a Minute M[r] Lopwood; and reconcile y[e] Father and y[e] son—

Exeunt Sir Harry & Leonard——

Scene Grange Continued—
Enter Bridget and Gibbet, (*With a Letter in his Hand*)

BRIDGET—Do, open it my Dear Gibbet: you are a Scholard and cun read—Let's have a Little fun with it——

GIBBET—(*Reading y[e] Direction*) To Miss Sophy Appleyard—As black as pepper itself——It was certainly wrote by some conjuror; with y[e] Devils ink—

BRIDGET—No matter what; I Long to Hear it—none of your Scrupolosities I beseech you:————

GIBBET—I am quite Afraid Bridget—We shall be Discoverd; I dont Like the business—my Heart trembles confoundedly——

BRIDGET—Po, Po, Have done with your Fantastarums—give it a flap with your finger thus; and make it fly all at once—I will seal it again with M[r] Thimble; and make it as well as Ever—

GIBBET—Will you indeed—(*looking at y[e] Seal*)——by Golds I have done it—and now Lets read it——*Reads slow*[177] My confinement hurts, my, mind, as well, as, my, body;—and, y[e], more, so, when, I think, of, your, present, condi,ti,on and my Utter in,a,bi,lity to Serve you—I write this to

175 i.e. 'O Gemini stars'. 'Gemini' could be used as an oath on its own and 'my stars' could similarly be used as an exclamation: *OED*. 'O Gemini stars' is also attested in *The Farmers Dialogue, on the Present State of Public Affairs* (London: J. Ridgwat, 1791), p. 12.

176 A strong beer: *VEA*.

177 i.e. not part of the dialogue but a stage direction for the actor to read slowly.

Guard you against wicked servants; Bridget is very Dishonest, and ye Boy you took from ye Charity School and Arrant Rascal, beware of both——I hope to Have my Liberty soon; & assure you I am faithfully yours—Jeremiah Wilson————so, so, this comes by our peeping truly—

BRIDGET—You must be upon Honor, Gibbet—

GIBBET—Yes, yes, all upon Honor, & burn ye Letter

BRIDGET—Lets away then, to prevent a Discovery——

Exeunt Gibbet and Bridget——

[*f. 25v*]

Scene y^{f} Last

Reenter Sir Harry; Leonard, Miss Meadows, Cub, and Sophy—

SIR HARRY—Then every thing is ready for ye Wedding you say?

CUB—Your commands Sir are only wanted

FANNY—My Life Sir, is at your Disposal; I have no Will of my own to oppose your measures—I can be but miserable If you will have it so——

SIR HARRY—You had my free consent Friend Daniel to marry Fanny Meadows; you have it from my Heart; she will make a very good Wife, or I am much mistaken——

LEONARD—I shall never be able to keep my patience; my Heart mutinys within—would to Heaven he had been Less indulgent—*Aside*—

SIR HARRY—M^{r}. Meadows declared before he Left ye kingdom; that by a Stratagem of his; you have sold some Lands to Clinch for half their value; & that he perswaded you to do this to procure money for himself; under ye pretence that you wanted it; for his sisters Wedding;—

CUB—Very true Sir.

SIR HARRY——You have been deceived young man and so has Clinch—ye Old Fox is caught in his own trap—those lands were Left you by your uncle as a Life Estate[178]—there is a Deed in my Hands y^{t} will explain it——And Let me tell it you Sir; He who is not Sufficient to manage his own Affairs, is a very Improper person; to manage a family——

FANNY—What can be ye meaning of all this; I tremble for ye event—*Aside*—

LEONARD—I begin to feel myself alive—*Aside*—

---

178 A type of property which is held for the duration of one's life and therefore cannot be sold, gifted, or otherwise disposed of: *OED*.

SIR HARRY—As soon as you please Friend Daniel; you may marry Miss Meadows——But this young Lady here is ye Daughter of Lord Mountairy——

LEONARD—Lord Mountairy?——

SOPHY—Lord Mountairy?

FANNY—I am all flutter and confusion (*Aside*)

CUB—Ah woe is me, for I wish it Otherwise—

SIR HARRY—His Lordship frequently hunted here When I kept my Hounds—there was an intimacy between him and my Housekeeper; she proved with child; and was Afterwards married to my [*f. 26r*] Tenant Meadows, with their mutual consent and good Liking——

SOPHY—I shall never envy Her ye first Fashions[179]——(*Aside*)

—SIR HARRY—Now this Discovery is made—will you Mr Lopwood be so wanting to yourself and family; as to Stain ye credit of your ancestry; by taking to your arms, a woman, so Dishonourably born——

LEONARD—We are answerable to Heavens S^r. Harry for our own faults only—ye vices of our Parents, do not belong to Us——

SIR HARRY—You seem to be resolute Sir—prithee be more considerate about it——it is a business of much Importance——

LEONARD—It is in your power Sir to break my Heart[—]my Affections for this excellent Creature, cannot be broken——(*Weeps*)——

SIR HARRY—Nay, Nay, no Tears my son—Mercy on me that Look of his will rend my Heart asunder——*Aside*——If you take her as a Friendless woman;—can you promise yourself that firmness of soul y^t would enable you to bear ye Insults of ye World; and ye frowns of Fortune—could you bear with patience those agonizing thoughts that would arise; from Giving Birth and misery, to a Helpless Offspring——

LEONARD—Reflections so deeply Laid as these S^r; are unnecessary restraints upon our innocent Amusements——

CUB—Oh that my Heart would burst——*Aside*——

SIR HARRY—Be not too resolute my son——few Have patience enough to bear afflictions——I feel my Breath Leaving me apace—*aside*—

LEONARD—Rocks,[180] banishment, or Prisons would be Eden with her—

FANNY—I can never support this much Longer—*Aside*

SIR HARRY—Know then Lord Mountairy died a Batchelor; and Left

179 Circumstances: *OED*.

180 'Rock' or 'rocks' in the figurative sense as a signifier of danger or destruction due to their common association with shipwreck: *OED*.

you a fortune of twenty thousand pounds[181]—Surely you will not be so Imprudent a young woman—As to throw it away upon a Young Fellow; whose Estates are Mortgaged for half their Value?——

FANNY—If I had a kingdom of my own; I would Lay it at Mr Lopwoods feet; and think it well disposed off——

SIR HARRY—O Fanny, Marriage is a business of the utmost consequence; both to your present, and future Happiness——Weigh it well I beseech you, madam—you have it in your power now, to be allied to Greatness——

FANNY—The Change of my Fortune makes me happier indeed by putting it into my power; to be more Grateful to so Deserving a Gentleman——

[*f. 26v*]

CUB—How sweet, How good she is——(*Aside*)

SIR HARRY—You are resolvd then?

FANNY—Nothing Sir, but your absolute commands, can alter my resolutions—

LEONARD—Incomparable woman—*Aside*——

SIR HARRY—Then am I blest indeed——Let me here join your Hands——and be as happy as ye Heart of a fond parent can wish you—

LEONARD—(*Embracing Fanny*) Oh Fanny thus Let me take you to my Arms—Thou as a Vessel tho once Shipwreckd to my fancy: Have now returnd to Port; a rich and a Welcome prize: Here shalt thou rest free from Storms;—be this thy faithful Hospitable Haven——

SOPHY——O, Wilson, you never Loved like this—(*Aside*)

SIR HARRY—Suppose Friend Daniel as you have Lost your mistress, you should offer your hand to Sophy Appleyard?

CUB—Never—

SOPHY—The wretch is as Obstinate as ye Millers Ass: I wish he was lodgd in a hollow tree and Stung to Death by Hornets—*Aside*—

LEONARD—Come, come, Master Cub; you are always upon cross purposes with ye Ladies; you must learn to be more civil to them; they are Given as to correct ye Severity of our tempers

CUB—Never—

FANNY——If you two were to come together Miss Appleyard; you must Remember to shut up poor Little Pug or he will shoot your favourite—He is very Philosotical you know Ha, ha ha!

181 Approximately £1,745,000 in today's money: *NACC*.

LEONARD—Creatures, of such mixed Qualities as these; When they are paird in Wedlock; commonly Leave to Society such a hash of Oddities; that y[e] world is y[e] worse for their Labours—

CUB—One word, & no more——be ye both as Happy; as I am miserable——Ah woe is me for I wish it otherwise (*Exit Cub*)

FANNY—Poor Creature, I pity him from my soul;——He has much Honesty at Heart——

[*f. 27r*]

SIR HARRY——And now M[r] Lopwood I relinquish to you y[e] better Half of my fortunes; and what I ever held more Dear and valuable to me, y[e] good will and affections, of my neighbours—

LEONARD—You are all goodness and generosity Sir——

SIR HARRY—As soon as y[e] wedding is over; I shall Leave you to yourselves; be you a Father to your people Here—Discountenance vice, and encourage virtue where you find it——so that by setting a good example in y[e] marriage State; you may by some measure recover y[e] credit of an Institution; that is now too much become; the ridicule of y[e] vitious[182]————

Twas taught of Old, in Wisdoms Sacred School:
"Worth makes y[e] Man; and y[e] want of it, y[e] Fool";
Let each from hence Learn this; himself to know;
Nor Idly soar too high; or sink too Low:
Walk Humbly forth; with cautious Steps & Even:
Humility's y[e] best; and Choicest Gift of Heaven.[183]

Prologue & Epilogue, y[e] next Page

turn over[184]

182 Alternative spelling of 'vicious'.

183 The manuscript has two sets of double quotation marks at the beginning of the quotation, one set immediately above the second set; we have transposed the second set to the end of the quotation.

184 We have placed the Prologue before the main text of the play.

[*f. 28v*]

Epilogue

Well, in my Life, I never saw before;
A face so frightful; at ye back stage door:
Fellow said I; what is your Business, Here?
Whose Wretch are you; whence come you, what, & where?
Tis mine he said; my Masters will to follow;—
Madam, I'm Bailiff to the God Apollo;
Sent from Parnassus by this God of Day;
To seize and take, the Author of your Play:
The court is met, an Honest Judge & Jury;
The suit commencd by all ye men of Drury;
Imprim[185]—that he having no fear before him;
In spite of all ye Nine,[186] and all Decorum
Has wrote a Play, and Pilferd Plot and Plan
Ma'am, will you tell me where to find ye Man?
Fellow said I, do Let Apollo know
Poets were Thieves, four Thousand years Ago:
Go back again, so, (tipt[187] the wretch a Crown)
For Earthly Thieves you need not to come down:
And if your Phœbus threatens him with jail;
We, ye Kings Servants here, will find him bail:—
The Fellow Grin'd, first made a leg,[188] and then
Flapt His broad wings, & sought Parnas Again;
Thus Having sav'ed[189] him from ye Bailiffs Hands
I wait on you to know your Just commands:
Will ye condemn him for this first Offence?
A naughty Man, to murder common sense;

185 Abbreviation for 'Imprimis' meaning 'firstly'.
186 i.e. the nine Muses.
187 i.e. tipped.
188 Bowed.
189 Perhaps Pratt was hesitating between writing 'saved' and 'sav'd'.

[*f. 29r*]

Yet should you pass, kind Sentence on his Play;
He may grow worse, and write another Day:
What's to be done—to you we must Submit;
What silent all, Box, Gallery, and Pit—?
Then Let me speak; tho partial to his cause;
For once transport[190] him—with your kind applause——

190 A pun on two senses of 'transport': (1) to transport the playwright with joy and (2) to transport him overseas, as many criminals were in the eighteenth century: *OED*.

'An Occasional Prologue to *The Clandestine Marriage*' (Print Version)

NRO PRA 664/26

Date: Printed as a standalone text in early 1779. There is no date on the standalone printed version of 'An Occasional Prologue to *The Clandestine Marriage*' reproduced here from the Pratt folder. The date given for the performance, 22 March 1779, suggests a date of composition in early 1779. Pratt's Occasional Prologue was printed along with the Epilogue Richard Gardiner wrote especially for the same production of *The Clandestine Marriage* in the *Norwich Mercury* for 3 April 1779, p. 3. The standalone print of the Prologue reproduced here was likely printed nearly contemporaneously with the newspaper version. Both Pratt's Occasional Prologue and Gardiner's Epilogue to *The Clandestine Marriage* are also reproduced in *Gard*, 185–8.

Authorship: Although the printing of the Occasional Prologue and Epilogue to *The Clandestine Marriage* in the *Norwich Mercury* only credits Richard Gardiner as the writer of the Epilogue, and does not identify the writer of the Prologue, the undated printing of 'An Occasional Prologue to *The Clandestine Marriage*' is credited to 'J. P.' of Watlington. Both this printing and the manuscript version of the Prologue in Pratt's hand are included in the Pratt folder. The Prologue can thus be confidently attributed to Pratt. The manuscript version of 'An Occasional Prologue to *The Clandestine Marriage*' is reproduced in Appendix 3.

Physical Description: Printed folio half-sheet measuring 20 cm by 33 cm.

[*p. 1*]

An OCCASIONAL

PROLOGUE

TO THE

CLANDESTINE MARRIAGE,

Perform'd by Gentlemen, for the Benefit of the Wives, Widows, and Families of Impress'd Men, for His Majesty's Sea-Service, in *LYNN* and its *Environs*, on MONDAY, the 22d *March*, 1779.

SPOKEN by

A GENTLEMAN.

AW'D to behold, these radiant Seats around,
Untrod before, I trembling touch the Ground:
Train'd to no Stage this Night we Humbly Strive,
To keep for once,—The COMIC MUSE alive.
Compassion gave those Hints, We here pursue,
And let Compassion, plead our Cause with you:
We claim the Feeling,[1] not the Actors part;
Our Wish to Please, our Aim to move the Heart,[2]
To sooth the Soul, to stop the trickling Tear:
For this We Act, for this you come to hear;
What-e'er our Fate, however understood,
We know, We feel, our Motive to be good.
Far from these peaceful Scenes, by Nature brave,
Our Sons of Neptune, mount the boist'rous Wave:
For Britains Weal, the Dang'rous Torrent stem,
They play their parts for us, and We for them:
Without their Aid, the blessings of our Isle,
Wou'd soon drop off, and Love forget to smile;

1 A question mark appears here instead of a comma in the original print.

2 c.f. the line 'His Wish to please; his Aim to mend ye Heart' in the Preface to *The Grange* [*f. 27v*, l. 14].

If thro' their Valour, we with comfort live,
Returns are claims! 'tis gratitude to give.
   But shou'd this Night some Critick rear his Head,
To strike us poor New-fangled Actors dead?
From you ye Fair, from you, one single Frown,
Will make all well, and dash the Monster down.[3]
Beauty has this peculiar art to Please,
You Charm with Rapture, and you Kill with Ease;
If ought this Night, your Nicer Ear offend?
Condemn the Actor!—But forgive the FRIEND.

J. P.
WATLINGTON.

---

3 c.f. the lines beginning 'Yet should some Critic, with his Pinch of Snuff' in the Prologue to *The Grange* [*f. 27v*, l. 15].

Longer Poems

(28)

Nor do our ſportſmen's labours of the day,
End with the ſun, tho' ſunk its Weſtern ray:
In dreams they ſtart, with more than labour' throes;
Whoup! Tally ho! Hark forward! there he goes!
Windſor is ſpur'd, or elſe in *Windſor*'s ſtead,
Their own *dear* wives‡ are tumbled out of bed:
Good ſenſe, good-nature too, muſt fix the bounds,
Men ſhould be men, not company for hounds.
Nor let old Thunder's praiſe be ever ſung,
When ſofter muſic flows from woman's tongue:
A thouſand charms in Charlotte's dimples dwell,
But thou art bleſt—young Sancho points ſo well.
What's wife, a daughter, or an angel's face,
To a net ſwelling with a good *five brace?*
Women may charm, and marriage joys delight,
But a full covey is a glorious ſight.
What! tho' thy pointers boaſt ſuperior ſpeed,
Range well and wide, and ſprung from *Doxy*'s breed;
Yet ſpare our ears, nor pour th' eternal tale;
Here *Turko* ſtood, there *Mungo* caught the gale:

From

‡ *Their own dear wives*----The power of the imagination in ſleep is very wonderful; whether the exertion of the ſoul at that time is greater than at another, muſt be left to the deciſion of the learned; but this we certainly know, that both our hands and feet are uncommonly merry and pleaſant in the time of dreaming.

Vide Prieſtly's Diſquiſitions.

Figure 8 *Page from* September: A Rural Poem

The Inundation or The Life of a Fen-Man

Source: We have used the copy of *The Inundation or The Life of a Fen-Man* at the British Library as our copy text (Shelfmark 11642. *f.* 4).

Date: Published in 1771.

Authorship: The attribution to Pratt is based on context. The title page lists a 'Fen Parson' as the author and the poem's form and style bear strong resemblance to Pratt's writings, in particular the long poem we are certain is by Pratt, *September: A Rural Poem*, with its extensive footnoting system and a combination of classical and local references. *September* and *The Inundation or The Life of a Fen-Man* were published by the Lynn printer William Whittingham, as was *The Coal-Heavers*. The reference to the hare and the partridge taken down from a tree at Downham Market is the kind of anecdote someone living in the area would be expected to know. However, there is an undated printing of *The Inundation or The Life of a Fen-Man* in the Wren Library at Cambridge University in which 'Thomas Boyce 1773' in Boyce's hand has been written on page 5 between the title and the first line of the poem. This has led to the poem to be attributed to Thomas Boyce (1732–1793) in the Cambridge University library catalogue. The annotation can, however, be read as simply a mark of ownership rather than a claim to authorship. Boyce was, moreover, not a parson who lived in the fens stretching from Cambridge to Lincolnshire: he was the curate of Cringleford near Norwich and Brampton east of Aylsham at the time that *The Inundation or The Life of a Fen-Man* was first published (see Boyce's entry in the *CDB*). Boyce's own elegies published as *A Specimen of Elegiac Poetry* (1773) and his later verse tragedy *Harold* (1786) show little of the imaginative energy of Pratt's writings. A piece of evidence in favour of Boyce's authorship of the poem is that he was a witness to the sale of a piece of fenland on 7 October 1775. See Cambridge University Library, University Library, 'Lease and release, Doddington, Cambridgeshire' GBR/0012/MS Doc. 1762. We think on balance, however, that Pratt is the more likely author of the poem.

Physical Description: Poem printed on pages bound together in a marbled booklet, the resulting booklet measuring 20 cm by 25 cm.

[*p. 1*]

THE

INUNDATION

OR

THE LIFE OF A

FEN-MAN,

A

POEM.

With Notes Critical and Explanatory.

By a FEN PARSON.

I thence
Invoke thy aid to my advent'rous song,
That with no middle flight intends to soar
Above th' AONIAN *mount, while it pursues*
Things unattempted yet in prose or rhyme.
Milt. Par. Lost. B. I.[1]

LYNN: Printed by W. WHITTINGHAM;
And sold by R. Baldwin, *Bookseller* in Pater-Noster-Row, London; Mr. KNAPP, at Peterborough; Mr. NICHOLSON, at Wisbich; Mr. HAYTT, at Bedford; MR. JENKINSON, at Huntingdon; MR. ALBIN, at Spalding; Mess. FLETCHER and HODSON, at Cambridge; and all other Booksellers. 1771.
(Price ONE SHILLING.)

1 *Milton*, 1:14–16.

[*p. 3*]

THE PREFACE.

THE *design of this little poetical piece is to instruct a race of men in their religious duties, and to inspire them with a chearful and patient submission to the will of divine providence, who are favoured with the smallest opportunities of availing themselves of instruction. The fen is a vast plain, intersected with various natural and artificial rivers, defended with high banks, to prevent the over-flowing of the high country floods in their passage to sea. On these banks the inhabitants, for their better security, erect their miserable dwellings, at great distance sometimes from each other, and very remote from their parish churches, to which they rarely resort, unless to a wedding, a christening, or a burying. So that they seem to be cut off from the community, and are deprived of almost every advantage of social life. It is a rare thing to meet with a village of twenty houses together, unless in their towns, from which they are many miles distant. They are, therefore, excluded every opportunity of the very lowest education, and few of them arrive at a higher erudition than to be able to read and write.*

The idiom of this poem is, in the general, calculated for the meridian of their understanding, some few instances only excepted, [*p. 4*] *where imitations of the most eminent Latin and English authors are introduced for the amusement of the learned. Frequent allusions are made to the sacred scriptures, as often as the nature of the subject would admit, this being perhaps the only book they ever read, probably the only one they have ever seen. Many moral reflections are also made to proceed out of the mouth of the poor fen-man, when he sees his fate determined, and no other resource left him, but the fortitude of his own mind, and the patience of his natural disposition, all tending to inspire a set of men with a calm resignation to the divine will, who, of all human beings, have the most frequent occasions to submit themselves to the absolute disposal of providence. To an upland farmer, the loss of his stock, or the failure of his crop, may be repaired by another more kindly season; but a drowned year strips the poor fen-man of every conveniency of life, his all is gone, he is compelled to abandon his dwelling, and has not an inch of dry land to set his foot on.*

If the rich and great, who are clothed in purple and fine linen, and fare sumptuously every day, should condescend to look into this humble performance, it cannot but awaken their sensibility with the distresses of many, who in this dreadful calamity, would be glad to be fed with the crumbs which fall from their table. The milkiness of human nature must overflow, to the relief of these miserable wretches, many of whom may be said to be even destitute of a place where to lay their head.

[*p.* 5]

THE INUNDATION.

OF sudden floods descending on the plain,
Which threat to drown a sinful land again,
Whose swelling surge with unresisted sway,
The lowly cot and cattle sweeps away,
Sing, heav'nly CLIO, thou that did'st inspire
Thy fav'rite NASO[2] with poetic fire;
Assist my weak endeavours to pursue
The similar tale, and make his fable true.

V. 1, 2, 3, 4. Expatiata ruunt per apertos flumina campos,
Cumq; satis arbusta simul, pecudesq; virosq;
Tectaq; cumq; suis rapiunt penetralia sacris.
Ovid. Met. lib. 1.[3]

V. 5. *Sing, heav'nly Clio.* She was one of the nine muses, the patroness of historic poetry. She derives her name from a Greek word, signifying Glory, in allusion to the honour and fame of the actions she records.

V. 8. *And make his fable true.* Alluding to the description of Deucalion's deluge in Ovid's Metamorphoses, which was in reality Noah's flood, disguised by poetical fiction, but is actually realized in the present situation of the Fens.[4]

---

2 The Roman poet Ovid, full name Publius Ovidius Naso.

3 *DLCL*: Ovid, *Metamorphoses*, 1:285–7 (p. 23) 'The rivers overleap all bounds and flood the open plains. And not alone orchards and herds, men and dwellings, but shrines as well and their sacred contents do they sweep away.'

4 See *DLCL*: Ovid, *Metamorphoses*, 1:253–380 (pp. 20–8). Deucalion and his wife Pyrrha were the only human beings left after the flood that Jove brought upon the world.

[*p. 6*]

And as thou mov'd the Grecian bard to write
Of frogs embattl'd for the bloody fight,
Strengthen the efforts of my trembling pen
To celebrate an humble race of men,
Alike amphibious, by kind Nature's hand
Form'd to exist on water or on land.

The glorious sun, bright regent of the day,
For five dry seasons with his sultry ray,
Had warm'd the earth, and in diurnal round,
Exhal'd the vapours from the fenny ground;
The less'ning flood relinquishes the strand,
And laughing CERES repossess'd the land.
As nature kindly had perform'd her part,
She meets assistance from her handmaid art.[5]
The banks are heighten'd, proper engines force
Th' expanded waters to their usual course.

V. 10. *Of frogs*, &c. Homer's battle of the frogs and mice.[6]

V. 15. *The glorious sun*, &c. In imitation of Milton.
First in the East the glorious lamp was seen,
Regent of day.

Par. Lost, *B*. 7.[7]

V. 20. *And laughing Ceres*, &c. In the ancient mythology Ceres was the goddess of husbandry.

5 Echoing stanza 155 of John Dryden's *Annus Mirabilis* (1667): 'By viewing Nature, Natures hand-maid, Art,/ Makes mighty things from small beginnings grow:/ Thus fishes first to shipping did impart/ Their tail the rudder, and their head the prow.' John Dryden, *The Works of John Dryden*, ed. Edward Niles Hooker and H.T. Swedenberg, Jr. et al. (20 vols., Berkeley: University of California Press, 1956–1989), vol. i, ll. 617–20, p. 83.

6 *Batrachomyomachia*, a Greek parody of the *Iliad*, traditionally attributed to Homer.

7 *Milton*, 7:370–1.

[*p*. 7]

The swampy bog now yields luxuriant grain,
And yellow harvests glad the low-land swain.

The patient FEN-MAN, who endur'd long time
The various hardships of the wat'ry clime,
Whose slaught'ring gun and faithful dog had fed
His wife and little family with bread,
Now holds the plough, turns up the moory soil,
And finds a vast increase reward his toil.
His fields are cropt with diff'rent sorts of grain,
His sheep and oxen graze the chearful plain.
He sees himself compleatly happy now,
And calm content sits smiling on his brow.

V. 26. *And yellow harvests glad,* &c. Quid faciat lætas segetes.
Virg. Geo. 1. *lin.* 1.[8]

V. 27. *The patient fen-man*, &c. This epithet is most strictly applied to him, since the life of a North-American savage is vastly preferable to his. They both live by their gun: the one traverses the woods and mountains in search of his prey, and retires at night to a warm cabin, with plenty of fuel to warm the rigour of the climate; the other in a little skiff, which a puff of wind would overset, paddles about the water till the evening, and comes home wet and cold to his miserable hut, and lies scarcely dry and warm all night in his bed. The American Indian also bears a near resemblance to our hero; as a fisherman, he has his canoe, and ventures upon the sholes in search of fish, he has also his favourite dog to attend him, and hopes that as he is his constant and faithful companion in this life, he will be in another.

But thinks, admitted to that equal sky,
His faithful dog shall bear him company.

Ess. on Man. B. 1.[9]

8 *DLCL*: Virgil, *Georgics*, 1:1 (p. 99) 'What makes the crops joyous …'

9 *Pope,* Epistle 1, 111–12.

[*p. 8*]

But when frail Fortune smiles, and goods increase,
Our pride and vanity keep equal pace.
He feels th' effects of more propitious climes,
And now his prospects alter with the times.
His little hut, which by the bankside stood,
Cover'd with coat of sedge, the walls of mud,
Where each domestic use one room supplies,
His victuals here he dresses, here he lies:
A little lattice to let in the day,
With half extinguish'd light and glimm'ring ray,
Appears contemptuous in his loftier eye,
And much too streighten'd for his family.
He builds a handsom box on purchas'd ground,
His fields and pastures lie contiguous round,
The neigh'bring hinds admiring as they pass
The red-bricked front, the sashes' glitt'ring glass.

V. 51. *The neighb'ring hinds, &c.* An old Saxon word signifying a servant or a labourer.

V. 52. *The red-brick'd front, the sashes' glitt'ring glass.* This whole character is realized in one JOHN LEAFORD: he was a common labourer in the fen, called a banker, and, in drowned years, provided for his family, according to the custom of the country, by killing wild fowl. He was employed by the corporation of adventurers in making and repairing their banks; got money, purchas'd adventurer's lands at a small price, and, by a happy succession of dry seasons, grew very rich. He built a handsom brick and sash'd house, near the bank of the hundred foot, at Oxload, in the parish of Downham, in the isle of Ely, which in a better country, would well deserve the name of a hall place, and become an elegant dwelling for a rural squire. He was employed as an officer under the corporation, and at last got to be a conservator. He was perfectly illiterate, but this was to his advantage; if his bills for works done by order of the board passed current, it was very well, if they were objected to, he screened himself, by saying it was the fault of his transcriber, for he could neither read nor write.[10]

10 For information on John Leaford (1685–1758), see our Introduction, pp. 11–12.

[*p. 9*]

Barns, yards, conveniences of ev'ry kind,
A useful garden shelter'd from the wind,
Hogs in the stye and pullets at the door,
And ducks and geese and turkeys, many a score.

Our troubles with our affluence increase,
Plagued with too much, and yet displeas'd with less.
His barns are now too little to contain
The plenteous produce of his annual grain.
He builds them larger, and contrives more room,
To hoard his goods and fruit for years to come.
Like the rich fool, to himself he fondly says,
"Be merry, eat and drink, and take thine ease."[11]

What is all earthly bliss, but infant's toys?
How vain our hopes! how fleeting are our joys!

11 An allusion to Luke 12:19: 'And I will say to my soul, Soul, thou hast much goods laid up for many years; take thine ease, eat, drink, and be merry' (*Oxford KJB*).

[*p. 10*]

The hour we think our happiness compleat,
The scene's revers'd, and we lament our fate.

For now rough winter comes, the welkin low'rs,
Pregnant with boist'rous storms and frequent show'rs,
The south wind rises on her madid wings,
And the low hov'ring clouds together brings.
As at the deluge forty days and nights
The rain descended from the mountain's heights,
As all the fountains of the deep broke forth,
And heaven's windows op'd to drown the earth;
So now three wat'ry moons' incessant rain,
Came pouring down upon the marshy plain.
From all the neighb'ring hills the torrents glide,
And meet the influx of the foaming tide.
Waves roll'd on waves accumulated rise,
And intermix their waters with the skies.
The stoutest banks in vain oppose their force,
In vain the art of man repels their course.

V. 69. *Welkin low'rs.* An old Saxon word signifying the sky.

V. 71, 72. *The south wind rises on her madid wings,*
And the low hov'ring clouds together brings. Alluding to Milton,
Mean while the south wind rose and with black wings
Wide hovering all the clouds together drove.
Par. Lost. B. 11.[12]

12 *Milton*, 11:738–9.

[*p. 11*]

A breach at last is made, the currents pour,
Thro' the deep chasm with tremendous roar.
Th' alarm'd inhabitants desert their home,
Whilst round their dwellings raging billows foam,
Betake them to their oars, and safely row
Over those very lands they us'd to plow.
Far as the wide horizon bounds the plain,
NEPTUNE extends his watery domain.
'Twixt land and wave the diff'rence is no more,
All is an open sea without a shore.
A vast expance, beyond what eye can ken,
From Ely's lofty tow'rs to Lincoln fen.
There the fam'd abby[13] strikes the gazer's sight,
At once with pleasing horror and delight.
The mighty ruins, mould'ring walls, express
The ancient grandeur of this sacred place.

V. 89, 90. *Betake them to their oars and safely row*
Over those very lands, they us'd to plow. In imitation of *Ovid*'s *Metam.*
———Cymbâ sedet alter aduncâ,
Et ducit remos illic, ubi nuper arârat.
L. 1.[14]

V. 93, 94. In imitation of ditto.
Jamq; mare et tellus nullum discrimen habebant.
Omnia pontus erant. Deerant quoq; littora ponto.[15]

13 Crowland Abbey in Lincolnshire. The abbey itself is apostrophized in line 101.

14 *DLCL*: Ovid, *Metamorphoses*, 1:293–4 (p. 23). 'Another man sits in his curved skiff, plying the oars where lately he has plowed.'

15 *DLCL*: Ovid, *Metamorphoses*, 1:291–2 (p. 23) 'And now the sea and land have no distinction. All is sea, but a sea without a shore.'

[*p. 12*]

"Where, CROWLAND, are thy domes, thy stately tow'rs?
"The rust of time thy priestly pride devours,
"Thy broken columns clasping ivy twines,
"And rev'rend moss surrounds thy mangled shrines.
"Where the loud organ charm'd the tuneful choir,
"The hooting owl and ominous bat retire."
Built and endow'd by MERCIA's princely hand,
The pamper'd ABBOT fixes here his stand,
To riot on the fatness of the land.[16]
Where verdant pastures were wont to feed
The fine-fleec'd sheep and ox of largest breed;

V. 101. *Where, Crowland*, &c. The reader will excuse this digression, when he reflects that it is designed as a compliment to the fen country, on recollecting the many noble religious foundations, which have formerly adorned it. Dearham, Shouldham, Marham, Pentney and Wormegay abbies, in Norfolk; Ramsey abby in the fens of Huntingtonshire, which was possessed of vast lordships and estates in Norfolk, great part of which are now in the possession of the antient family of the Hares of Stow Bardolph. In the fens of Lincolnshire, Thorney, Swinehead and Crowland abbies.

V. 107. *Built and endow'd by MERCIA's princely hand*, The abby of Crowland was built by Ethelbald, King of Mercia, at a vast expence, as the foundation was a morass, and they were forced to drive down strong piles of oak to support the noble superstructure; it was also largely endow'd by him: but to see the alteration of time! the remains of this magnificent edifice is now a parish church, and the vicarage 25*l. per ann.* and by contribution.

V. 108. *The pamper'd abbot*, &c. The present face of this country wears a very different aspect to what it did formerly; for it is a maxim, wherever we see a religious foundation, the circumjacent lands were rich and fertile. For as the ecclesiastics had the picking and culling of all the good things of the earth, they would never fix their residence but where they might be accommodated not only with the conveniences, but the delicacies of life, and their aquatic situation supplied them with plenty of fish for their fasting days.

V. 111. *The fine-fleec'd sheep, and ox of largest breed*. Lincolnshire is remarkable for the fineness of their wool, and the large breed of cattle.

16 Echoing Genesis 45:18: 'And take your father and your households, and come unto me: and I will give you the good of the land of Egypt, and ye shall eat the fat of the land' (*Oxford KJB*).

[*p. 13*]

Where rapid rivers yield the fishy prey,
To fast delicious on each maigre day.
But seasons change, the soil so rich before,
By frequent inundation's render'd poor.
The country's desolate, the people fled,
And in a safer climate seek their bread.
The rushing waters cover all the plain,
And the sea re-assumes her own again.
Devouring pyke o'er flow'ry meadows stray,
Where sportive lambkins us'd to frisk and play.

V. 113. *To fast delicious on each maigre day.* In popish countries, days of abstinence are called maigre days, from the French word maigre, i.e. lean; hence the phrase, faire maigre, to keep Lent.

V. 119. *And the sea reassumes her own again.* There is no doubt, but the fens and marshlands of Norfolk and Lincolnshire, were formerly recovered from the sea, which, as it gained upon other parts of the island, retreated on this. The names of places now existing, sufficiently prove this opinion; as Holbeach, in Lincolnshire, and Littleport, in the isle of Ely, which altho' now a village of no consequence, yet, by its many desolated streets and ruined buildings, appears to have been formerly a respectable place, and was no doubt a port of considerable traffick and merchandize.

V. 120. *Devouring pyke* &c. In imitation of *Ovid's Metam.*
Et modo qua graciles gramen carpsere capellæ,
Nunc ibi deformes ponunt sua corpora phocæ.
L. 1.[17]

17 *DLCL*: Ovid, *Metamorphoses*, 1:299–300 (p. 23) 'And where but now the slender goats had browsed, the ugly sea-calves rested.'

[*p. 14*]

The timorous hare, when all appear'd a sea,
Anxious for life, sits squat upon a tree.
The partridge, tir'd with flight, is glad to drop
Her wearied wings upon a willow top.
No living thing appears, but all is lost,
Or driven from th' inhospitable coast.
"Unhappy clime! malignant stars dispense,
"O'er thy devoted land their influence.
"Ev'n when rich plenty smiles upon thee most,
"Yet health, that healing balm of life, is lost.
The moory soil, the wat'ry atmosphere,
With damp, unhealthy moisture chills the air.
Thick, stinking fogs, and noxious vapours fall,
Agues and coughs are epidemical.
Hence ev'ry face presented to our view,
Looks of a pallid or a sallow hue.
Nor kindliest seasons these complaints redress,
They're owing to the GENIUS of the place.

V. 122. *The timorous hare*, &c. In imitation of the same.
Crura nec ablato prosunt velocia cervo,
Quæsitisq; diu terris ubi sidere detur,
In mare lassatis volucris vaga decidit alis.
L. 1.[18]

This extraordinary incident of the hare and the partridge, is a fact that in this drowned season actually happen'd, at Salter's Load, near Downham Market, in Norfolk. A large tract of land there, being kept dry by the continual attention of the owner, for a month after all the adjacent country was drowned, occasioned the little game in that district to resort thither for food and security, but a storm arising from the north west, broke the bank, and in an instant all was over-flown; the people employed to get the stock out of the ground took a hare and a partridge alive from the top of a willow tree.

---

18 *DLCL*: Ovid, *Metamorphoses*, 1:306–8 (p. 23) 'Nor [do] his swift limbs [save] the stag, since both [the stag and the board mentioned above] are alike swept away by the flood; and the wandering bird, after long searching for a place where it could settle, falls with weary wings into the sea.' (The Loeb edition has 'ubi sistere possit' in place of 'ubi sidere detur' and we have modified the translation to reflect this.)

[*p. 15*]

Near to the bank, in a dark dismal hut,
Made of the stern of an old shatter'd boat,
Pale FEBRIS[19] sat—her shrivel'd aspect shows
A shocking scene of sickness, pain and woes:
She shiver'd o'er a cow-dung's smoaky fire,
Squallid her looks and wretched her attire,
An old blue cloak was o'er her shoulders flung,
Her patch'd and tatter'd garments round her hung,
Her hollow eyes with scalding rheum look'd red,
And quiv'ring palsey shook her bending head;
Catarrhs and intermittings with her dwell,
And such the poison of her loathsom cell,
Whene'er she stirs abroad she taints the ground,
And spreads the dire pestilence around.

V. 141. *Made of the stern of an old shatter'd boat.* This, altho' made the cave of an evil dæmon, is of modern taste: the stern of an old lighter, ornamented with shell work, makes a handsom alcove seat, and is often to be met with in the gardens of the curious.

19 The Roman goddess of fever.

[*p. 16*]

But our Fen-hero her attacks defies,
Healthy by temp'rance and by exercise.
From early infancy to manhood's prime,
His constitution weathers with the clime.
But times and seasons are in God's own pow'r,[20]
He must submit, and waits th' approaching hour.
For now the BITTERN undulates her note,
Like a deep-mouth'd bassoon, and swells her throat.
The screaming seamows hover o'er the plain,
Portentous signs of gath'ring storms and rain.
He sees the coming flood, he hears the wind,
And meets his fate with a determin'd mind.
The sudden deluge overflows his ground,
And his fine stock is either starv'd or drown'd.
His barns, wherein his choicest grain he stores,
Lets in the water at the folding doors,
His corn-ricks are half drowned to the top,
Which like a SYPHON sucks the liquor up.
His stacks of hay are swimming o'er the mead,
Useless to him, his cattle want no feed.

20 Echoing Ecclesiastes 3:1–8: 'To every thing there is a season, and a time to every purpose under heaven' (*Oxford KJB*).

[*p. 17*]

At last his mansion, whose unusual load,
Ill suited to the soil whereon it stood,
The waters sapping the foundation round,
Falls an unwieldy ruin to the ground.
Whilst his deserted cot the storm derides,
And stands superior to the swelling tides.
He sees an end of all his toil and pain,
And hastens to his little hut again.
Renews his former life, and gets afloat,
With gun and spaniel in his cockle boat.

V. 174. *At last his mansion,* &c. The fen being generally a morass, will not support a foundation of brick or stone. This we find by many buildings therein, some in ruins, others in a leaning situation; particularly a house near Mepal bridge in the isle of Ely, formerly the mansion seat of Captain Fortree, built with stud work and turf between, instead of brick for lightness: the remains of it shew it to have been an elegant building, and ornaments of stucco are still to be seen in the front, a handsom walled-in court yard before, and gardens walled in behind, very plainly belonged to it formerly, by the ruins of them now visible.[21]

V. 177. *Falls an unwieldy,* &c. Et celsæ graviore casu, decidunt turres.
Hor. Od. 4. *l.* 2.[22]

V. 183. *With gun and spaniel in his cockle boat.* This is called a gunning boat, and is not much longer than his gun, which is made of a great length, to kill at a vast distance. This boat is constructed very light, that the fen-man can easily hawl it over the bank, when he wants to sail into other waters, in search of fowl: in a brisk gale it dances like a cockle shell upon the waves.

21 Fortree Hall in Mepal near Ely was built by Samuel Fortrey (1622–1681), a conservator in the Bedford Corporation engaged in draining the fens: *Oxford DNB*. Samuel Fortrey's third son James Fortrey (1656–1719) came into the possession of Fortrey Hall after Fortrey's death in 1681 and added several apartments and a large garden to it. James Fortrey was a Major in the Horse Guards under James II but left his command after the succession of William and Mary to the throne in 1688. See 'Fortrey of Byal Fen', *Fenland Notes and Queries*, 4 (1898–1900), p. 357. The original text has 'walledin behind.'

22 *DLCL*: Horace, *Odes 2,* 10:10–11 (p. 115) 'The collapse is more devastating when high towers fall.'

[*p. 18*]

He rises early, and he late takes rest,
And sails intrepid o'er the wat'ry waste;
Waits the return of *Shot-seal* on the lake,
And listens to the wild fowls distant quack,
At dusk steers homeward with a plenteous freight,
The crazy vessel groans beneath the weight,
A tidy house-wife waits his coming home,
Gets dry apparel and cleans up her room.
Prepares a chearful fire, brings out her hoard,
And spreads a homely plenty o'er his board.
To vend her fowl the dearest marts she tries,
And with the profit household wants supplies.
The capital's e'vn feasted with his store,
And London carriers whistle at his door.

V. 186. *Waits the return of shot-seal on the lake.* This is a term us'd in the fen country to denote the time, that is about sun set, when the wild fowl return from sea (which they are said to fly to every day) into the fresh waters.

Lake, in the fen language, is an open part of the river, or the waters in the fen, when a hard frost sets in, in a drowned year, to which the wild fowl resort for food.[23]

V. 197. *And London carriers whistle at his door.* As an instance of the luxury of the metropolis, there are a set of people call'd Kedgers, who, when the country can be travelled over, call regularly at the fen-men's houses to buy their fish and fowl at a vast price, and send them up to town, by the butter-boats, or sell them to the higlers that keep London market. But what is this to the extravagance of a Norwich weaver, who sends a special messenger from thence to Caxon, which is near 100 miles, to meet the north country carrier with fresh salmon?

23 'Seal' in the Norfolk dialect meant 'time' or 'season' so 'shot-seal' would have meant the time that birds could most easily be shot: *VEA*.

[*p. 19*]

Thus amply he his family maintains,
And of his change of fortune scarce complains.
His varied scenes of life, now make him see,
Nothing is certain, but uncertainty.[24]
That anxious fears attend our happiest state,
And greater grow, as we are growing great.
That who with higher affluence is blest,
Dreads more the loss of what he is possest.
That he alone is out of fortune's pow'r,
Who's sunk so low that he can sink no low'r.
And who life's comforts without pain would share,
Must very little have to hope or fear.
That cares and crosses every soul oppress,
And who with patience bears them, makes them less.

V. 198. *Thus amply he his family maintains.* It is almost incredible to believe, what great advantage the skilful fen-man makes of his winter shooting, in a drowned year, and in the following summer of his fish; by the overflowing of the Whittlesea Meer, and other great reservoirs of fish, the whole country is plentifully stocked with them.

The fen-men have a phrase for this, "that Whittlesea Meer has folded:" when the waters begin to abate upon the land, the fish retire into the dykes and rivers, and great quantities are taken: the traffick of fish, in general, is very lucrative to these people, and a single share of the smelt fishery, when they come to the rivers to spawn, has amounted to 50*l*.[25]

24 Proverbial. See *DOP*.

25 There is a comma at the end of this sentence rather than a full stop in the original text.

[*p. 20*]

That God's wise providence our lot hath thrown,
And the disposal of it is his own.
He once indeed was rich, and now he's poor,
But yet he is, but what he was before.
And all his interval of plenty seems,
As airy visions and delusive dreams.

FINIS.

The Coal-Heavers

NRO PRA 664/281

Date: Published in or soon before July 1774 (Since the review of the poem is in the July 1774 issue of the *Monthly Review* [p. 69]).

Authorship: There is no direct evidence that Pratt was the author. There are, however, two copies of the poem in the Pratt folder, like *September: A Rural Poem*, which we know to be by Pratt. The poem is also very much in the mock-heroic style that Pratt uses in *September*. In addition, the manuscript of *The Zgubbs* in the Pratt folder uses the similar subtitle 'Humbly Inscribed to all the Learned Societies in Europe'. We are confident in attributing the poem to Pratt.

Physical Description: Poem printed on pages bound together with string, the resulting booklet measuring 25.5 cm by 40 cm.

---

1 Another copy of the poem is also included in the Pratt folder under the reference code NRO PRA 664/27.

[*p. 1*]

THE

COAL-HEAVERS

A MOCK HEROIC POEM,

IN TWO CANTOS:

Humbly Inscribed to the

INHABITANTS OF

LYNN REGIS,

IN

NORFOLK.

CASTIGAT RIDENDO MORES.[2]

LYNN:

Printed and sold by W. WHITTINGHAM; and by Messrs.

CARNAN and NEWBERY, in St. *Paul's Churchyard*,

LONDON, and all other Booksellers.

MDCCLXXIV.

2 A phrase traditionally attributed to the poet Jean de Santeul (1630–1697), meaning 'one corrects customs by laughing at them'.

[*p. 3*]

The AUTHOR *of the following* POEM, *has made Use of fictitious Names, for two Reasons, the One to give no Offence to respectable Characters; the Other, not to magnify the Prowess of a Set of Men, who were deservedly punished for their Insurrection: The Poem took its Rise from a real Skirmish, which happened, but much of it may be ascribed to the Power of the Imagination!*

THE COAL-HEAVERS;

A MOCK HEROIC POEM,

In Two Cantos.

CANTO I.

THE Din of Arms, the deep embattled Field;
The warring Legions, and the batter'd Shield;
The neighing Steed; and Trumpet's horrid Sound;
And dying *Chiefs* who fall and bite the Ground:
Horrors like these, let HOMER'S Muse rehearse,
Where Terror stalks, majestic in the Verse;
Mine be the humbler Subject to relate
The bloody Nose, torn Shirt, and fractur'd Pate,
Dishevel'd Perukes, and bespatter'd Clothes;
And mingled Blood of Watermen and Beaux;
Parent of Gods and Men, Imperial Jove
Left his sweet HEBE[3] in the blest Alcove;

3 Greek goddess of youth, who served as a cupbearer for the other Olympian gods and goddesses. One of Hebe's duties was to serve the gods their nectar and ambrosia. She is sometimes depicted with wings and often accompanied by her father Zeus in the form of an eagle. The poem mixes Roman and Greek deities as it names Hebe's father as Jupiter.

[*p. 4*]

When rushing thro' the Air, with mighty Sound
Regain'd his Throne, and call'd the Gods around:
They to his Voice with swift Obedience ran,
When thus, th' Almighty Thund'rer, began:
"YE heav'nly Pow'rs, who have the Joy to share
"My choicest Gifts, and float with me in Air:
"Why do ye boast of Happiness supreme,
"Your flow of Nectar and Castalian Stream?[4]
"Why boast ye then, that here such Pleasures flow,
"When Men will live, like Deities below?
"There are, (O! Shame to Happiness divine)
"A Set of Men, who rival us in Wine:
"There are in *LYNN;* fast bound, in mutual Love,
"Mortals who dare to live, and act like Jove:
"But by myself, and this imperial Seat,
"Where Jove alone, will be compleatly great;
"Their boasted Union, shall not long remain,
"This Arm shall scourge these Children of the Main."
So spoke the GOD!----in deep Attention round,
The Heav'nly Host receiv'd the solemn Sound.
Th' imperial Sire with stern expecting Eye,
Survey'd them round, impatient of Reply.-----
When wild in Look, with rude dishevel'd Hair,
Discord arose, wide mouth'd, and Bosom bare;
Full many a Scar had mark'd her batter'd Frame;
Flat nos'd and toothless; and with Combat lame:----
"Mine be the Task, dread Sovereign, to fulfil
"Thy just Commands, and Jove's Almighty Will:
"Ye Gods, shall Men, vile Earth, inglorious Clods
"Live as ye live, and emulate the Gods?
"Shall LYNN's sleek Sons, like us Immortals shine,
"Tho' lin'd with Turtle, and Election Wine?[5]

4 The spring in a ravine near where the Delphian Oracle was located; those visiting the site would wash and refresh themselves there. It was also traditionally considered a source of poetic inspiration.

5 Candidates for election would 'treat' their supporters with food and drink to secure their votes.

"Shall pamper'd May'rs, or Aldermen presume
"To look like Jove and wear eternal Bloom?

[*p. 5*]

"By the dread Waves of Acheron, I swear,
"And you ye Gods, attend to what you hear:---
"Great Jove shall humble this imperious Race,
"And blast the Honors of their Town and Mace."
So spoke the Fiend[6]----No more, without Delay
Wrapt in pure Æther, wing'd her rapid Way:
Where *Marg'ret's* Tow'r,[7] in beauteous Pride surveys
The glorious Wonders of the Land and Seas:
There on a Turret, with a Demon's Frown,
The Fiend explor'd the Labours of the Town:
There, in deep Cell, where one dull Taper shines,
The mystic Cooper brew'd th' imported Wines![8]
Crabs, Chalk, and Egg Shells, in Profusion laid,
And all the kind Assistants of the Trade;
Like EGYPT'S Priest, the dark mysterious Sage

6 Quoting Book Four of *Paradise Lost* (*Milton*, 393).

7 St Margaret's Church, with its tall spire, dominated King's Lynn's skyline. Saint Margaret the Virgin is the patroness of King's Lynn.

8 The wine merchant James Fysh may be meant here, since he served on the jury that arraigned the labourers whose riot inspired *The Coal-Heavers*, or perhaps the cooper he employed named Edgly Smith, who wrote a short pamphlet complaining that officers in the Customs House at King's Lynn had withheld Fysh's customary 'present' of onions and plums from a ship carrying wine to King's Lynn, apparently on the grounds that Fysh had not paid his customs duties. See Edgly Smith, *The Case of James Fysh* (?King's Lynn, 1767). Fysh was mocked for this pamphlet by a supporter of the incumbent Sir John Turner in the King's Lynn election of 1768. See 'The Case of the Honourable Lynn Merchant' in *The Lynn Magazine: or A Collection of Papers, Published during the Contest in that Town* (?King's Lynn, 1768), pp. 29–30. If Pratt did intend a portrait of Fysh here, then he was satirizing someone who had been on his side in the 1768 election. An extract from an anonymous letter published in the *Cambridge Chronicle* describes how Fysh celebrated the revocation of John Wilkes' outlawry by displaying an illuminated 'ensign of liberty' on a turret on his house and 'gave wine to all that would drink to the success of that intrepid patron of British liberty, Mr. Wilkes'. See *Cambridge Chronicle*, 18 June 1768, p. 3. This letter is referenced in John Brewer, *Party Ideology and Popular Politics at the Accession of George III* (Cambridge: Cambridge University Press, 1976), p. 181.

Revives the Dead, and gives the New-born, Age.[9]
From Cask to Cask, the mingled Juice is tost,
Till *White* and *Red*, their dying Colours' lost:
So in MACBETH, in Midnight Storm and Rain,
The Wayward Sisters cook the Viper's Brain;
Dogs Flesh, and Newt, with Toads all savo'ry Chine[10]
Complete the Brewing of their Magic Wine:[11]
Next she survey'd the Yards, and Gran'ries round:
Where the Gaunt bushel stood, with Iron bound.
The Brewer's Art explor'd, the Market Scale[12]
And Wormwood sinking, in the *Murder'd* Ale.
Here as she stood, an uncouth Form appear'd
With round, big Belly, and neglected Beard;
The bursted Shoe betray'd the Gouty Toes;
Red were his Cheeks, and pimpled was his Nose.
The Demon eyed him in his hobbling Pace,
Rejoin'd his Side and star'd him in the Face:
She knew my Landlord of *Three Pi---n Street*,[13]
Where for good Cheer, the loud Coal-heavers meet.

[*p. 6*]

Pleas'd with the Hint, impatient of Delay
Sh' assum'd his Form; and cuts her liquid Way.----
There at the Club she stood my *Host* confess'd,

9 Priests in Ancient Egypt performed various rituals on the mummified bodies to prepare them for the journey into the afterlife. Illustrations of these practices in papyri and wall paintings were later sometimes misinterpreted in the sense that the dead are literally being brought back to life.

10 A joint of meat including all or part of the spine: *OED*.

11 Act Four of *Macbeth* opens with the witches dancing around a caldron and Macbeth enters soon after. The play-text does not include 'viper's brain', only 'filet of a fenny snake' (*Shak*, 4.1.12) and 'adder's fork' (*Shak*, 4.1.16), but 'tongue of dog' (*Shak*, 4.1.15) and 'eye of newt (*Shak*, 4.1.14) are among the ingredients mentioned by the witches.

12 Scales approved for use at a public market.

13 Skinner's Row in King's Lynn (nowadays known as St James Street) was popularly called 'Three Pigeon Street' because the public house there had a sign with three pigeons on it. See Henry J. Hillen, *History of the Borough of King's Lynn* (2 vols., Norwich: East of England Newspaper Company), ii, p. 731. On 2 December 1769, John Bagge leased the Three Pigeons, among other establishments, to William and Thomas Bagge for 34 years. NRO BL/BG 12/2/6.

And in the Form of Bl-----r[14] thus address'd
"MY jovial Friends, my ever honour'd *Blacks*;[15]
"Ye Men of Weight,[16] and Heroes form'd for Sacks:[17] ---
"Shall ye be bent to Earth, and parch'd with Heat
"Dine as ye do, on coarsest Joints of meat?
"Whilst Albions *(a)* Sons, on fatted Ven'son dine,
"And Lawyers *Clerks* are nightly drench'd with Wine.
"Shall Chariots roll, and *Whiskies* whirl around;
"Till our fam'd Cross re-ecchoes to the Sound?
"Whilst ye, (O sad and dismal to be told)
"Can only get six Quarts of Mild and Old:[18]
"Rise for your *Rights*, assert a nobler Pay:
"Let *Nog* inspire, and *Porter* lead the Way-----"
So spoke the Demon; and in Haste withdrew,
But first thrice cheer'd the bold advent'rous Crew:
As when the Gods from Heav'n's high Arch pour down
Their livid Lightnings on some guilty Town:
The rapid Flames in wild Disorder blaze,
And weeping Crouds in awful Wonder gaze.
From House to House, the horrid Scene's convey'd,
And all is in one mighty Ruin laid:-----
So *Discord's* Speech, imperious, bold, and loud,
From Man to Man inflamed th' attentive Crowd.----
Say, Heaven-born Muse, for thou can'st well describe
The March and Motions of the *Negro*[19] Tribe;
Thou canst, I ween, in comic Strains Declare
The Toil and Labours of the mimic[20] War:

14 We have not been able to identify who this person is—if he is not one a member of the Bagge family—though we guess the last name is supposed to be 'Blacker'.

15 Addressing the coal-heavers, who are all made black by their profession. There may also be a reference to the Waltham Blacks, who covered themselves with soot and intimidated people in a forest and engaged in poaching in the 1720s. See Katherine West Scheil, 'Early Georgian Politics and Shakespeare: The Black Act and Charles Johnson's *Love in a Forest* (1723)', *Shakespeare Survey*, 51 (1998), pp. 45–56.

16 Punning on two senses of 'weight' as heaviness and importance.

17 Alluding to the two senses of 'sack': to sack a city and a sack of coal.

18 Referring to ale: 'mild and old ale' as opposed to 'pale ale'.

19 i.e. the coal-heavers.

20 Mock or pretend: *OED*.

First in the Front, as some huge Turret, stood
The *Stern Entellus*[21] sprung from Butcher's Blood:

[a] *A Jovial Society in* LYNN.[22]

[*p. 7*]

From Sire to Sire in one Continued Line;
They peel'd the Souse,[23] and chopt the reeking Chine;
Down from his Lip the rich *Virginean* Weed[24]
Meandring flow'd and form'd a little *Tweed*;[25]
Him *Milo*[26] follow'd, of enormous Nose,
A living Anvil, well-inured to Blows;
Flat was his Face, and single was his Eye,
And shorten'd Wig fantastic hung a-wry:
Then Negro *Daniel* join'd the rebel Band,
The huge broad Thimble grac'd the Taylor's Hand:
Proud of himself, yet prouder of his Race,
And the full Glories of a sev'nfold Face[27]-----
Black George, well known to frame the fraudful Lye,
And Swearing *Joseph*, ever drunk, and dry:

21 Entellus is a figure from Greek mythology. In the *Aeneid* (Book 5) the Sicilian hero and friend of king Acestes defeats Dares in a boxing match held during the games commemorating the death of Aeneas's father. Entellus bloodies his opponent and then kills a sacrificial bull with a single blow in place of Dares to crown his achievement, which the poem's reference to a butcher seems to be echoing. For the names of the historical rioters see our Introduction, p. 42.

22 We have not been able to identify this society.

23 Pickled pork or other meat, often including feet or ears, of gelatinous consistency: *OED*.

24 Weed in the sense of tobacco: *OED*; the reference is to tobacco being chewed rather than smoked.

25 i.e. the River Tweed.

26 Milo of Croton (sixth century BC) was a famous wrestler, who had competed repeatedly in the Olympic games.

27 Echoing Alexander Pope's description of Colley Cibber's 'sev'nfold Face' in the first book of the final version of *The Dunciad* (1742–3), where it evokes both a heavy helmet (encased seven times in metal and impervious to criticism) but also Cibber's ability to personate many characters (Pope, 244). In Pratt's poem the epithet perhaps evokes the changing appearance of the soot-stained face of the coal heaver.

Him, Sun-burnt *Nancy* to his Father bore,
Nancy, who reign'd CZARINA[28] of the Shore:
The Sailor's Wish, and universal W---e:[29]
The dangling Shirt, snub Nose, and sooty Face;
Bespoke the Hero of the Sweeping Race;
Ah! what avail'd his Mother's briny Tears,
Salt as those Oysters, which she sold at Fairs-----
No Tears could keep him, or his Passions in:
Such is thy Pow'r, inexorable Gin!
Thus they condens'd in terrible Array
With loud Huzzas, pursued their noisy Way.
A Thousand Beldams[30] bless the marching Crowd,
And Pious Co-----r[31] wept, and pray'd aloud:-----
As when a Youth, of bold, unfeeling Breast;
Disturbs the Quiet of a Hornet's Nest;---
Th' insulted Reptiles first, by slow Degrees
Crawl from their Cells, and wind around the Trees----
But more disturb'd, in horrid Troops appear:
Hum round and buz, and blacken in the Air;

[*p. 8*]

Or, as a Ball, when roll'd along the Snows
Collects, improves, and thickens as it goes;
So, they by Numbers well enforc'd, and strong,
Go forth with mighty Shouts, and scour the Streets along.

CANTO II.

THE Heav'nly Pow'rs, in Jove's enamel'd Hall,
In full Assembly, grac'd the Midnight Ball;
CORNELY'S[32] Fame had reach'd the blest Abodes

---

28 A Czar's wife: *OED*.

29 i.e. 'Whore'.

30 Old women: *OED*.

31 Probably Robert Cooper (1741–1777), rector of Grimston (1767–77). Grimston is located approximately 6 miles northeast of King's Lynn.

32 Teresa Cornelys (birth name Anna Maria Teresa Imer, 1723–1797), an opera singer famous for hosting lavish balls and other social gatherings in Carlisle House in London and notorious for borrowing large sums of money. She died in the Fleet debtors' prison: *Oxford DNB*.

That Mortals there should *personate* the Gods:
They in their Turn would mask in human Shape,
The Cit,[33] the Clown, the Maceronian[34] Ape:
The God of Wine, full cheek'd and debonair,
With sleek round Sides, roar'd out, a jovial May'r[35]-----
Comus,[36] (good Quack) theatrically Loud;
In floating Peruke well harangu'd the Crowd;
Whilst mimic Momus,[37] in his comic Vein;
Held, as she stalk'd, Queen Dido's[38] sweeping Train.
Soft Dimpling Daphne[39] with her Heav'nly Grace
Usurp'd th' Shape of *Ey----s*,[40] and CHARLOTT'S sweeter Face.
Not so the Cyprian Queen[41]----Her gentle Heart
Knew well the Will of Jove, and Discord's cruel Art:
She lov'd her *Lynn*, for she from Ocean sprung
And once reign'd there when *Molly Cla--e*[42] was young.
As to our Minds, our Thoughts in Sleep convey
The Toils, and watchful Labours of the Day:[43]
So the good May'r revolving in his Breast,

33 i.e. citizen: *OED*.

34 i.e. a Macaroni in the sense of a dandy or pop: *OED*.

35 The Mayor of King's Lynn when the historical riot occurred was Thomas Somersby, Junior. Somersby was elected on 29 August 1773 and Horace Walpole wrote to congratulate him on his election on 23 September 1773. See Horace Walpole, *The Yale Edition of Horace Walpole's Correspondence*, ed. W. S. Lewis et al. (48 vols., New Haven: Yale University Press, 1937–83), xli, p. 262.

36 Comus is the Greek god of revels and festivities and son of the god of wine Dionysus.

37 Momus is the Greek god of satire.

38 Dido was the legendary founder and first queen of Carthage; in the *Aeneid* she has an affair with Aeneas and commits suicide after he leaves her. Virgil mentions Dido's train several times, although in the sense of her entourage rather than her outfit.

39 In Greek mythology, Daphne is one of the naiads (female nymphs associated with waterways and fountains). She turns into a laurel tree to escape the amorous advances of the god Apollo. The scene is depicted in detail in Ovid's *Metamorphoses*.

40 We have not been able to identify this woman.

41 Aphrodite.

42 Possibly 'Molly Clarke'. We have not been able to identify this woman.

43 Stephen Duck memorably calls attention to this phenomenon in his poem 'The Thresher's Labour': 'Think what a painful Life we daily lead;/ Each Morning early rise, go late to Bed:/ Nor, when asleep, are we secure from Pain;/ We then perform our Labours o'er again:/ Our mimic Fancy ever restless seems;/And what we act awake, she acts in Dreams./ Hard Fate! Our Labours ev'n in Sleep don't cease;/ Scarce HERCULES e'er felt such Toils as these!' in *Poems on Several Occasions* (London, 1736), p. 25.

The Town's great Good, and that *best* Good, the *Feast:*
He dreamt he saw, (O piteous to relate)
The tumbling Hall, and fractur'd Sword of State:[44]

[*p. 9*]

The Mace usurp'd, by some unhallow'd Hand;
The well-fring'd Cushion, rolling in the Sand;
The Hall's rich Paintings, all defac'd with Gore,
And poor Sir Ben,*(a)* now fall'n to rise no more.
As thus he laid disturb'd, with horrid Dream,
(The sad Effects, of indigested Cream)
Forth from the Wing of her own fav'rite Dove
A Milk-white Feather drew the Queen of Love;
Thrice round his Nose, she trail'd the tickling Down,
He winc'd, he woke, and found the World his own.
Now the big Voice of Fame had nois'd around;
The Mob had issued forth, and boldly chose the Ground.
The Council met----When Sage *TREBATIUS*[45] broke
The tedious Silence, and thus firmly spoke:
"MEN, Brethren, Friends, and my Companions dear!
"Ye Well-wig'd Chiefs, who long have pass'd the Chair:
"And you my Sons, whose glowing Cheeks confest
"The rosy Glories of our Godlike Feast:
"Must we be stunn'd, with Faction's giddy Roar,
"And see Rebellion stalk before the Door?
"A half cloth'd Mob such rude inglorious Foes
"Disdain our Laws and brave us to the Nose?
"Forbid it Heaven! and your just Decrees:
"Oh! fight for Freedom as we fight for Fees."
SOFT was his Speech, with just Expression fraught,
Mild as himself, and both without a Fault:

44 The sword of state has traditionally been part of the monarchical regalia symbolizing the monarch's power to protect the state from its enemies. The English crown jewels include a Sword of State made in 1678.

45 Trebatius Testa (fl. 84 BC–AD 4) a Roman jurist and a friend of Cicero, known for implementing the transfer of power from the Roman Senate to individual jurisconsults. The mayor of King's Lynn at the time of the historical riot was Thomas Somersby, Junior; see note 35 above.

As when a Pilgrim in the Summer's Heat
Squats on some Hillock, in a cool Retreat;
The Negro Ants, Bumb-shadow'd,[46] and opprest:
Run to and fro, not knowing where to rest;
So they disturb'd, from Place to Place proceed
Collect their Force, and form their Ranks with Speed:
Now they in close[47] Array embodied stand;
Nose threat'ning Nose, and Hand oppos'd to Hand:

(a) Alluding to the Picture of Sir Ben. Keene.[48]

[*p. 10*]

First, *Stout Entellus* levell'd with the Ground
The Cooper's heir,[49] in Calf-skin Waistcoat bound:
The rich Gilt Edging glitter'd to the View:
And from his Nose gush'd out the *Eau de Lue*;[50]
Four scented Clerks, (sweet Youths) with braided Hair
Fell by his Hand, and all perfum'd the Air:
Then Mighty *Milo* with incessant Blows
Drove at the Bridge, of Aldermanic Nose:
Him twice six Brethren of the common Weal
Seiz'd as he fell; and drag'd him by the Heel:-----
Forth from his Mouth gush'd out the mingled Stream
The Tail of Lobster, and the Ev'ning Cream:
Their prostrate Chief the gath'ring Host surround,
And his disdainful Wig, laid by him on the Ground.----
Jove weigh'd their Fate with new extended Scales,

---

46 i.e. the pilgrim's bum is blocking the sun. 'Bumb' is a recorded variant of 'bum' in the *OED*.

47 'inclose' in the original text.

48 Sir Benjamin Keene (1697–1757), from a prominent King's Lynn family, was a diplomat, particularly influential in his role as a British diplomat in Spain. Keene's portrait by Louis Michel van Loo still hangs in King's Lynn Townhall.

49 If our hypothesis that James Fysh is the poem's cooper is correct then this would presumably be his son. We have not been able to trace this person.

50 'Eau de' translates as 'water of' and 'lue' (now written 'lu') in French is the past participle for *lire*, which translates to English as the past participle of the verb 'read' ('read' pronounced the same as 'red'). Thus '*Eau de Lue*' would translate as 'Water of Read', with the 'lu' intended as an interlingual pun on 'read/red'.

And now the Court, and now the Mob prevails;
The Queen of Love enthron'd in heav'nly Light:
View'd from a Cloud, the Horrors of the Fight:
Loose was her Vest, redoubled were her Charms:
And sweetly lewd, she fought the God of Arms:[51]
Half she conceal'd, and half reveal'd her Breast,
Her Snowy Limbs th' admiring God possest:
She coax'd his Cheeks, she doff'd upon his Knee,
And thus in am'rous Mood the Goddess of the Sea:
"GREAT God of War, can'st thou unmov'd look down,
"And see the Ruin of my native Town:
"There *Mentor*[52] lies unnos'd; inglorious Sight----
"And clos'd those Eyes which lately shone so bright:
"Six Hams, Westphalian,[53] yearly grac'd his Board;
"And twice six Turkeys cram'd their mighty Lord."
The amorous God survey'd her beauteous Frame:
He leer'd, he sigh'd, and strangely eyed the Dame:
Then Mars inspir'd, with more than mortal Rage,
The young *Machaon*,[54] blooming in his Age,

[*p. 11*]

Fame call'd him forth, to leave the peaceful Still,
To roll down Heroes as he roll'd the Pill:----
Two sons of Slaughter first his Vengeance feel;
And *from* their Sides blaz'd out, the polish'd Steel:
Then sunk the Hero of the dangling shirt,
His Face *twice* cover'd with inglorious Dirt:

51 i.e. Mars, the god of war.

52 Mentor was a friend of Odysseus. Athena assumes his shape in order to advise Odysseus's son Telemachus to go to Nestor and Menelaus in order to ask them for information on his father's whereabouts in Homer's *The Odyssey*. It is not clear what King's Lynn figure Pratt means here.

53 Westphalian ham, made from pigs fed on acorn nuts and preserved by dry-curing and smoking, was a delicacy imported from Germany. For a contemporary description of this meat, see *The Critical Review or the Annals of Literature*, vol. 16 (London: A. Hamilton, 1796) p. 35.

54 In Greek mythology, Machaon, a son of Asclepius, fought in the Trojan war; he was also noted as a healer with a knowledge of medicinal herbs passed down from his father. It is not clear what King's Lynn figure Pratt means here.

There, mighty Vulcan with his mangled Eye:
Here, two twin Porters[55] undistinguish'd lie:
Well could he drench (good Leech) the ling'ring Steer,
Compose the Draught, and slily drink the Beer:
No fondling Mother *clos'd* the Warrior's Eyes,
No Child to lisp my *apron'd* Father,[56] rise-----
Far from his Forge, and its majectic Sound,
He roll'd a ROOD of Manhood on the Ground:
There, the torn Ruffle, late the Scriv'ner's Care,
And here, the Club's long Ribband wav'd in Air:
There, Man on Man, the horrid Scenes unfold;
And Wig, on Wig, voluminously roll'd:[57]
Where'er the Youth directs his rapid Speed,
Their brown Hides rattled, and the Victims bleed.
But what avail these Gifts the Gods bestow
When short and transient are our Joys below!
Where some huge Pointer of the Spanish Breed
Had laid his Tail a mighty Heap indeed:
There, where the Hero urged the flying Foe;
The smoking Pile betray'd his eager Toe:
He falls-----And lost in Air the meditated Blow:
A horrid Stench forth issued, far and wide,
But Pallas lov'd the Youth, and turn'd his *Nose* aside.----
Ah! hapless Youth, insulting *Trulla*[58] said,
Take my last Gift, and water'd on his Head;
Ah! hapless Youth, resounds from Shore to Shore;
Oh! that the Act had pass'd, and Dogs had been no more.[59]

55 Possibly two of the rioters who share the same last name, John and Thomas Austin, are referred to here.

56 A reference to Vulcan's vocation as a smith.

57 Echoing a line from Canto One of Alexander Pope's *The Rape of the Lock*: 'Where Wigs with Wigs, with Sword-knots Sword-knots strive' (*Pope*, 101) and also a line from his *Windsor-Forest*: 'The silver Eel, in shining Volumes roll'd' (*Pope*, 145).

58 A 'trull' is a prostitute: *OED*.

59 There were attempts to pass a Dog Act that would seek to limit the number of dogs by placing a tax on dog ownership in 1755 and 1761. See Ingrid H. Tague, 'Eighteenth-Century English Debates on a Dog Tax,' *The Historical Journal*, 51.4 (2008), p. 902. A short pamphlet opposing the proposals credited to 'A person without eyes from his birth' entitled *Crude Thoughts on the Dog-Act* was published in Norwich by J. Crouse in 1763.

[*p. 12*]

Thus they prevail'd, as Venus charm'd the God,
And Rebels tumbled as he gave the Nod:
Now they in slow, and solemn Triumph led,
Six mournful Captives of the fractur'd Head:
This with his Front, in colour'd Kerchief bound,
And this slow winding with his bleeding Wound:
Now all was hush'd, and they in Pudding Time,
Like Homer's Heroes, leave the Field, to dine.
The God of War, surveying from above,
With Accent mild address'd the Queen of Love:
"SWEET Heav'nly Maid, and Goddess of the Sea;
"Whom Gods and Men, and both the Worlds obey,
"No more shall Discord vex thy favo'rite Town;
"Mars will protect, and guard it as his own:
"Thou, Heav'nly Queen, shall deck the rising Fair,
"Play round their Heads and lead the aspiring Hair;
"A Thousand Loves their little Wings expand,
"To guard the Hoop from Man's rapacious Hand:
"Long as their *(a)Cup* shall grace the festive Board:
"Long as the Hand of Justice bears the Sword:
"Long as their Trade and happy Arts prevail:
"Long as their Ships shall crowd the swelling Sail:
"So long shall Feuds and civil Discord cease,
"And Lynn enjoy her *glorious Port* in Peace."
HE spoke, whilst JANUS[60] for his Order waits,
And shuts at once the Temples brazen Gates.

(*a*) *King John's Cup.*[61]

FINIS.

---

60 The two-faced Roman god of beginnings, transitions, doors, and gates and hence a fitting figure to end the poem by literally shutting the gates on it.

61 The lavishly decorated silver cup, which dates from around 1325 and has no documented connection to King John, first appears in historical records in 1548 as a gift to the city of King's Lynn from a merchant. It is notable as a rare example of secular silverwork and illustrations on its 31 enamel panels depict various hunting scenes. The poem evokes the cup as a symbol of King's Lynn affluence and prosperity. For more information on the artefact, see Ian Collins, *Masterpieces: Art and East Anglia* (Norwich: University of East Anglia Sainsbury Centre for Visual Arts, 2013), p. 82.

September: A Rural Poem

NRO PRA 664/311

Date: Published on 1 September 1780. This is the date advertised as the date the poems will be published in the advertisements printed in the *Cambridge Chronicle* and the *Norwich Mercury*.[2] The date is obviously appropriate for a poem concerning the hunting season, which traditionally began on 1 September.

Authorship: Although there is no known manuscript of this poem a copy of the advertisement that was printed in the *Cambridge Chronicle* and the *Norwich Mercury* in Pratt's hand is included in the folder of Pratt texts (PRA 664/11). The poem is independently attested to be by a 'J. P.' in the *Memoirs of Richard Gardiner*.[3] The poem can thus be confidently attributed to Pratt. The poem has been commonly misattributed to Richard Gardiner,[4] probably on the basis of a misreading of the mention of the poem in the *Memoirs of Richard Gardiner* as evidence of Gardiner's rather than Pratt's authorship.

Physical Description: Poem printed on pages bound together with string, the resulting booklet measuring 24 cm by 30.5 cm.

---

1 Another printed copy of the poem is also included in the Pratt folder under the reference code NRO PRA 664/30.

2 See Advertisement for *September: A Rural Poem* in *Norwich Mercury*, 26 August 1780, p. 3. The date of publication is advertised as '*the* Friday *of next Month*': i.e. Friday 1 September 1780.

3 *Gard*, 209–12.

4 See, e.g. Samuel Halkett and John Laing, *A Dictionary of the Anonymous and Pseudonymous Literature of Great Britain* (4 vols., Edinburgh: William Paterson, 1882), *s.v.* 'September. A Rural Poem'.

[*tp*]

SEPTEMBER.

A

RURAL POEM.

HUMBLY INSCRIBED TO ALL SPORTSMEN.

WITH NOTES AND ILLUSTRATIONS.

By a GENTLEMAN.

Imberbis juvenis, tandem custode remoto,
Gaudet equis, canibusq: et aprici gramine campi.

HOR.[5]

LYNN REGIS

Printed by W. WHITTINGHAM, and sold by R. BALDWIN, London, and all other Booksellers in Town and Country. 1780

(Price Two Shillings.)

5 *DLCL*: Horace, *Ars Poetica*, 161–2 (p. 464) 'The beardless youth, freed at last from his tutor finds joy in horses and hounds and the grass of the sunny Campus.' Pratt uses the same quotation in 'A Copy of an Advertisement sent to Cambridge'.

[*ad*]

Advertisement.

THE Writer of the following little Piece is well apprized, that he could have *served up* this his *Morsel* more agreeable to the public *Taste*, had he *shredded* in a few more *Blades*,[6] with a little of the *Coxcomb a-la-Creme:* But the Connoisseur must please to observe, that he is here invited, not to a *Feast*, but a *Snap*[7] only; we beg therefore our *Guests* would say *Grace* over this their *Morsel* in perfect Good-humour, and sit down with cheerfulness to a moderate Entertainment.[8]

[*p. 1*]

SEPTEMBER:

A

RURAL POEM.

HAIL, fair September![†] in whose gentle reign
The rural swains collect the golden grain:
Hail, wish'd for morn! whose fresh returning light
Has chac'd away the tedious hours of night.—

[†] *Hail fair September.* The month of September is now become the most respectable of the twelve; and as the game is a subject of serious controversy in most places, this passion is deservedly ridicul'd (with some degree of pleasantry) in the following little poem.

Scaliger natu Minimus——.[9]

6 The leaves of herbs used to garnish dishes: *OED.*

7 A snack or a small and quickly-eaten meal: *OED.*

8 The comparison of literary to gastronomic entertainment was much used in the eighteenth century. See, for example, the essay at the beginning of Book 1 in Henry Fielding's novel *Tom Jones* (1749).

9 Julius Caesar Scaliger (1484–1558) was an Italian writer of *Poetice* (1561), a tract on poetics. A '*filius natu minimus*' is a younger son. The note is therefore understood to having been written by a 'younger-born Scaliger'—in both the sense of being a critic born after Scaliger and in the sense of being a lesser Scaliger.

Brisk CHANTICLEER,[10] with proud erected crest,
Clap'd his gay wings, and strain'd his little breast:
Wide o'er the fields the lowing heifers stray,
And slip-shod gleaners brush'd the dews away.
   Where yon tall turrets proudly meet the skies;
The mansion clock strikes six, the Sportsmen rise;

[*p. 2*]

Deserted Fair Ones to their maids complain,
Stretch half awake, and ring their bells in vain:
Soft bridal Daphne to her[11] pillow sighs,
And hides in down those dear bewitching eyes;
They turn, they fret, and weep their own mistakes,
And wish that Pointers could be Wives for Rakes:
Now my good May'r unfolds the red streak'd eye,
Pants for his feast,* and the rich partridge pye:
Now mutt'ring grooms bend from the stable door,
Half shew themselves, and wish the breakfast o'er;
Maids scold at boys, and boys in turn reply,
Blows follow blows, and fractur'd china fly—
   But hark! the whistle gives its quiv'ring sound,
The Squire pours forth, the mansion roofs rebound;
The dancing sun-beams on his barrel play,
September smiles, and all her sons are gay.[12]
Sweet month, to thee thy jovial sportsmen bring,

* *Pants for his feast, and the rich partridge pye.* Partridge pye (says a bursar of a college) is excellent eating without doubt: but if we are to be cram'd at the same time with a detail of the whole day's diversion, it is very apt to rise in the stomach and make us sick.---The eternal subject of game is undoubtedly a heavy tax upon the time and patience of those gentlemen who are no sportsmen.

- - - - *loquacem*
Delassare valent Fabium - - - - Hor.[13]

---

10 Conventional literary name for a rooster.

11 'ner' in the original text is an obvious misprint.

12 c.f. a line in Canto Two of *The Rape of the Lock*: '*Belinda* smil'd, and all the World was gay' (*Pope*, 52).

13 *DLCL*: Horace, *Satires I*, 1:13–14 (p. 5) The context of the lines in question is a long list of examples of people not being content with what they had, all the instances of which 'could tire out the chatterbox Fabius'.

The first clipt feather from the partridge wing;
For thee, Collegians waste whole terms away,
Leave LOCKE and NEWTON† for a sporting day;

[*p. 3*]

The schools' loud wrangle for the covey[14] change,
And learn to dress old pointers for the mange.
  Goddess of Sports![15] O thou, whose virgin throng
Can lead the chace, and scour the fields along;
Not thou, chaste Dian, or thy sportive train,
Shall claim a Verse in soft September's reign:
The muse, exulting, now attempts to sing
The fresh-shorn fields, and covies proud of wing;
The pointers leaping at their masters' side,
And full-blown sportsmen in their autumn pride.
  Adieu the chace! to us a theme unsung;
To winter months those rougher sports belong:
Nor shall the loping, list'ning greyhounds claim,
One couplet here, as dogs of honest fame.
See, there they go! light bounding o'er the fern,

† *Leave Locke and Newton*. A tutor at Cambridge visiting his pupil, found his LOCKE open for a week together at the same page on Simple Ideas. "Child, says he, thou hast a strange affection for Simple Ideas," and he was right; for his pupil never went any where without them afterwards.

Voltaire, on empty bottles.[16]

---

14 Partridge brood or family that remains together for a season after the young are born: *OED*.

15 Diana, the Roman goddess of hunting.

16 The reference is to Voltaire's 1777 review of a French translation of *Tristram Shandy* in the *Journal de politique et de littérature*, in which Voltaire had retold the story that had already been told by Jean Baptiste Suard in his previous review of *Tristram Shandy* of a charlatan who promised to put himself into a bottle at the Haymarket. A large audience gathered there only to find an empty bottle on the stage and their money taken. Voltaire borrowed the previous review's *bon mot* that not even the bottle was emptier than the last two volumes of *Tristram Shandy*, applying the sentiment to the book as a whole. For a translation of Suard's review, including the anecdote, see B. Howes (ed.), *Laurence Sterne: The Critical Heritage* (London: Routledge, 1971), pp. 168–9. For Voltaire's review see Voltaire, *Les œuvres complètes de Voltaire*, ed. Theodore Besterman et al. (Geneva: Institut et Musée Voltaire; Oxford: Voltaire Foundation, 1968–), vol. 80, part 3 (2009), p. 38.

Whiff follows whiff, and turn succeeds to turn;
Distress'd, confus'd, the little victim flies,
Death follows close, she drops at once; she dies.
Mere woman's pastime! just alive to please,
To ride, chit-chat, and take our snuff with ease.
  Hush'd be the winds! nor let the wanton air
* Disturb the tresses of sweet Juliet's hair.
Guard her, ye Sylphs,[17] from falls, and man's approach!
And change the greyhounds for the burnish'd coach.

[*p. 4*]

The martial air, th' equestrian female pride,
Gives pain with pleasure, and our thoughts divide;
The graceful titt-up[18] may attract the eye,
But in the dance (sweet pow'r) we gaze to die.[19]
  Go then, ye coursers! shake your loaded sides,
The good Sir Loin repays your morning rides;
With many a wink the circling glass goes round,
And each applauds,† how well the Parson found.
Say, first! what dæmon, with infernal flame,

* *Disturb the tresses.* L——y T——d.[20]

† *And each applauds.* The clerical eye, at present, is in great repute for finding a hare sitting; owing perhaps to its extreme versability and occasional revolutions for many purposes.

Huc illuc oculos vertunt - - -[21]

17 Recalling the sylphs charged with guarding Belinda's chastity in Pope's *The Rape of the Lock*.

18 'Titt-up' can refer to the jerky movement of a horse's canter, the cantering horse itself, and figuratively an impudent woman: *OED*. All three senses seem to be in play here.

19 Female equestrians are also satirised in *Spectator* 435: 'Had one of these Hermaphrodites appeared in *Juvenal's* Days, with what an Indignation should we have seen her described by that excellent Satyrist. He would have represented her in her Riding Habit, as a greater Monster than the Centaur' (*Spec*, 4:28).

20 Probably Lucy Townshend (*c.* 1759–1786), a daughter of the Reverend Edward Townshend (1719–1765), Dean of Norwich (1761–65), who was in turn a son of Charles Townshend, 2nd Viscount Townshend (1675–1738). She is buried in St. James Church in West-Teignmouth in Devon. See Beatrix F. Cresswell, *Notes on the Churches of the Deanery of Kenn, Devon* (Exeter: James G. Commin, 1912), pp. 167–8.

21 'Turning their eyes now this way and now that'. A play on a line from Livy's *History*

Has fir'd this earth with such a lust for game:
Unmov'd by age, by widows', orphans' tears,
We feel all o'er for partridges and hares;
E'en gaunty quakers,‡ now so garish grown,
Can squint the eye, and pounce the partridge down.
Mad in our sports, we mix in fierce disputes,
And blood of man atones for blood of brutes.
Loose from his school, too dull for classic ground,[22]
The man-child claims his hunter and his hound:
Indulgent parents view their idol son,
Chum for his dog, and wedded to the gun;

[*p. 5*]

So sweet a stripling, so improv'd by years,
He grows a Midas,§ with the Ass's ears.
As vig'rous trees put forth luxuriant shoots,
Outgrow themselves, and shed their promis'd fruits;
So youth unprun'd, to manhood runs too fast,
Then stops, and proves unfruitful to the last.
Sweet is the sight the verdant meadows yield,
Yet sweeter far the new-reap'd summer field;
Try now the turnips, brush the stubbles round,[23]

‡ *E'en gaunty Quakers.* From the word quaker, and the tremor they are supposed to be under, we should suppose them to be but very indifferent sportsmen; but, alack-a-day, some of the friends can bring the creature down very abundantly, and eat him afterwards.

§ *He grows a Midas.*---This description of a Master Jacky from Eaton, or Westminster, is not to be applied to any one particular gentleman: we renounce all manner of personal severities in this work, and give our description herein to be divided amongst the multitude.

Qui capit, ille facit.[24]

---

of Rome: 'Samnites dum huc illuc signa vertunt' *DLCL*: Livy, *History of* Rome, 7:9 (p. 479) 'Samnites turning their standards now this way and now that.' Pratt substitutes 'oculos' ('eyes') for 'signa' ('standards').

22 Echoing Joseph Addison's *Letter from Italy* (1704), 'Poetick Fields encompass me around,/ And still I seem to tread on Classic Ground.' *Remarks on Several Parts of Italy, &c. in the Years 1701, 1702, 1703* (London: J. Tonson, 1718), p. ii.

23 The remnants of stalks left after the harvest: *OED*.

24 'He who takes it, has made it,' a Latin proverb.

And range the pointers o'er the furrow'd ground.
But let not these, ill-broke[25] and unconfin'd,
Rush lawless on, and idly sink the wind:[26]
Ill sport, with hoarseness, will your toils repay;
A lean light net,[27] and mother's white wine whey.[28]
  Now o'er the burning marl,[29] the gifted sons
Of mitred Aaron[30] wave their polish'd guns;
Earth from its centre feels the Demi-gods,
The green geese cackle,* and the gander nods:

[p. 6]

So notch'd, so peel'd, so primitive their dress,‖
Luther[31] might smile, and Saints could do no less.

* *The green geese cackle.*---Absurd to a degree! No green geese, as they are ridiculously called, in the month of September. The author probably means geese upon a green; we wish him to be more correct.

Dennis Redivivus.[32]

‖ *So notch'd, so peel'd, so primitive their dress.* A decency and distinction of dress is proper to be observed at all times; especially as black and white are so easily distinguished by the common people.

Ibidem.

---

25 The opposite of 'well-broke' meaning 'well-trained', a phrase usually used of horses but the phrase was applicable to other animals as well: *OED*.

26 For a hunted animal to move in the downwind direction during a hunt and so avoid being scented by the predator: *OED*.

27 i.e. the cloth used for straining whey.

28 White wine whey was used as a treatment for hoarseness: 'White Wine Whey [...] is of special Use in a Palsy, Lethargy, Epilepsy, Hysterics, Apoplexy, Dropsy, and Loss of Speech.' Thomas Short, *Medicina Britannica* (London: R. Manby and H. Shute Cox, 1746), p. 196.

29 A parody of the description of the devils in Book Five of *Paradise Lost*, who move with 'Uneasy steps/ Over the burning marl, not like those steps/ On heav'n's azure' (*Milton*, 117–19). Marl, a soil rich in clay and calcium deposits was widely used as a fertiliser in Norfolk. The term can also be used more generally to denote ground or earth: *OED*.

30 According to the Bible, Aaron was an older brother of Moses and the first High Priest of the Israelites. The Anglican clergy are here being referred to as Aaron's descendants.

31 Martin Luther (1483–1546), German theologian and central figure of the Protestant Reformation in the first half the sixteenth century.

32 'Redivivus' means 'brought back to life.' 'Dennis' is a reference to John Dennis (1658–1734), who wrote a pedantic catalogue of the supposed absurdities of Pope's *The Rape of the Lock*.

Soft be the verse, unwilling to offend,
Conceal all faults, except it be to mend;
Candour exclaims, O spare a brother's fame!
No poniard wounds so feelingly as shame:
Friend to your faults, wherever these abound,
We search the part, and gently dress the wound:
Yes, let me touch, not probe the wound too deep,
Whilst Folly laughs—to see Religion weep;
To see her sons to dissipation yield,
First in the dance,[‡] and foremost in the field;
Good rules, good order, decency aside,
Pert gawky pleasure mix'd with idle pride.
O Rome! no more thy papal pow'r shall rise;
We'll flush thy Pope, and shoot him as he flies:[33]
Prim'd at all points whatever sport invites,
Play, Ball, Bath, Bristol, or a game at White's:[§]

[p. 7]

There hov'ring round our sable troops appear,
To catch and spread the follies of the year:
But here discretion lets the curtain fall,
And sweet good-nature mourns, and covers all.

[‡] *First in the dance*——Nothing more is here intended but a kind and affectionate hint to some few of our younger clergy, not to batter themselves too much by dancing, for fear they should not be able to move afterwards on the hard road to preferment,

Vide Delany on David's dancing.[34]

[§] *Or a game at White's.* The firm of the house probably is still preserved.[35]

---

33 c.f. the couplet near the beginning of Alexander Pope's *Essay on Man*, which proposes to 'Eye Nature's walks, shoot folly as it flies,/ And catch the manners living as they rise.' (*Pope*, 1:13–14).

34 Patrick Delany, *An Historical Account of the Life and Reign of David, King of Israel* (London: 1742), pp. 162–83; Delaney defends King David's dancing as described in 2 Samuel 6:14–22 against the criticism of David's conduct in Pierre Bayle's biographical *Dictionnaire Historique et Critique* (1697; first English edition 1709).

35 White's Chocolate House in St James's Street in London was especially associated with gambling and gaming. The chocolate house itself burned down in 1773 but the club remained.

Clasp'd in those arms, where panting Gods might lie,
And Kings themselves be pleas'd, and proud to die;
What makes Hillario[36] (scarce one fortnight wed)
Leave thus betimes the new-deck'd bridal bed;
Thro' parched fields for feather'd vengeance roam,
When softer pleasures might be found at home?
O proof severe to man's internal eye!
That our best joys do but exist to die;
Thro' life we toil, its honey sweets to find,
Yet feel each pleasure leaves its sting behind.
Prone to condemn, let not old age presume,
To mix December with the flow'rs of June:
Youth's made for joy; 'tis nature's holiday;
And time soon steals the golden hours away.
A social heart, and ever cheerful face,
Bespeak no want of character or grace;
Pastimes and sports, by Heav'n's own will design'd,
Relieve the body, and assist the mind.
Live and enjoy,[‡] all nature's works declare;
He counter-acts, who bids us to forbear:

[*p. 8*]

Nature, and nature's lord delights to dwell,
Far from dull cloisters, and the hermit's cell;
Shuns dirty monks, who think their maker pleas'd,
To see them starv'd, neglected, and diseas'd.
Heav'n points the way, where sober pleasure lies,
And bids mankind be happy, and be wise;

‡ *Live and enjoy, all nature's works declare.* We have certainly a right to be as easy and happy as we can, provided we will suffer decency and good manners to be of the party with us.

Vide Secker's Remarks.[37]

36 Hillario is the name of the protagonist of Christopher Smart's mock epic poem *The Hilliad* (1753), satirizing the botanist and writer John Hill, and the eponymous dog's first English owner in Francis Coventry's novel *Pompey the Little* (1751).

37 Thomas Secker (1693–1768) was Archbishop of Canterbury between 1758 and 1768. It is not clear which remarks of Thomas Secker's are meant but the sentiment is common enough.

Excess alone leads all our thoughts astray,§
Whilst fashion lurks a serpent in our way.[38]
  But they live most, and nobler ends pursue,
Who live to pleasure, and their maker too.
Flush'd with rude health, and clos'd in triple steel,[39]
Young fiery sportsmen lose their pow'rs to feel:
To save their young, the screaming covies rise,
Unmanly shot! too near the mother dies.
The anxious fire exerts a father's care,
Wings off, and leaves his little soul in air.
O! where must now their wretched offspring fly?
No bush, no brake escapes the sportsman's eye:

[*p. 9*]

In turn progressive‡ each resigns its breath,
And close their eyes in agonizing death.

§ *Excess alone leads all our thoughts astray.* A reasonable equality amongst sportsmen is the one thing wanted: to promote this, a Minor Canon has advis'd, that all dead hands, and terrible shots, (as so commonly called) should all of them be properly weighted: to carry in their boots, or shoes, one gill, at least, of good, sound, unboil'd marrow-fat peas, or horse beans of two years old; or that the trigger finger should be handsomely capt, or cotted, with tin, leather, or cloth, so as to bring them to a fair equality with other sportsmen.

Vide Clergyman's Vade-Mecum.[40]

‡ *In turn progressive.*---Some gentlemen are so modest and sparing, as to confine themselves to five brace of partridges a day: this amounts to 120 brace for each person, for the first month of shooting; and yet these our modest gentlemen would take it ill to be call'd poachers.----How say you, critics?---Poachers, or not? Out with it freely.----*Poachers, murderers, Goths, Vandals, and Tuscans,* without dispute.

Legion.[41]

---

38 A play on Genesis, 49:17: 'Dan shall be a serpent by the way, an adder in the path, that biteth the horse heels, so that his rider shall fall backward' (*Oxford KJB*).

39 i.e. steel of extra thickness, used, for example, in armour plates. Some of the devils in Book Two of *Paradise Lost* are able for a time to 'arm th' obdured breast/ With stubborn patience as with triple steel' through their philosophical inquiries in hell (*Milton*, 569–70).

40 'Gill' as a unit of measure, equal to a quarter pint: *OED*; 'cotted': alternative spelling of 'coated'. The joke is that a 'vade mecum' or handbook literally means 'go with me'.

41 Here the word 'Legion' seems to apply both to the great numbers of gentlemen who kill too many birds during the shooting season and to the even greater numbers of their quarry.

Is this a triumph? This that manly pride,
Which boasts so much of reason for its guide?
To view unmov'd the mangled covies die,
And rob Creation to enrich a pye.
O, turn your arms to save a sinking land!
Britannia calls, and claims each active hand;
Leave fields of pleasure for the fields of fame,
The foes of Britain are the noblest game.
Comus,[42] dear droll! hold both thy sides, and see
Decrepid Threescore turnip'd to the knee;
Parch'd in the centre of the burning plain,
He stops, he pants, and rolls his eyes in vain;
Views the stiff point, each feeble effort tries;
Th' impatient dogs rush in—the covey flies.
Know then thyself, enervated Threescore,[§]
Now give and take the harmless Mattadore;[43]

[*p. 10*]

Or at back-gammon, in the ebb of life,
Size-ace[44] the vicar, or capot[45] his wife.*
O idle thought! with limbs and nerves unstrung,

§ *Know then thyself, enervated Threescore.* The poor climacterical sportsman, who bursted a string behind, when he was going fast to the dog then pointing, is a singular instance how very cautious we ought to be, not to lay open and naked the infirmities of old age to the eye of Ridicule.

Damnosa quid non imminuet dies.[46]

* *Size-ace the vicar, or capot his wife.* There can be no manner of harm in playing a game of Cribbage, or All-Fours, with a neighbour's wife, provided you do not sit so close together as to see each other's cards.

Take care how you turn up Jack?

HOYLE.[47]

42 Ancient Greek god of revels and festivities.

43 A card game: *OED*.

44 One of the varieties of backgammon: *OED*.

45 To succeed at taking all the tricks in the card game of piquet: *OED*.

46 *DLCL*: Horace, *Odes III*, 6:45 (p. 165) 'What does it not impair?'

47 Edmond Hoyle (1671/2–1769), expert on card games and author of several popular books and treatises on the subject: *Oxford DNB*.

That weak old age should covet to be young:
Vain is the wish; nor can our hopes succeed,
The old young man is impotent indeed.
See! thy stiff hunter, long inur'd to toil,
By years reduc'd, with patience breaks the soil:
But if he hears from far the op'ning hound,
He stops, he starts, he listens to the sound;
His lean shrunk sides will this one truth afford,
Time levels all, the hunter and his lord.
  Ye sons of rapine! tyrants of the chace!
Descended down from Nimrod's bloody race;[48]
Know, mercy is the attribute divine;[49]
'Tis Heav'n's own gift; and make that virtue thine.
Forbear, rash youth! nor with exulting eye,
Smile to behold thy feather'd victim die:
Nor with proud pleasure† crush the quiv'ring brain;
Or, unprovok'd, prolong one ling'ring pain;

[*p. 11*]

The meanest insect, with expiring breath,
Feels, as thou must, the bitter pangs of death.
  See at thy foot! in agonizing round,
In leaden death,[50] the flutt'rer beats the ground!
Say, now, wherein the mighty diff'rence lies!

† *Nor with proud pleasure*——Fiery young sportsmen will sometimes, we are informed, crush the head of a partridge in the mouth, to shorten the time of its dying: we wish this to proceed from an act of tenderness only, and not for the sake of expedition.

Monitor.[51]

48 Genesis mentions Nimrod in the so-called 'Generations on Noah' section as one of Noah's great grandsons and he is also mentioned as either the ruler or founder of several ancient cities. Various traditions name him among the builders of the Tower of Babel but the Bible does not mention this. Several Jewish and Islamic traditions also describe various versions of a confrontation or rivalry between Nimrod and Abraham, with Abraham representing good and Nimrod evil.

49 c.f. Pope, *An Essay on Criticism*: 'To Err is *Humane*; to Forgive, *Divine*' (*Pope*, 2:525).

50 A play on the literal and metaphorical senses of 'leaden'.

51 Monitor: Latin for 'warner'.

To-morrow thou, to-day the partridge dies.
Speak! is it pleasure, or the lust of food?
That makes thy arm thus prodigal of blood.
The new-fledg'd birds, now breathless at thy side,
This morn, like thee, were all their parents' pride;
Stretch'd their young wings, and fondly bask'd around,
And felt no torture,* till thou gav'st the wound.
Censure apart; if field amusements please,
The mind may be reliev'd with such as these.
This better far, (for this is lawful game)
Than plunge a dagger thro' a brother's fame:
Or let seduction poison the repose,
And give to age those wounds which never close.
Shun him who acts the vile seducer's part!
The wretch whose lips are foreign to his heart;
'Tis poor, 'tis wretched, and unmanly too,
To break a heart, which fondly bleeds for you.
The female tear, the lightest of its kind,
Dissolves the soul, and melts the feeling mind:

[*p. 12*]

We must be wretched, when the Fair complains;
Turn soft like them, and freely wear their chains!
Be every sportsman, every woman's friend,
Nor wound that honour† which you should defend.

* *And felt no torture*---Acts of cruelty are to be avoided as much as possible; the meanest insect being equally as susceptible of pain, as an elephant of the first magnitude.

Veritas.

† *Nor wound that honour.*---Nothing so mean and unmanly as the seduction of a young creature, because she loves you to distraction.

Bodney's Voyage to Loretto.[52]

---

52 Loreto, a town in Italy and the purported site to which Virgin Mary's house had been transported by angels from Palestine, was a popular destination for Catholic pilgrimages; we could not identify the author 'Bodney' nor a book by the title of *Voyage to Loreto* so this book it is likely Pratt's invention.

Forth from his farm, his mother's only care,
Dear Jacky scouts, the grazier's hopeful heir;
Half fool, half witling,[53] and a half pretence,
To something rumbling in the sound of sense;
Shot out[54] to manhood, pert with aukward pride,
The game bag dangling‡ at the booby's side:
Proud of the skirt,[55] to *varder*[56] tells the tale,
O'er the long sausage, and the ev'ning ale.
Once, sad event! with thee thy mother big,
Tore off in wrath thy father's woolly wig:
Terror to birds, aloft it wav'd in air;
You heard the tale, and chose the ribbon'd hair.
Thy club might now the peruke's place supply,
And birds would shun the monster as they fly.
You, my good dames, whose children are your care,
Let no frisseurs disturb the farmer's hair;*

‡ *The game bag dangling.*---Quere, says an old experienced sportsman, whether mother's darling, who seldom stirs a furlong from home, without a gun in his hand, and a lurcher at his heels, does not surreptitiously destroy more game than better and more experienced sportsmen.

Hunc tu, Romane, caveto.[57]

* *Let no frisseurs disturb the farmer's hair.*---Farms in general, upon an average in Norfolk, are supposed to be raised twenty per cent. since the introduction of knob'd hair, and nankeen breeches.

Vide Molesworth's Calculations.[58]

53 Someone who aspires to being a wit but falls short of being one: *OED*.

54 A play on the sense of 'shot out' as something carelessly or impulsively sent out and the sense as an area of countryside in which all the game has been removed through overhunting.

55 The skirt (i.e. the protective rim) of the game bag.

56 i.e. father.

57 *DLCL*: Horace, *Satires I*, 4:85 (p. 55) 'Of him beware, good Roman.'

58 John Molesworth (1751–1791), grandson of Robert Molesworth, first Viscount Molesworth. He became famous in the 1770s for claiming to be able to calculate winning numbers in lotteries and offering tickets for sale, which he claimed were likely to win. See Natasha Glaisyer, 'Calculation and Conjuring: John Molesworth and the Lottery in Late Eighteenth-Century Britain', *Journal for Eighteenth-Century Studies,* 43.2 (2019), pp. 135–55.

[*p. 13*]

The dangling club, long skirt, and simp'ring face,
With heads so marl'd,[59] make acres rise apace.
Nature on all bestows what's good and best,
But affectation's folly meanly drest;
All rank, all order, serves to some good use,
But swans deride the vain affected goose.
Be nature then your guide! your ruling star!
Nor strive to be more aukward than you are:
Time was, before prescription made us fools,
When men were wise, and follow'd Nature's rules;
Experience taught all field amusements good,
To brace the nerves, and purify the blood:
Law gave consent, that Britain's sons might know
To raise the tube, and level at the foe:
Now, sad reverse! despotic times succeed,
And men scarce know the very game they feed.†
  What, do they murmur? do they say, undone?
Seiz'd are their farms, the keeper takes the gun:
Mercy for all, e'en wretched rogues in jail,
But who forgives the murd'rer of a quail?
Not all the streams of Jordan's healing flood,[60]
Could cure this hot, rank fever of the blood.—

† *And men scarce know the very game they feed.*——To continue our sporting metaphors, we level our piece at the follies of men, and not their persons: if any random shot should reach any one particular gentleman, we heartily beg his pardon, and desire him to consider it as a scratch that can never injure him.

Vivas in amore jocisque.[61]

59 See note 29 above, p. 172 in our edition. The conceit is that the children's heads are well-fertilized and bear a plentiful crop of hair.

60 Reference to Naaman, a Syrian military commander, mentioned in 2 Kings 5, who is healed from leprosy after bathing in the Jordan River seven times on the advice of the prophet Elisha. The incident is also referenced in Luke 4:27: 'And many lepers were in Israel in the time of Eliseus the prophet; and none of them was cleansed, saving Naaman the Syrian' (*Oxford KJB*).

61 *DLCL*: Horace, *Epistles I*, 1:66 (p. 291) The full sentence is 'Mimnermus uti censet, sine amore iocisque nil est iucundum, vivas in amore iocisque.' 'If, without love and jests there is no joy, then live amid love and jests.'

[*p. 14*]

And what shall these defend our country's cause?
These guard our rights, and save our sinking laws?
Voters beware! despotic men disown!
You set them up, and you can pluck them down.
But in excess alone the mischief lies;
Men might be sportsmen, would they but be wise:
Manners with sense, and decency combin'd,
Need no restraint, nor want to be confin'd;
But in their sports men are unequal found,
These want indulgence, those too much abound.
   Fix'd to his cures, (say fifty pounds if clear)
Why boasts my priest his hundred brace each year?[†]
Or, what makes William sport throughout his life?
One hundred pounds per ann. in right of wife:
But these have worth, and many virtues hid;
Where? in the buskins,[62] and the pow'rful quid.

† *Why boasts my priest his hundred brace each year.*--It is a fact of notoriety, that some of the clergy in Norfolk destroy with a single gun three or four-score brace of partridges and pheasants in one season. To prevent this excess, some have advised, that a text should be given after service for the following Sunday--but Gediccus[63] has well observed, (*De decimando et non decimando*,[64] and in the case of *Pepper versus Splash*[65]) that where tithes are taken in kind, the text must not be intrusted with the Squire, or parish officers.

Est modus *in Rebus*.[66]

62 A type of leather boot: *OED*.

63 Simon Geddicus (1551–1631) was a Lutheran theologian, most famous for his *Defence of the Female Sex* (1595), written against Valentius Acidalius's hoaxing tract in which he appeared to argue that women do not have souls. See Manfred P. Fleischer, '"Are Women Human?"—The Debate of 1595 between Valens Acidalius and Simon Geddicus,' *Sixteenth-Century Journal*, 12.2 (1981), pp. 107–20.

64 'To be tithed and not to be tithed' (our translation). 'De non decimando' in ecclesiastical law was a right or claim not to have to pay tithes.

65 Obviously, a made-up lawsuit.

66 *DLCL*: Horace, *Satires I*, 1:106 (p. 13) 'There is measure in all things.' The phrase can be found in a number of other classical authors but is most frequently associated with this occurrence in Horace.

Away distinctions, and each vain pretence!
The wholesale murd'rer gives to all offence:
Define who will, be his the poacher's fame,
Whose life's a kennel, and profession game—

[*p. 15*]

And should there live a youth, so lost to sense,
Who knows no bounds, but sports to give offence;
Who hurls defiance at his patron's head,
And poaches fields, which freely yield him bread:
If such there be, may I, good Heav'n! decline
To mix with such, or call that friendship mine.
Say then, where must our game contentions end?†
That each may trust his neighbour, or his friend:
When must suspicion drop the fev'rish fear,
Nor guns roar down distraction on the ear.
Thou must, discretion, hold the equal scale,
And honour bind superior to a jail.
Lords of our fields! to whose despotic sway,
Mortals must bend, and laws themselves obey;

† *Say then, where must*——The various disputes about the game in many places become daily an interesting subject to the public in general; as lives, fortunes, peace, and good neighbourhood are too frequently sacrificed to the capricious and ridiculous idol.

Mungo Campbell.[67]

67 Mungo Campbell (1712–1770) was an excise officer, who fatally shot Alexander Montgomerie, 10th Earl of Eglinton (1723–1769), during a dispute over hunting rights on Eglinton's lands in Ayrshire, Scotland. Campbell was sentenced to death but hanged himself before the sentence could be carried out. See *The Trial of Mungo Campbell* (London: D. Wilson and G. Nicol, 1770). Closer to home, the story of how George Townshend had challenged his neighbor Thomas Coke, Earl of Leicester to a duel in part over a dispute over game in 1759 was well known in Norfolk, although it is not clear that the duel ever took place. See Susanna Wade Martins, *Coke of Norfolk (1754–1842): A Biography* (Woodbridge: Boydell Press, 2009), p. 11.

Mortgage, or bond,‖ at all events defend,
And save the partridge, tho' you lose the friend.
But what is friendship? what a brother's blood?
To live and reign, sole tyrant of a wood;
To hear at once a hundred pheasants rise,
To feel a triumph, when a poacher dies;

[*p. 16*]

O heav'nly conquest to a virtuous mind,
To live and die, the scourge of half mankind!
    But, see he comes!—A cherub's form appears,
Edg'd with white hat, and tipt with ass's ears:
O! for the hartshorn,[68] or we die away,
To see such softness, in the form of clay:
Waft all his sweets, ye gentle gales, around!
Wheree'er he treads, fresh odours scent the ground!*—
Ye, once un-acred, nor e'en blest with roods,[69]

‖ *Mortgage, or bond*—— It is a mortifying reflection, that some gentlemen, by an over avidity to preserve game, have very much shortened those acres whereunto they belonged.

- - - *In jus*
Acres procurrent - - -[70]

* *Wheree'er he treads, fresh odours scent the ground.*——Who is this? A question more easily asked than answered. It is, my good reader, any body, nobody, or whom you please. The daubings of this writer have this quality of your Fuller's Earth;[71] designed to take out your spots, and make your garment better, but not to injure it.

- - - - *Non ego paucis*
Offendar maculis - - - -[72]

68 See note 45 in *The Grange*, p. 68 of our edition.

69 Unit of measurement of land equal to a quarter of an acre: *OED*.

70 *DLCL*: Horace, *Satires I*, 20:1 (p. 93) 'Keenly they rush into court.' Pratt probably intends a play on the Latin 'acres' (keenly) and English 'acres' as a unit of land measurement.

71 Fuller's earth was a type of clay used to clean clothes: *OED*.

72 'I shall not take offence at a few blots'. *DLCL*: Horace, *Ars Poetica*, 351–2 (p. 479) the whole sentence is 'Non ego paucis offendar maculis, quas aut incuria fudit aut humana parum cavit natura.' 'I shall not take offence at a few blots, which a careless hand has let drop or human frailty has failed to avert.'

Tho' now ye boast fair fields, and stately woods;
Feels not your cheek the conscious glow of shame,
For legions slaughter'd of unnumber'd game.
Why then thus rigid? why so lordly grown?
We hail your manors, tho' of late your own:
Go make your tenants covenant by lease,
To strain the laws, and wound the public peace;
Juries, no doubt, will aid the righteous cause,
And prosecutions thrive from injur'd laws.
But why those sullen shrugs, that cinic[73] sneer?
That cits[74] should taste a partridge once a year:
Why thus disturb'd, and peevish to a fault?
Look up, my lords! good news—a poacher's caught!

[*p. 17*]

Jail him, they cry;* zounds! have him fast and bound!
O glorious deed! Th' unshirted villain's found.
The triumph ended—restless as before—
For why? My lord has fifty pheasants more.
What will suffice? what suits your present taste?
The full, the sole dominion of the waste.
All game is ours. What all? delicious word!
This smooths the front, makes peace, and sheaths the sword.
   But hold—Shall little men, deputed too,
Rave round our fields, and be as fierce as you?
Shall these, (O force of second-handed pow'r!)

* *Jail him, they cry*——It is a truth, not to be controverted with success, that many of our most rigid preservers of game were, a few years backwards, the most notorious free-booters on the manors of other gentlemen.

——*Tempora mutantur, et nos mutamur in illis.*[75]

73 i.e. 'cynic'.

74 A contraction of 'citizen'. The term 'cit' was usually tinged with derision and applied to town-dwellers as opposed to country-dwellers or merchants as opposed to the landed gentry: *OED.*

75 'Times change and we are changed with them' (our own translation); a Latin adage of uncertain authorship often erroneously attributed to Cicero; in classical Latin the correct word order is: 'Tempora mutantur, nos et mutamur in illis.'

Strut out the puny tyrants of an hour?
So down the stream,[†] cry'd out, in pert array;
See, see, we swim!—we pippins[76] of a day.
What pity then my lord, whose goodness charms,
Whose life's a lesson, and whose friendship warms;
Should wear a speck so fest'ring at the heart,
This game disease, beyond the pow'r of art:
Lose half his virtues, and be deem'd severe,
To save that poor mean animal—a hare.

[*p. 18*]

Men should be decent—yes, 'tis very true;
Men should be decent, so my lords should you:
What if to cure this phrenzy of the brain,
We should confine our curates on the chain;
Tie up our sportsmen till the season's done;
And then let loose to air, and feel the sun;
Sweet, heav'nly balm, to ease the tortur'd breast,
And rock the minds of busy men to rest.
But know, no creature walks the earth so mean,
But wears resentment, tho' it lurks unseen;
Nature bestows on all a self-defence;
Brutes have their claws, and man is arm'd with sense.
Contempt and scorn, those horrid plagues to teaze,
These all men have, and use them as they please.

† So down the stream——Under the idea of representation, deputation, or more properly perhaps, defamation, some of our second-hand deputed lords of manors, frequently exceed their originals in every degree of pedantry and ostentation.

O imitatores! servum pecus——[77]

76 The game keepers are here compared to the image of apples bobbing down the stream but the line also evokes the image of a 'pippin squire' as a gigolo or a prostitute's pimp: *OED*.

77 *DLCL*: Horace, *Epistles I*, 19:19 (p. 383) 'O you mimics, o you slavish herd!'

Thrice happy ISLE![‡][78] where ev'ry *seventh* year[79]
Calls forth the pleasing gewgaw[80] of a chair:
When tost in air, triumphant members ride;
So smooth, so pleasant, and so *free from pride.*
"Dear Sir! good creature! my obliging friend!
"You know my soul, you know you may depend;
"You know my int'rest must at last succeed,
"And Tom shall be an officer, indeed:

[*p. 19*]

"Do all you can, secure your cousin's vote,
"And take this trifle—to repair his coat:
"Friends of my soul, be free; apply, command,
"You have my house, my manors, and my land;
"For you we live, for you we dare to die;

‡ *Thrice happy Isle*——It is wonderful to consider, how smooth, and how very much in season great men are, on the approach of an election year; occasioned, it is said, by a certain *political rouge*, which clarifies the face, and gives a delightful simmering to the whole countenance, keeping all the muscles and dimples for a time, at least, in excellent preservation.

C. Warren, perfumer, Parliament-Street.[81]

---

78 Recalling the lines describing the stars as seen by Satan in his descent towards earth in John Milton's *Paradise Lost*: 'Like those Hesperian gardens famed of old,/ Fortunate fields, and groves, and flowery vales,/ Thrice happy isles.' (*Milton*, 3: 568–70).

79 After the Septennial Act of 1716, elections were held every seven years in the eighteenth century.

80 A garish object of little value: *OED*.

81 A perfumer named Richard Warren (fl. 1769–1784) had addresses in Cheapside and Golden Square. A trade card in the British Museum (Heal Collection Heal, 93.35+) advertises: 'Richard Warren Perfumer … Imports, Makes & Sells All Sorts of the Richest Perfumery Goods in all its branches & greatest perfection, Wholesale, Retail & for Export … In Adoration to the God of Day/ Rich Sweet Perfumes the Eastern Princes Pay/ In Jewish Temples the Fragrant Scent/ And Christian Churches where the Knees are bent.'

"Save, save yourselves;† save us; save Liberty!"
  But what is this? mere gilding of a day,
One month elaps'd, the varnish melts away;
Then each freeholder, with extatic stare,
Cries, *Marcy, Sars*! how strange these *great men* are!
"For six long years they lead us in a chain,
"Then smooth and polish for their *chairs* again."
And it is thus, by low and mean deceit,
Our patriots rise to honours and a seat?
Suspended Justice mourns our fate, too near,
Looks down, and weeps o'er poor Britannia's bier.
  O! how unlike to this is his good name,
Whose virtues are as public as his fame;
His country's idol, and the good man's praise,
And uncorrupted in the worst of days:
Statesmen and Peers, if this be worth approv'd,
Know A——y[82] lives, thus honour'd and belov'd.

[*p. 20*]

  Sad, horrid tale! by much too often told;
My worth is acres, and my virtues gold:
But as one blemish marrs an angel's face,
So wealth alone is coupled with disgrace.
Wealth without worth, serves only to assert,

† *Save, save yourselves*——The beauty of this line depends, in a great measure, upon the manner of speaking it; the closing of the eyes, the stretching out of the fingers, and mode of elevation: Borough Members have fine advantages this way, on a market day, from such spirited exertions.

- - - *Quem mirabantur Athenæ,*
Torrentem——[83]

82 Sir Edward Astley (1729–1802) MP for Norfolk (1768–1790): *Oxford DNB*. Pratt's brother Edward had married Blanche, Sir Edward Astley's sister, in 1751.

83 *DLCL*: Juvenal, *Satires*, 10:126–8 (p. 377). 'The object of Athens' admiration [was] twisting.' The full line reads 'Saevus et illum/ exitus eripuit, quem mirabantur Athenae/ torquentem et pleni moderantem frena theatri.' 'A harsh death snatched him away, too, the object of Athens' admiration when he was twisting and controlling the reins of her packed assembly.' The reference in the original satire is to Demosthenes, who committed suicide after speaking against Philip of Macedon in 322 B.C.

The rich man's claim to gilded hoards of dirt:
Inglorious triumph, when each sober clown,
Lives more at ease, less mean, with half-a-crown.
Fortune, blind dame! derides our mimic state,
Bends rich men down, and makes the needy, great;
Pours gifts and favours wheresoe'er she please,
And lifts a Curate—to a coach of ease:†
Then smiles to see her new-rais'd prelate ride,
To see him bend, and nod with holy pride:
The triple cure, and Sunday splash forgot;
'Tis now, *Jehu!*[84] Your *Honour!* and what not!
Smote with surprize, we stand aloof, and stare;
We gaze, we think, and wonder what we are—
These are thy whims, O Fortune! these thy deeds;
'Tis thou canst turn to joy the widow's weeds:
By thee th' apprentice,§ long inur'd to wipe,
The rich adhesions of the ivory pipe,

[*p. 21*]

Mounts up to honours, and a full display,
And reigns the *pestled*[85] monarch of a day.——
  Grant me, good Heav'n! my humble wish to live,
Pleas'd and contented, with the gifts you give:
Nor be my lot so high, that with disdain,
The looking down may turn my giddy brain:

† *And lifts a Curate——Ut tu fortunam, sic nos te, Celse, feremus.*[86]

§ *By thee th' apprentice*----Sudden elevation in life is frequently too rapid for tender spirits to undergo: when the deputy grave-digger of a certain parish was told, that he would certainly be made under-sexton at the Easter meeting, the poor fellow went away overjoy'd, with tears in his eyes, muttering to himself - - - The Lord's will be done, for it is his doing, and not mine——

84 A king of Israel who lived *c.* 842–815 BC. He appears in 1 and 2 Kings and 1 and 2 Chronicles in the Bible.

85 Forced into a shape or role: *OED*.

86 *DLCL*: Horace, *Epistles I*, 8:17 (p. 307) 'As you bear your fortune, Celsus, so we shall bear with you.'

Teach me to shun each dangerous extream,
Not idly poor, nor opulently mean.——
   And should there be superior plagues design'd,
One greater curse than all, to blast mankind;
His be that lot, who with a tyrant's frown,
Lives and presumes—this world to be his own;
Who joys to fill the aching heart with fear,
To bind no wound, nor stop the trickling tear;
A mean self-love, and over-weening pride,
Ill-natur'd spleen, and passion for his guide.—
   Foul fiend, avaunt![§] griping monopoly!
To thee the churl, the niggard bends the knee;
Thy baleful taint corrodes the lib'ral mind,
The heart which loves, and lives for all mankind.---

[*p. 22*]

The love of pow'r, and horrid rage of sway,
Oft leads good-nature, and good sense astray.--
Yes, he was once both good and gentle found,
Till Fortune curs'd him—with some miles of ground:
Now *manor-mad*, he dreams of slaughter'd game,
And Heav'n is storm'd,* if Pero[87] should be lame.

§ *Foul fiend, avaunt*!-----Where a turbulent, inordinate passion for game prevails, too many instances are not wanting to prove, that neither vicinity, affinity, or the most amiable qualities of the heart, can possibly preserve for a time the peace and good fellowship of a neighbourhood.

Bella, horrida bella——[88]

* And Heav'n is storm'd----It is almost impossible to conceive, what a hurricane is made in a family from the trivial accident of a scalded puppy, or from the impression of the maid's patten on the ear of Juba.

Miscentur; Magnisq; vocant clamoribus hostem.[89]

87 This dog is named after a princess from Pylos, whose father tried to keep her away from her many suitors, mentioned in Homer's *Odyssey* and in the writings of Apollodorus.

88 *DLCL*: Virgil, *Aeneid*, 6:86 (p. 539) 'wars, grim wars'.

89 *DLCL*: Virgil, *Georgics*, 4:76 (p. 223) 'with loud cries [they] challenge the foe'.

Him, skill'd in sports, sleek Obadiah[90] bred,[§]
And Ruth's fair hand would often pat his head:
What heart so hard, but must for Pero bleed,
Sweet son of Don, and sprung from Dido's[91] breed.
The fabled youth[†] embrac'd his cat for life;
Take thou, sweet boy, thy Sappho for a wife.---
Not Mira's smiles, or Delia's charms avail,
Love rides triumphant on the pointer's tail;
All hearts give way to see Castalia drest,
But then dear Juno holds her head the best:
We mourn a parent, and lament his end,
But Don, dear dog, is father, wife, and friend;
Our waking thoughts, our ev'ning theme the same,
The one dear subject of eternal game.---

[*p. 23*]

Minions attend! my noble Sir declares,
"Zounds! Fire and blood! I'm plunder'd of my hares."
Curst be the thought! shall little tradesmen join,
To roast our game, and drench themselves with wine?
O, horrid times, and greatly to be fear'd,

§ - - - *Sleek Obadiah bred*. Vide Barclay's Apology.[92]

† *The fabled youth*----In Æsops Fables, a young man is married to his cat.[93]

---

90 This dog is named after prophet Obadiah, who, according to the Bible, though originally an Edomite, converted to Judaism and used all his wealth to shelter 100 prophets from Jezebel's persecution, for which God bestowed on him the gift of prophecy.

91 On Dido see *The Coal-Heavers*, note 38 (p. 158 in this edition).

92 Pratt refers to the attack on sports made by Robert Barclay (1648–1690), an influential Quaker leader from Scotland. See Barclay, *An Apology for the True Christian Divinity* (?London, 1678), pp. 366–9. Pratt had this book in his library (Octavos, 98).

93 In Aesop's fables, either Jupiter or Venus (depending on the version of the fable) turns a cat into a young woman and a young man marries her but when the maiden sees a mouse, she starts chasing it, which proves that nature is stronger than nurture, and the gods change transform the woman back into her original feline form.

When bread-sauce trickles down† the trader's beard!
Portentous times, with ev'ry ill replete,
When little souls inordinately eat!
O! but my passion is too strong to last,
All order dies, and decency is past;
Pertness and folly mark each flippant owl,
And starv'd attornies perk their ears, and growl.
Gods! shall our tradesmen sit with horrid grin,
O'er roasted pheasants, napkin'd to the chin?
Stretch out their limbs, with pert Parnassian sneer,
And drink Madeira, like a banker's heir;
With noise and nonsense ev'ry ear confound,
Then break, and pay five shillings to the pound?
Alas! alas! good sisters§ of the loom,
Cut short our thread, and seal Britannia's doom.---

[*p. 24*]

"Go forth, my men,* set all your traps around,
"No foot unpunish'd treads my hallow'd ground.

† *When bread-sauce trickles down*----We will not pronounce it felony, or sacrilege, for a tradesman to eat bread-sauce; but we will venture to prophesy, that except they are paid their demands better, than some of them are at present, they will have little or no bread to eat.

Waste book, page 45, *&c. &c. &c*

§ *Alas! alas! good sisters*----Alluding to the three sisters, who are supposed to spin the thread of man's life.[94]

* *Go forth, my men*-----Patent man-traps are soon expected in Norfolk, so curiously contrived, as to evacuate the body at once of all its blood, juices and marrow, with the greatest freedom; dragging out, and destroying in the nearest manner, every nerve, muscle and sinew; so that the person trap'd must expire immediately in the most pleasing and agreeable agonies.----*Suetonius Life of Nero.*[95]

Messrs. Buller & Co. Birmingham.[96]

94 According to Greek mythology, the three fates (Μοῖραι) spun the thread of every person's life and controlled its length.

95 Gaius Suetonius Tranquillus (*c.* AD 69–after 122) wrote biographies of the first twelve Roman emperors. His chapter on Nero's reign became a chief source for accounts of the emperor's many eccentricities, perversions, and acts of cruelty.

96 Presumably the firm of Buller & Co. in Birmingham were involved in the construction and selling of man traps, but we have not found evidence of the business operating.

"Hark! Do I hear? A dog! a dog! Pursue!
"Run, Sam! ride, Joseph! follow you and you!
"Off with his head†—so much for curs like these;
"Be this my fiat, and my heart's at ease."
My great Achilles, (thus old Homer speaks)
And if we moderns might translate from Greeks,
Such were his words—"Pelides, born to wield,
"Tame thy big soul, thou thund'rer of the field."[97]---
Smote with concern, we trembling drop the pen,
And grieve to find such rage in *little* men.
But let not here pert fancy's busy tongue,
Condemn the verse, and think our labours wrong:
No foul detractions reach the muse's ear;
She draws from life, and paints what mortals are;
Holds up the mirror, as they pass in view,
Yet grieves to find her portraits should be true.
  Pleas'd with a whim, let fancy here describe,
The sporting Squiret[98] in his autumn pride;

[*p. 25*]

Neat in nankeen,[99] of form genteel and strait,
In gentle sing-song, swinging in his gait---
As much of man, as nature chose to give,
As much the maid, as could with manhood live:
The folded arms around his gun are seen,
With white-topt gloves, and net extremely clean;
The club's long ribbon waving in the wind,
With flint half out, and powder left behind.

† *Off with his head*----Alluding to one of Shakespeare's plays:
"Off with his head---so much for Buckingham."[100]

97 An alternative name for Achilles (after his father Peleus).

98 i.e. a little squire.

99 A type of cotton cloth, originally made in Nanking, China: *OED*.

100 The line is actually from Colley Cibber's adaptation of Shakespeare's *Richard III* (1699) and does not appear in Shakespeare's quarto or folio versions of *Richard III* (*c.* 1592–1594). The words 'Off with his head' (*Shak*, 3.4.75) does, however, appear in Shakespeare's *Richard III*, but refers to Hastings rather than Buckingham.

Old sullen pointers, half asham'd to go,
Sneak close behind, and slily snuff the beau.
Partridge, or pigeon, 'tis the same to him,
John grins applause, and Master has his whim:
Proceed, dear creature, and your sports pursue,
We only wish one thousand such as you.*
   Come, my adepts! my abler sportsmen, say!
Ye who can stop the whirring pheasant's way;
Fam'd for your sports, and mighty scenes of blood,
Dash thro' the ford; or rush along the wood:
Must we all listen, and your tales attend?
Told twenty times, yet never to the end:
Must half your kennels round the hearths extend,
And, unmolested, poison wife or friend?

[*p. 26*]

Pour forth rich scents of meals, in full decay,
Till Miss turns sick, and Madam faints away?
"O! I shall die! Good Gods! What must be done?
"Pho! bring the drops;† my dearest Betsy, run!
"Die? No, good Ladies, that's a horrid sight—
"The *School for Scandal*[101] claims your hearts to-night."—
Or, shall young Fop with poultry limbs be fed,
And saucy pointers snatch the children's bread?
Wives, half asham'd, put forth the serious pish,

* *We only wish one thousand such as you.----Noverint universi*[102]----That the characters here drawn by this writer have the quality of the trooper's boot, that would fit any leg whatever. If any description here suits any one particular gentleman, and fits easy with him, he is welcome to use it at his own discretion.

† *Pho! bring the drops*——Too many dogs in a parlour, must be *fundamentally* wrong, and hurtful to the olfactory nerves of those gentlemen in the Minority, who are smelling out the foul Works of the Ministry with great discernment.

NASO.[103]

---

101 A 1777 play by Richard Sheridan (1751–1816).

102 The Latin phrase '*Noverint universi*' is common in legal documents and means 'let all men know'.

103 A play on the Latin for nose (nasus) and on Ovid's full name Publius Ovidius Naso.

And gently whisper, "Pray, Sir, change the dish."
Coarse wit, with freedom, hurts the tender wife,
And courtship should be kept alive for life.---
Nor can the muse, without a blush, impart,
How wives, with hunters, share the sportsman's heart:
The doctor wanted---"Sir, may Bumper go?"
"No, John. The filly?" "No. Your honour? No.
"The chestnut gelding, now his sweats are o'er,
"Might"—"Curse the fellow! leave me, shut the door."
The tenant's hack, poor jaded, borrow'd wretch,
Gallops for all, from fevers to the itch.
  Say next, what storms the smallest ills produce?
Jack sinew-strain'd, or Pero kills a goose;

[*p. 27*]

Or, worse than death, the Curate in the wood;
Trap him, by G—, and sluice him of his blood:
"Shall he, shall they, shall these my covers[104] force?
"A horse! a horse! my manors for a horse!"[105]
Good Heav'n! are these for marriage rites design'd?
(O lost to sense, and impotent of mind!)
Unhappy women! for such arms decreed;---
Mere sportsmen are---mere animals indeed.‡—
  Blest be that maid, whose soft persuasive charms,
Can draw the sporting ideot to her arms:
Blest wives, to hear the early flounce from bed,
The deep hoarse cough, and doors that split the head;
The hall's loud eccho, and the thund'ring sounds
Of ham-stuff'd sportsmen, and the roar of hounds!
Each place a chaos, in confusion lies;

‡ *Mere sportsmen are---mere animals indeed.*---Field amusements are joyous, rational and manly; but the eternal pursuit of game, as the practice of some of our modern sportsmen is, makes it rather a nusance than an entertainment.

Ne quid nimis——[106]

---

104 In the sense of foliage in which game animals and birds can be found: *OED*.

105 Parodying King Richard's line from *Richard III*: 'A horse! A horse! My kingdom for a horse!' (*Shak*, 5.3.361).

106 A common Latin phrase meaning 'nothing in excess'.

Rolls pil'd on rolls, and pigeons torn from pies:
Rush on to horse: hark forward! and away;
And yawning maids sit down to toast and tea.
Wives, piteous things! drag on the winter day,
With squalling brats, and dinners burnt away;
Behold at night their dear *adorers* doze,
And pour the concert thro' the vocal nose.---

[*p. 28*]

Nor do our sportsmen's labours of the day,
End with the sun, tho' sunk its Western ray:
In dreams they start, with more than labour's[107] throes;
Whoup! Tally ho! Hark forward! there he goes!
Windsor is spur'd, or else in *Windsor*'s stead,
Their own *dear* wives[‡] are tumbled out of bed:
Good sense, good-nature too, must fix the bounds,
Men should be men, not company for hounds.
Nor let old Thunder's praise be ever sung,
When softer music flows from woman's tongue:
A thousand charms in Charlotte's dimples dwell,
But thou art blest—young Sancho points so well.
What's wife, a daughter, or an angel's face,
To a net swelling with a good *five brace?*
Women may charm, and marriage joys delight,
But a full covey is a glorious sight.

‡ *Their own dear wives*----The power of the imagination in sleep is very wonderful; whether the exertion of the soul at that time is greater than at another, must be left to the decision of the learned; but this we certainly know, that both our hands and feet are uncommonly merry and pleasant in the time of dreaming,
Vide Priestly's Disquisitions.[108]

107 'Labour" in the original text.

108 Joseph Priestley (1733–1804), was a unitarian theologian, natural philosopher, and polymath, known in particular for his liberal theology and advocacy for political reforms. In *Disquisitions Relating to Matter and Spirit* (1777), he argues against the view that the phenomenon of people seeing objects while dreaming and sleepwalking implies that the mind is not a material or extended substance. See Joseph Priestley, *Disquisitions Relating to Matter and Spirit* (London: J. Johnson, 1777), pp. 38–9. Pratt had a copy of Priestley's *Disquisitions* in his library (Octavo, no.19). We cite the edition that Pratt had in his library.

What! tho' thy pointers boast superior speed,
Range well and wide, and sprung from *Doxy*'s breed;
Yet spare our ears, nor pour th' eternal tale;
Here *Turko* stood, there *Mungo* caught the gale:

[*p. 29*]

From hill to vale, we drove the covey round,
Till the last bird,[§] with vengeance, thump'd the ground.---
So strange thy tale, the very servants stare,
And seem to say, by G— he was not there.---
Minor, attend! nor let thy throbbing heart,
Pant to possess those joys the fields impart:
Maturer age holds up this wholesome truth;
No time redeems the idle hours of youth.
Art thou a clerk? ingross in sober peace,
Remove the pointer, and renew the lease.
Doom'd to a shop?* be thy attention there,
Nor lose the Squire, by coursing of a hare:
Fix'd in thy calling, shun each roving thought,
One plan is best——Variety a fault.—
Prudence forewarns, and sober laws prescribe
Just bounds, that sportsmen may not err too wide;
Yet idle pleasure, play-thing of a day,
Calls forth her sons, and folly leads the way;

§ *Till the last bird*-----Nothing so kind and affectionate as game is; by the use of a certain *machine*, you may turn it into lamb, brawn, sturgeon, or any thing you choose to have: in some families, the game is supposed to be a saving of near twenty pounds a year, in the great article of houskeeping.

Hinc illæ Lachrymæ. - - -[109]

* *Doom'd to a shop*----Unexperienced young gentlemen will sometimes purchase a little game, when it can be had, to save appearances; and this is certainly better, than stuffing the dumb bag with brown paper, dog's couples, or turnip tops.

- - - *Æternæ quærens præconia famæ*.[110]

109 A common Latin phrase meaning 'hence those tears'.

110 'Braggarts seeking eternal fame' (our translation). The phrase appears in many thesauruses of Latin phrases from the sixteenth century onwards.

[*p. 30*]

Too soon undone, they sink in sad despair,
And lose in jail,† their liberty and air.—
Madness severe! just twenty-one--Canst thou
Waste the hard savings of thy father's plow?
Drove out from men, unpity'd and unknown,
To glean those acres, which were once your own.—
Distress and want the fractur'd spendthrift feels,
Yet whistles on, with pointer at his heels.—
Say then, ye wise! for ye can well define,
Where must good sense, and order draw the line?
Where fix the bounds, that sportsmen should obey,
'Twixt lawless insult, and the love of sway?
Far from the mind be that injurious thought;
In distant fields, no murder is a fault:
These dire Macbeths cry out, "Lay on, Macduff,
"And damn'd be he, who first calls, Hold, enough."[111]
But stay, free-booter! stop thy murd'ring hand,
Nor claim dominion o'er another's land:
Know, Moderation‡ is of heav'nly mien,
And of all virtues, Decency is queen.

[*p. 31*]

What, but the law, defends thy flocks and fleece,
Secures thy house, and makes thee sleep in peace?
The same good laws defend another's right,

† *And lose in jail*-----It was very unfortunate for a certain gentleman to be hurried to prison before the hunting season was entirely over; as he had certainly an estate of one hundred pounds a year, with a mortgage upon it of very little more than two thousand pounds.

VERITAS.

‡ *Know, Moderation*-----Instances are not wanted to prove, that those over-tenacious gentlemen of their own game at home, in an enemy's country (that is, from home) are very inordinate in their sporting.

---

111 Slightly misquoting Shakespeare's *Macbeth*: 'Lay on, Macduff,/ And damned be him, that first cries, "Hold, enough"' (*Shak*, 5.7.72–3).

His game by day, his property by night.
Weigh well their force; be decency your rule,
He who breaks thro', is wantonly a fool.—
And should ill-fortune place thy manors there,
Where corp'rate troops descend without a fear;
Where stiff mechanics leave the council board,
To ride down pudding, and to stare abroad;
Bear it with patience, for their trade is such,
They give too little, and they take too much.—
   True sporting is true honour, temper'd right,
Not the dumb-bag[112] that's disembogued by night:
Not him, who spares no sex, no times, no age,
But deals his fire with unremitting rage;
Not him, whose vacant mind for ever loves
To haunt the fields, the meadows, and the groves;
Mere winter drudge, a dull, laborious ass,
Who half exists, the hunters turn'd to grass:
Nor let the priesthood idly entertain,
The thought—their Master liv'd and dy'd in vain:
His was the seed, but theirs the full increase,
And they should labour, who would share the fleece:

[*p. 32*]

Nor trudge the field, in one eternal round,
Whilst Jerom moulds,[‡][113] and Austin lies unbound.
   No! he sports best, and with the most applause,
Who hunts for wisdom, and consults her laws;
Beats classic ground,[114] where sportive muses twine

‡ *Whilst Jerom moulds*-----Poor dear Jerom---you must never expect a better coat, whilst your master has almost his own by the thorns and bushes.---Nothing so subject to be torn as black cloth.

112 We have not found this phrase attested elsewhere, but presumably it refers to the poacher's bag for game.

113 i.e. moults.

114 See note 22 above, p. 171 of our edition.

Their laureat wreaths for brows, soft GRAY,[115] like thine;
Where bards seraphic tun'd their lyres to please,
Where MILTON soar'd, and HORACE walk'd with ease:
Above the sportsman's rant, the loud regale,
The song, the bumper,[116] and the thread-bare tale.
   Nor yet un-nerv'd, nor yet without the pride,
To hang the first dear woodcock at my side;
Teach me, sweet month, thy jovial rites to praise,
And hug the thought of youthful, sporting days:
Sweet are the tales, and pleasant to rehearse,
Are youthful deeds, when dignify'd with verse:
Sweet days! when joy stood tip-toe in the eye,
And pulse beat quicker, as the covies fly:
The breezy morn, the gun's imperial roar;
The pointers bursting from the kennel door;
The maid's long visage, and obdurate frown,
The sly arch boy, the muffins tumbled down;

[*p. 33*]

The wayward hobby, seldom to be caught,
The dog run home, (sad dog!) too dearly bought;
The busy bustle,* and the ideot stare,
And things mislaid, and gone--the lord knows where--
Life's giddy rage, when rapid blood flows on;

* *The busy bustle*-----This description of a sporting morning is undoubtedly natural, if not political. The writer, we suspect, is a man of fire himself, (a sad dog most likely) but whether he shoots clean, or mangles his game in this work, must be left to his readers to determine.

Monthly Reviewers.

115 Thomas Gray (1716–1771), poet and scholar at Pembroke College, Cambridge University. Gray was offered the poet laureateship but declined it. His 'An Elegy Written in a Country Churchyard' (1751) became one of the most well-known poems of the mid-eighteenth century.

116 A glass completely filled with an alcoholic beverage: *OED*.

"Farewell! farewell![†] my occupation's gone."---
Now wrapt in thought, I strole the wat'ry mead,
The woodcock twitt'ring o'er my pensive head;
Fond to explore what pleasures make us blest,
What part of life is fittest and the best.
Whether in youth, when fev'rish blood runs high,
And mounting fire darts trembling from the eye;
The frolic dance, soft sounds, and rosy feast,
Or the sweet snow which heaves on Kitty's breast?
Or, are our joys to sober years confin'd?
When kind reflection jogs the absent mind;
When prudence shews the paths we should pursue,
And age finds out, that life has nothing new.

[*p. 34*]

My reason starts, and sober truths prevail,
And future hopes drop in and turn the scale.--
What tho' our summer days too fast decline,
And winter life* can scarce be said to shine;
Yet age has this one blessing left---to hear
Faults once its own with mild attentive ear;
To judge with candour, and with truth defend;

† *Farewell*! *Farewell!*----By this and the following lines, we may easily perceive the decline of the old sportsman, Dead, Dead, Dead! To save the Reviewers the trouble of hulking him, we recommend to him the following adage:

Lustisti satis, edisti satis, atq; *bibisti,*
Tempus abire tibi est——[117]

* *And winter life*---Old men should never forget that they have been young, as the utmost allowance should be made for the indiscretions of youth, and the extravagance of the passions.

Seneca, de Senectute.[118]

117 *DLCL*: Horace, *Epistles II*, 2:214–15 (p. 441) 'You have played enough, have eaten and drunk enough. 'Tis time to quit the feast.'

118 'De Senectute', an essay on the subject of growing old and dying, is actually by Cicero but Pratt is probably misattributing it on purpose for the sake of the chime of 'Seneca' and 'Senectute'.

And sportsman once,† be ev'ry sportsman's friend.
O PHAON!‡[119] blest with nature's richest store,
So well accomplish'd, that we wish no more;
O thou! all but the very thing approv'd,
Of virtues shaded, yet by all belov'd:
Life's greatest ills from high examples flow,
As smallest specks are soon observ'd on snow:
Pleas'd with thy youth, thy virtues were our boast;
But, ah! how soon were all thy blossoms lost.

[*p. 35*]

Thus early fruits, which most attract the eye,
Fall with the whirlwind and untimely die.---
Too early lost, a prey to woman's art,
Love finds no way to reach thy captur'd heart.
Shun woman's wiles, is wisdom's wholesome rule;
Bad custom's vice, and fashion makes the fool:
Time wipes the honey from the flatt'rer's tongue,
And future years will prove thy passion wrong:
Pass but a time, thy fields, thy manors gone,

† *And sportsman once*----Anonymous advertisements have often appeared in the Norwich Mercury, for the meeting of Gentlemen at Swaffham in Norfolk to protect their tenants: Old Sportsmen, who can smell a fox at a distance, suppose this to mean nothing more than the protection of their own game.——Quere, If it may not be necessary soon for qualified gentlemen to associate in turn, to protect themselves and their own rights.

——*Timeo Danaos, et dona ferentes.*[120]

‡ *O Phaon*!---This Gentleman is of an amiable disposition, but lives unmarried.
SUFFOLK[121]

---

119 Phaon was Sappho's lover, who abandoned her and drove her to despair and suicide. The genders are reversed in the story that follows.

120 *DLCL*: Virgil, *Aeneid*, 2:49 (p. 319) 'I fear the Greeks, even when bringing gifts.' For the advertisements notifying the meeting of the 'Swaffham Association' 'THE Gentelmen associated for the Protecion of their Tenants at the Crown in Swaffham', see Saturday 6 December 1777, 25 September 1779, 27 February 1779, and 2 December 1780 in the *Norwich Mercury*.

121 'SUFFOLK' suggests that the gentleman in question is a bachelor residing in Suffolk—it is not clear who is meant.

And thy dear creature[122] drops a wife to John:
Then all thy faults† to ev'ry fool are known,
She stabs thy virtues to repair her own.
O gratitude, sweet boon! that Heav'n bestows
On feeling minds, to soften human woes;
The tainted soul thy blessing seldom knows,
Thy seat is there, where truth and virtue grows.
Like Ætna's flames, superior[123] as they rise,
The harlot's fire breaks forth at once and dies:
Superior joy to wedded love's confin'd,‖
Grows at the heart, and captivates the mind.

[*p. 36*]

Life of my life! O thou, whose gentle breast
Can sooth my soul and lull my thoughts to rest!
Source of my joy, by rites connubial mine,
Be all my life and all my thoughts like thine!
With thee conversing, each returning day
Springs with fresh joy, and sheds a brighter ray:
When fev'rish heats, or anxious thoughts molest,
Thy arm sustains and holds me to thy breast:
Not winter's spite or low'ring clouds displease,
If thou art there, my soul, my heart's at ease.

† *Then all thy faults*----Strange, indeed, that those very creatures, who are too frequently the successful instruments of ruining a man's fortune and character, should be (which is often the case) the first to censure and condemn him. Vice of every sort is mean and despicable.

‖ *Superior joy to wedded love's confin'd.*----This uxorious scribbler we suspect to be a surrogate himself by his recommending of matrimony so much; but the immorality of the times bids fair at present to set aside the use of licences and wedding fees.

- - - - - - *Mea Delia, Tecum*
Dummodo sim; quæso, segnis inersq; vocer.[124]

122 i.e. 'thy dear mistress'.

123 See the erratum at the end of the poem, which instructs the reader to read 'impetuous' for 'superior'—probably to avoid the repetition of 'superior' in line 705.

124 *DLCL*: Tibullus, *Elegies*, 1:57–8 (p. 197) 'Delia dear; let me only be with thee, and I will pray folk call me sluggard and idler'.

Accept, dear partner of my bed, my lays,
Unsung the theme---a married woman's praise!
Phaon, to thee this moral lay—attend!
Nor lost to virtue, rashly blame a friend---
If all thy actions on thy will depend,
Thine's mere existence to no useful end:
Slave to thy passions, hug thy gilded chain,
Tho' blest with fortunes and a wide domain;
The heart bleeds inward, tho' the face is gay,
Nor can forc'd mirth drive guilty thoughts away.
Ty'd to his stall, the poor unthinking beast,
The fatted ox, like you, enjoys the feast;
Snorts o'er his heap and proud disdainful breath,
Nor knows, poor fool, his feasting ends with death.
So thy own gifts abus'd and misapply'd,
Mean only this—he feasted, and he dy'd.

[p. 37]

Seek then a wife![†] let wedlock set you free,
And then my Phaon[125] may be blest as me.
Good sense, good conduct will her steps attend,
And wife be then united to the friend:
Fair peace, soft dalliance, and domestic ease,
Sweet mutual love, and ev'ry wish to please;
Life's thorny way with due contentment trod,

† *Seek then a wife*---The prevailing custom of keeping Mistresses, not only amongst the rich and great, but amongst inferiors of every sort, by the modern and fashionable appellation of House-keepers, becomes daily more alarming than ever: If this evil is not properly attended to, both by Magistrates and Clergy, the rebukes of such a writer as this are not worth regarding.

——*Quis enim non vicus abundat*
Tristibus obscenis? —— JUV.[126]

125 See note 119 above.

126 *DLCL*: Juvenal, *Satires*, 2:8–9 (p. 149) 'After all, isn't every street packed with grim-looking perverts?'

And easy faith,‖ which lifts the mind to God.--
Now free as air, and wanton as the wind,
Soft pleasure charms, and folly sooths thy mind:
But when Old Time shall brush thy hours away,
And future life breaks forth to open day;
Where then thy courser's pride, the goblet's charms,
Or the lewd surfeit of forbidden arms?
When strong convulsions tear thy lab'ring breath,
What friend has thou to smooth the bed of death?
In that sad hour what female hand applies,
To sooth thy pains, or close thy dying eyes?

[*p. 38*]

Too late convinc'd, you'll find the sure deceit,
Pleasure is vain, and idle life a cheat.
O! blest with sense, with judgment just and right,
Why should a wanton cloud my Phaon's sight?
Think, for thou must, a reck'ning to be fear'd,
Time flies apace and conscience will be heard;
And should (Heav'n grant it!) thy reforming life
Be blest with thought, with ease, and sober wife;
Pleas'd thou wilt say, (thy former faults forgot)
How blest, how happy is the *Husband*'s lot!
Surrounding cares and ev'ry pang will cease,
And thou, like me, shalt live and die in peace.

FINIS.

‖ *And easy faith*---By faith in this place is to be understood, that believing scriptural faith, that is neither alarmed at the disquisitions of Dr. P——y, or the heterogeneous publications of Mr. Th—— L-——y.[127]

Casaubon.[128]

127 On Joseph Priestley see note 108 (p. 195 in our edition) above; Theophilus Lindsey (1723–1808) was a unitarian minister and theologian and one of the signatories of the Feathers Tavern Petition. Priestley was among the friends who supported Lindsey financially after he resigned from his post in Catterick in protest over the Parliament's rejection of the petition: *Oxford DNB*.

128 Either the classical scholar Isaac Casaubon (1559–1614) or his son Méric (1599–1671), also a classical scholar. Probably the former, notorious for his pedantry, is meant.

[*p. 39*]

ERRATUM.

Page 35, Line 17, for *superior*, read, impetuous.[129]

129 We have let 'superior' stand in our edition.

Shorter Poems

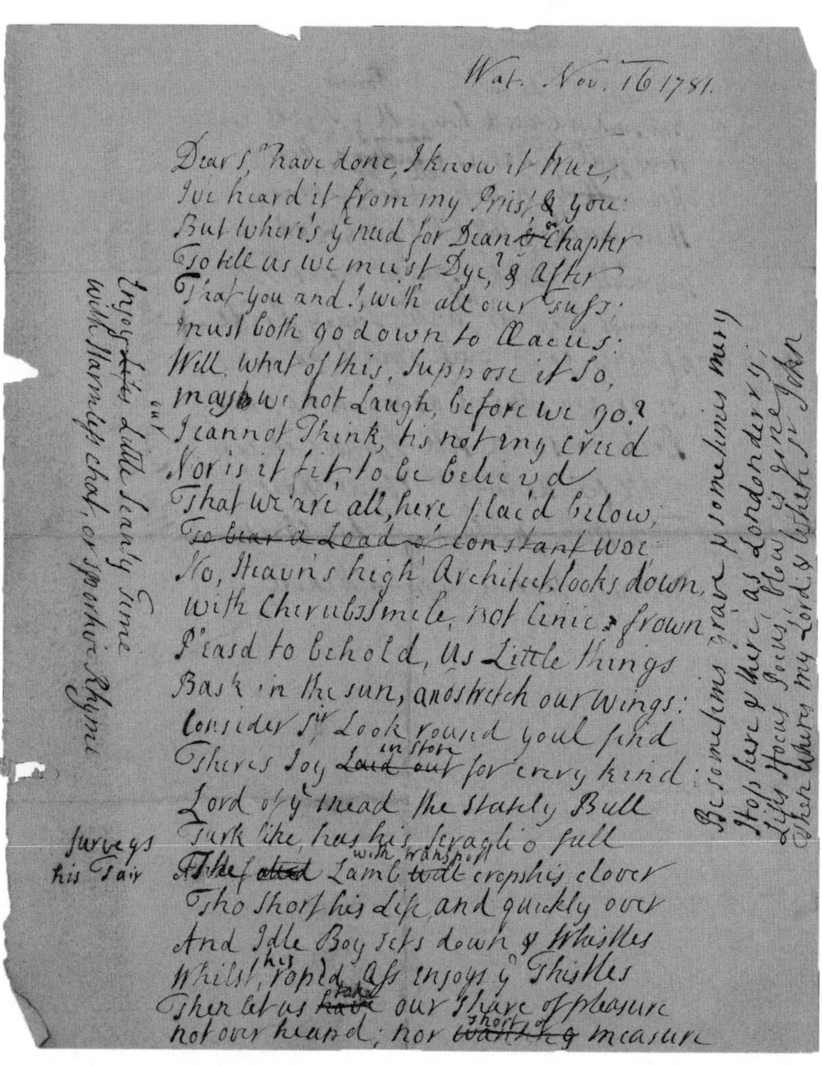

Wat. Nov. 16 1781.

Dear S, I have done, I know it true,
I've heard it from my Pris', & you:
But where's ye need for Dean & Chapter
To tell us we must Dye? & after
That you and I, with all our stuff,
must both go down to Aeacus:
Well. what of this, suppose it so,
may we not Laugh, before we go?
I cannot Think, tis not my creed
Nor is it fit, to be believ'd
That we're all, here plac'd below,
~~To bear a Load o' constant woe~~
No, Heav'n's high Architect, looks down,
with Cherub smile, not Cinic frown
Pleas'd to behold, us Little things
Bask in the sun, and stretch our Wings:
Consider Sr Look round you'l find
There's Joy ~~Laid out~~ in store for every kind:
Lord of ye mead the stately Bull
Turk like, has his Seraglio full
~~At the fatted~~ Lamb with transport crops his clover
Tho short his Life and quickly over
And Idle Boy sits down & Whistles
Whilst his roped Ass enjoys ye Thistles
Then let us ~~have~~ take our share of pleasure
not over heap'd; nor ~~wanting~~ short of measure

Enjoy ~~Life~~ our Little Scanty time
with Harmless chat, or sportive Rhyme

Surveys his Fair

Be sometimes grave & sometimes merry
Hop here & there, as Londonderry;
Life's Hocus Pocus; How is gone
Then where's my Lord & where's Sr John

Figure 9 *Page from 'Watlington, November 16, 1781'*

'Grunnelia or the Sow in the Dumps'

NRO WKC 7/56/7, 404X3

Date: Written soon before 22 February 1760 (the date of the letter itself).

Authorship: The poem is enclosed in a letter to William Windham and both the letter and the poem are in Pratt's hand.[1] The poem and letter is almost certainly by Pratt.

Physical Description: Letter and accompanying poem handwritten in ink on three sides of a single sheet of paper, folded once, in Pratt's hand, measuring (in its folded state) 20 cm by 32 cm.

[*f. 1r*]

To

Colonel Windham

[*f. 1v*]

Sir

Every thing y^{t} can be said to you of Mrs Windham by way of return, fuss, or compliment, would be so infinitely short of my design, y^{t} it must be inadequate to ye purpose; I must leave it to your own benevolence to repay you with interest, every sort of kindness, you so feelingly bestowd upon me & my poor sister[2]: I have now ye blessedness of being in my own great chair by my own still fire; I can now look down upon my Knucle of veal with

1 William Windham, Sr (1717–1761) of Felbrigg Hall in North Norfolk. Windham served as the lieutenant-colonel of the Western Battalion of the Norfolk Militia.

2 Pratt's sister Harriot had recently lost her husband Thurlow Stafford and she must have been visiting the Windhams at their seat at Felbrigg Hall when Jermyn was writing his letter.

wonderful composure, where a sly strip of bacon peeps from behind a colony of cabbage with smoaking alacrity: Grunnelia, (a Hampshire beauty) waits upon colonel Windham, If you find her too indelicate & dirty in expression consider her as she is, a Sow, & how difficult it is to pervert or stop y[e] powerul operations of nature: I must think most of our Writers of Pastoral extremely faulty for giving y[e] Sentiments of a Newton to y[e] carrier of a Pitch-fork: Their Shepherds & Shepherdesses (for no one Else is permitted to Love) put forth such exaggerated complimen^ts^, irregular wishes, & impracticable undertakings, y[t] they are frequently as Absurd, as even y[e] renonnd Orontes:[3] I sent Grunnelia some time since, to Soame Jenyns Esq[r4] & he was pleased to like it, If you find a few lines y[t] are natural or comical & should make you smile, it will answer every intention of sending it, and give real pleasure to him who begs leave to subscribe himself y[r] most ob:[t] & obliged Hum.[e] Sert

Stoake[5] Feb[y] 22[d] 1760 Jermyn Pratt

I beg our Compliments to M[rs] Windham & y[e] young Ladies, in my next to M[rs] Stafford,[6] you will receive (inclosed in her letter) some choice, & familiar words in the Norfolk phraseology.[7] Mention it not to M[rs] Stafford but a certain r[e]d coat with black buttons, appeared upon a great Occasion, Dii Superi.[8]

3 A reference to Oronte (often rendered 'Orontes' in English-language texts in the eighteenth century), a character in Molière's *The Misanthrope*, who uses an artificial and pretentious sonnet in an unsuccessful attempt to woo Célimène in the play.

4 Soame Jenyns (1704–1787), a writer of tracts and light verse, author of *A Free Enquiry into the Nature and Origin of Evil* (1756); successively MP for Cambridgeshire (1741–1754), Dunwich (1754–58), and Cambridge (1758–1780).

5 Stoke Ferry, just to the east of the parishes of Wereham and Wretton, which Pratt served as perpetual curate.

6 'M[rs] Stafford' is Harriot Stafford, Pratt's sister and the 'poor sister' referred to above, whose husband, Thurlow Stafford had died the month before on 29 January 1760. Thurlow Stafford had been a captain in the West Norfolk Militia.

7 This letter seems not to have survived.

8 'The gods above'. The 'r[e]d coat with black buttons' may have been a member of the Eastern Regiment of the Norfolk Militia, but not the Western Regiment, which used a grey uniform. The person referred to could also have been a regular soldier in the British Army. It is possible that Richard Gardiner is referred to here: he is said to have arrived back at Spithead from his adventures fighting in the Caribbean during the Seven Year's War on 5 October 1759: *Gard*, 71.

[*f.* 2*r*]

Grunnelia or ye Sow in the Dumps

Beneath an ample stys refreshing Shade,
In doleful dumps, a gentle Sow in laid,
When heaving from her breast a rueful groan,
She scrubd her A—e[9] & thus was heard to moan.
Ah! woeful day, Ah! day of woe she Cryd!
When tho' these pales my Grunnions Chap I spied.
His tinkling Eye-balls set my heart on fire
My Wriggling Tail betrayd a fierce desire
To the cleft door my tingling tail I turn'd
He lickt beneath and with vexation churnd,
A thousand kinder things entraptured said
And curst the day that ever Stys were made.
False were his vows, Alas! In vain I grieve,
But boars were born to swear, & sows believe,
Canst thou forget the time, ungrateful Hog?
I, saved thine ears from Goody Dobsons Dog,
Yet there her measley sow engaged thy Love
These Eyes were witness to the parting shove,
Yet then I hid thee, strove to Ease thy Smart,
And pist a flood upon the wounded part:
Say, would that sullen Dowdy do the Same?
Her neck is scaby, & one foot is Lame;
A wayward temper in her looks is Seen
But Love is blind, to every fault I ween;
Return my Grunnion, come my lovely Swine
My milk, my Acrons,[10] all I have is thine.
Two dainty T—s[11] each morn our Ploughmen S—e[12]
And thou my Love shall have ye biggest bite
When in ye Autumnal heat we range ye grove,
I'll bring the Juiciest crabs to cool my Love:
And when ye winter snows upon our Shed

9 i.e. 'Arse'.
10 Acorns.
11 i.e. 'Turds'.
12 i.e. 'Shite'.

I'll bring the clean Horse-muck for my Grunnions bed.
Ah! silly sow he Views thee with disdain
Vain are thy Gifts thy proferd service vain
In that Loved breast no longer claim a part,
Dame Dobsons sow<'s> is Mistress of his heart:
Yet once my form his fickle mind could please
When first he twigd me in the Parsons pease:

[*f. 2v*]

And sure my beauty is not altered quite
My eyes still sparkle, & my teeth are white;
The neighbouring boars to me their homage pay
Why art thou prouder & more hard than they?
Our Vicars brawn the Stoutest of his kind,
Whose double wallet sways a load behind
An humble suitor at my roof appears
And hazards for my sake his small remains of Ears.
Pignelion too ye widows Dapper boar
Whose dainty frame ne'er felt ye cold before,
His love all night, grunts to ye Inclement Sky
Proud to catch cold beneath my dripping Sty
In vain they Sue, I scorn their Odious Love
No sighs can soften, or distress can move;
Constant for thee my heart forever burns
As in thy absence it forever mourns.
O! could my amorous wishes ought avail
An humble Louse Id live beneath thy tail
To range those fragrant hills of sweetness o'er
Could mortal<'s> sows ambition covet more?
Yet what were Life If I must still dispair,
His Love alone can make it worth my care.
Die, Die, Gurnnelia, End thy fatal smart
Dame Dobsons sow is mistress of his heart
Thus wailed she tearful to herself alone
Y^e hollow tubs reecchoing every groan,
When Cicely from ye Dairy screamd aloud
Whose well known voice collects ye grunting croud
Hogs, boars, Pigs, Pignies, with discordant din
Rush to her Pail and dash through thick & thin,

She starts, she cocks y[e] remnant of her Ears
Her Grunnions voice she hears, or thinks she hears;
And now his honest front appears in view
And her heart flutt'erd as he nearer drew
His short, snub snout, he thrust beneath ye floor
And with one heave, he swangs it on y[e] floor.
Neglects his supper to remove her pain,
And bottle-screw'd her, till she squeakd again.

‘The Death of the Woodcock’

PRA 664: ***Norwich Mercury*****, 19 October 1765, p. 2.**

Date: 19 October 1765 (date of publication).

Authorship: There is a strong possibility Pratt wrote this poem on the basis of the clipping of the poem being included in the Pratt folder, which also includes a clipping of the poems ‘Political Duck-Hunting’ and ‘The Sunday Visit’ from the *Norwich Mercury*, which we are confident in attributing to him. The clipping has not been given its own reference code.

Physical Description: Newspaper clipping of a poem measuring 7.5 cm by 12.5 cm.

[*f. 1r*]

For the NORWICH MERCURY.

As the approaching Moon gives us the pleasing expectation of that Illustrious Foreigner, the WOODCOCK,[1] the following VERSES perhaps may be agreeable to some of your Readers.

The Death of the WOODCOCK.

Up rose the Morn; and with the Herculean Stride,
The well-nerved Sportsman, flushed with rosy Joy,
Springs o’er the Dale, to reach the distant Hill,
To wake the WOODCOCK in his thorny Bed.

1 Woodcocks are game birds with a wide range across Europe and Asia, prized for both their meat and feathers. Until the middle of the nineteenth century, when large scale creation of pheasant coverts facilitated their breeding and led to increase in their numbers, they were more commonly to be found in the winter months, hence Pratt’s designation of the woodcock as a ‘foreigner’.

Say, was it not O Cynthio[2] speak! A Cock
Who twitterd from the left with hasty Glide.——
Thrice hail, Illustrious Bird—O Juba,[3] Bounce,
Ye Friends, by Goodness, as in Blood allied?
Remember Hoary Whipster's[4] matchless deeds,
Whipster's high fame, and emulate your Sire.
Big Expectation, with obsequious Leer
Dance in their Eyes, with sympathizing Glee
They kiss the Hand—Then with impetuous rush
Dart on, and make the quivering Thicket crack;
Climb the steep Bank, and pry the scooped Ditch.
Upwards he tow'rs, and for a Time impends;
Oh! Spare him yet, Inexorable Wretch
And save a helpless Foreigner from Death.
In vain—'tis off—the fiery Engine smokes
A thousand Deaths, and gives a thousand Wounds:
Writhing in Air with agonizing Lead
Drops on a Bough, his momentary stay;
Then falls a victim to th' exulting Crew.
Ill-fated Bird, where Instinct seems to act
With niggardly Affection—doomed to fly
Thy native Soil, for Fields of Foreign woe!
Ah, what avails thy full-orb'd lucid Eye,
Thy rich-waved Breast, and Feathers dropt with gold.
O blind to Fate, and prodigal of Life,
No more shalt thou in sportive Mazes, play
Thy twittering Gambols, in the liquid Air:
Nought can escape the Curate's ravening Maw.
More fell than Storms or Wind, that waft thee here.
And thou, proud Youth, now flush'd, with giddy Joy,
Beware in Time, of Sappho's matchless Charms:
Thou too, may'st fall a Victim to the Fair;
Fade in thy Bloom, and die in hopeless Love.

2 Nickname of Giovanni Battista Giraldi (1504–1573), a notable Italian author of poetry, prose, and drama. Shakespeare used his stories from *Hecatommithi* for the plots of *Othello* and *Measure for Measure*. In the poem, 'Cynthio', 'Juba', and 'Bounce' are names given to hunting dogs.

3 Foliage of trees: *OED*.

4 One who drives horses with a whip: *OED*. 'Whipster' is the name of the dog who was the father of Juba and Bounce, now deceased.

Two Squibs on the 1768 Norfolk Election

Norwich Mercury, **2 January 1768, p. 3. (The mock newspaper article)**

Norwich Mercury, **16 January 1768, p. 3. ('To Mr. Anti-Puff')**

Dates: 1 January 1768 (date given as the date of composition for the mock newspaper article) and 13 January 1768 (date given as the date of composition for 'Mr. Anti-Puff').

Authorship: The attribution to Pratt for both the mock newspaper article and 'Mr. Anti-Puff' is on the basis of the reference to Pratt's brother Edward as 'Pretty Pratty' and to Jermyn Pratt himself as 'J——n P——-' in the answer poem 'To Mr. Ranti-Puff' (reproduced in Appendix 1) as well as Pratt's connection with Downham Market and his involvement in the Norfolk elections and local politics. The likely author of the response to the first squib is the Reverend Robert Potter, based on the fact that the poem 'To Mr. Ranti-Puff' is attributed to Potter in a handwritten note in one of the copies of *The Contest* in the British Library (shelfmark 8135.bb.85.(5.), p. 68), in which both the squibs are reproduced. For an overview of the exchange see our Introduction, pp. 41–2. For Potter's letter replying to the mock newspaper article and verse reply to Pratt's 'Mr. Anti-Puff' ('To Mr. Ranti-Puff') see the appendix.

Physical Description: A mock-newspaper article measuring 7 cm by 4.2 cm (A Mock Newspaper Article on the Canvassing at Downham Market) and a newspaper poem measuring 7 cm by 6 cm '(To Mr. Anti-Puff').

a) A Mock Newspaper Article on the Canvassing at Downham Market[1]

[*p. 3*]

NORWICH, Jan. 1, 1768.

We hear from Downham, that Colonels W——and D——[2] marched into the Town Monday the 28th of December last, preceded by the *Military Insignia* of Colours, Drums and Fifes, to beat up for VOLUNTEERS, but it so unluckily happened, that not one *single Recruit* appeared, either at the *Drum's-Head* or at their *Quarters*.

The Sons of FREEDOM, to the Number of *Ninety-four*, having *previously* and *constitutionally inlisted* themselves in the honourable Corps of A—— and C——[3] under the Banner of LIBERTY, and were inrolled accordingly; upon which Occasion, the Evening was concluded with the utmost Unanimity, Joy and Harmony.

1 This mock newspaper article was also published in the *Cambridge Chronicle*, 2 January 1768, p. 2 and the *Ipswich Journal*, 2 January 1768, p. 3.

2 Sir Armine Wodehouse (1714–1777), MP for Norfolk and colonel of the East Norfolk Militia and Thomas De Grey (1717–1781), MP for Norfolk and lieutenant-colonel of the West Norfolk Militia.

3 Wenman Coke (1717–1776) and Sir Edward Astley (1729–1802), the challengers of De Grey and Wodehouse for the Norfolk county seat.

b) 'To Mr. Anti-Puff'[4]

[*p. 3*]

To Mr. ANTI-PUFF.

Hit 'em again Chicken.[5]

DOWNHAM, *Jan.* 14, 1768

I.

WHO first began to puff and crack and boast
From Yarmouth, Wells—and down along the Coast?
HOLKHAM'S rich Heir?[6] or sweet Sir ARM—, say?
Imperious AST—Y? or the meek De G—Y,
Whose gentle Carriage steals all Hearts away,

II.

ILLEGAL and not warranted by Law,
Who from these Words could *different* Meanings draw?
HOLKHAM's rich Heir? or sweet Sir ARM—, say
Imperious AST—Y? or the meek De G—Y,
Whose gentle Carriage steals all Hearts away,

HARK FORWARD! RANTI-PUFF.

And if you have Sense to balance a Straw,
You'll soon take a Hint from the Picture I draw, &c.

---

4 This squib was also published in the *Cambridge Chronicle*, 16 January 1768, p. 2.

5 Richard Gardiner had used this phrase as one of the two epitaphs for *A Letter to John Shadwell, Esq; of the County of N--rf--lk* (London: J. Swan, 1754).

6 Wenman Coke, whose residence was at Holkham Hall in North Norfolk.

Cinderetta

NRO PRA 664/251

Date: 19 March 1768 (as recorded in the poem itself).

Authorship: There is no manuscript in Pratt's hand but there are two copies of the printed poem in the Pratt folder. The poem also appears in *The Contest* (1768), a miscellany of material in both verse and prose published on the occasion of the contested 1768 election. It is noted that the poem is said to be by Pratt in a handwritten note in one of the two copies of *The Contest* in the British Library (Shelfmark 8135.bb.85.(5.), p. 129). The poem is also clearly modelled on 'Grunnelia or the Sow in the Dumps' which we are sure is by Pratt. We are confident in attributing this poem to Pratt.

Physical description: A single-sided printed poem measuring 21 cm by 33 cm.

[*f. 1r*]

CINDERETTA:

A MOCK-PASTORAL.

Detur Digniori.[2]

DOWN dropt her Brush; the Dish-cloth thrown aside;
And lost was all the Kitchen's silver Pride;
Scarce would the deep majestic Bellows blow,

1 There is also another printing of *Cinderetta* in the Pratt folder that has not been given its own reference code.

2 A common Latin phrase meaning 'let it be given to the worthier'.

The lab'ring Jack[3] would hardly, hardly go;
Dull was the Brass, unwash'd her Earthen-Ware,
And *Tabby* slept neglected in the Chair:
LOVE wrought the Change, 'twas LOVE that had betray'd,
When thus in doleful Dumps[4] bewail'd the Maid:
"Go, gentle Gales! And bear my Sighs away,
"Ah! Why so long does HURLO-THRUMBO[5] stay?
"Why form'd Dame Nature Woman's Love so *strong*,
"Or, why art thou so *Tempting* and so *Long?*
"Resound my Tubs, my *hollow* Tubs resound;[6]
"Ah me! That Love should give so *deep* a Wound!
"Why in that House[*] shouldst[7] thou so strive to Shine,
"Is it more *clean* or better *kept* than Mine?
"Alas! I'm told (but they are Lies, I ween)
"That *dirty* House, no Mortal yet could *clean*:
"*Rub* as they will, and Polish as they can,
"PENSIONS and BRIBES will *Iron-mould* the Man:
"Go, gentle Gales! And bear my Sighs away!
"Ah! why so long does HURLO-THRUMBO stay?
"Why seeks my Soldier *Forts*, or *City*-Walls,
"When I can make my Love *less hurtful* Balls[8]?
"Why to the *Camp* must HURLO-THRUMBO fly,
"When *I* can *raise*, and you *besiege* a Pye?
"If thou *must* Fight, for thou art born to Wield,

---

3 See *The Grange*, note 112.

4 c.f. Grunnelia's 'doleful dumps' in 'Grunnelia or the Sow in the Dumps', [*f. 2r*, l. 2].

5 Hurlothrumbo is a foolish and cowardly soldier in the play of the same name by Samuel Johnson of Cheshire, published in 1729. The Norfolk MP Thomas De Grey (1717–1781) is identified as the man Richard Gardiner satirised as 'Hurlo-Thrumbo' in *Miscellaneous Pieces in Prose and Verse: Relative to the Contested Elections, for Members of Parliament for the County of Norfolk and City and County of Norwich* (Norwich: S. White, 1768), p. 32. He is also presumably the target of *Cinderetta* as well. In the contested election of 1768, Sir Armine Wodehouse and Thomas De Grey were painted by their opponents as supporters of 'General Warrants'. They were opposed by the anti-administration candidates Sir Edward Astley and Wenman Coke. Astley and De Grey were elected.

6 c.f. Grunnelia's 'hollow tubs reecchoing every groan' [*f. 2v*, l. 64].

7 The 'u' in 'shoulst' was erroneously inverted in the original print of the poem.

8 i.e. boluses, large edible balls taken as medicine: *OED*.

"O! Fight in *Paste*[9] the Heroes of the Field:
"When yester Morn I turn'd my *Jack* around,
"The *Salt-box* fell portentous to the Ground:
"Thrice mew'd the Cat, and thrice she flew on *Tray*;
"Oh! Think on this, and thy *Election Day*[10]*!*
"Die, CINDERETTA! Ease thy hateful Smart,
"Ambition's now the Mistress of his Heart:
"Ah me! Each Object that these Eyes can View,
"Brings to my Mind some pleasing Form of *You:*
"When in this Hand the polish'd *Spit* I hold,
"Thy *Shape* is here, for thou art *Long* and *Cold*:
"If I the *Cleaver* take, the Joint to part,
"Thy absence then is *cleaving* of my Heart;
"Or, if I strive the Kitchen-*Fire* to mend,
"Those *Eyes* are *flaming* at the *Poker*'s end:
"Go, gentle Gales! And bear my Sighs away!
"Ah! Why so long does HURLO-THRUMBO stay?"
Thus wail'd She tearful to herself alone,
The *hollow* Tubs re-Ecchoing every Groan:
When lo! her much-*Lov'd Hero* stood to View,
And her Heart flutter'd as he *nearer* drew:
She sought the *Garret* for her *Sunday*'s Pride,
Pinn'd on her *Nims*[†], and brush'd the Fleas aside.
The busy *Sylphs* attend the dressing *Fair*,[11]
This clears the *Scurf*, and this *Pork*-Lards her Hair:
This with its *Breath* reduc'd her *Tear-swoln* Eye,
Another *fans* the *pouting* Nostrils *dry:*
Down came the *Damsel* with superior Grace,
With all the *Stew-pan*'s radiance in her Face:
So *dredg'd*, so *finish'd*, and so *soft* her Look,
Now Trips a GODDESS, and now Smiles a *Cook*[12]*:*
Flies to Her HERO, with resistless Charms,

9 i.e. dough.

10 The day of the contested election of 1768 held for the Norfolk seats on 23 March 1768.

11 The reference is to the sylphs in Alexander Pope's *The Rape of the Lock*.

12 Echoing the description of 'Sporus' (John Hervey, 1695–1743) in *Epistle to Dr Arbuthnot* as a man who 'Now trips a Lady, and now struts a Lord' (*Pope*, 329).

And clasps the *Long, Cold* C——EL[13] in her *Arms.*

* Parliament.
† Shirt-sleeves.

Norwich, March 19, 1768. White-Swan.[14]

13 i.e. 'Colonel'.

14 An inn in Swan Lane in Norwich, also known as 'Swan Inn' and 'Swan Hotel', which operated from the early seventeenth to the late nineteenth century. The supporters of Sir Edward Astley and Wenman Coke reconvened at the White Swan after the nomination of the four candidates: *Contest*, 6. With the Pope's Head the White Swan acted as one of the two headquarters of the Free Blues who supported Astley and Coke. See John A. Phillips, *Electoral Behavior in Unreformed England: Plumpers, Splitters, and Straights* (Princeton: Princeton University Press, 1982), p. 129.

Mr. and Mrs. Clagett's Epitaph (Monumental Inscription)

Date: After Mary Clagett's death on 24 July 1775.

Authorship: The manuscript of the epitaph in Pratt's hand is included in the Pratt folder and Mary Clagett was Pratt's sister-in-law. The poem is almost certainly by Pratt. The manuscript version is reproduced in Appendix 2.

Physical Description: Monumental inscription on brown marble plaque 50 cm x 250 cm, on the south interior wall of St Michael at Plea Church, Norwich.

Sacred

To the Memory of

The Rev^{d}. WILLIAM CLAGETT. A:M.

And MARY his second Wife[1]:

He died suddenly on ye 14th. Day of December

In the Year 1774. Aged 48.

1 William Clagett (1726–1774) and Mary Clagett, née Stanforth (1725–1775). William was the rector of Mundeseley and Trimingham, adjoining parishes on the north-east Norfolk coast. Mary Clagett was a younger sister of Ann Pratt, Jermyn Pratt's wife, who was living at Watlington at the time of her marriage. William and Mary married on 5 January 1773. See NRO ANW 24/47/170. A monumental inscription containing a slightly different version of the epitaph is in St Michael at Plea in Norwich, where both William and Mary are buried. See Parish Records of St Michael at Plea, Norwich NRO PD 66/3. According to the inscription, William died on 14 December 1774 and Mary on 24 July 1775.

MARY his beloved Wife

Survived him seven Months.

And died on the 24th. of July

In the same Year of her Age.

Stay Moralist—and with one transient View
Read oe'r these Lines, which friendly speak to you:
If through Life's waves, thy Bark serenely glides,
Trust not too far, nor dare the adverse Tides:
Here rests a Pair, to whom Indulgent Heav'n
Had ev'ry Wish, and ev'ry Virtue giv'n:
But Joys like theirs, too exquisite to Last
In one sad Hour, receiv'd the fatal Blast
So the best Fruits of most distinguishd Worth
Shrink at the Storm and drop at once to Earth:
Such are thy ways, Thou Providence Divine,
And blessed be the unerring Hand of Thine.

'If tis no Crime to Give the Just Applause'

NRO PRA 664/23

Date: ?*c.* 1776. After the physician Robert James's death on 23 March 1776. The paper on which the poem is written has the same watermark as the manuscript version of 'Political Duck Hunting' (*c.* 1779), 'The Jay a Fable', and 'To 'N. S.' suggesting that all these poems may all have been composed in the same general period of time.

Authorship: The poem is in Pratt's hand and can be confidently be attributed to him.

Physical Description: Poem handwritten in ink on both sides of single piece of paper, folded once in half, in Pratt's hand, measuring (in its folded state) 18.5 cm by 30.5 cm.

[*f. 1r*]

If tis no crime to give the just applause:
And conscience dares to plead in merits cause.
If in this age of wrath and thirst for blood,
One Honest Heart may feel for public<k>[1] good.
Accept O! James![2] what gratitude can give
By whom with (Gods permission) thousands live—
Had thy blest genius lived in better days;
When ye famed Græcian[3] sung Machaons[4] praise;
Or, when proud Athens wept her Heroes lost;
Her Sickning <heroes> ^legions^ and deserted coast.

1 The 'k' is cancelled in the manuscript.

2 The occasion for the poem is the death of the physician Robert James (1703–1776), a member of Samuel Johnson's Literary Club: *Oxford DNB*.

3 Homer.

4 Machaon, one of the sons of Asclepius, fighting on the Greek side in the Trojan Wars.

Athens had then immortalized thy name!
And thou hadst lived ye favourite son of fame—
Stranger to thee, which way thou man of Art
Canst thou accept the fulness of my heart?
Poor is the praise a worthless muse can Give
For him who Saves and gives <y^{e}> ^a^ power to live—
For from ye muse be flatterys tainted breath
Or falsehoods tongue which stings desert to death
Truth heaven born truth is <midwife to> ^parent of^ desert
And honest praise is seated in the heart
When all <is> ^was^ sad and nature still as death
Seemed just expiring with ye parting breath;
When ye big tear distilld from Sapphos Eyes[5]
Thy medicine saved, & <bids> ^bad^[6] ye patient rise
As If some God the mighty cure had wrought
We Stand Amazed and wrapt in holy thought
If there should live a wretch so lost to shame
Whom In'trest prompts to blast a brothers fame—
Whose mind approves & conscience must commend
Yet damns thy powder[7] for a selfish End

[*f. 1v*]

May all the Ghosts by long prescription made
Haunt when he sleeps this, murtherer in trade.
Blenheim[8] and Wealth to Malbro' <Britain> ^Britons^[9] gave:

5 Ovid's *Heroides* 15, which takes the form of Sappho's complaint about her abandonment by Phaon, has multiple references to Sappho's tears as she initially finds herself unable to weep, but later cannot stop.

6 In the MS, Pratt cancels the 'ds' in 'bids' to turn the verb into the past tense 'bad', an alternate form of 'bade': *OED*.

7 James was noted as the inventor of a popular 'fever powder', although the product's popularity also led to him being accused by some of his adversaries of quackery: *Oxford DNB*.

8 The military hero, John Churchill, first Duke of Marlborough (1650–1722) was richly rewarded for his successful campaigns on the continent during the War of the Spanish Succession, including the Battle of Blenheim in 1704; his existing grant of £5,000 a year was made permanent, he was given the entire hundred of Wotton and the manor of Woodstock, whose stones were later used to build Blenheim Palace, though Blenheim was unfinished at the time of his death: *Oxford DNB*.

9 Pratt cancelled the 'a' in 'Britain' and wrote 'ons' directly above to change the word to 'Britons'.

He slaughterd legions, and you legions save:
Then Stephens[10] merit catchd the senates Ear
The pension flowed, & fortune Haild ye fair
But you to who great Phœbus <gave> ^willd^ ye Art:
To turn deaths Javelin pointed at ye Heart
To whom your loved, Hippocrates[11] would bend:—
And Galen's[12] self be proud to call you friend;
Must live to Merit and Desert alone
And take this short inscription, for yr stone[13]
<To James his country pasd no Just regard>
But be ?all to Heav'n to give ye Just reward>
X X X X X X X
Here, What could die, of James, ye Mortal Part:
Death has subdued, & triumphd over Art:——
The force of Medicine could no further go—
His cures were such, Death markd him as his foe
To <thee thy> ^him his^ country paid, no Just regard
But left to Heaven, to give thee great reward

10 William Stephens, Rector of Sutton (1649/50–1718), who published a letter criticizing Marlborough's military campaign. He was successfully sued by the Duke for libel and sentenced to the pillory and a fine. Queen Anne, however, granted Stephens a remission from the corporal punishment after the Duchess of Marlborough interceded on his behalf: *Oxford DNB*.

11 Hippocrates of Kos, also known as Hippocrates II (*c.* 460–370 BC), Greek physician.

12 Galen, Aelius Galenos in Greek and Claudius Galenus in Latin (AD 129–*c.* 216), Greek physician and philosopher.

13 Two lines of illegible crossed-out text follow this line.

'Political Duck-Hunting' (Newspaper Version)

Norwich Mercury, **18 September 1779, p. 2.**

Date: 18 September 1779 (date of publication).

Authorship: The newspaper version of this poem is not in the Pratt folder but the manuscript of the poem in Pratt's hand is included in the Pratt folder. The manuscript version of 'Political Duck-Hunting' is reproduced in Appendix 4. The poem is almost certainly by Pratt.

Physical Description: Newspaper printing of the poem in two columns, measuring 7 cm x 12.5 cm in total.

Note: This poem was subsequently republished with the prefatory letter (probably not by Pratt) addressed to the printer in the *Newcastle Chronicle* on 25 September 1779, p. 4.

[*p. 4*]

For the NORWICH MERCURY.

POLITICAL *DUCK-HUNTING*.[1]

I.

Once on a Time some idle Folks
Who lov'd to laugh and cut their Jokes,
(For idle Folks love fun:)
Duck-hunting went, their favourite Sport,
And if it suits the vulgar Sort
Why! let their will be done.

II.

Down Severn's[2] Stream they did discern
A *Mallard*,[3] deck'd from Head to Stern
A First Rate, of his Line:
Tray[4] wagg'd his Tail and seem to say
Whoof! we shall have fine Sport To day,
That *Mallard* shall be mine.

1 This poem depicts the engagement between the French and British navies at the Battle of Ushant, fought on 27 July 1778, but it also stands as an allegory for the American Revolutionary War as a whole. For more information on the background to the poem see our Introduction, pp. 45–6.

2 The Severn stands in for the English Channel.

3 The mallard duck represents France.

4 Tray the dog represents the fleet of British ships that fought at the Battle of Ushant and Britain more generally.

III.

But, as in merry Æsop's Days
When Birds were wise and had sly Ways,
So this sagacious Fowl,
Knowing old *Tray* was cursed tough
And that he ne'er could swim enough
Call'd in her Neighbour *Owl.*[5]

IV.

Her Neighbour came with solemn Pride,
She dropt a-stern the *Mallard*'s Side
Now cheer'd, and now saluted:
Tray thought it best to swim around,
Was sometimes lost and sometimes found,
Mal quack'd, and *Madg'y* hooted.

V.

To-day they sink, To-day alive,
Now *Tray* gets hold, now *Mallard* dive;
Now running, now pursuing:
The common People swore by G—d
They never saw a sight so odd,
Such Fuss—and nothing doing.[6]

5 The owl, later in the poem named as 'Madge', represents Spain, which entered the American Revolutionary War in June 1779, three months before the poem appeared in the *Norwich Mercury*.

6 The 'such Fuss and Nothing doing' people can be taken to refer not only to the fact that there was no clear victor of the Battle of Ushant but also the perception that the American Revolutionary War was dragging on without any clear victor.

VI.

When Lo! three sturdy Farmers Sons*
Came Down that Way with Loaded Guns
  And Swore they'd have no more:
Madge took the Hint; and sought her Nest
The *Mallard* wing'd his way for B—[7]
And *Tray*; got safe to Shore. Z.

* *Russia*, *Prussia*, & *Holland*.[8]

7 i.e. 'Brest'.

8 Catherine the Great of Russia would soon form the League of Armed Neutrality in 1780 to protect trade during the American Revolutionary War. The League included Holland, which was the first country to recognise the United States of America. Holland would, however, enter the war against Britain in 1780. Prussia remained neutral throughout the American Revolutionary War but even before the beginning of this conflict the relations between Britain and Prussia were tense, following Britain's abandonment of an alliance with Prussia during the Seven Years' War. Prussia, however, engaged in trade with the newly independent America first through France as an intermediary and then through a private company. It officially recognized the United States only after Britain had already done so.

'The Sunday Visit' (Newspaper Version)

PRA 664: ***Norwich Mercury*****, 31 March 1781, p. 3.**

Date: Published 31 March 1781.

Authorship: A working draft of the poem in Pratt's hand is included in the Pratt folder. A clipping of the poem from the *Norwich Mercury* is also included in the Pratt folder. (The clipping has not been given its own reference code). The manuscript version of 'The Sunday Visit' is reproduced in Appendix 5. The poem is almost certainly by Pratt.

Physical Description: Newspaper clipping of a poem measuring 8.5 cm by 40 cm.

The SUNDAY VISIT;

In a Letter from Brother WILLIAM to Brother GREGORY.

Non satis est, pulchra esse poemata: dulcia sunto.

HOR.[1]

[*p. 3*]

BROTHER Greg, you enjoin'd, and I'm proud to obey,
To send you in verse, how we spent the Lord's Day;
My good Wife, you well know, was the Niece of a Priest,
So she loves to ride out and partake of a Feast.

1 *DLCL*: Horace, *Ars Poetica*, 99 (p. 459) 'It is not enough for poems to be beautiful, they must also be pleasing.' The poem's manuscript version does not include this epigraph.

T'other Night she began when we both were in Bed,
"Billy (pray now, my dear, take your Hand from my Head)
"I should like, if you please, just by way of a change[2]
"To dine, Sunday next, at old guzzle-down Grange;
"Cousin Hollocks oft says—and I know he speaks true—
"Mrs. Hunter, my Wife would be proud to see you."
We rose at the time, and I made our Jade ready,
Little Bet was soon up, and quite smart was my Lady;
The dear Child pack'd before, and my Wife hung behind,
And our Bobby plac'd by on a Hobby[3] that's blind;
Then we chatted and trotted, and made our Remarks,
Whilst our Bobby was driving and chasing the Larks:
"That's a sweet pretty Seat, what a pity his Honor
"Has laid such a weight of some Thousands upon her:
"By Gowls said our Bet, I could wish from my Soul,
"That my Nurse, and our Ned, were possess'd of the whole."
When we came to the Grange, Cousin Hollocks came out,
And he crys, "What a pox have ye all been about!
"What, ye took the wrong Turn when ye came into Town"—
Then he kis'd little Bet, as he took the Child down,
And Bobby, said he, you're as smart as your Sister,
But the Boy look'd confus'd, for he'd rode up a Blister.
When we enter'd the House, at the end of her Fork,
The Maid ran away with a Huge Leg of Pork;
And she staring at us, it drop'd from her Hand,
So she rubb'd it, and blow'd it, and clear'd it of sand.
Then we sat down to dine, and we merrily drank,
"Mrs. Hunter your Health;" "I'm oblig'd to you Frank;"
"Master Bobby is grown quite a sweet handsome Fellow,
"And Miss never look'd half so well as in yellow:
"Nelly, pray tuck the Cloth round my dear Bobby's Throat,
"For fear the sweet Boy should *contamin*[4] his Coat.
"Mrs. Hunter, my dear, now I beg you be free,
"Is the Goose to your mind? do our Tatus[5] agree?

---

2 The 'n' in 'change' was erroneously inverted in the newspaper printing.

3 See *The Grange*, note 102.

4 Malapropism for 'contaminate'.

5 The MS version has 'tastes'; in the newspaper version Pratt probably changed the word to represent Mrs. Hunter garbling the word.

"Our Tradesmen don't send the best things to the Grange,
"But, my dear, I *subsist*[6] that we soon make a Change,"
The Dinner remov'd, you will think it a sin,
That we walk'd round the Farm, with the Bells ringing in:
"By the Lord said old Hol, 'tis a sad burning shame,
"That these sweet Fields of Corn should be ruin'd by Game,
"They subscribe and protect, and their Tenants defend,
"Yes afaith[7] so they will, for to serve their own end."
Now suppose, Brother Greg, the Clock half after four,
Tea and *Toast* swallow'd down, and our Jade at the Door—
Many Curtsies and Bows, now returning and passing,
With nodding, and squinting, and curvetting and a——g,[8]
With the Handkerchief shak'd, and held up in the Air,
Bye, Bye, little Souls, Oh! I wish ye liv'd here.
When we rode half a Mile, most unhappy to tell you,
Little Bet found the Cheese-Curd besieging her Belly;
So I drop'd the Child down, and she ran to a Hedge,
And laid a good Heap on a Bundle of Sedge:
Misfortunes, dear Greg, are not oft unattended,
For our Bob broke his Girth,[9] which so lately was mended,
And in turning a Lane, the Lord Harry knows how,
The old Saddle came round, and he dropt in a Slough:
Here my Wife she shriek'd out, and she scolded and grumbled,
Her Tooth was so bad, and her Cloaths were so tumbled;
If she came abroad, it was always the same,
Willy, Child kick the Jade, for the Devil is lame.
When I got to my home, comes my Aunt with her Bible,
In a black tatter'd Bonnet, well whited with Crible;[10]
So, so, she began, here's your very fine doing,
No wonder, say I, that some Folks come to ruin;
My dear first Husband said, and he always spoke true,
If you slight the Lord's Day, that the Lord will slight you:
Not a Man could I get, not a Soul to my aid,

6 Malapropism for 'insist'.

7 i.e. 'I'faith', a contraction of 'in faith', a mild oath.

8 The manuscript version has 'ar——.' The word intended is 'arsing'.

9 A belt securing the saddle of a horse: *OED*.

10 Presumably full of holes, and so reminiscent of the *criblé* technique of engraving on metal or wood.

There's our Ralph hobbled off with the old Parson's Maid;
And the Boy watch'd ye all from the Cheese Chamber Wicket,
Then away ran the Rogue, like a Devil, to Cricket;
Old Crump's in the Ditch, and so bruis'd is her Back,
That I vow it will turn to a mortify'd black;
And the Sow that's shut up with her Tribe of fifteen,
Has swallow'd the whole—not a pig to be seen.—
Here she stopt her Harangue, and I drew off the Pillion,[11]
And found both my Cheeks of a blessed Vermillion.
  O! Greg, without doubt, these are sad horrid Times,
When we Farmers ride out, in the hearing of Chimes:
You remember the time, when with Family pride,
How we all ran to Church by the Minister's Side;
When we join'd in the Psalm, thought the Sermon had Good in,
Though we sometimes believ'd that it ruin'd the Pudding;
For the Term of my Lease, for my Years yet to come,
I will ne'er on the Sabbath be rambling from home;
For as my Aunt says, "We shall all find it true,
"If ye slight the Lord's Day, that the Lord will slight you."

Z.

11 A 'pillion' or 'male-pillion' is a stuffed cushion used for carrying luggage on a horse behind the rider: *VEA*.

'Watlington, November 16, 1781'

NRO PRA 664/14

Date: 16 November 1781 (the date of composition given in the poem's title).

Authorship: The manuscript of the poem in Pratt's hand is included in the Pratt folder and Pratt was rector of Watlington Church. It is a near certainty that the poem is by Pratt.

Physical description: Poem handwritten in ink on both sides of single piece of paper in Pratt's hand, 18.5 cm by 23 cm.

Note: Given the complexity of Pratt's revisions to this poem, we have chosen to present a diplomatic transcription, with reconstructed line readings provided in the footnotes where necessary.

[*f. 1r*]

Wat.[1] Nov. 16 1781.

Dear S^{r}, have done, I know it true,
I've heard it from my Priest, & you:
or
But where's ye need for Dean ~~&~~ Chapter
To tell us we must Dye? & After
That you and I, with all our Fuss;
Must both go down to Æacus:[2]
Well, what of this, Suppose it So,
May ~~to~~ we not Laugh, before we go?

1 i.e. Watlington.

2 Aeacus was one of the three judges of the dead in Greek mythology.

our
Enjoy ~~Lifes~~ Little scanty Time
With Harmless chat, or sportive Rhyme[3]
I cannot Think, tis not my creed
Nor is it fit, to be believd
That we are all, here, plac'd below;
~~To bear a Load of constant woe;~~
No, Heavn's high Architect, looks down,
With Cherubs Smile, not Cinic~~s~~[4] frown;
Pleasd to behold, ~~Us~~ Little things
Bask in the sun, and stretch our wings:
Be sometimes grave & sometimes mery
Hop here & there, as Londonderry;[5]
Lifes Hocus Pocus, blow is gone[6]
Then where's my Lord; & where St John[7]

Consider Sir, Look round youl find
in store
There's Joy ~~Laid out~~ for every kind:
Lord of ye mead the stately Bull
Surveys Turk like, has his Seraglio full[8]

3 These two lines are written vertically in the left-hand margin, taking up space between lines 5 and 18.

4 The final 's' has been cancelled.

5 A manuscript of musical pieces created by someone named John Miller between 1799 and 1801, now in the A.K. Bell Library, Perth, Scotland, includes a dance he labelled as 'Londonderry', which Celia Pendlebury describes as a 'quick step'. See her 'Reels and Hornpipes: A History of "Traditional" Dance Tunes of Britain and Ireland,' unpublished MA thesis, University of Sheffield, 1958, p. 67. Our thanks to Rebecca Haidt for this reference.

6 Reference to the so-called legerdemain tricks, in which the audience is tricked into thinking that an object has disappeared and sometimes involves a member of the audience or the performer blowing air to supposedly bring about the disappearance or subsequent reappearance of the item. See *Hocus Pocus Junior. The Anatomy Of Legerdemain* (London, 1656). There is also a pun on a flower's 'blow' or bloom being gone: *OED*.

7 These lines are written vertically in the right-hand margin, taking up space between lines 5 and 20. 'St John' recalls the opening couplet of the first epistle of Alexander Pope's *Essay on Man* (1733–34), dedicated to Henry St John, Viscount Bolingbroke: 'Awake, my ST. JOHN! leave all meaner things/ To low ambition, and the pride of kings' (*Pope*, 1–2).

8 Our best guess is that Pratt intends this line to read 'Turk Like Surveys his fair Seraglio full'.

with transport
his fair ~~And~~ The ~~fatted~~ Lamb ~~well~~- crops his clover
Tho Short his Life, and quickly over
And Idle Boy sets down & Whistles
his
Whilst, roped Ass enjoys ye Thistles
take
Then let us ~~have~~ our share of pleasure
short of
Not over heapd; nor ~~wanting~~ measure
Let know Brisk
But ~~send~~ me ~~word~~ how ~~well~~ yr spouse is[9]
~~& how well~~
How well yr Barns, ~~the Shalterd~~ Houses
are all of them
How ~~well~~ yr Tenants, ~~pleased &~~ ready
How much yr betterd by my Lady
are Did
How ~~well~~ yr Banks ~~If~~ Last moons Tide
ye top
~~Did~~ not Peep oer, with Saucy Pride +
What Present want, what future Evil
And how goes——with ye Devil[10]
&
Do all things If things go on, quite smooth ~~or~~ dear
Gibe Or are you plagud as much as ever:
Be this reservd till Xstmas cheer
both
Shall fix Us ~~in~~ yr Elbow chair—
~~Then~~, Mark, no Stirring till eleven
Except yr Orderd up; to Heav'n

with wig awry, &[11]

9 This short poem is on the reverse side of the sheet; in the original, 'let' is inserted above 'send', 'know' is inserted above 'word', and 'brisk' is inserted above 'well'.

10 The final two lines are written vertically into the right-hand margin and '+' after 'Pride' indicates that they are meant to be inserted here.

11 This phrase is written vertically at the bottom of the left-hand margin—it would make sense for Pratt and his addressee be ordered up to heaven 'with wig awry'.

‘To Christopher Anstey’

NRO PRA 664/15

Date: ?*c.* 1781. A comparison of the watermark for the piece of paper on which this poem was written and the one ‘Watlington, November 16, 1781’ was written shows that both poems were written on the same sheet of paper, which was cut in half. Therefore it is probable that this poem was composed at the same time as ‘Watlington, November 16, 1781’—or at least was written down at this time.

Authorship: The manuscript of the poem in Pratt’s hand is included in the Pratt folder. Christopher Anstey was a student at King Edward VI. School in Bury St. Edmunds at the same time as Pratt. The poem is also signed ‘J:P:’. It is a near certainty that the poem is by Pratt.

Physical description: Poem handwritten in ink on both sides of single piece of paper in Pratt’s hand, measuring measuring 18 cm by 23 cm.

[*f. 1r*]

To C. Anstey Esq.[1]

Brought up with you, & Taught by Rule;
The slow, dull work, of Grammar school:
Where, yok'd betimes, to Classic Team;
We Drag'd up Hill, our Loaded Theme;
With Kin'smans Grins; & <sad> ^vile^ Grimaces[2]
Wheel up my lads & mend y^{r} paces—
Slow winding thro fatigueing Tupto[3]
Long Istemi[4] and heavy Crupto:[5]
When; oft we tuggd, and oft stood still;
To reach the Steep, Parnassian Hill[6]—
I own it would augment, my Pride
To see once more; the new Bath, guide
You, Happy Sir, are Smoothly coated;
Well Litterd down; and sweetly Oated;[7]
Can run a Distance when you please;
Walk oe'r ye course; or, Frisk with ease;
Yet, as Superior Parts, are join'd
To a Superior gentle mind;
You will not Spurn; or Lift ye Heel
Tho you, fore horse, And I at Wheel:
For when Lifes Little drag; is over,
And you turn'd out, of worldly clover

---

1 Christopher Anstey (1724–1805), author of *The New Bath Guide*, a satirical poem on the city of Bath, first published in 1762, and very popular at the time.

2 In the original the following four lines are written on the first page vertically in the left-hand margin. Arthur Kynnesman (1682–1770) was the headmaster of Edward VI. School in Bury St Edmunds when Pratt and Anstey were students there. For more information on Kynnesman's pedagogy see our Introduction, p. 18.

3 Greek τύπτω meaning 'to strike', 'to beat', and 'to slog'. In *Tristram Shandy*, Tristram observes that a typical student of Greek will be 'Seven long years and more τύπτω-ing it, at Greek and Latin' (*Sterne*, 2:483). The editors of the Florida *Tristram Shandy* note that it was commonly used as a paradigm to teach this particular conjugation. (*Sterne*, 3:389).

4 Greek *isthimi* meaning 'to stand'.

5 Greek *krypho-* meaning 'hidden' or 'secret'.

6 The home of the Greek Muses.

7 Of a horse, to be provided with bedding and sustenance: *OED*. There is also a play on the oaten pipe played by shepherds in pastoral poetry, a symbol of poetic powers in general.

Then you; as well as Hacks,[8] like us:
Xanthus;[9] Old <Pad> ^Peg^;[10] Beucephalus;[11]
The state Horse; War Horse; naval Poney.
The braided, Ambling Maceroni;[12]
Girth galld, or not; with Splint[13] or Spavin;[14]
Must feel Deaths all destroying Jav'lin
<And whether yok'd, or not, together>
<Must shoot our Coates and Hides for Leather:>
Must all Lie down in Dust together[15]
& Leave behind these Hides for Leather[16]
When ye <full> ^rich^ Sieve no man shall rattle
To feed you Pampered Happy Cattle

[*f. 1v*]

Since then Lifes, but a human ^mortal^[17] race;
Where some move slow, some run apace:
You first in speed, & quite new market
I yok'd To Tithes, and forc'd to cart it;
(Tho, Thank my stars, good Provender
Has made me sleek, and Loth to Stir:)
And since, Heav'n Wills, it should be So,
May we not Bait,[18] before we go?
Just Hynnhmm[19] it,— <as> ^since^ Life's so short
Here Samuel, your Masters Port

J:P:

---

8 A play on the two senses of 'hacks' as 'horses' and 'hack-writers': *OED*.

9 One of the two horses of Achilles.

10 Only the final 'ad' is crossed out in the original.

11 The horse of Alexander the Great.

12 i.e. 'macaroni' in the sense of a dandy or fop: *OED*.

13 A callous tumour that effects the leg of a hose: *OED*.

14 A hard and bony tumour that effects the leg of a horse: *OED*.

15 In the original these two lines are written on the first page vertically in the right-hand margin.

16 This and the following line are written perpendicularly along the left-hand margin.

17 In the manuscript 'human' is not crossed through but 'mortal' is written above it, suggesting that Pratt meant to replace 'human' with 'mortal'.

18 'Bait' in the sense of stopping at an inn to feed the horses or more generally to rest: *OED*.

19 A reference to the 'Houyhnhnms', an intelligent race of horses from Jonathan Swift's Book 4 of *Gulliver's Travels*.

‘To N. S.’

NRO PRA 664/17

Date: ?*c.* 1781. Our best guess is that this poem was written around the same time as ‘Watlington’ and ‘To Christopher Anstey’ given the similar concerns of all three poems with friendship and ageing. The poem was presumably written before 1787, the year Ann Pratt (‘my Jewel’) died. Styleman died in 1788.

Authorship: The manuscript of the poem in Pratt’s hand is included in the Pratt folder.

Physical description: Poem handwritten in ink on both sides of single piece of paper in Pratt’s hand, measuring 19 cm by 30.5 cm.

Note: We believe ‘N.S.’ to be Nicholas Styleman (1722–1788) because he is the only person with those initials who attended Cambridge University in the years when Pratt was also a student there. Styleman (entered in the school register as ‘Stileman’) was also a student at King Edward VI School at the same time Pratt was there (*BEKE*, 372). We have taken Styleman’s birth and death dates from the ‘Parish Records of Snettisham’, NRO, PD 304. Styleman is often identified in *The Contest* as a supporter of Edward Astley and Wenman Coke, whom Pratt also supported.

[*f. 1r*]

To N; S: Esqr

Yes I am old, tis true at Last
I feel the Glorious Hours are past
When Youth sat Smiling on my Brow
And Lud I felt, I knew not How—
Armd with round Cap and Caian[1] Gown
(If eer the Gods to Earth came down)
I felt myself a very God
And hardly touchd ye Ground I trod:
Farewell blest Days forever Gone
And thou Sweet College Hour of One
When Rohoust, Puffendorf, & Rowning[2]
Gave way to Love & Nancy Downing
And If Dear Pollys Ivory Hand
Would Pat ye Cheek or Stroke ye Band[3]
Not Persian Kings in all their state
Were half so blest, or half so Great—

Now when I rise, to pray my Jewel
Do Heat again my water Gruel
O Lord my Head, this nose of mine
Which once was broke in Drapers[4] time
Fills me so full with pain & sorrow
Child, I cannot go out to morrow—
Do Send the Boy, and tell my Friend

---

1 Belonging to Gonville and Caius College (Cambridge).

2 Jacques Rohault (1620–1672), author of texts on physics; Samuel von Pufendorf (1632–1694), author of texts on jurisprudence; John Rowning (1701?–1771), author of texts on mathematics. Texts by Rohault and Pufendorf are listed among the volumes in Pratt's library upon his death.

3 Part of an academic or clerical gown, which developed out of the so-called falling collar. Parson Woodforde also attests to having close relations with young women during his days at Oxford University between 1759 and 1761 in his diary (*Woodforde*, 1:15–16), including exchanging snuffboxes with a Nancy Rooke 'by way of a Remembrance of her' (*Woodforde*, 1:18).

4 Jonathan Swift (1667–1745) published a series of tracts against the English government's mismanagement of Ireland, under the pseudonym 'M. B. Drapier' between 1724 and 1725. We do not know how Pratt broke his nose, if he indeed did.

I am half Dead from End to End:
Then I Look up, with bloodshot Eye
Lord save us! What a Horrid sky!
These clouds so black to Northward bending
Are full of Storms and just descending
Child stand aside, & don’t be teazing
This Cursed Cough; this Horrid Sneazing
Is Hasho, Hasho, so provoking
All night I felt ye dread of choking
Turn up <a>[5] my Nose at this and that
Whip out the Dog; or kick the Cat——

[*f. 1v*]

Friend of my Youth, together Joind
With one Consent of Heart and Mind
Say is there not some <Sober> Joys in store
When Lifes Fantastic Scenes are o’er
Or, must we Middle Aged complain
That Half our Days are sent in Vain
No, mayst thou Long my Honest Nic
(As a Huge <Bark> ^ship^ in Adriatic)
Roll in thy chair from side to side
Without a Storm or adverse Tide:
And may my Little Baark[6] Attend
Close by thy side and Rudders End—
Together oer Lifes Ocean sail
Partake ye Storm, or share ye Gale.
In every State propitious Heaven
Enough to all hers [*sic*] Sons has Given;
Holds up to all this <moral> ^certain^ rule
God is all wise, and mans ye fool:
Times iron Hand has batterd Down
Great Babilon and, Priams Town[7]
Time makes ye rose & Lillies Dye

---

5 Pratt was beginning to write a word beginning with ‘a’ but then decided not to and this whole area of the page is smeared out.

6 i.e. ‘Bark’, another name for a ship.

7 i.e. Troy.

On Sapphos Cheek and Juliets Eye
Mixes great Potentates with Dust
Nor spares the monumental Bust:
<Then> ^Yet^ Let him known with all his rage
Our FriendShip[8] shall Improve with Age
That Heavenly ray shall brighter shine;
Nor feel the Sad Effects of Time
<Then> ^And^ Since it is the fixd Decree
That Such a Thing as man <should> ^must^ be
Whatever is your Lot or mine
Does prove alike, the Hand Divine:
And Whether we are Crossd or blest
Whatever is, is Good and best[9]—
^May we frail Lamps^ <Then Brother Lamp>[10] prest in our Sockets
Wasting away in Life and pockets
That we to Lifes dull end may Shine—
<Lets> Trim ^up^ our wick afresh with balm
Banish each anxious thought & care————
And wish to be, Just what we Are[11]

8 'Ship' is deliberately capitalized in order to draw attention to the metaphor of the two friends as ships.

9 Echoing the conclusion of the first epistle of Alexander Pope's *Essay on Man*: '"Whatever IS, is RIGHT"' (*Pope*, 294).

10 'may we frail lamps' is written in the left-hand margin immediately before '<Then Brother Lamp>'.

11 These final four lines are written perpendicularly to the main text in the right-hand margin.

‘The Jay a Fable’

NRO PRA 664/16

Date: ?*c.* 1781. This poem was probably written around the same time as “To N. S.’ as both the sheets of paper on which the poems are written share the same watermark and are of similar sizes. We have tentatively dated ‘To N. S.’ to the same period of ‘To Christopher Anstey’ and ‘Watlington, 16 November 1781’ and our best guess is that ‘The Jay a Fable’ was also probably written around this time.

Authorship: The manuscript of the poem in Pratt’s hand is included in the Pratt folder and concerns clerical matters. We are confident in attributing the poem to Pratt.

Physical description: Poem handwritten in ink on both sides of single piece of paper in Pratt’s hand, 18.5 cm by 23 cm.

Note: Given the complexity of Pratt’s revisions to this poem, we have chosen to present a diplomatic transcription.

[*f. 1r*]

The Jay a Fable—

Prudence, an Heiress sprung from Marle[1];
But too much freckled for an Earl:
Suppos’d a Living would produce,
A Husband, or at least a goose[2];
So being not of heart Obdurate

1 See note 29 in *September: A Rural Poem*, p. 172 in our edition.

2 In the figurative sense of a foolish person: *OED*.

She bought ye Tithes, & took the curate
Reubens,[3] good Soul of Sober Life
Was Dignified with y^{s} said wife
And took the Dear Delicious curse
As others do for good or worse
Ten Horrid tedious years or more
Poor Reubens tugd ye Marriage Oar:
Found no Philosophy, or books
Or Evening walks, or happier Rooks
No Friends or Patience could contribute
To Save him from this Earthly Gibbet
From morn to night, her restless tongue
Was ever loud, and always wrong;
Around ye House for ever bawling
Fretting, fuming, Scolding, calling
Each Day produced a thousand evils
The Boy was bad, ye maids were devils
Her things, were never worth a Farthing
Her Pig was always in the garden:
Betsey had burnt her Sunday gown;
And Jackeys Frock was all unsown:——   so unthinking
Child, there is you and that dog Tray
Forever in our ironing way:—   you men are always
~~How should we get the things together~~   Sarah; those sheets
~~But some folks mind no times~~ or weather
~~Poor~~ Reubens starts ^up^ ye tear conceals   must have a Sprinkling[4]
And Tray close follows at his heels—
Now Sauntering o'er less hardned stones
Down dropt the Priest on marrow bones:
he weeping said
O Jupiter ~~whom mortals dread~~
Showr down thy curses on my Head
Or blast me; If I so deserve

3 A simple rustic person, a yokel; derived from the name of Jacob's and Leah's son Reuben in Genesis: *OED*.

4 Possibly Pratt meant to insert the lines 'You men are always so unthinking/ Sarah; those sheets must have a sprinkling' in place of 'How should we get the things together/ But some folks mind no times nor weather.'

Why did I not a curate starve?[5]
Gave up my Ease, and Chrysistom[6]
For a shrill Wife and noisy Home
Whateever my crimes, however wrong
O Save me from a Womans tongue
Jove, who knew well ye tricks of Marriage[7]
And all the taunts of female carriage
Said Mercury[8] my Boy, descend;
And be for once y^s poor mans Friend.

[*f. 1v*]

Do my good Cock,[9] your Jove Obey
And turn this Vixen to a Jay:
No sooner spoke, but in a Jerk
Down to the Earth descended Merc[10]
Found maids, and madam in debate
The Subject, what? a broken plate.
Merc waved his wand, but did not shew it
He touchd her, but she did not know it:
Strait underneath her Grogoram Gown[11]
She felt a rising dove Like down
Which sprouting round, her stays of Leather
Grew thro ye Holes; and turnd to feather:
Her Nose which did her face adorn
became at once, a beak of Horn—

5 Curacies were notoriously unstable forms of employment as well as being poorly paid.

6 John Chrysostom (*c.* 347–407), an early Church Father, who early in his life had lived as a hermit and was noted for his ascetism.

7 Jupiter was married to his sister Juno but was notorious for cheating on her with both humans and other gods, which enraged Juno and inspired various retaliations by her.

8 Mercury is the Roman messenger god, often depicted with wings at his feet; he is also the god of commerce, hence the irony in the following line about him being 'for once the poor man's friend'.

9 Mercury is sometimes depicted with a rooster, symbolizing the start of a new day.

10 i.e. Mercury.

11 Alternative spelling of 'grogram', a mixture of silk, wool and/or mohair, usually of a somewhat coarse texture due to being stiffened with gum: *OED*.

Her pocket string, thro' Placket[12] Hole
Stood a stiff Tail as Barbers Pole[13]
Her arms dropt off & lost their Springs
And all at once were changd to wings
Strange to behold, and odd ye cause
Her feet were now no feet, but claws
Good lack quoth she, (her favourite word)
Good lack, I'm quite a finishd Bird:
Thus changd to Jay, she reind her Neck
Began to Chatter, Hop and Peck
Retains the same Loquacious nature
A Busy, Bawling, flippant creature[14]
Ask all the Birds, and not a fowle
But shuns the noisy Screaming owle
With neither mate, or Bird Agrees
        Bawls
But ~~Prates~~ Eternaly to Trees;—
The moral shews in Humble Measure
What mischiefs flow from thirst of Treasure
How wild Ambitions Giddy Glare
Sets in our way the marriage Snare
And whilst we Gaudy schemes pursue
We frequently ourselves undo:
Would you ye priests Lead Happy Lives.
Take not for wealth these Jays for wives
Let Merit Lead you to preferment:
A Jay at best is but Interment.

12 A slit in clothing which gives access to a pocket: *OED*.

13 Since a placket often referred to a slit in a woman's apron and could also denote a vagina, there is likely a jocular phallic reference intended in the turning of the pocket string that was hanging out of the placket into a 'stiff tail as Barbers Pole'.

14 The description of the dramatic transformation echoes the technique in Ovid's *Metamorphoses*, which feature around twenty instances of humans turning into birds (though none explicitly into jays).

'Give up the world?—By Heaven not I'

NRO PRA 664/10

Date: ?*c.* 1781. Our best guess is that this poem belongs to the period in which Pratt was writing similarly themed poems on the subject of ageing as 'To N. S.' and 'To Christopher Anstey' and 'Watlington, 16 November 1781'.

Authorship: The manuscript of the poem in Pratt's hand is included in the Pratt folder. We are confident the poem is by Pratt.

Physical Description: Poem handwritten in ink on both sides of single piece of paper in Pratt's hand, measuring 19.5 cm by 32 cm.

[*f. 1r*]

Give up ye world?—By Heavn not I

Give up ye world?—By Heavn not I
Give up ye world—Id sooner dye
What shall old Lady Wrinkle prance it
And Miss Rump-wriggle nightly dance it
Whilst I set moping by myself
And take my pray'r Book from the shelf
What I, who have without rebukes
<Mind> ^Run^ carriages with Earls and Dukes
Drove down Lord Puppets Phaeton
When Miss Screamd, out Lud, Lud, undone:
Bet, reach my Drops (that Little Phial)
Give up the world?—O Horrid Trial
Fetch me my fan, I shant recover
Dear Little World, What give thee over—

O Bet, Bet, Bet, I faint I dye
Give up the world, in Dear July?
What set within, in Smoakey Houses
And eat fat meat with Sleepy Spouses
Set down <and> ^to^ hear ye Footmen swear
Puss Lick her Paw's, or wash her Ear
No, I am still, and will Inherit
Each Particle of Womans Spirit
Give up the World?—come hither Stephen
Be ready, with ye coach at Seven:
I must see, Dear Sir Francis Grog
Good Soul, Half poisond with his nog:
And I must call, just as I go
On poor Bet Gallops mangled toe
That Nasty, Heavy, Justice Brewin
Stampt on her foot, & caus'd its ruin:
Molly, Has Fizgig brought my Caps?
Dear ma'am not she, good God, perhaps
Sal Pinkaway—(is Sally marryd)
Yes ma'am, & has they say, miscarryd——
Now Jonathan, good Lad, make ready
Wheel up ye coach, & take your Lady:
"You Irish Dog, you son of Whore
"Fall back, nor crowd ye Carriage door
"By G—d Ill cut your backs to pieces[1]
"Make way, for Mad'm & her Nieces"—

[*f. 1v*]

Away they Whirl and Sing Te Deum[2]
At <Ranelap>[3] ^dear vauxhall^,[4] or some museum:

---

1 There are double quotation marks in the original manuscript at the beginning of this line.

2 An early Christian Latin hymn, of praise and thanksgiving, included in the Book of Common Prayer as part of the Morning Prayer.

3 Alternative spelling of 'Ranelagh'. The Ranelagh Gardens were pleasure gardens in Chelsea and included an impressive rococo rotunda.

4 Vauxhall Gardens. Both Chelsea and Vauxhall were located outside London itself in the eighteenth century. Ranelagh Gardens were newer and charged a higher admission fee than its rival gardens in Vauxhall. In 1744 Horace Walpole wrote: 'Every night constantly

The coach now gone; & bustle horrid
The Poet comes and Wipes his forehead
And beg you would, (from Histry Oral)
Accept from him, a bit of moral <—>
Lifes Brightest Day, with wishes granted
Will Always have, a Some thing wanted
There is (Dear Peg be grave) youl find
A Huge deep Gravel pit of Mind
Which all ye Spades, our Towns produce
Can near[5] fill up for present Use—
Have you not seen, th Assembly night
When Pulse beats high, and Tapers bright
When Totty stands, in sweet Surprize
To see Miss Biddy's Flummry[6] rise
When all is Flutter, Joy, Parade
Cold Tea, bad Wine, and Lemonade
Hackd out at Last: ye clock past four
Their spirits sunk, ye Candles Low'r
When Captain Brass, full mouthd, & Mellow
"Balls out play up, you sleepy Fellow
Fidlers, play up, or Else by God
Ill kick you, to the Land of Nod
Coaches away; to cool their Pride
Then those Tramp home, who cannot ride
Miss of Threescore pins up her cloaths
And Lanthor[7] Boys fall out with Oath's
"Wheres Mr Shuffletoes great coat
"Dear Sir tye something round your throat
Then Arm in Arm, they hobble down
This has a Beau, and this a Frown
Is Mr Alsops Servant there

[...] I go to Ranelagh; which has totally beat Vauxhall. Nobody goes anywhere else,—everybody goes there [...] you can't set your foot without treading on a Prince of Wales or Duke of Cumberland.' Walpole to Henry Seymour Conway, 29 June 1744, *The Yale Edition of Horace Walpole's Correspondence*, vol. 37 (New Haven: Yale University Press, 1937–1983), p. 164.

5 i.e. 'never'.

6 Insincere compliments: *OED*.

7 i.e. 'lanthorn', an alternative spelling of 'lantern'; 'lantern-boys' could be hired to light the way for those travelling by night where street lighting was not available.

Good God—Where is Pol Wollops chair:
Scud different ways, some slow, some fast
And tumble down, by too much haste
Thus tis in Life, with merry glee
We dance out youths, Fair Jubilee
Join hands & prance, and frisk about
As If Lifes Joys, would near wear out
But when Old Master Time advances
Come Boys, he cries, have done with dances
Here's Master Death and I are come
With Lanthorns for to Light you home:
Come come make Haste; y^{r} dance is done
Bid Master Kirk, engrave ye Stone
Here, ends ye verse, good Night, no quarrel
You've sense enough, to find ye Moral[8]——

8 The last six lines are written vertically in the left-hand margin.

'A Hint for the Year'

Norwich Mercury, **6 August 1785, p. 4.**

Date: 6 August 1785.

Authorship: There is no manuscript in Pratt's hand but the presence of the clipping in the Pratt folder, the fact that the poem concerns a clergyman, and the mock-learned reference to Diomedes of Thrace makes us think there is a strong possibility that the poem is by Pratt. The clipping has not been given its own reference code.

Physical description: Newspaper clipping measuring 7 cm by 10 cm.

[*p. 4*]

A HINT FOR THE YEAR

A Thracian King,[1] a bloody King indeed,
With human flesh was known his nags to feed:
So mean a wretch, and of such saving knowledge,
He'd rack[2] his steeds, with Fellows of a College:
Sometimes perhaps, when plump upon the rib,
A huge fat lawyer tumbled in his crib,
Doctors and proctors, shovell'd in by dozens,
And what was worse, good God, he rack'd with cousins:
Old Hercules,[3] who lov'd good deeds they tell ye

1 Diomedes of Thrace, notorious for his man-eating horses.

2 A rack is a frame containing animal fodder. 'Rack' could also be used verbally in the sense of providing animals with fodder: *OED*.

3 Hercules's eighth labour was to catch the horses and bring them back to Greece; in the process Hercules killed Diomedes and fed him to the mares.

With his own pitchfork ran him thro' the belly;
Wreathing[4] he bore him, to his own good horses:
"Here, nags he cry'd, here's first and second courses;
"Here's a tit bit, who once so fiercely rid,
At him my boys, and chew the royal quid.[5]—
You laugh, my Lord, and you my good Sir John
Hold, hold awhile, my tale is not yet done:
When you great folks, with legions at your heels,
With men and nags, who want a hundred meals,
When you to visit some good priest drive on
You'l knaw his flesh; you pick him to the bone:
Take here a hint, enlarge your own good rack,
And save this year the Vicar's infant stack.[6]

4 i.e. 'writhing'.

5 A small lump of chewable substance, often tobacco: *OED*. Here it figuratively refers to the Thracian king, who is also likened to a 'tit bit' in the preceding line.

6 Hay or straw arranged in a pile, often with a thatched top for protection: *OED*.

Longer Prose Writings

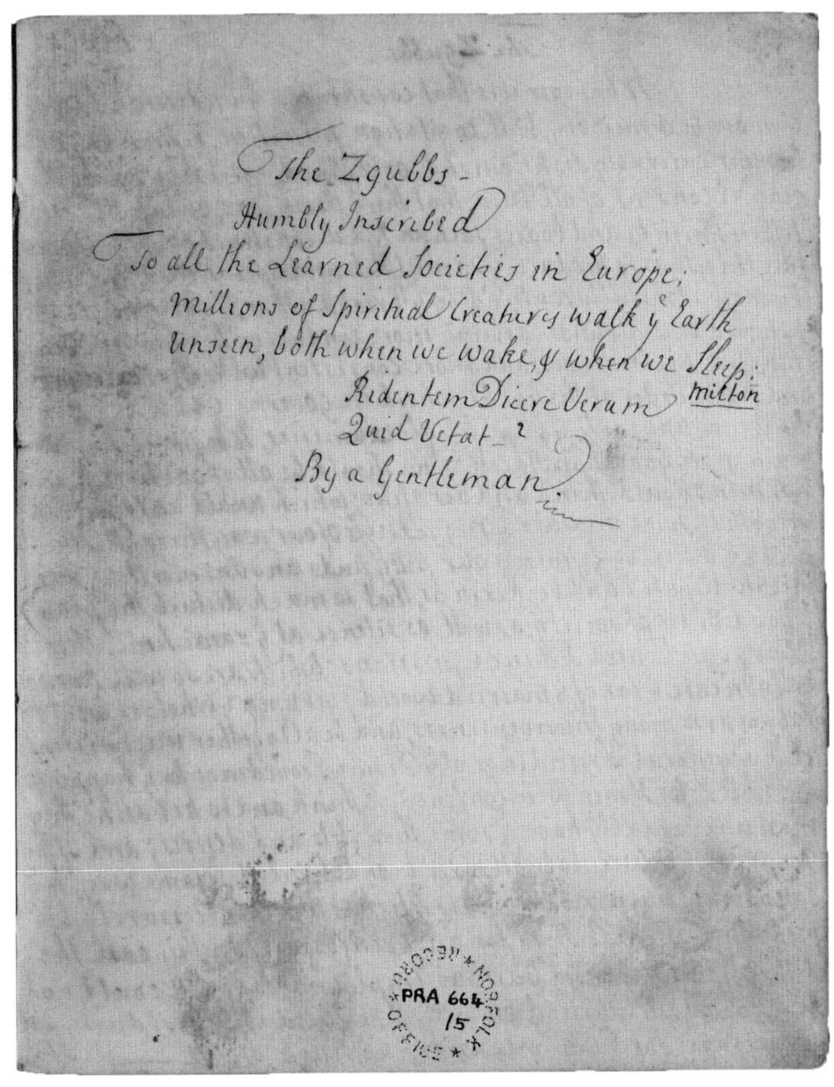

The Zgubbs -

Humbly Inscribed

To all the Learned Societies in Europe;

Millions of Spiritual Creatures walk ye Earth
Unseen, both when we wake, & when we Sleep: Milton

Ridentem Dicere Verum
Quid Vetat - ?

By a Gentleman

Figure 10 *The Title Page of* The Zgubbs

The Zgubbs

NRO PRA 664/5

Date: 1782 or later (based on an apparent reference to an essay by Vicesimus Knox first published in 1782).

Authorship: The manuscript is in Pratt's hand and is included in the Pratt folder. We are confident in attributing the long essay to Pratt.

Physical description: Long comic essay handwritten in ink on a single page at the back of a sewn paper booklet with a marbled cover in Pratt's hand, measuring 19.5 cm by 24 cm.

[*tp*]

The Zgubbs—

Humbly Inscribed

To all the Learned Societies in Europe;

Millions of Spiritual Creatures walk ye Earth

Unseen, both when we wake, & when we Sleep:[1]

Milton

Ridentem Dicere Verum

Quid Vetat—?[2]

By a Gentleman.

1 The lines are spoken by Adam to Eve in Book Four of *Paradise Lost* (*Milton*, 677–8). Joseph Addison also quotes the lines in *Spectator* 12. As we note in our Introduction (p. 22) the argument about the Zgubbs also recalls Soame Jenyns's serious proposal that evil events may be attributed to malevolent spirits in *A Free Inquiry into the Nature and Origin of Evil* (1756). Pratt had sent a copy of his poem 'Grunnelia or the Sow in the Dumps' to Jenyns before February 1760 so he was likely familiar with Jenyns's work.

2 *DLCL*: Horace, *Satires I*, 1:24–5 (p. 7) 'What is to prevent one from telling truth as he laughs.'

[*p. 1*]

The Zgubbs—

Whatever it is that constitutes ye understanding of man, be it memory, Will, cogitation, perception, reflection, or however curiously distinguishd or Defined, yet it seems to be the general consent of all Men, that there never was, or can be in different minds and bodies; such an Equal construction of parts and faculties, so as to produce ye same Effects and Operations—And indeed it is most admirably contriv'd by ye Great Author of our nature y^t it should be Otherwise; as being more conducive to ye General Happiness of his Creatures, and more consistent with that excellent and fixed Order of things, by which he governs ye World; For, tho it may appear to ye superficial examiner, to be productive of much more good than Harm; y^t we should be all of one mind, and that men should think and act alike; which would undoubtedly smooth in some measure ye ruggedness of our way through this Life to a better; by Lessning our petty feuds and animosities, our private disputes and bickerings, that so much disturb the peace & good Order of Society, as well as silence at ye same time, those Silver sounds and Silkey expressions; Which are so well known to Lubricate ye ear of ye married World; yet upon ye Whole it would subject us to many Inconveniences, and be altogether inconsistent with ye general Proceedings of ye Divine Providence for ye happiness of ye World: for, If men were confined to think and to act alike, they must unavoidably have ye same thoughts and desires; and if the Powers of men were to be all turn'd and directed ye same way, to ye same sort of purposes and pursuits; this would necessarily be productive of great disorder and confusion: In this case the different businesses and various Employments of Life could not be followed and carried on with that Laudable Assiduity so necessary for the good and Happiness of All——If [*p. 2*] things were to be thus orderd; ye mind for want of a proper exertion and a necessary variety, would in a great measure grow Languid and Loose its force, being Eternaly pointed to one and ye same Object—to be more easily understood—Suppose half a million of men for instance, were all resolute and Dertermin'd to pursue the great profession of ye Law; or, If as many would be sweating & shoving their way to Warwick Lane;[3] ye consequences in both these instances would be dreadful; in ye first, ye courts of a thousand Westminster Halls, could never possibly contain them; besides there must be such a wretched want of Employment; that they would soon

3 The Royal College of Physicians was located in Warwick Lane in London.

be in the miserable condition of Starved fish in a Pond; and so Obliged by necessity to turn Short[4] and Destroy each other, and ye consequence would be ye same were as many Determined to be Physicians; in this case which of them do you think would undergo their own prescriptions? And If they would not as certainly would be ye case, we may easily suppose men to Live to a much Longer period. Now if things were to be thus managed; How effectualy would it ruin ye clergy and Laity too, such I mean who depend upon their burial fees[5] (as is the case in most cities) not to mention ye good Society of Undertakers, coffin-makers, Grave-diggers[,] Parish Clerks, and Others, who by this means would be deprived of their bread, and turn'd adrift to a merciless world; besides, If so many were so ridiculously intent upon ye same employments; Where would there be found Hands Sufficient, for the furnishing out such a variety of Perukes as would be wanted? (I need not mention ye danger of wearing their own Hairs) Where too would be found, such a quantity of Green Bayes:[6] Parchment,[7] canes, snuff-boxes, Nosegays and rings, If such a Scheme could be brought to practise to furnish out these mighty professions—? It is then most true and Evident, that for men to be of one mind and to think and to act always alike, is by no means for the general good of the [*p. 3*] whole, ye different pursuits men have, and ye different operations and modifications their minds undergo; ye different Trades & occupations they are engaged in, rouzes ye soul to a variety of Action, and which occasions at ye same time ye most pleasing and valuable productions; and as both Air and Wind are allow'd to be good and necessary for ye moving and purifying of our waters; so a different mode of thinking is equaly necessary for ye minds and bodies of men; to keep them in a reasonable and necessary agitation[8]——

As it is then most admirably contrived, that ye minds and faculties of men should be opposite, and differently modified for their respective

4 Turn around suddenly: *OED*.

5 Fees charged by the parish for the interment in a particular burial plot; the amounts varied across parishes and even within a particular parish, depending on the location and size of the particular plot. See Peter C. Jupp and Clare Gittings, eds, *Death in England: An Illustrated History* (Manchester: Manchester University Press, 1999), p. 76.

6 Bay leaves, from the bay laurel plant, have been used for medicinal purposes at least since antiquity.

7 Used presumably for the writing of the life-extending prescriptions.

8 c.f. Anthony Ashley Cooper, Third Earl of Shaftesbury's famous argument in his *Sensus Communis: An Essay on the Freedom of Wit and Humour* (1709) for the benefits of friendly raillery: 'We polish one another and rub off our corners and rough sides by a sort of amicable collision.' *Characteristicks of Men, Manners, Opinions, Times*, ed. Lawrence E. Klein (Cambridge: Cambridge University Press, 1999), p. 31.

Operations and employments; so it is no less a proof of infinite care and Wisdom; that y[e] bodies and Shapes of men should be as different as their minds; If it was Otherwise and we had all y[e] same kind of features, and were all exactly of y[e] same mould and Stature; y[e] inconveniences arising from hence would be such, as effectually to destroy y[e] peace and Happiness of thousands—for tho' it might afford much agreable fun to a modern set of young fellows, to out face, and out Lye an innocent Neighbour, by asserting roundly and swearing heartily for each other; y[t] it was not his wife, or his daughter who was debauchd; but that it was another mans wife or relation, and that they would undertake to prove it so by y[e] exact Symmetry of the features, and y[e] peculiar proportion of y[e] Woman; yet how great and manifest would be y[e] Mischeifs & injuries y[t] must arise from hence?—for If men and women could not be distinguishd y[e] one from y[e] Other by their outward Form and figure; they would be so Jumbled and mixed together; that except they were all to be markd and branded like Cattle; it would be as difficult to distinguish them; as it would be for a [*p. 4*] Gardiner to know every distinct Pea in his basket; and supposing this was to be y[e] case, we might frequently see an honest man, Harried away for another by mistake, to execution—y[e] Heir in the clothes of his Fathers Steward and running off with the money; women mistaking other men for their Husbands; and Husbands as mistaking in their wives; y[e] Taylor fitting one mans coat upon y[e] shoulders of another; y[s] eating anothers meat by mistake of the Butcher; and y[e] world would be (If possible) much worse than it is at present—Now it must be granted by every thinking person; that it is much better for y[e] General good of y[e] Whole, that there should be that inequality and variety that now is, both with respect to y[e] minds & persons of men; and from hence it will follow; that as there are no two minds and persons alike; so every one has a full and absolute right to y[e] Enjoyment of his own mind; and may so think & maintain his opinion of things; y[t] no power on Earth can challenge any right to deprive him of it——We are indeed so truly sensible of this; y[t] If you or I (my Intelligent Reader) were to take an Opinion; (suppose it to be that of our Lawyer, or Physician[)]; we become immediatly conscious to ourselves, that this his private Opinion, is private property with him; and that we must Leave with either of them a reasonable consideration, before we dare Venture to take it from them; and therefore so Long as men are quiet and peacible in their several Stations and occupations, and do no manner of Harm in the world by word or deed; and do cautiously avoid all manner of clamor and faction; they have an Absolute and unquestionable right to frame and enjoy What notions and Theories they please: And should it be said to me here in this place; that a man has no more a right to be ye Maker of his own Opinion; than he has to be the maker of his own Garment; that If all men were [*p. 5*] allow'd to think and Judge for themselves, this would necessarily involve us in great confusion; yet I must beg Leave to Observe by way of reply: that If I am to follow an Opinion, because it is backd by another person, without ye consent and approbation of my own understanding; by ye same rule I might be inducd to admire ye Rosary itself; or to believe ye good Old Stories of Ghosts & Goblins[9] ye Clanking of Chains, and Shrieks in ye Chimnies Corner, as both my Nurse and my Grandmother ^God bless them^ believed most cordialy.——

And here I shall pause a moment to satisfy my fears and apprehensions, and to bespeak ye Readers patience not to grow restless and peevish with me, nor to cry with an Insolent Pish, What ye Devil can there be in these Zgubbs—Let us not fall out by ye way for we are men and Brethren; ye Works of Authors Like ye flowers in your Garden (If you have one Gentle Reader) will not all open and blow alike; they have their times and their Seasons and most of us know that ye finest Pearls are frequently found in those shells that are most difficult to open; Do not think it then so easy a matter as some men may Idly suppose for a man[10] to bring into ye world his first born Hypothesis in full proportion; ye throes and pangs of Authors are dreadful upon such Occasions, (Oh! Heaven what do I feel this minute) and a Writer must be inclosed in triple brass[11] at Least, or have a heart of Adamant, If he does not Shake and tremble all over, when he reflects on ye Grin of ye Critic, ye Sneer of the Pedant; and ye formidable talons of ye Reviewers[12] so ready to fall upon him and souse him to Atoms; but I am determined however to take a Little courage and turn about in ye face of my pursuers and plead ye privilege of an Author; for tho it may not be in my

9 'Goblins' appears on the unnumbered page facing p. 5, which otherwise is blank. Since it is obvious where the word is to go in the sentence, we have inserted it into the relevant place.

10 Each letter in the word has been underlined individually in the manuscript.

11 In the third ode of Book 1 of Horace's *Odes*, the heart of the first sailor is described as being encircled by triple brass and oak. Brad Pasanek notes that this ode 'is a favorite of those eighteenth-century British audiences that pride themselves on their nation's naval victories' and that many poets in this period, including Christopher Smart, either imitated the ode or referenced it. See his *Metaphors of Mind: An Eighteenth-Century Dictionary* (Baltimore: Johns Hopkins University Press, 2016), p. 180.

12 Compare Tristram's address to the reviewers in *Tristram Shandy*: '— You Messrs. the monthly Reviewers——how could you cut and slash my jerkin as you did? ——how did you know, that you would cut my lining too?' (*Sterne*, 1:190–1).

power to build a Sty for my pig, or a Heet[13] for my Winters firing, yet as ye materials are all my own, I will build my Hypothesis [*p. 6*] in spite of ye world, and in that way which pleases me best[14]——

—It can never be denied by persons of any tolerable candour, but that the wildest Parodoxes, even of the Wildest Writers are sometimes mixed with material truths, and ye world has been long amused with variety of Systems, Theories, Phenomenons, and ye Lord knows what; The Great Plato (God bless him) had his Anima mundi;[15] Epicurus his Atoms to play with,[16] and ye good Bishop of our own kept his flying Chariot to take a trip now and then to ye moon,[17] (tho he never paid a Farthing for ye Wheels)—Varro[18] himself has told us long enough ago, that there were eighty eight opinions concerning ye summum bonum;[19] Cartesius enjoyd his Nullibists[20] Hobbs chuckled over his Leviathan;[21] Whiston and Burnet,[22] Idolized their Theories, Descartes had his flings and his Jerks as well as the rest

13 A fireplace: *OED*.

14 The building of and stubborn adherence to absurd hypotheses is recurrent theme in *Tristram Shandy*, in which Tristram observes 'It is the nature of an hypothesis, when once a man has conceived it, that it assimilates every thing to itself as proper nourishment: and, from the first moment of your begetting it, it generally grows the stronger by every thing you see, hear, read, or understand' (*Sterne*, 1:177).

15 '[T]he animating principle, a power or spirit supposed by early philosophers to be present throughout the material universe, organizing and giving form to the whole and to all its parts, and regulating change and movement': *OED*.

16 Epicurus (341–270 BC) held that all phenomena could be explained through the motions of atoms.

17 John Wilkins (1614–1672), Bishop of Chester and a Fellow and founding member of the Royal Society. Wilkins wrote *A Discovery of a New World* (published posthumously in 1684), in which he proposed that a winged chariot propelled by sails could be used for an expedition to the moon and predicted that such a journey would happen in his own lifetime.

18 Marcus Terentius Varro (116–27 BC), Roman polymath and author, whose *De Philosophia* actually includes 288 opinions.

19 'The highest or supreme good, as the ultimate goal according to which values and priorities are established in an ethical system': *OED*.

20 René Descartes (Latinized as 'Cartesius') argued, like the Nullibists, that the soul is separate from the body. He is, however, more often associated with the so-called Holenmerists, who claimed that the mind is located in the body though it is different from it, whereas the Nullibists claimed that souls or spirits do not exist in physical space: *SEP*.

21 Thomas Hobbes in his *Leviathan* (1651) developed a theory of the commonwealth as a corporate person represented and brought into being by the sovereign. A leviathan itself is an enormous aquatic animal often mentioned in the Hebrew Bible: *OED*.

22 William Whiston (1667–1752) and Thomas Burnet (1635?–1715), proponents of a new cosmogony, noted and initially criticised for disagreeing on various points with the biblical account of creation: *Oxford DNB* and *SEP*.

but unfortunately loosing his clew at ye first setting out, he was Afterward most miserably shut up in a Labyrinth of his own contriving[23]——Was I indeed to go forth in ye Armour of those invincible Theorists who challenge ye world of Criticks to Oppose them; such as ye fugitive m'P—[24] or ye dull and Elaborate D^{r} S;[25] (for I will mention no names in this work—^nor touch any mans sore except it be with a design to heal it——^) was I to go forth I say with ye spouts and foam of those doughty Champions and Lovers of System, who will rage, swear, and blaspheme If you will not think with them, and swallow all they have to Offer you; I might then indeed deserve ye Lash of ye Critic; but Alas! Alas! I am Little more than a youth, and cannot go forth with such weapons as theirs, I have never as yet proved them; nor can I boast at present of that sevenfold impenetrable Assurance, y^{t} distinguishes those hardy Veterans; this is so far from being my case, y^{t} I do not desire one man upon Earth to think as I do except he chooses it; I had much rather Jibe with you in matter of Opinion, (my Intelligent Reader) and probably we shall think alike before we part; But if a man is so unfortunate as to be sent into the world, as it [*p. 7*] may be with a dislocated understanding, If he feels a strange uncomfortable twist in his Noddle; it is better & more Charitable surely, to receive such a one ^as^ a Little out of ye way; and not altogether as an Object for our contempt and ridicule:——

Let it be known then to such who choose it; that ye Land of conjecture is wide and Open, and every one has an unquestionable right to a Share therein; and he who knows not how to Cultivate and make his improvements in it ye public has a right to divest him of it, and give it to him who has better talents; in this Land of uncertainty and darkness there are many Labourers; great application and Industry is frequently used, and no pains are wanted to cultivate this Stubborn & barren soil; and after all that is done or can be done in it Little or no fruit is to be had to reward their Labours: It is here we may find Metaphysicians, Opticians, Mathematicians, Physicians, and a thousand Others; ye refiners of Theology, Astrology, Zoology, Physiology & ye Lord knows who, most incessantly hard at Work: Here they are digging

23 In *Rules for the Direction of the Mind* (composed 1626–1628; published posthumously 1684), Descartes compares the whole world to Daedalus's Labyrinth and his own scientific methods to the string that had guided Theseus out of the Labyrinth.

24 Probably a reference to James Macpherson, the author of *Fingal* (1762), what he claimed to be a translation of an ancient Gaelic epic. Pratt had a first edition of Fingal in his library. It was common to use the abbreviation 'm'' for 'Mac' in the eighteenth century. Our thanks to Amanda Louise Johnson for this suggestion.

25 Probably Dr Philip Skelton (1707–1787), Irish cleric and author of short theological treatises and satirical pieces: *Oxford DNB*.

and Delving; clearing and making their way in ye highest spirits, each expecting to be blest with some new discovery; and whether it is owing to ye natural barrenness of the soil itself, or to ye improper method of cultivation; to the badness of ye seed that is sown, or to whatever cause it may be attributed yet it is certain and beyond all doubt, there is Little or no Increase to ye Public; It is here ye Theologist sows most plentifully and expects ye reaping a full harvest of Grace, Free will, predestination[,] Original sin, and so forth; but it commonly turns out in the end y^{t} his seed falls on so dry and barren a soil that nothing will come up that is worth ye reaping: in this Land of conjecture, ye Physician[,] the Antiquarian and many Others, will put in their claim [*p. 8*] for discovery; Here Muscle and Vein, Nerve and Artery, are carefully examin'd and dissected; and when he thinks he has made ye most important Discoveries ye Earth was ever blest with; ye Animal Spirits, or nervous fluid commonly springs upon his way, and overflows all his works, with a mighty torrent: nor indeed is it any thing better with ye Antiquarian and Others, in y^{s} wide Land of uncertainty; for tho he will use no other tools, but such as the Grecian and Roman Artists have Long approved of; yet after a number of researches in ye dark, and a great deal of Hunting to Little or no good purpose; he stumbles at Last on ye head of an Otho,[26] which so miserably turns ye Edge of his Tool; that nothing can Afterwards be done, to bring his work to perfection:—and should there now & then be found a Husbandman who knows very well, how to sow his seed in due season; and from whence we might expect a tolerable increase; yet even then ye Sly Deceiver will come within the month[27] and scatter his tares amongs[28] it; and where then are ye hopes of his harvest;—? If then it is evident to all men; that this Land of conjecture is so dry and barren; If so Little encouragement is to be given to ye slaves who do ye Drudgery; If our critical Masters will have their tale of Brick, when so Little Straw is to be allowed;[29] we must not think it strange, or expect any thing better, than a Zgubb, or a Gomma, instead of ye fair flowers of Tristram, and ye shrubs of

26 A coin from the reign of Marcus Salvius Otho Caesar Augustus (AD 32–69), who was Roman emperor for three months in AD 69, and due to his reign's brevity, few coins with his portrait were minted.

27 The manuscript uses a dotted line under 'month'.

28 Variant spelling of 'amongst': *OED*.

29 Reference to the phrase 'bricks without straw', based on the account of the Jews' plight in Egypt in Exodus 5, where the Pharaoh punishes Moses for requesting the permission to leave by making the Jewish brick-makers gather their own straw required for brick-making while requiring the same level of productivity as when the straw had been supplied to them.

Gulliver:[30]—If this then be ye state of ye Land and with ye Slaves who people it; and If every one has a right to conjecture, as he certainly has in ye way he chooses; and If these kind of visionary buildings are as Easily destroyd as built, we beg ye Indulgence to put in our claim with ye rest of our Utopian Brethren, and to Offer our Hypothesis to the world without offending——

[*p. 9*]

There are according to a certain medico-physical society, certain natural excavations in ye head of man, wherein every one may be supposed to have a sort of twisting Mill, or Gig[31] of his own; to work and bring forward his Ideas; and whatever happens either to Obstruct or Impel ye Working of this machine gives such wonderful Alterations to ye brain; y^t^ a man feels himself better milld at some seasons of ye year than he does at another. And this in some measure Accounts why there are some heads so strange and Whimsical, without any fixed Ideas at all, some exceeding heavy and confusd; some working and whirling along with amazing rapidity, depending in a great measure upon ye different movements of ye machine as it works and mills ye Imagination; and from hence we may probably Account for ye strange mistakes of our medical people concerning ye various Disorders of ye Head; for whatever has been said or wrote, of the Cephalagia, the Cephalea; ye Hemicranier, ye Clavis Hystericus[32] and so forth; yet After all; most of ye Disorders of ye head may proceed and be occasion'd by ye over friction of ye Gig, or its strange inequalities in the working; should it be granted me then that there is or may be such a machine or Gig in every mans head; that thus works and mills his Ideas, yet it may be questiond perhaps After all, what it is that can give it its first motion; Give me Leave to Observe in this place;

30 Here, Pratt modestly compares *The Zgubbs* to Laurence Sterne's *Tristram Shandy* and Jonathan Swift's *Gulliver's Travels.*

31 A twisting mill or a gig mill was a machine designed for creating cloth. The *OED* describes a gig-mill as 'a machine for raising a nap on cloth by the use of teazles or wire-cards', with examples dating from 1551 to 1879. In *Tristram Shandy* Uncle Toby compares the revolutions of his own mind to those of a 'smoak-jack' (*Sterne,* 1:226). On eighteenth-century metaphors of mind in general, see also Brad Pasanek, *Metaphors of Mind: An Eighteenth-Century Dictionary* (Baltimore: The Johns Hopkins University Press, 2016) and its accompanying internet database *The Mind is a Metaphor,* which can be accessed at http://metaphors.iath.virginia.edu.

32 All terms for different kinds of headache: Cephalagia and Cephalea are more general while Hemicrania (in the eighteenth century called 'Hemicranier') denotes pain concentrated on one side of the head and Clavus Hystericus to an intense pain in the forehead (formerly assumed to be brought on by Hysteria): *OED.*

that all our motions and sensations are executed by ye help of ye nervous fluid[,][33] now the first movement of this Machine or Gig in the head may be accounted for two ways; either by ye influx of this nervous fluid[34] into ye brain, (very near to Descartes pineal Gland)[35] w[h]ere ye Nerves are said all to terminate; or by ye outward air taken up and received at ye mouth, ye Ear, or Nostril; Now the cortical part of the Brain being allowd to be exceeding Vascular;[36] A quantity of this nervous [*p. 10*] fluid may be taken up and conveyd to ye brain, by ye coroted and vertebral Arteries,[37] and so set ye machine a working; or it is possible to be, yt ye air received by ye mouth, ye Ear, ye Nostril, or ye very common Operations of Breathing, Sneezing, coughing, Ventilating and so forth, or ye very motion of ye Limbs and body, may serve to cooperate with ye Gig in its different motions—I do not take upon me to say, yt it is thus absolutely performd; I will be ye Director of no mans Opinion but he who is anatomicaly acquainted with ye processus Zygomaticus,[38] ye processus Hyloides,[39] or ye processus Mammillaris;[40] will easily grant me all this may be performd by ye Air that is received by the Ear, or mouth only; so that it is reasonable to conclude that every one has a Gig or mill of his own, to bring forward and work his Ideas and ye irregularity of its motion at different times, may occasion (observe that I say may occasion) ye very different productions we meet within ye world; and many times I have observd; from the same Authors:—Having thus far paved ye way for ye introducing of my own opinion of things, (which may be thought perhaps to be a Little whimsical) I feel myself more enlarged & comfortable at ye heart, and shall go on with much better Spirits; and whatever shall be said of these my Zgubbs; that it is a strange & ridiculous Undertaking; so mix'd

33 Some punctuation would be expected here but as the word appears at the right-hand margin of the page there is no punctuation.

34 In early modern medical theories, fluid was believed to travel around the nervous system and thereby transmit nervous impulses to the brain: *OED*.

35 The pineal gland, a structure deep in the brain, was supposed to function as the interface between the body and the soul. Joseph Addison writes in *Spectator* 275 that 'The Pineal Gland, which many of our Modern Philosophers suppose to be the Seat of the Soul' (*Spec*, 4:89).

36 The cerebral cortex; what Pratt is here terming the 'vascular' part of the brain probably refers to the concentration of folds in this area of the brain in addition to veins and arteries.

37 Carotid and vertebral arteries, which supply blood to the brain: *OED*.

38 The zygomatic process is the section of the bone in the skull articulating with the zygomatic bone or cheekbone: *OED*.

39 The styloid process refers to several protrusions of bones where muscles are attached: *OED*.

40 The mammillary process refers to the protrusions in the lumbar vertebrae where muscles are attached: *OED*.

and confused a performance; and so totaly unconnected throughout, that a Reader can neither be pleas'd or instructed by it; yet so Long as it is a Child of my own Fancy, tho it is not perhaps in every feature Like ye rest of the family, or so agreable as Papa could wish it, yet I cannot find it in my heart to disown the Bantling;[41] for If every common Baker in ye composition of a Farthing cake,[42] can Stick his plumb here, or his comfort there, as it pleases his Fancy [*p. 11*] best, can Glaze and mingle his work as he chooses to have it; Let me humbly entreat ye public to give me Leave, to raise this my Theological meslin[43] in ye way that I Like, as no one is Obliged to purchase, except he chooses it[44]——

Our excellent Milton has Long ago Observ'd that there are (or may be) millions of Beings continualy surrounding this Earth of ours, and occupying Every part of it, tho invisible to us, and beyond ye reach of our discovery; and If we may be allow'd to reason from analogy and ye Wo[r]ks of nature, (which is but fair and reasonable;) If every part of this small spot of ours which we call earth, seems to be so plentifully fill'd in all its parts, so yt immense space which surrounds us here, cannot be supposed to want its Inhabitants any more than ye earth itself: Now if there be as we may Suppose a regular gradation of Beings there may be such things as ye Zgubbs, or Gommas,[45] such kind of

41 See *The Grange*, note 5, p. 57 in our edition.

42 A farthing cake, named so because it cost a single farthing, was a simple flat cake made with flour, water, and sometimes raisins, glazing, plums, preserves ('plumbs' and 'comforts' [confits] in the sentence above): *OED*. In the word 'comforts', Pratt presumably underlines 'ort' to make it clear that it is 'comfort' in the sense of 'confit' that is intended, but a pun on 'comfort' is also possible.

43 A variant of 'maslin', a mix of different types of grain or a bread made from such a mixture: *OED*. Here the term is used metaphorically for the mixture of different ideas from theology and natural philosophy presented by Pratt in his essay.

44 c.f. Tristram's plea to the reader in *Tristram Shandy* to let him 'tell my story my own way' (*Sterne*, 1:9).

45 The name given to these immaterial beings the 'Zgubbs' is obviously a nonsense word. It does, however, phonetically resemble the 'grubs' that were the bane of Norfolk farmers. In the *Norwich Mercury* a letter writer reported his conversation with one farmer on the plague of grubs: 'The Increase of these destructive Vermin is so great, that, as I have been inform'd, this Man has positively asserted that he has sometimes destroyed fourscore Bushes of them in one Season upon his own Farm only; and that for several Years, whilst he continued to use this Method, he received little or no Damage from them; but being hindered by Illneses from doing it one Season as usual, a great Part of his Crops, both of Grass and Corn, were destroyed by them in the two following Years.' See *Norwich Mercury*, 22 June 1771, p. 2. Grubs, in turn, are not too far from 'maggots', which could refer both to the larvae of flies and to strange fancies born of the brain: *OED*. The alternate name for the Zgubbs, 'Gommas' suggests 'commas': grub-like little typographical marks that authors employ to help get their 'maggots' out of their minds and onto the page.

airy substances I mean, as are freed from ye Incumbrances of flesh, Attending and surrounding us in every part, not inattentive to our Actions, and moving in a Sphere of activity beyond our own; I do not take upon me to say that this is matter of fact; let ye hardy Disputant disprove it If he can; It is sufficient for my purpose to Urge y^t it is impossible for him to prove it Otherwise, Leaving ye following remark with our grave Philosophers and men of System; that there is no one instance they can give of superior pride and perverseness, than to Disbelieve every thing they meet with; because it is beyond their power to comprehend how, & in what manner it exists—For if in ye material world Almost every thing we meet with, tho within ye compass of our knowledge, is more than Sufficient to puzzle the acutest Philosophers to Account for; in [*p. 12*] what way is it possible to us to explain ye nature of those worlds y^t are so far beyond us[46]—? And for a man to Affirm that he cannot rise from his chair, or view a Star in ye Heavens because he cannot explain how seeing or motion are effected, is ye most deplorable of all absurdities, for after all we know so Little of what an immaterial substance is; How it subsists and Operates; and what are its peculiar properties, that there may be myriads of Zgubbs around us in all directions; tho we are not able to say in what manner they exist. Whatever then is, or may be ye employment of these my Zgubbs; whether they float in air, or flutter at ye elbow whether they have any existence at all, which I own is much to be questiond, whether they constantly Attend our motions or superintend our Actions, or how far they are disposed to promote our pleasures or oppose them, is rather a matter of inquisitive speculation; for If we know so Little of unembodied substances, what qualities or properties they have it is impossible to explain ye nature of their agency with respect to us, or what kind of relation or fellowship they carry on in the world——It has been reported indeed of one Hieronymus Cardanus[47] a native of Milan, that he was constantly Attended by an aerial spirit; but whether it was an actual existing Zgubb or Gomma, does not appear from his History at this distance of time; and as it was observd before, we cannot possibly know what are ye modes and Qualities of unembodied Substances, so is it impossible to explain their nature and agency with respect

46 In *Entretiens sur la pluralité des mondes* (*Conversations on the Plurality of Worlds*), first published in 1701, Bernard le Bovier de Fontenelle popularised the thesis that the sun and its planets comprised only a small part of the universe and that the fixed stars were suns with planets of their own, with the corollary that there were millions of 'worlds' in existence beside our own: *SEP*.

47 Hieronymus Cardanus (1501–1576), an Italian mathematician and physician. John Beaumont discusses Cardanus's writings on spirits, including his account of the spirit that attended him, in *An Historical, Physiological and Theological Treatise of Spirits* (London: D. Browne et al., 1705), pp. 50–7.

to ourselves; yet after all I do most Seriously confess; y^{t} I cannot altogether think with those persons; who are not willing to ascribe anything, to ye possible Agency of the Zgubbs, not even Any of the Lesser provocations we meet With in the World [*p. 13*] but will account for every thing that falls in their way; as if all was by chance or accident, or by our own folly & mismanagement, and not a single Zgubb concernd in those many teazing perplexities and provocations that so frequently fall in our way tho' at ye same time I do confess, (and give it here under my hand) that this my Hypothesis of ye Zgubbs, may be nothing more than a creature of my own brain, without any real foundation to support it——————————

In ye year of our Lord 1734 (If I remember aright) dropping a Shilling by accident at our club, it so unaccountably wheeled away on its Edge, y^{t} I stood frighted for a time, and under ye Greatest embarrassment: I turn'd myself to ye Left, Lo! It was not there, to ye right it was not there; this way and that way, twisting around a hundred times, muttering to myself at ye same time, bless me, Dear Heart, mercy on me, where can it be and so forth; till at last I it at a considerable distance, standing Edge way against ye foot of a Chair; and as I thought with a kind of Leering alacrity to play at Bopeep with ye company; from that time I began to think more seriously than ever of ye reality of these Zgubbs, or Gommas, whether it was not possible (I say possible) that some of them might be concernd in driving away ye Shilling, in ye manner the School Boys do their hoops; what power if any they have over us Mortals; and in what way we may account for those many perplexing Incidents and Little teazing provocations that are so frequently to be met with; tho often unobserv'd by us, in ye common transactions of our worldly business— Everydays Observation convincd me more and more, that notwithstanding how Chimerical and Absurd this Hypothesis of mine might be thought by some; However Whimsical and particular it may Appear to the inquisitive sceptical Theologist who will dive to [*p. 14*] ye bottom of every thing that comes in his way; yet there are and will be still a thousand difficulties y^{t} do happen to us all every moment of our Lives, a thousand Oddities in our way, wonderful in their Effects and altogether above ye boasted Sufficiency of the most consummate Philosopher to account for—for my own part I detest from my heart ye insolence of those Writers, who will not even allow a thing to be possible (which is ye most I contend for) because it will not square with their own notions of things; they will be so hardy as to deny ye real existence of a Zgubb, because Neither Kepler nor Galileo[48] forsooth, could

48 Johannes Kepler (1571–1630) German astronomer; Galileo Galilei (1564–1642) Italian astronomer.

ever discover by any of their Glasses a real existing Zgubb; If they do not set up an Hypothesis of their own making, they are sure to condemn and pull down ye visionary Labours of other men; and will be even so unmerciful, as to deny a man ye reasonable satisfaction of supposing a thing to be Matter of fact because it may be different from their own way of thinking and take from yt majesty they would Usurp, over ye minds and consciences of their Brethren:——

There will be scarce now I hope either man or woman to be found as this our History of ye Zgubbs is laid open to common Observation, but will be able to bring to their memories, ye many horrid and teazing provocations they have frequently under gone; tho ye reason of such their sufferings have hitherto been undiscovered: It must now appear plain and manifest to a thinking mind; that what has hitherto passd so long in ye world; by ye name of Accident, casuality,[49] want of memory, unlucky incidents, and so forth, might be Attributed perhaps with more propriety to ye agency of the Zgubbs and their horrid fun of tormenting us; There is not a man in ye world who does not know the difficulty there is in keeping ye gloves and Hankerchief together in the same pocket; that a Paper, Book, or writing, most wanted [*p. 15*] Should always be ye most difficult to be found, and after escaping our most diligent enquiry should at Last be found <so> snug at ye elbow; That a Parlour Chimney should so occasionaly smoke when a Holiday is at hand, and ye dinner so uncommonly spoiled when there is most company to partake of it——that even ye younger Linen horse[50] should go over and over again so very uncommonly where there is most dirt to receive it; that a Hedge Stake[51] should be so exceedingly fond of Growing where it is not wanted, when our plantations and Nurseries are raised with ye greatest difficulty:—yt ye innocent Lamb as he is Idly calle'd [*sic*], should have such an exquisite pleasure in running down a new bank, or cropping ye new made fence; and yt all Animals in General should be so exceedingly Obliging, as to rub and frisk against every thing yt is newly painted; that our very Brick and Timber, should be all of them so Affectionately disposed to fall upon our feet & Limbs and to give us ye most exquisite refreshment; yt ye Button on a mans shirt collar should so unaccountably fly off on ye Sunday morning when no work is to be done; yt even ye very Nails, bolts, catches, Hedges and thorns, with all ye good fraternity both of iron and wooden instruments, should all

49 The condition of being contingent or caused by chance: *OED*.

50 Frame for drying cloths and clothes indoors or outdoors: *OED*.

51 Vertical stakes are either initially or periodically inserted into laid hedges for reinforcement or decoration; Pratt's reference to them 'growing' is thus obviously intended as a joke.

of them be so ready and willing to tear our clothes and flesh to pieces, catching at us with ye most malevolent Asperity, are things common enough in ye world; and yet such as betray such an Original (what shall I call it) Whimsicality in ye things themselves, as is to me most wonderful and extraordinary to account for—I do not desire a man in ye World to think with me on this Subject; I had much rather my Reader should think otherwise; I only desire ye Liberty of enjoying my own opinion, and surely neither council or Parliament should take it [*p. 16*] from me; I do confess here (and Let those Laugh who Like it;) that I seldom put on my shirt without first putting my sleeve-buttons in to my mouth, for If they are once laid down, Lord bless me! What a Hurricane do they make in ye family!—I have more than once stood over ye Little carpenter at his Bench, and have pityd him from my heart, to see ye poor fellow twisting and turning himself about so often, fumbling in all his pockets, Scratching ye dirt over and over again; squirting his Tobacco in all directions and muttering to himself what ye Devil is become of this Little Gimblet,[52] when I have Observd perhaps at ye same time; a Little bit of Shaving dragd as it were most artfully upon ye Gimblet, and ye Glue Pot covering at ye same time ye small paper of Sprigs,[53] as If all was done on purpose to torment him; It may be said perhaps that few have made such trifling Observations as these are, but as I am rather of a Philosophical turn of mind, and much giving to musing these sort of trifles do not escape me: I have more than once pitied our Rose from my heart when I have stood near to ye churn; to see ye horrid distress ye poor thing has been in; such twitching and tugging, so fretted and melted; & so Effectualy worn out by fatigue yt ye poor Girl gradualy proceeding from crying to sobbing, & then from cursing to swearing; that at Last overpowerd with passion, she has snatchd up ye Crank in her hand, and drives at ye head of William for Laughing at a distance; roaring out with an abominable Oath; that mother Nog[54] had bewitchd her butter.—I will not Affirm in these instances that ye Zgubbs were concernd in either of them; nor do I positively say that they were perch'd on ye tops of ye churn to Let in ye Air and prevent its working: nor would I aver for a kingdom; that they [*p. 17*] certainly held back ye crank, and so kept it from turning properly, or that they hauled ye Glue pot over ye paper of Sprigs; or that it was they who secreted ye Little Gimblet; as it is impossible to be absolutely assured of all this; but I will

52 Eighteenth-century spelling of 'gimlet', a boring tool: *OED*.

53 A small nail, peg, or pin: *OED*.

54 A long tradition in English folklore attributed mishaps with milk curdling to witches and fairies. Compare Puck's enumeration of the curdling of milk among the mischiefs he has wrought on humans in *A Midsummer Night's Dream* (*Shak*, 2.1.35–6).

venture to assert at ye same time, that not a Theologist on earth can prove it otherwise—I will here take upon me to call on ye Hardest of Unbelievers, and desire him to account for ye conduct of my good and valuable Friend who being sent for to attend a ^female^ patient went away from his own home with two different coloured Stockings, and ye one with so remarkable a clock[55] that easily distinguishd it to be a womans stocking: Is it possible now to suppose that as sensible and good a man as can exist, would have gone forth with his green bag, and with a white and a black Stocking? Or that he himself would have published in y^{s} manner that he had a favourite at home? It can never be reconciled with common prudence; and to urge that he rose in the dark is begging ye Question; I say that he had a candle; and let others think as they please, for my own part I can easily figure to myself, a Squadron or two of ye Zgubbs attending him, some turning down ye White Stocking, some tugging on ye black one, some Hauling his Garters on ye floor; some putting ye night cap over his Eyes, and using every art and Stratagem in their power to conceal and bring forward, their wicked purposes——there are a thousand Storys of this sort in every ones mouth;—there is Hardly a Boy, or Girl who does not know ye roguery of ye Zgubbs:—How easily are ye best ruffles or apron, torn to pieces, and how seldom will ye Scissors associate with their own case? <and> how [*p. 18*] impetuously let me ask, will ye Ironing box burn & scald things to pieces, If left for a single minute; as If peevish by ye Inflammation that it has within—; and what a mighty bustle is commonly made when ye ivory Egg[56] is wanted for a Slice of nutmeg? I might Stop here and summons [*sic*] a thousand Witnesses to Attest ye truth of these things: How easily will ye Breath of a single Zgubb occasion ye Gun to flash in ye pan When ye Game is just at ye end of it; and how frequently do we Stunt[57] at ye toe, or deliciously fall on our faces when we are hurrying away to a Dog when pointing[58]—? And indeed the Story of poor Mr Twist is as extraordinary as ye former—Mr Twist it was very well known served a triple curacy for a very small Stipend (ye great Tithes were all in ye Bishop) and by ye great fatigue from his duty was supposed to be in what is commonly calld a Galloping

55 A silk decoration sewn on a stocking: *OED*.

56 A grater for nutmeg seed inside an egg-shaped ivory case, usually designed to serve concurrently as a small storage case for the nutmeg between uses: *OED*. In the eighteenth century, grated nutmeg was commonly added to punch and pocket-sized nutmeg graters were frequently carried around in pockets for this purpose. See John D. Davis, *The Robert and Meredith Green Collection of Silver Nutmeg Graters* (Williamsburg, VA: The Colonial Williamsburg Foundation, 2002).

57 An alternative term for stubbing one's toe: *OED*.

58 i.e. when the dog is 'pointing' to the presence of game by standing rigidly: *OED*.

consumption:[59] Mr Twist being appointed to preach a visitation Sermon,[60] it most unfortunately I, that as he was so exceedingly thin, yt ye sermon case slipt away between the cassock & waistcoat, and which ye poor Gentleman never miss'd till he appeard in ye Pulpit—The Reader may best figure to himself Mr Twists confusion; O! Horror, of all Horrors ye worst, and most distracting! Ye poor man coughd and Humd up ye best apology he could and so it ended—Now, shall any man on Earth perswade me to believe, that this accident was entirely owing to Mr Twists want of care and attention? I know he was thin; I allow him to be consumptive; and that there was a considerable cavity in ye Middle of his stomach, and that ye sermon case might possibly Slip away between ye cassock and waistcoat: I would have believed all this with all my heart, and that ye whole was mistake or [*p. 19*] Accident had not the Gentleman himself Observd when he told ye story; that there was a green string in ye sermon case which hung down a considerable Length—Now as this was so very inviting for ye Zgubbs to tug at, and waved as it were for a pleasant hint; why was it not probable Let me ask, yt ye Zgubbs, or Gommas, might be concernd in this roguery, to put him into so horrid a confusion.

Great and Glorious without doubt are ye abilities of our Collegians & men of System, in their own opinion at Least, and yet I very much doubt whether there has as yet been one Almighty Theorist; be he either Histriographer,[61] Cosmographer; Archytopographer,[62] Geographer, Zoographer;[63] or Hydriographer,[64] who has been able to shake himself Loose from these notions of ye Zgubs [*sic*] & who dares assert, that he has never once been under their power and direction; for tho it may be allowd to be better for the interest of society, for men to reason deeply & philosophicaly than to be Left to their own vague notions of things; yet tho a man is read in Didactic and exegetic theology up to ye very chin, and is Acquainted with all that has been wrote by ye monothelites,[65] or ye monophysites;[66] by ye followers

59 An especially rapidly progressing case of tuberculosis: *OED*.

60 Sermon preached to the local bishop during one of his visitations: *OED*.

61 Alternative spelling of 'historiographer'.

62 i.e. a principal topographer, an expert in topography: *OED*.

63 A scholar of descriptive zoology: *OED*.

64 Alternative spelling of 'hydrographer': an expert in hydrography, the subdiscipline of geography and geology dealing with earth's water: *OED*.

65 Monothelitism is a Christological doctrine dating back to seventh-century Syria and Armenia, according to which Christ possesses both a divine and human nature but only a single divine will. This doctrine arose as an attempt to find a common ground or compromise between Monophysitism (see below) and Dyophisitism (which claimed that post incarnation Christ had two separate natures, divine and human): *Oxford DCC*.

66 Monophysitism is a Christological doctrine dating back to the fifth century, according

of Zosimus[67] and Ziska;[68] yet the Instances I shall give will prove, y^t men of y^e most redoubtable abilities are not always able to protect themselves from y^e mischeivous persecutions of y^e Zgubbs————M$^{r.}$ Jeremy Simkin was a very good Scholar, and was fellow of a College too, many a cap was doft to Mr Simkim [*sic*] as he was y^e first of y^e family who had enjoyd such Honors, not a man of his time could [*p. 20*] untwist a syllogism better than Little Jerry; or split an argument so nicely, as to make it fly all to pieces at once, and was at ye same time a profound mathematician: madam Deborah Simkin his Affectionate Aunt, as he was an Only child, sent him annually to College a cask of her excellent October,[69] knowing it to contain such knock him down Arguments, as neither Soph,[70] moderator, or ye very professor himself could easily take off: Mr Simkin as was usual with him, invited four or five of his most intimate Friends to partake of this excellent Liquor: they met with ye Glow of Cherubims; and they who have experienc'd ye comforts, or rather Glorious Enthusiasm of a College Evening, where Mirth, good Humour and Cordiality are so happily united; may easily suppose Mr Simkin and his Friends ye Happiest of mortals;————

Animæ quales, neque Candidiores
Terra tulit[71]————

The pipes were laid out in order, the Oyster barrel well heapd with coals, and ye Gip waited with very near Half a shirt;[72] Mr Simkin retired to pierce ye vessel it was fine, it smiled in his face, it was excellent in taste and colour;

---

to which Christ has a single nature, either divine or an indivisible composite of human and divine: *Oxford DCC.*

67 Zosimus (living in the late fourth and early fifth century), a Greek polytheist historian based in Constantinople; he is the author of *Historia Nova*, which records the decline of the Roman Empire from a perspective hostile to the rise of Christianity: *Oxford DCC.*

68 Jan Žižka (1360?–1424), a Czech Hussite general, noted for winning numerous battles against the various configurations of Catholic forces during the Hussite wars in Central Europe: *Oxford DCC.* His mention by Pratt is curious as he did not author any texts and, while he can be considered a radical Hussite, he was primarily a military leader and is not known to have been involved in setting the Hussite religious doctrines. Pratt might have mixed him up with the radical religious reformer Jan Hus (1369?–1415), whose ideological follower Žižka was and after whom the Hussites named themselves, or chose him as a proxy for Hus to achieve a kind of phonetic symmetry between the 'Z's and the 'M's in the sentence, next to Zosimus and Monothelites and Monophysites.

69 An ale with high alcohol content historically usually brewed around October: *OED.*

70 Abbreviation of 'Sophister' and a term for a second or third-year student at Cambridge: *OED.*

71 *DLCL*: Horace, *Satires I*, 5:41–2 (p. 67) 'whitest souls earth ever bore'.

72 A variant spelling of 'Gyp'—a Cambridge term for a college servant; a half-shirt denotes a shirt front for men, a chemisette for women: *OED.*

ye good man in ye Gayety of his heart snap'd his fingers and Chuckled exceedingly; but unfortunately in his hurry, being a little absent as he was to keep a divinity Act in ye schools, and having perhaps ye ten predicaments of Aristotle[73] a Little too much in his head; or, whether he was thinking of ye square of ye line bisecting ye Verticle[74] [*p. 21*] Angle of any triangle, together with ye rectangle under ye segment of ye base made thereby; is equal to ye rectangle under ye sides containing y^{t} angle; is of very little Use to be known in ye present business; be this as it will he unfortunately laid hold of ye Spigot of ye Vessel instead of ye candle; and returnd to his Friends with ye glass in his hand which would have charmd an Anchorite; ye company Approved of it & smiled approbation; it smiled in turn and look'ed deliciously, when one of ye company observing Mr Simkin had left the candle in ye cellar, it filld him immediatly with ye Utmost terror—Alas! it was too Late to save it; ye Beer had unfortunately meanderd itself along to every part of ye cellar; disposing of itself as it went to ye coals, to ye pavement, to ye old red slippers, and even to ye very boot Jack[75] itself; and general was the consternation of ye company—Now if were[76] to Argue ever so long, or so closely upon this Intricate Subject, it would be impossible to suppose Mr Simkin himself concernd in y^{s} horrid mistake; It could not possibly be any act of his own; for is it probable, (let us reason cooly) that a fellow of a college, a great and profound mathematician; would have assembled his best Friends together for no other purpose but to Lay 'em under so horrid a disappointment?—would Mr Simkin think ye have paid ye carriage of ye cask, and have bungd it down with so much caution; cutting ye vent Peg[77] himself with his own mathematical Instrument; and doing all this in his white topt Gloves, had he at all suspected what would have been ye terrible consequence? Can we suppose him to have calld so many [*p. 22*] convivial souls together, for no other reason in ye world, but to see them sit Licking their Lips, twirling their thumbs over & over again; Leering at one another, and now and then looking most wishfully at ye cellar door with ye most flattering expectation?

---

73 The ten categories of things which can be the subject or predicate of a proposition, based on the four basic forms of predication (and hence called 'predicaments' by Pratt, or 'praedicamenta' in Latin) as described in Aristotle's *Categories,* included in his *Organon.* These categories would have been a standard part of an eighteenth-century university curriculum and students would have been expected to memorize them.

74 Alternative spelling of 'vertical'. Vertical angles are angles opposite one another when two lines cross. These angles have the same vertex, hence their name.

75 An implement for removing boots: *OED.*

76 A pronoun like 'I', 'we', or 'one' would be expected before 'were' but Pratt omits it.

77 In a cask or a barrel, a peg for closing the vent-hole, which allows the passage of air as opposed to the bung-hole, which is for liquid: *OED.*

I will not believe it on any Account; it is impossible to reconcile it with common prudence; for tho I will not take upon me to say, why no friendly Zgubb would interpose with a thumb or a foot to save ye beer, as ye Spiggot hole might have been stopt at first yet as Mr Simkin always Observ'd when he told ye Story himself, that there was certainly a kind of uncommon hissing at the bung hole which he took for ye working of ye Ale; which probably might be nothing more, than ye Shouts of ye Zgubbs, and their immoderate tittering among themselves, to see so solemn and consummate a Mathematician; in such a doleful and wretched situation————

If then ye proofs yt are here advanc'd do not convince ye deepest Philosophers, and Lovers of System & men of ye most enlarg'd Abilities, that they may be under ye Influence of ye Zgubbs tho they do not perceive it; I can only enforce ye supposition by one or two melancholy cases with respect to myself; and then Leave it for every man to think and to Judge us as he pleases: but before I proceed any further in ys intricate undertaking; Give me leave to Observe in this place; That nothing ye Lord God has given to man is half so frightful and Vexatious as yt Eternal Egotism of <some> Authors, and ye horrid dominion they would exercise over ye minds and consciences of their Brethren; this self-sufficient and petulant Temper; is a Weed of so rank and poisonous a Quality; that it is as baneful [*p. 23*] to a Liberal mind as either night-Shade or mandagora[78] is to ye body; and it should be a caution to every man of candour to turn away from that detestable monster of self-Opinion—And therefore do you, ye Leviathans,[79] who take your Pastime in the circles of Literature give to Others ye Liberty of thinking for themselves; nor Idly suppose ye whole compass of nature lies open to such as you; And I confess I am a little afraid; that it may be said to me in turn, dost thou that Judgest another, commit—? Alas! I am open to conviction and modestly kiss ye rod; but when a man sets up a new and favourite Hypothesis of his own; and brings into ye World with some pain and Labour, a few odd & singular notions, that may be opposite to common Opinion; it becomes necessary for him in some measure to call to his Assistance every art and Stratagem in his power to furnish out his Hypothesis, to the best advantage: I here ask my Readers forgiveness for stepping a Little out of ye way from my Subject & will immediatly return to things of much greater consequence—

78 An alternative spelling of 'mandragora', in English also known as 'mandrake', a plant originally from the Mediterranean region noted for both its poisonous and narcotic qualities: *OED*.

79 The *OED* notes that the term was applied to wealthy and powerful men; here Pratt applies it ironically to men of vast erudition.

Suppose me then in my black waistcoat—ye transition perhaps is a Little unexpected but I could not help it; and that I may not appear too familiar & unreasonable with my Reader, Let me beg of him to suppose once or twice more before we part, (I feel myself much Affected) and I promise him to ask no more for a twelve month or two——Suppose then ye shaving apparatus before me, ye razor well set, ye soap Scented, ye strap in good Order, and myself Looking at ye glass and thinking (O force of human vanity!) there were worse features in ye world than my own; what a proof said I to myself, (beating up the larder at ye same time) is [*p. 24*] this arrangement of features of mine of ye Almightys wisdom and caution, for tho he has sent into ye world so many generations of men, so many Millions of souls, yet there never have been two faces in every respect alike, nor ever will be, but that the one might be distinguishd from ye Other; I was in this pleasing reverie when ye provoking piece of soap so amazingly bolted forth from my hand, bespattering ye wainscot as it flew, and then totaly disappear'd at once——I believe I said to myself Hey! Day what is ye matter now, but won't be positive of saying this, and then turning myself round and round in ye greatest perplexity; I found it had Nestled itself into ye corner of ye room, where there was most sand to receive it; and stood so conceal'd for a time at the foot of a Little Table; and in such a way conceald, yt upon my Stooping to take it up, (for I use no shaving cloth) ye Larder plentifuly bedewd my bosom: I shall not stop here to make any remarks upon this sad accident; as I have only one instance more to produce to shew as far as we know; that it is possible; that we may all thus suffer by ye Zgubbs, and yt when these kind of fortunate Discoveries are once made and lighted up to ye world what pity it is they should be given up without further enquiry—Suppose it then for ye Last time ye sweetest morn that ever shone from ye heavens, and suppose as you may ye Author of the Zgubbs the happiest of mortals—my Little gardening bag tied most Affectionately before me; ye Ladder against ye Wall; ye black breeches cut into Shreds, and ye Hammer and nails in readiness——In this manner I was Laying out ye twigs of ye Apricot to the best advantage cutting this out, bringing this in, altering and realtering, nailing and unnailing my Tree with infinite pleasure [*p. 25*] and satisfaction—I thank thee O, Father of Heaven, I believe I said to myself (or ought to have done it) and you my excellent Friend——for giving me this blessed retirement and Days of Ease & comfort and which ye first Minister of State would be pleas'd to call his own: On a sudden ye Sun shone out with peculiar freedom, and in the midst of my work, I found there was a something that tickled my cheek a little—I suppos'd it at first to be a Little Midge, or some Other insect that might have crawled from ye tree——It grew more troublesome—I then gently rubd my Cheek on ye side of my Waistcoat sleeve; to brush it off If I could——It was more troublesome than ever, when turning my head aside in a Hurry towards my Left shoulder, ye confounded little Hammer dropt immediatly thump, upon my poor thumb nail——I cannot endure to think of it even now—I fell from ye Ladder, ye tears came into my Eyes I stood confounded for a considerable time, and then Whipping my thumb into my mouth, waddled away to ye House under ye most uncomfortable feelings—Now, in both these instances I am hard to believe that they could either of them be Occasiond by any carelessness of mine, or be imputed to my being thoughtful; I was never in better spirits, or more carefully Larded[80] in all my Life; and it is wonderful to conceive that a square piece of soap, not more than four cubical inches, should so preposterously bolt away in a room of twelve feet Square; and be so strangely directed to no Other part, but where it was most difficult to be got at; and as to ye idle supposition as some will have it that there must have been a midge at my Cheek; I am altogether convincd and assured to ye contrary I have I'd strange things before then—It is not the first time I have been alarmd; and If others do not choose to believe as I do, they are welcome to believe as they please: [*p. 26*] I have lived thank Heaven long enough in ye world to dispise ye censures of it: It is impossible we should think all alike in all things. No, No, I did not stand in such a ninny Like way to no purpose, I knew their intentions very well; and it was very evident to me what it was yt occasiond the thump of ye Hammer:

With inconceivable Labour and trouble to myself and with much injury to my Inventive faculties, I have been at last able to bring out to ye world, this my first born Hypothesis of ye Zgubbs ye extreme diffidence I have hitherto entertaind of my own abilities, and ye horror of being ridicul'd by a barbarous world, for such singular notions as they will be thought by some: have hitherto kept this my Laborious undertaking from ye press, and ye discovery has long rested with me: But if this my work of Labour, & great application is to weigh nothing with our Theological Writers and men of System: If ye arguments I have herein urged; ye particular cases that have been related; are to be considerd as carrying no manner of conviction with them: it must be imputed surely to ye obstinacy of men's hearts, or to ye weakness of their heads; as every thoughtful and intelligent person must be convincd of ye reality of ye Zgubbs, as much as ye Author himself—And after all it is a very unthankful as well as a painful undertaking, for a man

80 Presumably in the sense of being carefully 'lathered' with soap (although this sense is not attested in the *OED*). Lard was a common ingredient of soap in the eighteenth century.

to turn all his powers to study and application; to give up all his time and pleasing avocations; & to leave no stone unturnd to light up these important Discoveries to ye world: If a few wayward men; who being armd with ye thunder and Logomachy[81] of ye Schools; (blessed word how it rolls in ye mouth) because they know forsooth a few of the [*p. 27*] Jerks and turnings, y^t^ belong to ye mystic, ye Adiaphoristic,[82] and fiddlestick arguments, because they can Collegize and flourish a Little, about mode and figure, object and affection, substance & attribute; and are a little Acquainted with ye writings of good Father Simon, and sweet master Timon;[83] y^t^ they should inhumanly set their shoulders to overturn this my work, & even crush it in its very production; for, would it not be Let me ask ye greatest of all hardships If a man might not enjoy his own opinion of things; when not a soul upon earth can be injur'd by it?—And If my Sentiments of a Zgubb, or ^a^ Gomma, Guelph or a Gibbeline,[84] or y^t^ of a cloak or a surplice,[85] be different from y^t^ of my neighbour; there is no reason in ye world If we should be Enemies on this occasion: I never assume to say y^t^ ye thing is so, must be so, and shall be so, and Zouns swallow it as we please to give it you. I hint a suspicion only of my own opinion and there I Leave it—I never affirmd in my Life, that it was either a Zgubb, or Gomma, that Elbowd in ye Middleton[86] Chaise into ye ten foot drain; & so plentifully refreshd the good vicar thereof, in his way to Cambridge: but I do and will assert in spite of ye world; y^t^ it is neither absurd, or improbable to suppose, that there might be a something about ye head of his horse, I say a

81 An argument about the meaning of words; from the Greek logos (word) and machia (fight): *OED*.

82 The Adiaphoristic Controversy was a conflict in the German Lutheran Church in the middle of the sixteenth century between orthodox and moderate factions over the proposed return to certain Catholic practices: *Oxford DCC*.

83 The paired terms 'mode and figure, object and affection, substance & attribute' were used in the eighteenth century to translate technical terms in scholastic philosophy into English. For more explanation on them see the headnotes for these terms in Ephraim Chambers, or, *Cyclopaedia or an Universal Dictionary of Arts and Sciences*, 4th ed. (2 vols., London: D. Midwinter et. al, 1741). 'Father Simon' refers to the Byzantine monk Saint Symeon the New Theologian (*c.* 949–1022) and 'Timon' to the Greek philosopher Timon of Phlius (*c.* 320–*c.* 230 BCE).

84 In the early Middle Ages, German and Italian politics were broadly divided between supporters of the Pope, the Guelphs, and of the Holy Roman Emperor, the Ghibellines.

85 A reference to the so-called 'Vestments Controversy', which started under the reign of Edward VI and continued under Elizabeth I and revolved around debates over what outfits were to be worn by Church of England ministers during religious services: *Oxford DCC*.

86 A village approximately three miles to the south-east of King's Lynn.

something twittering & glimmering before him, which might be ye means of making ye Beast to start, and so occasion that horrid Immersion: and Notwithstanding what has been said already so much to my disadvantage; I never affirmd it openly to ye world: that it was an actual Zgubb, y^t^ traild away my Friend ye Barristers nightcap; When his Bride Look'd so much at her watch, & was ^so^ Gloriously disposed for Slumber; but we Live in a Splenetic[87] world and must Submit to it———

[*p. 28*]

———Having now run over ye greatest part of my work; preserving I hope ye forehead of my Reader in tolerable smoothness, by now and then exciting an innocent smile; I must here call upon him in y^s^ place to put on a more ^solemn^ countenance; being now to be unexpectedly introduced to a Subject of a Graver nature; & to ye conduct of those wise Theologists; who by very uncommon application and great abilities, have Left things much worse than they found them; Who by being over nice and scrupulous in ye preserving of mint & Cummin, and over resolute not to part with a single advantage; who by passing over ye Weightier considerations of morality & by writing upon Subjects which they never understood, and by disputing for things of Little or no Importance, have unfortunately left behind them a wide and unbounded field, for cavil and Disputation—— and whatever Critick may arise in this place to condemn the unnatural attempt of our Author here, (as may be ye case with many) for uniting such Opposite Subjects as are here to be found such too as can never be forc'd (according to them) into tolerable union: yet as it is somewhere Observ'd, y^t^ even a want of connection may have its beauties, and there may be such a thing as an agreable disorder in composition; (examine If you please ye Ars Poetica of Horace for a proof of this)[88] and as a Writer would choose now and then, to step a little aside from ye common path to get away from

87 Relating to the spleen and hence often connected to melancholia and/or hypochondria, which were believed to arise from disorders or imbalances in this organ: *OED*.

88 No lines correspond to this point in Horace's *Ars Poetica*. The superstitious figure who is presented as the writer of *The Zgubbs* seems rather to be remembering Alexander Pope's *Essay on Criticism*, in which it is observed that 'Great Wits sometimes may *gloriously offend*,/ And *rise* to *Faults* true Criticks *dare not mend*:/ From *vulgar* Bounds with *brave Disorder* part,/ And *snatch* a *Grace* beyond the Reach of Art,/ Which, without passing thro' the *Judgement*, gains/ The *Heart*, and all its End *at once* attains' (*Pope*, 152–7). *The Essay on Criticism* was modelled on the *Ars Poetica* and is full of echoes of Horace's poem. But here and elsewhere, Pope's poem deviates from the classical poem's doctrines.

ye dash of ye Critick, I shall only say for myself in this, that I write as ye Flash shall come upon me with freedom and without hesitation; preferring in writing as I do in music those pieces best, provided they bring some graces and decorations with them; tho they may be a Little [*p. 29*] out of Order, to those more solemn and formal compositions which have Little or no variety to recommend them; And here before I carry my Reader he knows not where, (& probably out of his Depth and mine) I would beg and beseech him once for all to be reconciled, to ye very different Subjects, that are here to be united; and If my Joining ye Serpentes Avibus, and ye tigribus Agni, which Old Horace so obstinately forbids,[89] should arise in his thoughts, as they do in mine; yet Let it soften the peevishness of his Lip; when ye same Old Jovial Rake has assur'd both him & me, y^{t} a man may Laugh and speak truth at ye same time:[90]—and whatever may have been said by our ablest Writers, upon the subject of mixing Opposites, and ye violence there, must be always Used in hauling together things of different natures & Qualities yet I am well Assured; Mr Mayor[91] lookd uncommonly well in his Sattin[92] Waistcoat; tho it was very well known to half ye court, y^{t} both ye back part & ye Sleeves were made of a Serge[93] from his own materials; and If things of Opposite Qualities may be so mix'd and Artfully put together, so as to accord and agree tolerable well; and it is no very uncommon sight; to see a short Little Wig most affectionately adhering to a full and plentiful countenance, (you must remember him at Trinity College)[94] so I cannot think myself ye worst in ye world, for ye Shaking up together, for ye smoothing ye muscles of ye face, this my innocent & Zgubbical mixture; and If every Boy and Girl when they are eating their cherries do all of them know what they are to take and what refuse,[95]

---

89 At the beginning of *Ars Poetica*, Horace warns the prospective poet against combining serpents with birds or lambs with tigers as a metaphor for mixing together incompatible styles or subjects: 'non ut/ serpentes avibus geminentur, tigribus agni' *DLCL*: Horace, *Ars Poetica*, 12–13 (p. 451) '[but not so far that] … serpents couple with birds, lambs with tigers'.]

90 A reference to the lines from Horace's *Satires, 'Ridentem Dicere Verum'*, used as the text's epigraph, see note 2 above, p. 264 of our edition.

91 Perhaps Sir Samuel Fludyer (1705–1768), a clothier who was Lord Mayor of London between 1761 and 1762: *Oxford DNB*. Fludyer's unusual periwig was featured in William Hogarth's satirical print 'The Five Orders of Periwigs; As they were Worn at the Coronation of George the Third' (1761). Thanks to Linda Troost for this suggestion.

92 Alternative spelling of 'satin'.

93 A fabric or garment made of wool: *OED*.

94 Trinity College Cambridge.

95 Reference 'cherry-picking' in the sense of carefully selecting only the best items or opportunities from an available group.

so it would be a disparagement to ye Understanding of our Readers, not to suppose them able to choose for themselves [*p. 30*] and to pick out If they can, what is best and most agreable to their palates:————

Amongst all ye bubbles[96] y^t have appear'd in the world, there has not been any perhaps more common or Vexatious to men; then y^t of System; Theory; prescriptive authority, Fundamentals, and such, Like Frippery: these sort of Zgubbical feathers have been long toss'd and blown about ye world from one end to ye other of it; and whoever examines ye Operose and JeJune[97] Labours of ye school men; their minute investigations, and the miserable jargon they maintaind for so many centuries together; ye wretched credulity they have shewn upon all occasions, and the violence they have been for usurping over private Judgement; will find in many of their writings, as Little consistency and improvement as in this our History of ye Zgubbs——I would not here be thought to depreciate ye Laudable endeavours of such men; who have Used their Utmost abilities to stop ye Growth of ye Superstition in ye times they lived by venturing to follow their own opinions; nor would I wish to check ye Laudable endeavours of a respectable society, who are now opening a way for greater Latitude of Opinion and free devotion; yet If we seriously consider and Lay to heart, ye many Deplorable heresies and Schisms y^t have been Long propogated in ye world by so many of our redoubtable Theologists; ye number of Heterogenious publications that have swarmd from the press ye Great discredit religion has undergone by controversies so imprudently manag'd: ye strange want of temper and candour; y^t declamatory rudeness & sometimes ye most bitter revilings; with which these meek Defenders of our faith, have been bespattering One another with the dirt of their own making; it may [*p. 31*] be much question'd after all (very much indeed) whether ye world is ye better, or ye worse, for such their Zgubbical Labours; For, if after all; ten thousand Volumes could be added to those already receiv'ed, it would still be Evident to common sense; y^t every mans opinion is inseparable from his nature, and makes a part of himself, and a man cannot possibly think otherwise than his faculties will permit him to Judge and think; And, what heart is there that is not past feeling, y^t does not Lament in Secret; that so many should be so Early calld, to ye Subscription of Doctrines, ye most Abstruse in their nature y^t

96 Foolish or empty notions: *OED*. For a study of the semantics of the word see Sarah Tindal Kareem, 'Enlightenment Bubbles, Romantic Worlds', *The Eighteenth Century: Theory and Interpretation*, 56.1 (2015), pp. 85–104.

97 Pratt capitalizes both 'J's in 'jejune'.

could possibly be put together & ye most difficult to be reconciled to ye understanding, such too as admit of different explanations, and never can be reasonably confined to one meanning[98]——^to have so many under ye hard condition of wanting bread; or consenting to ye most mystical doctrines, invented and set forth by fallible men; when a less exceptionable way might easily be found; and ye peace and good order of ye church, more Effectualy preservd——^: Besides If ye religion which is called Xtian,[99] gives to every man ye Liberty of thinking for himself, independent of all Authority but y^t of ye holy Scriptures; If y^s religion as it certainly is, is a plain easy System of morality: If neither its great author or those who were commission'd by him; did Lay any sort of Stress, upon abstruse points; Scholastic Opinions and peculiar modes of worship; ye tying men down as it were to the narrow tenets and confined notions of other men; (whose disputes had nothing more than Victory for their Object and not ye truth,) is Laying them under such disagreable restraints, as neither Xst[100] or his Apostles intended——

Whatever then is here offer'd to the world by ye name and Title of ye Zgubbs; however strange & whimsical it may appear to many, or however fantastically it will be rec^d by others; it is much to be questioned after all; whether any thing herein advancd, is either more Childish or ridiculous [*p. 32*] than ye several Systems and Theories, ye incredible tales and Idle storys, ye world has been so long receiving for so many Centuries together: The opinion of ye Gnostics,[101] even in the first Century that there were malevolent Genii, who occasion'd perplexities and distresses to mankind;

98 On *f. 31r* the following instructions appear: '—ye four underwritten Lines are to be inserted after ye words, confined to one meanning——'. The lines of inserted text beginning 'to have so many' and ending 'more Effectualy preservd' then follow after a gap of approximately three lines on *f. 31r*. We have inserted the relevant text from *f. 31r* into *f. 31v* accordingly. Although the Feathers Tavern Association is mocked in *The Grange*, here the work of the former members of the Association in advocating for the abolition of clerical subscription to the Thirty-nine Articles is presented sympathetically. See note 151 to *The Grange*, p. 105 of our edition.

99 Christian. See following note.

100 Abbreviated form of Christ's name from Greek, in use in writing since Anglo-Saxon times, with a switch in usage from Xp (the Greek letters chi and rho) to the semi-anglicized Xt (and Xpian to Xtian for the adjectival form) occurring between the sixteenth and seventeenth centuries: *OED*.

101 A set of Judeo-Christian religious systems in existence during AD 1, which combined ideas from non-rabbinical Judaism and early Christianity and variously emphasized the concept of an unknowable God and importance of knowledge. The genii Pratt is referring to here are spiritual emanations of God, which different brands of Gnosticism termed and understood differently: *Oxford DCC.*

may be as difficult to prove perhaps as this our fable: ye wonderful tale of ye Aons[102] who were sent from ye Celestial regions to such who were under any bodily afflictions and to deliver men from ye Oppression of Demons, carrys with it Little more probability (If any) than ys our Hypothesis of the Zgubbs—and it is wonderful to conceive what an idle & uncommon veneration has been so implicitly paid to those Spiritual Writers (of ye first six centuries especialy;) receiving every thing that dropt from them as ye most precious and infallible truths; tho frequently upon subjects of ye most trifling nature, and such as they themselves never sufficiently understood: And If it appears as was Observd before yt ye holy Writings alone are sufficient for our instruction and salvation, what occasion can there possibly be, to use these men as such infallible Guides, to follow them as such precious Interpreters of Scripture; wading after them, through such dirty waters, When they were so far from removing ye darkness religion was then under; that they causd ye film which had partly coverd it, to be much more difficult to be remov'd——follow them If you please and with all my heart, where they are consistent with truth and sound doctrine; read them where it is to be had for instruction, but at ye same time Let us have no fellowship with their Mistakes and Errors: nor is it necessary for us now to be drawn aside by their forc'd Allegories and ridiculous Interpretations, frequently turning aside the holy Writings [*p. 33*] from their natural meaning, & setting 'em at variance with one another: for Let me ask any reasonable person, what have all the controversies of Alexander and Arius,[103] of Jerome and Vigilantius[104] and a thousand Others contributed to ye peace and Happiness of society? What benefit has ye world rec'd, from ye School men and their Zgubbical writings, their Mystic and fiddlestick nonsense? In what way are we ye better for ye creed of Irenæus, ye creed of Origin, or even thine (it may be said by many,) most

102 Variant spelling of 'aeon/eon': the Gnostics believed that aeons were emanations that fulfilled God's purposes: *OED*.

103 Arius and Alexander represented the two sides in the so-called Trinity or Arian Controversy in the fourth century; Arius, a Berber presbyter and ascetic, disagreed with the prevalent view of the church that the Father, the Son, and the Holy Spirit were all equal, claiming instead that the Son could not be considered to be an equal of the Father; Alexander, the 19th Pope of Alexandria and later St Alexander, defended the official position: *Oxford DCC*.

104 The disagreement between Vigilantius, a presbyter from Gaul (modern day France), and Jerome (later St Jerome), occurred around the year 400 and was caused by Vigilantius's rejection of a variety of practices, such as the sending of alms to Jerusalem, veneration of saints and their relics, holding of vigils in basilicas of the martyrs, and veneration of the unmarried state: *Oxford DCC*.

excellent Athanasius?[105] What a jot of improvement has ye church rec^{d}, from all ye abstruse contentions; Scholastic opinions, and points of speculation, which have been buffeted about to ye worlds end; and which has so miserably twisted and turnd about ye Heads of so many good men, to ye keeping up such a Theological uproar; that the very disputants themselves have been frequently lost in ye Dust of their own procuring: and it is indeed most sad and dismal to consider what bloodshed, excommunications, and massacres have ensued concerning ye meaning of a few trifling Insignificant words; which they themselves never sufficiently understood; as If any man was to be excluded ye kingdom of heaven, because he could not distinguish ye nature of Being, person, or Substance, Original sin, Interior generation and procession,[106] with a thousand Quirks and metaphysical distinctions about things, which were confessedly at ye same time beyond ye power of comprehension and After all what a bundle of Rubbish has been sent into the world, about ye Doctrine of ye Trinity, ye immaculate conception, ye doctrine of free-will, Grace, predestination and so forth; ye various Heterogenious publications of ye almost innumerable Sectaries; Ebionites, Ophites, Antidicomarianites [*p. 34*] the Anthropomorphites[107] and ye Lord knows who; ye followers of Arianism, Pelagianism, Nestorianism[108] and a Hundred others insomuch,

---

105 Irenaeus (*c.* 130–*c.* 202) Greek cleric and important early Christian theologian; Origen (*c.* 184–253), whose name Pratt spells 'Origin', was an important early Christian scholar and prolific theologian from Alexandria; Athanasius (*c.* 296/98–373) was a bishop of Alexandria, theologian, and an important early defender of the concept of Trinity: *Oxford DCC.*

106 For 'substance', see note 83 above, p. 286 of our edition; 'interior generation' refers to the theological argument, deployed in discussions of the nature of the Trinity, that Christ is the Son of God without division or separate existence from God the Father: *SEP.*

107 Ebionites: a Jewish-Christian sect which accepted Christ as a Messiah but not as God; Ophites (or Ophians): a Christian gnostic sect, whose beliefs and practices supposedly included the serpent worship, mentioned by Origen; Antidicomarianites held that Jesus's siblings mentioned in the Bible were Mary's younger children rather than Joseph's children from a previous marriage as per the mainstream view; Anthropomorphites (or Audians): an early Christian sect which maintained that God literally created humans in his own image: *Oxford DCC.*

108 Arianism, a non-Trinitarian doctrine originating in early fourth century and asserting that Christ as God's Son is subordinate to God the Father. The Athanasian Creed, a statement of Christian faith created in the sixth century and since then in use by most major Western Christian churches, which emphasizes the equality of the Holy Trinity's three constituents and was originally intended to set Nicene Christianity apart from Arianism and its supposedly heretical views on the Trinity. It was traditionally believed to have been authored by Athanasius but more recent scholarship has concluded that it was written approximately a century after his death. Pelagianism, an early Christian doctrine according to which humans have free will and can attain salvation without God's intervention.

that If all was to be collected into one mighty mass together, it would equal mount Olympus itself in height; and yet retain at ye same time ye property of ye other mountain, which the fable mentions, that brought forth a mouse from a mighty Labour[109]— —And If there is a man upon earth unwilling to believe all this; let him sit down and turn over ye pleasing tales of ye thundering Legion; ye snug little Phial of Oyl that was brought by a pigeon at ye baptism of Clovis, with ye unaccountable trials by cold water and fire Ordeal;[110] & If he can sweetly suck in and digest this sort of coagulated Theology; I shall not in ye Least despair but that he will have, after all this, a swallow Sufficient to take down and digest ye savoury morsel of ye Zgubbs————

I must here repeat it again for fear of being misunderstood in this place; that I would by no means be thought to depreciate ye good intentions and honest endeavours of such men, who have both wrote and Sufferd in ye defence of ye Xtian doctrine; these[111] superstition and whim apart, can never be too sufficiently approvd: I mean only to censure y^{t} ridiculous and precipitate Zeal of too many Xtian Writers, their strange battles of words only; ye religious Phrenzy and Philosophical Scuffle of those Christian Worriors;[112] their trifling investigations, replications and triplications, their modalities, Suppositalities[113] and ye Lord knows what; and that horrid effusion of blood, y^{t} was sometimes mixed with the very sacrifices themselves, upon ye meer ceremony perhaps of who should Enter first into the holy

---

Nestorianism is a set of early Christian doctrines, notable especially for emphasizing the dual (human and divine) nature of Christ: *Oxford DCC*.

109 Reference to an Aesopian fable (n. 520 in the Perry Index to *Aesop's Fables*), in which a mountain gives birth to mouse.

110 The Frankish king Clovis I converted from Arianism to Catholicism in the last years of the third century. According to Gregory of Tours, his baptism by Saint Remigius in Reims in 496 was supposed to be marked by a white dove, which brought a vial of holy oil to the event, and during his subsequent conquest of much of Gaul, God had indicated his favour for Clovis through omens including a ball of fire emanating from a church and a hind signalling a safe place for crossing a river. Gregory of Tours, *History of the Franks*, trans. Ernest Brehaut (New York: Columbia University Press, 1916), Book 2, pp. 28–43.

111 'These' refers back to the men who have written and suffered in defence of the Christian doctrine.

112 'Warriors' is spelt 'Worriors' to make the pun on 'worriers' explicit.

113 Reference to the theological debates about the nature of the Trinity; c.f. 'These men, discoursing of the Nature and Subsistence of God in a Language neither warrantable nor apprehensible, have, by their Modalities, Suppositalies, Circumincessions, and twenty such other Chimeras, so misrepresented this Adorable Article of the Trinity to Men's reason, as to bring them first to loath, and then at length to deny it', Robert South, *Thirty Six Sermons and Discourses, on Several Subjects and Occasions*, vol. 2, 5th ed. (Dublin, 1720), p. 100. Pratt had the 1737 London edition of this text in his library.

Sepulchre;[114] together [*p. 35*] with their outrageous disputes about ye time of Easter[115] when ye best Astronomers could never perfectly determine it; that uncommon credulity which so many (Otherwise good men) had so unhappily Imbib'd and for which they are so deservedly condemnd ^& their nakedness exposd^ by our ablest Writers:—And if we bring ye Scene still nearer to ourselves; If we consider of all that has been wrote or said, of a cloak or a surplice, a table or Pulpit;[116] ye turning to ye East or West,[117] ye Use of ye cross in Baptism,[118] and other fancies as unimportant as these are, as If our Lord and his Apostles had ordaind, that every one should undergo ye fire and faggot, bonds[119] and Imprisonments, because he could not Subscribe forsooth to ye Opinion of such, who had little or no Other merit perhaps, except (If it must be allowd) of coming into ye world some ages sooner: And strange it is to believe, y^t^ we should be now, at y^s^ distance of time, still gathering of weeds instead of flowers; considering our church as already arriv'd to a Settled degree of perfection, and y^t^ nothing is now necessary for her improvement; when so many Stumbling blocks are still in our way, & so much might be done, for ye quieting ye minds and consciences of men; had we but ye patience and moderation to Effect it—And if amongst many others that might be mentiond, (I speak it with ye utmost Submission) a more proper occasional service was offerd for ye thanksgiving of women After delivery; than that which is now in Use;[120] as nothing perhaps can be more improperly

114 Between 1555 and 1767, control over the Church of the Holy Sepulcher shifted several times between the Orthodox and Catholic Churches (specifically the Franciscans) and in 1767 a power-sharing agreement among all the claimant churches was worked out, which has been in operation since then although various disagreements and conflicts continue to the present day: *Oxford DCC*.

115 Since the early Christian era, controversies have been waged over the date of Easter Sunday. For a history of these disputes, see E. G. Richards, *Mapping Time: The Calendar and Its History* (Oxford: Oxford University Press, 1998), pp. 354–78.

116 Another reference to a debate within the Church of England, over whether a simple table rather than an altar should be used for celebrating the Eucharist.

117 Reference to the debate over which direction the priest celebrating the Eucharist should be facing, which has varied across Christian denominations. The Reformation generally abandoned the tradition, dating back to early Christianity, that the celebrant should face the east, but Archbishop Laud sought to reinstate the practice although it was not commonly adopted again until the Oxford movement in the nineteenth century: *Oxford DCC*.

118 Reference to another Reformation debate, over the making of the sign of the cross during Baptism rituals.

119 'Bonds' in the sense of physical confinement: *OED*.

120 The Book of Common Prayer stipulated that the priest should read Psalm 116 to women after they had given birth to children. The Psalm gives thanks to God for delivery from 'The cords of death'.

applied than that occasional Psalm; or were we sufferd to follow a Brother to ye grave; without thanking God for taking him to himself, when we know him to have Lived most notoriously wicked, for by their fruits we must know em;[121] Or, were we permitted to dispense with Sponsors for Children [*p. 36*] at ye time of baptism; when no good purpose Attends it at present, but a bold and daring prevarication which is too frequently the case; or If ye exhortation before communion, whereby ye people are taught to believe, y^t ye Devil will enter into them as he did once into Judas was to be totaly laid aside, or more fully explaind;[122] Or if ye absolution y^t is given to ye sick was made Less exceptionable & better understood; what offence could it give to ye most feeling mind; or who prejudice apart, could be offended, were we to be blest with a review of such things, and made happy at ye same time, by some such necessary and reasonable alterations?, And should it here be replied as it may if when once we begin to make alterations and amendments in our forms of worship, ye business will never be ended; that things are all very well as they are at present, were we so wise as to be satisfied with them; yet I must own ye Argument would weigh no more with me, than that of ye Ideot with his nurse, who would not suffer his Eyes to be washd in ye morning, for fear he should see more than he liked;[123] and should be entertaind with a more Agreable prospect——And what pity it is after all y^t can be said; as we have their mistakes and errors to correct our own; and are at ye same time boasting of greater light and better discoveries than they were blest with: that there should be still such a Love of victory and dominion over ye minds and consciences of our Dissenting brethren; such a miserable want of Love and Charity such an expanded violence of Temper; that it is but Little better at present; than an unnatural and horrid Struggle to see, who should be the most provoking, or who the most violent Declaimers.————

[*p. 37*]

Be Learned then (as much as you please) ye Spiritual Judges of ye Earth, but at ye same time be humble and modest with it, nor do ye Idly

121 Echoing Matthew 7:16: 'You shall know them by their fruits' (*Oxford KJB*).

122 Luke 22:30: 'Then entered Satan into Judas surnamed Iscariot, being of the number of the twelve' (*Oxford KJB*). This is another long-standing Reformation controversy. Whereas in the Catholic doctrine the Devil could possess people and priests are authorised to conduct exorcisms, in the Church of England, the interpretation was much more cautious, generally considering claims of possessions by the devil as hoaxes and frauds: *Oxford DCC*.

123 Pratt tells the story as if it were a proverbial one, but we have not been able to discover another instance of this story being told.

suppose, ye whole compass of nature Lies open to you alone; every soil has a something to boast of its own. However barren and uncultivated it <ye soil> may appear to you, & every man has a right to the Use of his own understanding; and If ye good Emoluments of our church had not made it so palatable & necessary to believe and to Subscribe so much; If ye Loaves and ye fishes had not stood so invitingly in our way; we never should have had such violent Struggles and disorders in our church in ye defence of such things, as are neither of consequence enough to promote our knowledge; or concern our Salvation; and Whatever may be said on ye opposite side of ye Question; it will ever Appear to a sober and thinking person; that we are still retaining, (may I not say Little more than trifles,) and by ye strength of ye same good Argument, which our Neighbours ye Dutch make Use of, for their being so Long confined to their Wooden shoes, because their wise fore-fathers forsooth,[124] did so before em[.] And as a proof of ye truth of this; yt we are still snarling for things of ye Least importance, & such as cannot Affect ye conscience of any, give me Leave to put ye Question to you ^my^ Reverend Gentlemen who should walk together in ye House of God as Friends—suppose it to be now enacted by royal Authority; that whoever of you persisted in ye reading of ye Athanasian creed;[125] ye use of ye cross in Baptism, ye turning to ye East or West; ye wearing a Hood or surplice; or ye retaining of Sponsors in our church, when Little or nothing Else is intended but ye feast of the Ham & Chickens[126] must give up and Loose your preferments;? Would you Mr Rector or you Mr Vicar; Give up ye snug Little whited manse, with [*p. 38*] the comfortable Glebe around it; for ye retaining of these things which are confessedly of no great use at present; and such as can in no way Affect ye salvation of a Xtian;[127] ^Alas! Alas! under these sort of restrictions we should all kiss, coalesce, and be Friends ^^at once^^ and ye good things of ye church would soon determine it————^ but it may be necessary here to be properly understood, to put in ye following caution: yt tho it is much to be wish'd by many good men; that there might be a review of our Liturgy, and ye Articles of our Church revised, and men of ye most sensible feelings, would be Glad to see some necessary and reasonable Alterations, which are undoubtedly much wanted

124 Wooden clogs were (and still are) one of the items traditionally associated with the Dutch.

125 See note 108 above on Arian versus Nicene Christianity, pp. 292–3 of our edition.

126 Festivities accompanying baptisms.

127 Pratt's own insertion is indicated here, which in the manuscript is written on the (unnumbered) page facing [*p. 38*], to be inserted after the semicolon following 'Xtian'. We have inserted the relevant text from the unnumbered page into [*p. 38*] accordingly.

at present; for what is there that is perfect of mans invention? Yet the daring innovations of some men in their Late religious enquiries & yᵉ reviving at this time those heresies, which were almost fortunately extinguishd; and yᵉ resurrection of Arguments which had Long sunk in Obscurity; can never be yᵉ right and proper method to heal our divisions and make us Friends; nor answer indeed any one good purpose, except it be to display a superiority of Genius, to unsheathe yᵉ sword of Goliath, and to challenge yᵉ whole armies of Israel: and after all our Learned disputes and pride of contention[,] After all our discoveries and boast of abilities; it may be much Questiond still; whether he who shoes yᵉ horse for yᵉ market, or she who carries our provision thither, are not both in their way as great and Useful to yᵉ world as yᵉ most solemn & profound Theologist? For Let any man but of common Observation Look into the societies of yᵉ Learned; and he will frequently find these prodigies of learning (as they choose to be thought in their own way) are not always to be received even as prodigies of common sense; and it is no very uncommon thing to find such a Farrago of Learning so Stuffd and ^so^ kneaded into one theological head; (where Ideas Like yᵉ Ribbands in her Ladyships toilet; are all twisted & [*p. 39*] Jumbled together;) so as to Leave it in a worse condition; than any man could possibly experience from yᵉ most invincible ignorance: these sort of Cloysterd proficients, do frequently Live so Abstractedly from yᵉ world; & so much in yᵉ shade of retirement; that they ^frequently^ chill the friendly affections of yᵉ heart, and ^may be said^ rather to vegetate than Live; under yᵉ most uncomfortable feelings:———— If it be evident then from what is herein Observd; yᵗ yᵉ greatest Learning and yᵉ most extended abilities, do not always accompany & refine yᵉ social Affections, but contribute too frequently to make men proud, insolent, capricious, and self-admirers; let it be known to ^you^ Arch-bishops, and Bishops; Convocations and Chancellors, Treasurers, Precentors, exarchs, and all yᵉ rich and good furniture of our Church; yᵗ yᵉ best and most amiable Study the heart of man can be engaged in; is an Endeavour to be easy and happy in ourselves, and to extend this good and amiable intention towards all mankind in general; and If this excellent and happy temper of brotherly Love & moderation was to become yᵉ common practise of yᵉ World; it would soon cool and Abate yᵉ influenza of yᵉ brain; yᵗ itching spirit for dominion & power, & we should then indeed in reality be Little Lower than yᵉ Angels themselves; And what pity it is when heaven has so created us, as to make us more capable of contributing to our Brothers happiness, than all the other creatures yᵗ God has made; yᵗ man should be so terribly imbruted, as to deal more unfriendly with his Brother, and to occasion him more uneasiness and distress, than all the other creatures yᵉ Lord God has made; and If we are made ye only Laughing Animals[128] on this side heaven; If our [*p. 40*] Creator Loveth a Cheerful worshipper, as well as a Cheerful giver; If according to Ragbag, Bangswanger,[129] and Other Anatomists, who never did or will exist; (you need not look into your index) ye muscles of our faces, are all so exquisitely contrivd and framed, as to dilate and contract with ye greatest freedom and we may so manage ye machinery of our faces, so as to laugh out with ye greatest Ease; surely it would be better for us all, to Lay aside ye Grin of ye Critic, ye sneer of ye Pedant, those engaging Qualities of ye monster; and Laugh out heartily, what say you, good Reader, are you now ready to do so? (with all my heart) Ha! Ha! Ha[!] without guile and without Hypocrisy— And here I must pause a minute to Lament ye Sequesterd abilities of my much loved Friend; who tho posterity[130] may be ye better for his Learned Labours upon ye subject of Chitterlings;[131] and my own head has been frequently ye better for his kind and friendly remarks; yet alas no recompense can be made me; for ye Loss of those happy and convivial hours (ye supreme happiness of this Life) y^t^ Harmony of mind, freedom of sentiment, and social Affections, of more worth and value to me, than all ye labours of ye Vatican—

Grant it me then and we shall all be Friends y^t^ we Live in a strange and Zgubbical world; where we seem to be moving at present upon our heads and not on our heels, every one working his way to ye national whirl-pool which is to ingulph and to take us in; And as it would require more than the Labours of Hercules to untwist and make strait, either our Civil or spiritual dislocations; it may be as well perhaps for a man to fix himself in thy Easy Chair[132] (O Tristram!)[133] & Laugh at a whimsical Age, than to set down under a Philosophical Gloom, and a disturbd countenance; to find fault with [*p. 41*] those things which we do not design to remedy: It is somewhere said of ye good Socrates himself that he rode ye School Boys Hobby,[134] and ye amiable Agesilaus[135] would now and then mount on his

128 There is a long tradition dating back to Aristotle of identifying laughter as one of the key qualities distinguishing humans from animals.

129 As Pratt reveals later in the sentence, these are jocular made-up names.

130 The 'o' in the manuscript is not completed but 'posterity' was clearly intended as it fits the sense of the sentence.

131 A type of sausage made from small intestines of pigs or other animals and usually filled with minced meat and fried: *OED*.

132 A remembrance of the line 'Or laugh and shake in Rabelais' easy chair' in the first book of *The Dunciad* (*Pope*, 22). We quote from the 1741 version.

133 Tristram Shandy from the book of the same name.

134 i.e. a hobby-horse, a children's toy but also a slang term for a prostitute: *OED*.

135 Agesilaus II (444/3–360 BC), king of Sparta noted for his personal as well as leadership qualities in ancient historiography. A story about him pretending to ride

reed, and take a frisk with ye children; and If a man has now and then a mind to mount his Zgubb;[136] (and who is he who never rode out in y^s^ way, in all his Life?) and take a Little excursion; to unbend himself from more Laborious applications; it would be ye cruellest thing in ye world to Unzgubb him and take him down; Genius says a certain great Writer,[137] (I know not who) is one of ye best of goods that heaven has bestowd upon us poor mortals; but If it be sequesterd and confind at home it becomes a disease to the constitution and will soon waste and consume it; Our Fancy may pleasantly sport itself without Offence; and ye faculties we have are allowd their innocent gratifications; we may Laugh and grow fat If we can, and it is more especially necessary at this time so to do, when provisions are so hard to be met with, and I will venture to say for one; that I would sooner be master of thy happy and amiable disposition Good Arch-D—n[138] of Norfolk than be Stuffd out with all ye swell and turgid abilities of ye great Master of ye C——r H——e[139]—We are now, my Affectionate Reader, (and who can give you better Language) most probably in ye good and happy condition of man and wife, most heartily tired with one another; and both of us ardently wishing for a speedy and eternal separation; you shall have your divorce immediatly; but before we part never to meet again; I must admonish you hereby: that If thou thinkest any thing that is herein contained, is intended to censure any one man Living, or to cast any sort

a stick-horse when playing with his children served as an illustration of his amicable fatherly persona. Arthur Hugh Clough, 'Agesilaus II', in William Smith, ed., *Dictionary of Greek and Roman Biography and Mythology*, vol. 1 (Boston: Little, Brown and Company), pp. 69–70.

136 c.f. Tristram's account of mental hobbyhorses in *Tristram Shandy*: *Sterne*, 1:12–14.

137 Probably Pratt means Vicesimus Knox (1752–1821), who wrote of genius in the second edition of his *Essays Moral and Literary* that 'it appears to me that this glorious gift of heaven, ought not to be so lightly esteemed.' See *Essays Moral and Literary* (Charles Dilly: London, 1782), 2:311. Pratt had a copy of the 1782 edition of the *Essays* in his library. The fact that the essay from which this quotation comes ('On the Best Method of Exciting Literary Genius in Boys who Possess it') appeared for the first time in edition strengthens the likelihood that Pratt had Knox in mind. Pratt seems to be both invoking Knox and subtly revising his advice on how to develop genius, since Knox writes in the same essay 'the most effectual method of restraining young people from vice, is to watch them circumspectly, to keep them at home, and at a distance from temptation' (2:312).

138 Thomas Warburton (1719?–1798) was Archdeacon of Norfolk (1744–1798): *CDB*. He overlapped with Pratt at Cambridge: *AC*.

139 Pratt probably means Samuel Salter (1713–1778), the Master of Charterhouse (1761–1778). As the Master of Charterhouse Salter, 'tried to regularize inefficiencies perhaps too pedantically; he soon developed acrimonious relationships with his registrars and officials over bureaucratic minutiae': *Oxford DNB*.

of reflections upon ye best religious Establishment, some things excepted the world can boast of; you are much & [*p. 42*] very much mistaken; If you find in this work numberless faults as you very well may, have you perfection in yourself—? If not be charitable with your censures: If you find it to be a motley composition, borrow'd, Jumbled, and most whimsicaly packd together it was so designd: you are to Laugh, or be angry Just as you please. Object or approve as you are in ye Humour; If it occasions thy face to pucker into an innocent smile; it will make me happy because it has made you so: If ye Joining of these my Zgubbs, to so serious a subject as y^{t} which follows should give offence to any; consider it rather as a stratagem in ye Author for ye avoiding a greater Labour or an artful spreading of ye cloth to excite your Appetite, when he knows there is so Little to set before you; and If ye publick taste at present is so nice and squeamish that nothing will go down without its trufles, ye Reader must excuse ye mental as well as ye common mountebank; If he will not purchase his Packet, and take it in the way prescribd, (when it is honestly worth ye sixpence); If instead of ye joining ye knive, or razor to it,[140] as is common in other instances, he should give you a Zgubb, or a Gomma, or any thing that comes in his way, to make you swallow it—If it offends in any respect I am sorry for it; but after all that has been said, or can be said on ye subject; and whatever shall be ye fate of these my Zgubbs; I do give it here under my hand; that I will most freely forgive from my Heart every kind of Critick, Viewer, Reviewer, or common Sewer; with every sort of Literary Insect, who shall Attempt to torment, bite or bedaub an innocent Writer provided he or they will read over with attention, the following concluding Paragraph; which in fact [*p. 43*] comprehends ye meanning of all y^{t} is containd in this pamphlet—and is neither more or Less, than ye sum & Substance of ye whole together, That whatever restraints are Laid upon our Xtian Liberty in any church, or churches whatever; they both are and will ever continue to be ye Object of concern and dislike to many sober and considerate persons: and however Gilded ye chains may be, which some men are wearing at present; yet ye weight of them is sensibly felt within, under these sort of burthens too many good men inwardly groan; and from which (I am speaking ye minds of thousands) may ye wisdom of this nation Deliver us.

---

140 i.e. if the physician should give the reader as patient a quack medicine (the medicinal equivalent of a mental Zgubb or a Gomma) rather than using a knife or razor on them (which would presumably be worse if the physician is a fraud.)

A Modest Address to Lewis Lord Bishop of Norwich

NRO PRA 664/4

Date: After Lewis Bagot's primary visitation in the Diocese of Norwich in 1784 and the publication of *A Charge Delivered To The Clergy At The Primary Visitation Of Lewis, Lord Bishop Of Norwich* in the same year.

Authorship: The manuscript of the address is in Pratt's hand and is included in the Pratt folder. The autobiographical details given in the address (like the author's 'very near to forty years' in the church [*p. 5*]) match Pratt's closely. We are confident in attributing the address to Pratt.

Physical description: Prose address handwritten in ink in a sewn paper booklet with a marbled cover in Pratt's hand, measuring 18.5 cm by 23 cm.

[*tp*]

A modest Address to Lewis[1]
Lord Bishop of Norwich
by a Clergyman of his Diocese
Publishd with his Lordships Permission—
Pudet Hæc opprobia Nobis
et Dici potuisse, et non potuisse refelli.[2]

---

1 Lewis Bagot (1740–1802) served as Bishop of Norwich between 1783 and 1790. He had previously been Bishop of Bristol and Canon of Christ Church at Oxford: *Oxford DNB*. For a discussion of the circumstances that led to Pratt writing the *Modest Address to Lewis*, see our Introduction, p. 36.

2 *DLCL*: Ovid, *Metamorphoses*, 1:758–9 (p. 57) 'Ashamed am I that such an insult could have been uttered and yet could not be answered.'

[*p. 1*]

My Lord—

—your Clergy, and their Parishioners with them esteem themselves ^happy^ that ye Providence of God has appointed you to bear rule & authority over them, whose abilities and exemplary conduct (as hitherto reported) has fill'd us, with ye most pleasing expectations that your zeal & exertions will not be wanting in the high Office you are in, to revive ye Credit of religion; to give conduct & stability to your Clergy; that by your exemplary labours and diligence with them, the overflowings of ungodliness (now at our doors) may be retarded at least, If not prevented; and those sheep brought home to their folds again, who have Straggled from us; the Writer my Lord of this Little hasty production, has no desing[3] to fill your Lordships ear with Flattery; or, to varnish over a Character y^{t} does not want it, a liberal mind detests this kind of incense, and I would rather undergo ye hard Duty of my triple curacies again; than Offer the sacrifice of praise where it is not deserv'd; or ^endeavour^ to blow up another mans vanity, (could it be done at any time) to serve some designs of my own; but as this particular manner of application to your Lordship, may be suppos'd to carry with it an unwarrantable air of Freedom with some, and by others to be founded, on a ridiculous and presuming vanity and hopes of Applause; yet, as no man can be ^more^ proper than a Protestant Bishop, (and who more worthy by report than Doctor Baggot) to be calld out in ye defence of our religion; so I trust from ye acknowledgd good qualities of your heart and mind, that If the Facts and grievances, here after set forth in this Little Treatise, should Suffer by an improper and injudicious arrangement of the truths in question, (as may be the case) the good intentions [*p. 2*] of ye Writer, may plead his forgiveness with you, and ye Public,—nor would y^{s} slender performance have intruded itself upon your patience and y^{t} of ye Reader had you not so feelingly put ye Question in ye late Queries[4] you sent your Clergy,—"Is there any thing you can communicate to me for ye promoting of religion, and ye cause of our common master?["]—Every good man your Lordship very well knows, is ye natural guardian of Morality and must be materialy hurt at heart; when ye religion of his country is derided

3 i.e. 'design'; this is either a mistake or an intentionally archaic spelling of 'design' as the *OED* attests 'desing' as a common spelling of the word before the seventeenth century.

4 Pratt is referring to Bagot's *A Charge Delivered to the Clergy of the Diocese of Norwich* (1784), which criticized the Norfolk clergy and to which Pratt's text is a response. For more information see our Introduction, p. 36.

and set at nought, and when its divine influence on the heart becomes every day more feeble, and ineffectual, for we, my Brother, (of ye same Family without disparagement, my Lord,)[5] tho very differently employd ^I confess^ in our masters service, Who should walk in ye house of God as Friends, defending & preserving it from all pollution ordaind and set apart for ye arduous undertaking of the Ministry; We I say, of all men Living, must not set down with our hands before us as if nothing was to be done & expected from us; must not suffer the vanities and ye soft allurements of ye World; or ye treachery of our own hearts to divert our attention from ye one thing needful; for If the watchmen will not blow ye trumpet to give ye people warning of their approaching danger; their blood will be requird at their hands, a Languid indifference in us, is criminality without excuse, it is a desertion of our sacred trust with cowardice, & it would be a proof to ye World, (ready enough to believe it of us,) y^{t} we live to ourselves altogether; for what an Opinion would any of us, your Clergy entertain of those men; who could look on with indifference, in Less weighty concerns than these; to see ^for instance^ a noble Edifice in flames, recommending what might be done to save it, and yet doing nothing at ye same time to Stop ye violence and progress of the flames: A Careless indifference in these things, must be odious in the [*p. 3*] sight of God:—ye case Let me say is much ye same with ourselves, we are as it were my Lord, in flames all over; ye flames of corruption, and a general depravity of manners, have reach'd to our very Vitals; and except such men as you, to whom we look up upon such Occasions, with a degree of reverence: & holy awe, will stand up and help us against ye evil doers; we shall soon bid Adieu to ye protestant religion in these kingdoms: for these reasons and weighty considerations my Lord; you are thus addressd; as your elevated station in ye church, your Family connections and honourable seat in Parliament give you both power & Authority to be <both> useful & active in ye Preservation[6] of our Faith ^& mortals^; God himself has set you apart amongst others, in ye high Office you are in as chosen Vessels in this great purpose; he uses you and such good men as you, (I doubt not but I may add with pleasure and truth) as instruments in his hands; not meerely to Dress and ornament his Vineyard, and to be filld with ye good things yourselves ^(as ye Idle & Illiberal may suppose it of you)^ but to Labour diligently therein, that when he comes again to visit his vineyard, he may receive his fruits in due

5 Bagot and Pratt were not related but Pratt means they are of the same figurative family as men of the cloth.

6 A portion of the text has been erased and 'Preservation' has been written over it.

Season, when this is not ye case our ministry becomes meer formality, and religion Lies bleeding at every Pore, by ye wounds of our own inflicting[7]—your Lordship will pardon I hope, this boldness of application to one, Who is so abundantly Watchful; & well experienc'd in these matters; but ye necessity of ye times, must plead my apology for it,: we are not yet we have hopes, so miserably sunk in national Wickedness, but we still have chances, y^t some remedies may be Applyd, to check and prevent y^e [*p. 4*] growth of it; for, tho it is almost a disgrace now, to pretend to be moral; & fashionable Life, is become ye Supporter of Infamy, to excess; yet we have still the Happiness to be assurd; y^t bad and desperate as our condition may be at present; yet there are some thousands of knees y^t will not bend to Baal[8]; there are even yet, those men to be found y^t will not blush, to own, that they Love and reverence their maker, and are not afraid to confess him;—there is not yet (God be thankd) so total an Apostacy from all goodness, nor will we suppose ourselves so Lost, as to be beyond every degree of recovery—ye Salvation of Sinners is a serious business my Lord; and well worth ye notice of us all, it will come home to ye most improvident heart, and eternal punishment must be dreaded as well as felt; nor do I believe depravd as we are represented to be from head to foot, but there is even yet amongst ye rude multitudes at Large, dispositions and hearts to be reclaimd: your Clergy my Lord, must set them good examples by being in earnest themselves; our Light in particular, should so shine before em that they may see our good Works; without the emoluments of our church to persuade us; y^e[9] clergy must seriously and often examine their own hearts; whether it was not ye good things of ye World altogether; that has brought so many of us into the gainful Office of thy ministry; and whether ye misconduct of some amongst us;[10] have not contributed too much, to make others, more dissolute and Wicked than they otherwise would have been; and would but such men who are high & eminent in rank & Station, Laity and Clergy together be but as proportionably good & distinguishable for their morals and good behaviour: could we but see the upper Part [*p. 5*] of ye world putting forth[11] good examples to their Dependants & inferiors:

---

7 A portion of the text once occupying the space between the words 'ministry' and 'inflicting'—has been erased and written over—it is not possible to know what Pratt originally wrote.

8 Baal is one of the rival deities to the God in the Bible.

9 A portion of the text has been erased and 'putting forth' written over it.

10 The words 'amongst us' were originally cancelled and new text was written above the line; Pratt later elected to keep the original text and erased the text above the line.

11 A portion of the text has been erased and 'putting forth' written over it.

would these be[12] sober, temperate, & frugal in their Families, setting Fashions in doing good; rebuking vice and its Abettors we might soon be more than Conquerors over sin & Satan; we might[13] then hope to find those, who have turnd aside from our mild Establishment; returning[14] to their own Shepherds again; Hallelujah might be sung in our Streets and righteousness run down Like a torrent[15]— — — — — — —

To address your Lordship, on a Subject so much your own, (and which requires ye support and protection of all good men, & all ye exertions y^{t} ye Law can give it;) Will Subject no doubt a subordinate and inferior Brother to ye imputation of being too free and presuming; with unavailing and ridiculous complaints for national reformation; for it is a well known Fact; y^{t} no service a man can possibly be engaged in; is so much censurd & discouragd and so disgustful; to ye public Palate, as y^{t} of a capricious reformer,—this is a kind of soil that will return Little or no increase to the owner of it, this kind of Ismael,[16] is singled out at all times, and set apart for abuse and ye Public ridicule, and every mans hand is against him; for there is commonly such a bitterness in this kind of moral prescription; that tho it may make men better afterwards yet few will be found to Attempt ye trial of it,—ye moral as well as ye state Empirick[17] has ever had, and will have their enemies, but whoever acts from ye integrity of his own heart, is above all censure whatever:—ye Long services I have undergone in y^{e} <great> work of ye ministry, (very near to forty years,)[18] may be admitted I hope as a reasonable proof at Least of a competent knowledge and [*p. 6*] experience, in ye Duties of a Clergyman: ye remarks & Observations y^{t} are herein offrd, may be depended upon, as unquestionable truths and it is with pain & reluctance too, y^{t} I do so earnestly believe and assert, y^{t} we are every day growing worse, & more hardned with respect to ye general behaviour, and good Order of our People; and I hope to be forgiven

12 An insert sign appears after 'be' but no text for insertion appears.

13 A portion of the text has been erased and 'might' written over it.

14 A portion of the text between 'turnd' and 'returning' has been erased and written over.

15 An allusion to Amos 5:24: 'But let judgment run down as waters, and righteousness as a mighty stream' (*Oxford KJB*).

16 i.e. Ishmael, the first son of Abraham and Hagar. Hagar was a servant to Abraham's wife Sarah. Sarah subsequently gave birth to her own son Isaac and expelled Hagar and Ishmael into the Beersheba desert. Pratt's allusion to Ishmael as inferior evokes this trajectory and his status as the ancestor of the Arab people in contrast with Isaac as the progenitor of God's chosen Jewish people.

17 'Empiric' in this context means 'medical': Pratt means to say that there are people who inhibit the state of being physically healthy just as there are those who inhibit the state of being spiritually healthy.

18 In the year 1784 Pratt had served 37 years in the church.

when I add; our church establishment in particular for where is there to be found at this time of ye Day that Subordination and Decency of manners, that Sobriety and Simplicity of heart; that civility & modest deportment, yt so eminently distinguishd ye Lower class of our people half a Century backward!: for, is there not, in many places to be found; even at ye Ploughs tail, as great and as accomplishd a Libertine, as any where to be seen in ye purlieus of Covent-Garden? and where is ye man to be met with now; so contemptible in his own Opinion of himself, but he can defy & abuse his minister; disown and find fault with ye authority, both of church & State, Living frequently in open defiance of all those checks, & reasonable restraints, that reason & Christianity require? and where now let me ask, do we find at this time; those connubial and sober joys, that Domestic Love and Union, that once gave Lustre and Credit to the marriage bed, in more honest, tho less fashionable Days? instead of these things, have we not reason every day to lament, a forward assurance, an ungovernable rage for Idleness and Dissipation; so generally possessing ye other sex, so greatly distinguishd a few years backward for their modesty & good behaviour? and how horrid it is to have it known, yt <those> Lascivious <trials for adultery[19]> ^& most impure Books^[20] should have found their [*p. 7*] Way into some female Libraries; & how hurtful ye conversation yt is sometimes to be heard[21] that idle and dissolute men are ye best and most eligible for Husbands:—But I am here aware of an objection that may be thrown in my way, that If the world in common is so dissolute and so corrupted throughout, as is here reported, of what use, or advantage are our clergy to us?, or why do those watchful guardians of our morals, look on with so much indifference and so Little seemingly concernd; as if all was well at ye heart;—should these men slumber or sleep, say ye soft sons of pleasure and Idle Life, When ye storm is gathering so fast around us, and we are every day in danger of Sinking!; If such a charge as this is designd for ye clergy in general; I believe it to be as Illiberal as it is void of truth; for there is not we hope, and are assurd, that indifference for ye Salvation of sinners, as ye revilers of our Order do frequently pretend; there are few in comparison of ye rest, (and God grant there were fewer still) tho men with Like passions as their accusers; who are so divested of Feeling for ye happiness and well doing of their people, as not to be willing and ready to give Happiness and Salvation to Sinners; but suppose it was otherwise, for of

---

19 The title of a book compiling divorce cases. See *Trials for Adultery: Or, the History of Divorces* (7 vols., London: S. Bladon, 1777).

20 There is illegible cancelled text underneath the inserted text.

21 An insert symbol appears here but there is no text for insertion.

What Order of men must they be, who can claim perfection for themselves?—ye good man would Lament that it should be so, & candour would favourably draw ye vail over our unworthiness and imperfections. It is painful indeed to urge, but I believe there is too much truth to justify the Observation; that ye most [*p. 8*] animated zeal of your Clergy, when there is such a general want of morality amongst us; will not be sufficient of itself; (circumstanc'd as we are at present,) to recover ye credit of religion and to give establishment to Order & Virtue;—your Lordship will not suppose that I mean in this place, your ministry is of no consequence to ye World in general for such an undertaking; far be it from me to think after y^{s} manner;—but my Opinion & Meaning is, y^{t} we cannot Effectualy do this of ourselves alone, & by our own authority with ye People; ye Laity must unite and Assist our endeavours, If we expect to return to our senses again, or If ever religion be able to lift up its head <again> over Infamy disgrace, and opposition: you have ye happiness my Lord to reside in a great and flourishing city; you are surrounded with Clergy, that do honorir [*sic*] to their profession & you: you have magistrates ^(I am speaking in a general way)^ upon <all> occasions that are Watchful over ye morals of your people in common; Citizens of zeal and decency to preserve our Laws; & resolute to enforc[e] Authority when wanted; and Happy let me add are ye People who are in such a case, & comfortable is ye Lott of those Ministers, who are thus supported; but this is far from being ye case in the more distant parts of your Lordships Diocese, where men are not even apparently decent, (should it prove no more than this) as those men are in common, who live within the precincts of cities or Larger Parishes; for tho we all live under, and claim ye same protection and benefits of the Laws [*p. 9*] and are under ye same Obligations to Observe em; yet in places w^h^ere Magistrates are thinly Scatterd; not to be found perhaps in ye distance of twenty miles, (which is sometimes ye case) ye refractory and Lawless multitude; will avail themselves of this fortunate circumstance for them, committing Violence and smaller thefts without ye dread of a Prison: and should it so happen, and God knows that it sometimes will; that some Opulent and unprincipled Person; should be at ye head of a Village whose power and overgrown Fortunes, stamps authority with ye vulgar in what they do; If these men encourage Sensuality & prostitution by their own examples; If they have their mistresses in their Families; ye fashion becomes Epidemical & rapid in the Village ye Tenants will have their Housekeepers, in turn; (a new adopted word for ye same good purposes,) their Dependants & Servants under em, will imitate & out do If they can their betters; from hence arises such a want of Decency and Subordination, such a total indifference to every thing y^{t} is commendable and praise-worthy, such a shameful desertion of ye Sabbath

Day in particular & such an avowd contempt of the blessed sacrament that an almost irreparable injury is done to ye morals of ye people in common; by these means they Live in too general a way; as loose and disengaged, from all ye restraints and Obligations of a Xtian Life, as ye inhabitants of Otahite:[22] Under such circumstances as these my Lord and in this situation, What is there that can be done by ye minister of a Parish unsupported and almost Left alone, to prevent or to Stop these growing Evils? [*p. 10*] If he acts from an honest & good Conscience to discharge his duty, and has sometimes a recourse to the Magistrate; to enable him to punish an Offender, ye alarm takes wing at once in the Parish, and ye majority of ye Parishioners (from a conviction frequently, y^{t} too many live under Similar sins) will neither join, or assist him: they are not worse you are told, than other men are in other Parishes; Adultery, Fornication[,] Sabbath Breaking, theft, and Drunkenness are vices, that are nothing new or uncommon; they are as frequent & more so, in other villages: and what a Strange unwillingness is almost every where to be found to Suppress these Evils:*—ye next Step to this is often, a confederacy to plague ye Parson; and to do this Effectualy some Leering Pettifogger of ye Law; a shame to his profession and all that is good and moral, will advise the meanest of these inconsiderate people; not to go home and behave respectfully as they ought to do, but to make ye Parson take his tithes in kind (if it be almost impracticable to be done) and If this will not do ye business for you: Saddle & Load him with rates of every kind; this will serve either to break or bend ^him^ and ye probable consequence from such good advice is, tedious and vexatious Law-suits; dissentions and contentions, in ye Parish where it happens; ye people Alienated in their Affections from their Ministers, they in turn indifferent to ye behaviour of their people; by this means a good man often Looses his own Peace of mind, reducing frequently an income

* And if this kind of relaxd indifference had not been so common as it is amongst Parish Officers ^in general^ we had never been so infested as we are at present, with such numbers of Villains of every kind, Disembogud as it were from our great Metropolis, to spread terror & desolation in our Lesser Villages.[23]

22 Tahiti in the South Pacific Ocean was commonly known in the eighteenth-century English speaking world as 'Otaheite' based on a misunderstanding that the article 'o' was part of the island's name. As a result of reports of the voyage from Samuel Wallis's *Dolphin* voyage (1766–1768) and James Cook's *Endeavour* voyage (1768–1771) among others, Tahitians were associated with a perceived lack of sexual inhibition.

23 In the manuscript Pratt has glued a separate slip of paper containing this text to the top of page 10 on the left-hand side. We have treated the text on the slip of paper as a note rather than an insertion.

[*p. 11*]

too slender of it self, and all this at ye same time from an honest and disinterested design, for ye Salvation and preservation of his people: I would not here be thought to have my colouring too coarse and glaring; I am rather perswaded ye picture is too much Like, I have not a single doubt my Lord; but there are good and principled people to be found in all places, and we hope not a few amongst ourselves; and for ye sake of these it may probably be, that God has hitherto preserv'd this nation: but with ye majority of ye people in common, it is far Otherwise, these like ye wild Asses colt are not to be restraind; these and such as these, are not to be governd by reason or mild persuasion, & when civility[,] reason, and good Advice Loose their power and influence with ye unthinking multitude, ye terror of ye magistrate must be exerted to enforce Obedience: our admirable constitution has given us without doubt, a System of Laws that are truly excellent in themselves, but If they are not properly enforcd, to what purpose serveth ye Law? ye difficulty of doing this will appear hereafter, and except we had an easier and less incumberd method to put them into execution, except as one man with heart and mind; ye body of our people will stand up and take our part against ye Evil doers; except we resolve to lay aside that coldness and indifference for ye honor of God and his beloved son, & become more animated and in earnest to promote Morality & national good behaviour both in our selves and Others; it is not, nor will it be in the Power of ye Clergy, only to restore Order and Virtue [*p. 12*] in their different Parishes — — — — — — — — — — — —

Suppose then; (and God grant that it was not so common as it is), an outrageous Brawler[24], and Blasphemer with ye bitterest Oaths and imprecations let Loose in a Parish, when ye sober part of ye Parishioners are assembling together for ye Public Worship of God, on his own Day?; so hardned a wretch, y^{t} he will be heard, & so indecent in his behaviour that he must be noticed: Suppose too, ye Parish Officers should apprehend such a Wretch as this, & commit him to ye Parish Stocks, Legaly considerd by some, as a place of Security and not of punishment: If the magistrates should Live twenty miles from ye place where ye Offence is committed, (ye very case from whence I am writing this,) or If these Magistrates will act but one day in ye Week; or should not be at home at ye time of ye mans commitment; or this should happen in ye winter season as it thus might be; Whether or not, ye Prisoner suffers in his health, as may sometimes be

24 A portion of the text has been erased and 'Brawler' written over.

ye case by too Long a confinement, or ye severity of ye Weather; there is ever a Pettifogger of ye Law at hand to start up & undertake ye poor mans sufferings; as those merciful and immaculate good men would term them; ye consequence that then ensues, is dreadful prosecution for ^Long or^ false imprisonment, and ye vengeance of ye Law is pourd forth, with all its horrors, on those innocent Parish Officers who have acted to the best of their knowledge to preserve decency & Decorum: & ye same want of enforcing ye Laws with less <fatigue> than at present, Operates also as powerfully, in other instances [*p. 13*] We need no other proofs of this than ye Scandalous passing of carts and waggons so frequently; on ye Sabbath Day, the shameful carrying on mens common Trades & Employments in our Lesser Villages in particular; as at Other times and without distinction; ye rude assembling of mobs to ye very doors of our Parish churches; for ye joining in riotous sports & pastimes; when God knows at ye same time our churches are so miserably thin and naked; & ye Public Worship of God so shamefully Deserted:—by these, & such like enormities as these arise in a great measure, those streams of bitterness, that are so ready to break in and Overwhelm us; to have it so daringly Asserted by Servants and others, with them; that the Sabbath day is entirely their own and not their masters; and therefore they will use it as they please; from this kind of unparr^al^ell'd Assurance, good men are deterrd too often; from defending or assisting in ye cause of Virtue; they shrink aside to avoid ye terrors of ye Law; afraid they should plunge themselves into mistakes & difficulties; so that morality is every day Loosing ground; a cold indifference to devotion & good behaviour takes place in the hearts of thousands; & Villainy of every kind; Lifts up its head in triumph— — —

To Lessen these growing Evils, (so much to be wishd by all good men,) I cannot apprehend (tho I speak it with utmost Submission to better judgement) any inconveniency or Injury, could Possibly arise [*p. 14*] to ye Public in general, were the Clergy permitted to act as mag<g>istrates for ye Sabbath only, or at most in such cases as relate to the preservation of our morals; Alas! Alas! there would be no occasion to fear or alarm our apprehensions, was this to be ye case, that ye clergy would Acquire too much power and consequence in such a Licentious age as the present is, when ye most cautious and prudent of our Order, with ye most becoming Sobriety and decency of manners cannot <cannot> always escape disrespect and rudeness*: we my Lord are undoubtedly ye natural Guardians and Defenders of our masters day; and I hope I may add, our Hearts and Principles as intentionaly good; as ye best of other men; and as the Clergy are more particularly engagd in ye duty & Service of ye Sabbath and can administer Oaths by Authority in many instances; what should hinder them, under mild and merciful Laws, (provided for this purpose,) from protecting ye Sabbath day from pollution; ye restraining those common & Scandalous Offences on that Day, (now, probably become ye wors<e>t<day> of the Seven) as are a disgrace to ye establishd religion of our country, & ye horrid relax'd state & condition of our Laws in general.——

But it may be said perhaps (and Let it be granted If you will,) that Reformation of this sort; is of itself a great, and arduous undertaking; and when necessity makes it become national; it is then ye most

* But why should I say in y^{s} place for ye Sabbath only? for if ye Clergy have as much merit and ability as other Gentlemen as may be reasonably granted beyond all doubt, & are frequently men of property too why are they to be set aside & excluded from ye participation of ye Public Services or, what is there to justify such unequal treatment, except it be <to Humour> ^y^{e} determind^ ye Whim and caprice of a man of Power— — — —[25]

[*p. 15*]

difficult of all our Labours, it is nothing Less than to combat ye vices and follies of mankind, ye Ill will and prejudices of ye world in general, and such endeavours, however intentionaly good are as buffeting ye Air to make it return with greater violence, and are seldom crownd with Success; If this be ye case, must we give it up at Once, & attempt no further? there may be indeed some truth in this, for, give advice to the Libertine and man of Pleasure, and you make him your enemy at once; you Loose your Authority with him, when you expostulate & would become his Friend; there is an Impatience of Spirit in Wicked men that they will not be governd they are continually starting aside Like ye broken bow; they hear not ye voice of ye charmer, but with ye gratitude of ye Serpent ye Fable mentions;[26] do commonly wound and injure ye bosom y^{t} is most ready to cherish them;— But, If this be ye case with us says ye Scoffer, as you describe it;—to what

---

25 In the manuscript Pratt has glued a separate slip of paper containing this text halfway down page 14 on the left-hand side. We have treated the text on the slip of paper as a note rather than an insertion.

26 A reference to the Aesopian fable 'The Farmer and the Viper', in which a kind-hearted peasant finds a freezing serpent in the snow and saves it by warming it up (in some versions on his own bosom) only to be killed by the revived beast. The tale appears in the earliest collections of the tales by Babrius and Phaedrus and is meant to illustrate the moral that evil will repay good only with evil. In some later versions the farmer's wife is killed instead or the farmer manages to kill the serpent before it can cause any harm. In the Perry Index to Aesop's Fables, it is fable number 176.

purpose are your designs to reform and to make us better? If ye whole body is diseasd from head to foot, and ye disease has nearly coverd the whole; to what purpose are ye hopes of reforming?—It is in moral, as well as in medical cases; a disease may be general and almost mortal; but not altogether incurable and beyond ye hopes of ye Skilful; In such dangerous and Obstinate cases, the best endeavours must be used and no time Longer delayd;—exertion is a necessary Qualification for a Christian; save thy self and others: We must set aside in both these instances all Pretenders to healing; must call in the Able Physicians of ye Soul [*p. 16*] to advise and administer comfort; and as (God be thank'd) tho our case be dangerous; it is not quite hopeless, circumstancd as we are at present even up to ye Lip in wickedness; your Clergy must not of all men set down my Lord, under a timid and cool indifference without Stretching out ye hand to help them: It is not us to Look on; and pass away on ye other side, as our Brother once did in ye Parable;[27] when religion lies bleeding at every Pore and cover'd with wounds; and ye very constitutions itself at ye Last gasp;—But ye man of Wit and Humour exclaims, why are we so repeatedly torturd to Death, with this Old stale tale of reformation?; That ye world is every day growing worse & that our iniquities will Speedily overwhelm us: When time after time, years after years, & even Centurys After Centurys, ye same sad threatnings have been used, and yet ye corruptions of ye present times are pritty much ye same as they were; some centuries backward. Tush, say these men; tell us not, that ye nation is quite undone; but give us remedies to remove these Evils, and make us better— there seems to be a mistake in this favourite reply of ye Scoffer—we wish from ye heart that it could be prov'd, that we are not worse than those who have gone before us, but is this any reason at all to prevent our Amendment?—Would to god We were all much better: but as in those Natural calamities yt God sometimes sends to Afflict different nations with; we know them to be <tho> most terrible and dreadful Visitations; tho we [*p. 17*] cannot find out a remedy to explain or prevent em (Witness those once flourishing kingdoms, yt are now no more, and thou Depopulated Messina[28] amongst ye rest) so, in the moral world, there are remedies not always at hand, to remove our Evils, which ye Providence of God may

27 Reference to The Parable of the Good Samaritan from the Gospel of Luke, in which Christ relates how a priest and a Levite ignore a man whom robbers had beaten and left lying by the road between Jerusalem and Jericho, and only the Samaritan passing by later helps him.

28 Likely a reference to a series of earthquakes and related tsunamis that struck Calabria in 1783; the first tremor destroyed much of Messina on 5 February, killing around 25,000 in the city and the surrounding villages.

Allott for us; tho we must always use our best endeavours to prevent such national judgements, and leave ye rest to ye merciful dispensations of Gods Providence:—the facts and Truths that are here set forth; with some few and imperfect Hints for redress that are occasionally interspert in this Work, do not Originate my Lord; either from a querulous disposition to find fault without reason; or, from a petulant and uneasy temper to be displeasd with every thing about me, nor are they owing to any over weening conceit of my own conduct; or from any complaints that God has hedg'd me in as it were with poverty, or disappointments; this is so far from being ye case, y^{t} few men have more comforts, or enjoyments in ye World, or have more reason to be thankful than myself; nor do I design to set forth and remark, y^{t} some Particular Parishes are more reprobate and worse than <Others> ^their neighbour Parishes^; or, that some of our Brethren are more relax'd & remiss in their duties than others are, (tho this is apparently true to every Observer) as candour is ye most becoming Ornament or our Lords disciples; yet I had rather go forth under the Safety of general Assertions, confessedly true in themselves; [*p. 18*] than wound ye peace of another, by holding him forth as an Object, of Public censure;—

The annual returns of our Parish Register Bills, are melancholy proofs to your Lordship of ye great increase of Bastardy from every Quarter, and ye exertions of our Laws at present, too feeble & ineffectual to suppress these growing Evils; we Live at y^{s} time, in no common Age but in one, more bold & fearless than ever; when ye crying sin of adultery, & Whoredom keep each other in countenance, and go as it were hand in hand as Sister vices; and as ye harmless, & familiar corruptions of ye times we Live in; when such impurities as these, and such Illicit pleasures are made ye prevailing Vices, and such as men not only commit <and> ^but^ glory in them; ye dreadful consequences must ever be poverty and Wretchedness to private Families; confusion and disorder to ye State itself; Let me here in this place appeal to ye common notice of ye world in general; do not many thousands, live in such a way; as If they expected neither Death or Judgement? do they at ye close of Life apply to their Parish minister, or, ^rather^ is not ye passing Bell, too frequently, ye first notice y^{t} the Clergyman receives, of a souls departure—? Nor is it to be wonderd at that we are thus loose & relaxd in our manners & in want of all manner of discipline; when our Vices & their vicious adherents have such numbers of open Votaries to plead in their behalf, for; let but a well disposd person examine into ye Licentious practices of ye fashionable [*p. 19*] World in general, let him but Observe how indiscriminately our vices and follies are mixd together; how easy and undisturbd we Live, under ye most Scandalous Offences and he would almost suppose us

Acting with ye authority of ye Laws, and not perpetrating such atrocious crimes as are totally Subversive of all Order & national happiness.

It is a confession that all must own, that ye mutual desires and inclinations of the Sexes are ye most difficult without doubt, of all our Struggles, so ye pursuit of these Libidinous pleasures stand foremost in the Catalogue of our present Vices, ye best of men have ever acknowledgd this to be ye sin y^{t} so easily besets them; <and> and even they who are separated for better purposes, ye most immaculate of all ever had & will have in all Ages their failings and infirmities with ye rest of their Brethren, & had he that is possest of so much hardy virtue as to say, I am free from <this enticing sin> ^y^{e} temptations of y^{s} sin^; Let him take heed Lest he fall let him be careful that he so regulates and subdues his own private thoughts and ye inward feelings of his own heart, that there be no secret Longing for ye indulgence of <this sin> ^such unlawful pleasures^; so as to become almost; If not altogether as criminal in ye sight of God, as by ye commitment of ye sin itself:—this vice is become so familiar & so common a practise, that it is almost I was going to say expected in most places, for whenever connections and intercourses are formd Amongst ye Lower class of our people; unhappy in ye want of Education and where bad examples are set them by their Parents and [*p. 20*] others, & when no punishment is expected: it is rec^{d} with no degree of surprize, (so common is ye case), when ever as it is calld, ye misfortune happens; I would not here insinuate that the Lower class of our people are more vicious & inordinate than their betters are; but as their tresspasses in y^{s} sin in particular must be known to prevent distresses and Starving, whilst ye rich are acting by ye kind interference of their attorneys; (a new and Fashionable mode to promote iniquity,) so such instances of Offence are not made so public, at Least not so generaly known amongst men; in higher Stations—Nor is it to be wonderd at in ye least, that there should be such a rapid increase of prostitution and Bastardy, when so Little notice is taken of ye commoness of ye vice & so little done by ye Authority of ye Laws to prevent ye practice—If in most instances of this sort securities can be had, so y^{t} ye Parish does not suffer in the rise & increase of their rates; If Bonds of Indemnity can be Obtaind; tho frequently of Little or no signification, ye Parishioners become easy and satisfyd at once, & it is wonderful what a peculiar tenderness and partiality is paid to y^{s} prevailing sin in particular probably from a genral perswasion, that it will soon come home to themselves, or amongst their nearest connections; for supposing a Pauper should make a complaint at a Vestry for even one additional sixpence per week, or even for a Petticoat to cover a Womans nakedness; ye Vestry takes fire at once on such complaints as these; ye poor rates are declard to be excessive, and the Parishioners all ruind at once: it was once my Lord, ye usual Sense and practise of the Magistrates, in Less fashionable [*p. 21*] times that all Lewd and abandond women should be punishd and immorality of every sort ^checkd^ prevented[29] as much as possible; but ye sin of Bastardy is hardly considerd as a fault at present nor is any kind of punishment expected, for If any thing like security can be had, for ye maintenance of a Bastard child no kind of interruption is then given to these Amours; Parish Officers swallow their Oaths, so easily, that they are digested at once without thought or concern; and so long as ye Parish rates are but moderate and easy; Little or no Attention is shewn to ye Act itself—But ye wise Preachers for hire, crys the Libertine and man of pleasure; shew us ye times If you can; in which ye intercourses of ye sexes were not common; And when y^t Age and time so pure & i^m^maculate that ye Love & practise of these Libidinous pleasures was not known? there certainly never was a time when men were found to be without passions and follies, nor never will; and what ye sage once said, I love the Vice but I dare not use it; was speaking ye Sentiments of the word in general, men of former ages undoubtedly had their follies as well as ourselves ^Human nature was ever fallible & must be so—^ but they mixd let me say, some Degree of modesty with their Vices; they did not boast and glory in their shame; they strove not to be partakers in Other mens sins; nor were their vices so common and general as they are at present[.] ye vices of the former times like ye coins of ye curious; were kept as it were out of ye way of ye common people; they were chiefly confind to courts, and amongst men of distinction: nor were they then (as will appear hereafter,) so common & dreadful in their consequences to Society; as they are found to be at present: but under our present Improvements in Wickedness [*p. 22*] we are now become Open, and avowd Offenders; above all restraints and management of ye Law, above shame, or ye power of Conscience: <And it is easy to produce as accomplishd a Libertine in a cot[30] or even at ^a^ common work house, as is any where to be found in this Majesty's dominions>——————————

We will try our Assertions my Lord; by the practice of ye times we Live in, and we will suppose for once, a common Prostitute complaind of at ye Sessions, as incorrigible & under ye infamy If you please of a third Bastard, If application is made to punish so old an Offender, as reasonably might be expected; it becomes a question of enquiry immediatly with ye Magistrates,

29 Apparently 'checked' is to replace 'prevented' but Pratt has not cancelled 'prevented' in the manuscript.

30 i.e. a cottage.

Whether; ye woman is chargeable to the Parish or not; If it appears y^t ye Parish Officers have accepted a Bond for ye security of ye Parish, you are then told that you have your satisfaction; y^t ye Parish can receive no injury at all, and so long as this Affectionate care is taken to prevent Parish expenses, ye bad conduct of ye woman shall pass unpunished & ye Vice itself permitted to continue in full perfection: it is not now as it was once, woman go home and do no more so wickedly[31] but woman go home and Oblige your Neighbours—and sad it is to consider, What innumerable Evils do arise to the public, from the partiality and wonderful indulgence that is too commonly shewn to this prevailing Vice, Hinc Illæ Lachrymæ[32] ye consequences y^t arise from it are of ye most alarming Nature to society in common, and so long as there is no Punishment to stop the progress of such proceedings; there can be no [*p. 23*] manner of wonder, that it should, so increase and abound.

And here my Lord I must beg Leave to appeal to ye sober and well disposd in heart and mind: If this kind of connivance does not amount to an almost tolerated indulgence in this sin: When ye Magistrates themselves are often so tender and well disposd; ye Parish where Bastardy is committed so perfectly satisfyd and good Humourd, (the clergy so entirely out of ye Question, and ye Partys themselves as easy and unmolested, as If there was no fault or crime in ye Act itself: Let any man in Orders, who has made ye internal state of his Parish his care & concern; (an attention my Lord that is greatly wanted;) let him declare from his own experience & observation, whether those illegitimate Children I have been considering ^of^, have ye common chance of Living with those who are born in Wedlock; I do not say they are violently pushd out of Life all at once; ye Laws are their protection and defence; but If they are sufferd to want, as they frequently are the common necessaries of Life; If they are permitted to linger in filth and Wretchedness, without ye care and Attention of their Parents in their helpless condition, it must be (Whereever it happens) ye most unnatural of all Deaths; and God only knows how often it is ye case, but If we may judge from ye desperate behaviour of some of these hardned Prostitutes, with what Affected and constraind devotion; they sometimes Lift up their Eyes to God to take such infants to himself: tho they seldom [*p. 24*] mention his name at any other time: except with a wish to blast and to destroy each other; and when we seriously consider what a variety of hardships some of these women have to struggle with & undergo, in many of our Parish houses;

31 The reference is to the unnamed woman accused of adultery in John 8:11: 'And Jesus said unto her, Neither do I condemn thee: go, and sin no more' (*Oxford KJV*).

32 *DLCL*: Terence, *The Woman of Andros*, 126 (p. 61).'This is the explanation of his tears.'

there is too much reason to fear it is much too frequent: and as women of this sort have a right (as certainly they have,) to ye Labours & Attendance of their ministers, as well as ye rest of their Parishioners, it is wonderful to see what uncommon Zeal and diligence, is sometimes used amongst them, to hasten ye Christning of this sort of child, that they <most> probably wish dead in their own minds most heartily; And If a Bastard Child Lives thro ye month, and is then, or before yt time buried with ^(some thing Like ye)^[33] ye <common> Solemnity yt is used on such Occasions; ye good mother is so easy & comforted in her own mind; that she has done all that was in her power and all that was wanted; her child was properly baptized; and buried by ye minister, in his surplice, yt probably ye good creature takes all ye care that a woman can; that she may be as decent and comforted again one twelve months after ^when things are thus as they certainly are^: <and here my Lord> on ye behalf of many of my Suffering Brethren the clergy; and on ye behalf of my own feelings in particular; Let me Lament ^my Lord^ the Hardships We sometimes Undergo; by reading over, our excellent burial Service to half a dozen children perhaps, (dancing ^<& Merrying> Leaping frequently^ after a funeral of this sort,) and over a Dearly belovd Brother, of five days existence:—If things are thus as they too frequently Are; what remedies have we my Lord [*p. 25*] at hand to prevent these increasing Evils?, do we your clergy, or can we suppose, that it is not worth our while, to make some Attempts at Least,[34] to Lessen ye dissipation & mad extravagancies of ye times we Live in; or, are We prepard to meet the Visitations of God and defy his vengeance?—When a nation becomes thus unprincipled in common in their several stations & employments, & so satisfyd & easy to see national Depravity <so> ^thus^ flourish and abound; is it possible to expect ye blessings and favours of God, or ye continuance of our national happiness? we may complain ^of^ & Lament If we will, <of> ye unfavourable changes both of times & Seasons; and how unprosperous all our undertakings have been, both in Peace and War; How discontented and dissatisfyd most of us are with ye Governing Party; and how ready for insurrections upon all Occasions; but Look into ourselves, & we shall soon find ye source & origin of all our misfortunes; Dissolute men will ever occasion dissolute times; & If we are so determinately wicked & fearless as to wage war with heaven itself, we must be an undone and miserable people; but w[h]ere there are willing minds and good intentions, something may be done let us hope, (before it be too Late;) to avert those Judgements, and Visitations, which all Historys

33 Pratt inadvertently inserted a second 'ye' above the line in the manuscript.

34 A portion of the text has been erased and 'at Least' written over.

announce have been, and ever will be ye portion, of over Obstinate & sinful Nations[,] the ax has Long been lifted up as it were against y^s^ unthankful kingdom but blessed be God not as yet Laid to ye root: nor would I have these reflections to pass with the multitude; [*p. 26*] as ye forebodings of a Gloomy and fretful mind, or from any worldly chagrin or disappointment ^of my own^: this is so far from being ye case y^t^ they are ye sober thoughts of truth and sincerity; and they are ye sentiments of one affectionately disposd to have all men happy, and brought to Salvation:————————

To you then; ye magistrates of this realm we must first Lift up our Eyes, for safety and preservation as much is to be expected from your authority & good examples be ye then in earnest to do your duty; for when ye Laws, are properly enforcd, & magistrates themselves are both good and active Vice will naturally hide its head and shrink away from ye terror of ye Law: were we then once so happy as to see ye time; when ye Love and rage of pleasure and dissipation, shall be Less than it is at present, when both Clergy and Laity shall be cordially united substantial & serious advocates in ye cause of Virtue; great and salutary effects would naturally spring up and abound in all places but If in stead of this, Debauchery and Lewdness are permitted to go on so fast, and so unmolested; If Whoredom and the sin of Bastardy, are to be got thro in so cheap a manner, without any dread of punishment or even rebuke; If ye crying sin of Adultery is to pass, as a common & harmless failing (a sin of the first magnitude with heaven) we must not wonder at the infamy and disgrace of ye times we Live in:—If for instance a Farmers Servant can have fourteen or sixteen pounds a year for his Service and ye great sum at present for ye maintenance, ye cloathing, & Education of a Bastard child: is so mercifully Agreed [*p. 27*] and Stipulated to be one shilling and sixpence per week (ye cheapest of all things at present) ye man will tell you ^to your face^ he can afford to be vicious If he pleases; and if the Law is satisfyd in this particular; as it commonly is, and he keeps up to the Obligation of his Bond; what has ye Minister of the Parish, or any one else to do with him, when the magistrates have so effectually Settled ye Business for him?—from y^s^ shameful and pitiful provision that is often made for a Bastard child, for (ye aid & assistance of ye mother cannot reasonably be expected for the first Quarter at least) great & manifold are the hardships & inconveniences y^t^ must follow; and how frequently are those solemn vows & promises that are made in ye time of seduction forgot and evaded, by such an easy & scandalous commutation and what numbers of Friendless young women, and sometimes for ye first Offence; by being brought[35] to poverty and Wretchedness by y^e^

35 A portion of the text has been erased and 'brought' written over it.

distresses of a town house, have been renderd irrecoverably Lost to themselves and ye community they belong to; who by ^proper^ reproof and better treatment, might have been reclaimd and brought back to repentance and good behaviour: but as these things are commonly managd in many Parishes, these kind of women are permitted to go on from one degree of Wickedness to another; by this means numbers of children are Lost to ye public in general: town Houses become Little better than common brothels & numbers of hands shamefully employd in every kind of pill<e>fering villainy which should have been preservd and [*p. 28*] and ought to have been employd in ye Service of the Public; If then a better provision was to be made for a Bastard Child[36] which in so dear a time, Humanity itself requires; supposing half a crown or three shillings per week was allowd by ye magistrates in such cases; it would then be, (in some measure) in ye first place, a restraint upon ye Illicit amours of Servants & inferiors, and If in such cases ye mothers of these children should be judgd improper as disqualifyd by their vices; (too often ye case:) to have ye management of their own children, then ye Elder women of a Parish would become willing & proper nurses: as three shillings per week would enable em to be careful & to do their duty to such infants: and should it be here remarkd that this would be ye readiest way to encrease ye Evil I am here complaining ^of^ now even supposing yt it should be so; which is by no means to be granted, yet it would certainly be ye saving of many <infants> ^Lives^; and If ye magistrates would Attempt to check in earnest this prevailing sin; If ye woman for instance was to wear a badge ^of distinction^ on her arm with ye Letter—W at large for two or three sundays together in ye Parish church where ye Bastard was born,[37] or in any other; or, in case of

36 A portion of the text has been erased after 'Child'.

37 Forcing women accused of engaging in sex outside marriage to wear a badge with 'A' or 'AD' (standing for 'adultery'), as famously depicted in Nathaniel Hawthorne's *The Scarlet Letter* (1850), was a documented practice in New England in the seventeenth and eighteenth centuries: see George P. Howard, *A History of Matrimonial Institutions: Chiefly in England and the United States* (Ithaca: Cornell University Library, 2009) rpt. of 1904 edition. In England the Poor Act of 1697 required paupers in receipt of support from their parishes to wear identifying badges on their right shoulders with the letter 'P' preceded by the first letter of the respective parish. Single mothers with illegitimate children were sometimes among those badged welfare recipients but were not specifically singled out or penalized. Norwich was one of the parishes where these so-called 'badging laws' were actively enforced in the late seventeenth century; in some parts of England they were still in use in the 1790s. See Steve Hindle, 'Dependency, Shame, and Belonging: Badging the Deserving Poor, *c.* 1550–1750', *Cultural and Social History* 1 (2004), pp. 6–35 and Edgar J. McManus, *Law and Liberty in Early New England: Criminal Justice and Due Process, 1620–1692* (Amherst: The University of Massachusetts Press, 1993), pp. 201–10.

Obstinacy and disobedience was to be sent to ye common prison, (for one month at least) or to pay a sum of money not less than twenty Shillings, for ye Use of ye Parish poor where ye Bastard was born; or; If for ye second Offence or more; ye persons so offending should be oblig'd to marry; or, the refusing party in such cases, or both; should be made [*p. 29*] Subject to a Heavy Fine; and If not able to pay ye Fine (to be Levyd by Order of magistrate,) then to be committed to ye common Jail for six months ^imprisonment^, (If ye magistrate allowd it) good & salutary effects might be expected from such; or similar exertions: and tho tis certainly difficult to point out the ways & means to Subdue & remove our vices, especialy those of this sort which so easily beset us and are so common, and tho ye Hints that are herein offerd may be ^thought^ nugatory; & of small esteem with some (as probably, will[38] be ye case,) yet men of ability and more experience in ye world, might be easily found, to assist and improve upon such a plan; were we but once in earnest to be truly serious in a business, of so much Importance and it is certainly worth ye while of such who are men of property in ye nation; If for no Other reason, than ye following to stop ye spreading of this iniquitous practise, as ye increase of ye poor rates will be speedily such, as to ruin and destroy their ^States, &^ Fortunes; And If ever there was a Period in the Annals of this country, in which it was incumbent upon ye Laity and Clergy together, to be more watchful & diligent than ever,[39] it is ye present time, when shameless profligacy & avow'd Libertinism go hand in hand, when <we> ^men^ are grown so very hardned as not only to commit ye most scandalous Offences but even to boast and glory in <u>their</u> sins when they are committed, as if there was a contest <amongst us> ^in general^, who should be ye most notorious Offenders;—when matters are run out to these sad extremities; there can be no Occasion [*p. 30*] to tell us my Brethren, and companions of ye Altar; how necessary and useful our zeal & Labours must be; were we permitted to act as magistrates; to recover and bring us back to Sobriety and good behaviour:—to do this as it should be done it will be necessary for us to lay some Useful restraints upon ourselves even in ye usage & enjoyments of our common pleasures, yt more of our time may be set apart for such important purposes; And If such attempts as these were made with heart & hand, were we ^to^ stand up in earnest as one man, against ye Evil doers, ye good & mighty influence it would have, from such good examples, would descend to our Parish Officers and our Parishioners with them, we should not then have such frequent Perjuries as we now have such reason to

38 A portion of the text has been erased and 'will' written over it.

39 A portion of the text has been erased and 'than ever' written over it.

complain of; nor such a breach of those customary oaths of office as are a disgrace and scandal to ye community we Live in;—for should a stranger to this country be introduc'd at ye time of our visitations, those solemn courts of enquiry into Parochial duties, would he not suppose us to be the most pure and immaculate of all nations?: No kind of presentment is ever offerd, (or at most but seldom) no common Drunkard or Adulterer is any where to be found; but all is peace & well, all perfectly chaste and pure[40] tho we know very well and are at ye same time assurd, that those kind of sinners against themselves and their Own souls, do every where increase and abound—to remedy in some measure [*p. 31*] these growing Evils, & others (as notorious as these,)[41] nothing can more Effectually contribute; (as has been before observd) as ye making our Clergy magistrates in common, and If this should be thought too much, then let it be for the sabbath only,—by this means a nearer access would be had to Justice, proper punishments more at hand, which are so much wanted, Authority would be more extended & ye morals of our people more easily preservd—

It must then my Lord, be ye work not of a few only, but ye join'd Labours of ye whole together everyone, as we may say, at his Oar; If we yet can have hopes to be savd from national ruin: it is not in your Clergy alone deserted & unsupported as they sometimes are, were they more ready & diligent than they are at present, (or, were they even permitted to act as magistrates upon ye Sabbaths ^or at Large^) to bring us back to order & reformation by their own authority; or even by their good examples: it is not in ye magistrates themselves few and scatterd as they are over ye face of this county in particular; were they more interested than they are in the cause of religion to replace us within ye bounds of Decency & Decorum; no, it must be ye general Endeavours of all parties the rich and poor; one with Another, If any thing is to be done to continue to us those blessings of Providence we have so long experiencd; for when we Live so unprincipled in our Lives and actions, when almost ever sin has its avowd [*p. 32*] abettors, when scarce any man is valued or more Esteemd for his modesty and good behaviour; when all distinctions of Good & bad becomes every day a meer matter of indifference with ye fashionable world in general ^what is there y^t can save us from ruin?^ It is not therefore my Lord <our> ^an^ enquiry at present, whether we are more profligate and abandond than those men were who have lived before us; this is rather a matter of inquisitive curiosity than of real use, for these sort of comparisons are generaly made in ye favour of former times;

40 An insert mark appears here but there is no text for insertion.

41 We have deleted a single parentheses before 'others'.

as it is confessedly granted on all sides that we are more than sufficiently sinful;—as a proof of this, let us look up to the alarming increase of public robberies, the numerous murthers & perjuries from every Quarter, and ye sad Spectacles that ye Jails & Gibbets are exhibiting every year, insomuch that they almost cease to affect us, when these things become national Evils more than in common, it is more than time to infuse into ye rising generation solid, and sober principles of religion of more real use to make men better, than all our Jails or ^knotted^ Gibbets and to do this Effectually it should be done in their early years; Parents should become good Examples to their own Children & Others, in temperance, sobriety, and good behaviour, they should teach em frugality at home; a Love of industry in their respective callings, reverence to their superiors, civility to inferiors, and benevolence to all; they must endeavour to Lessen that Love of pleasure and Idle Life so early introduced in their [*p. 33*] younger years to Lessen that vanity of dress & forwardness of behaviour: that is not becoming,—to keep them within ye bounds of decency and moderation, for when this is not ye case, ye early pursuit of pleasure & Fashionable Life will ripen ye passions too fast, and the follies of the world will usurp the places of Sobriety, & candid reasoning and let all such who are plac'd in ye capacity of masters and mistresses in their respective families; suppose themselves, in some measure responsible to God (as they certainly are) for the conduct of their inferiors & dependants Let them be inure'd [*sic*] to family devotion in their own houses, make them truly ye Servants of God at all times as well as your own, and Suffer them not to suppose that the Sabbath Day is entirely their own, and which may be employd as they think proper; a prevailing notion with some that is attended with ye very worst of consequences, nor Let the Idle and inconsiderate be so easy of belief, as to Suppose (as too many do,) that we are still going on in a safe and good way; and that we are not in any thing worse than those ^men were^, who have lived some Ages before us; for tho it has hitherto been our good fortune, as well as our happiness at present, to have escapd those horrid calamities, with which God has visited so many of our Neighbour nations, yet [*p. 34*] If these warnings do not reach us; If we will not Learn instruction from their Sufferings and distresses; so as to bring us home to ourselves, to sobriety & effectual reformation, I think I may venture to pronounce; and this without a gift of Prophecy; Delenda est Carthago[42]—

42 'Carthage must (or is to be) destroyed.' The quotation is attributed to Marcus Porcius Cato (234–149 BC), who is supposed to have used it repeatedly in the Roman Senate, ending all of his public speeches with it. The intended parallel is with the urgency of necessity for combatting sin in England.

Shorter Prose Writings

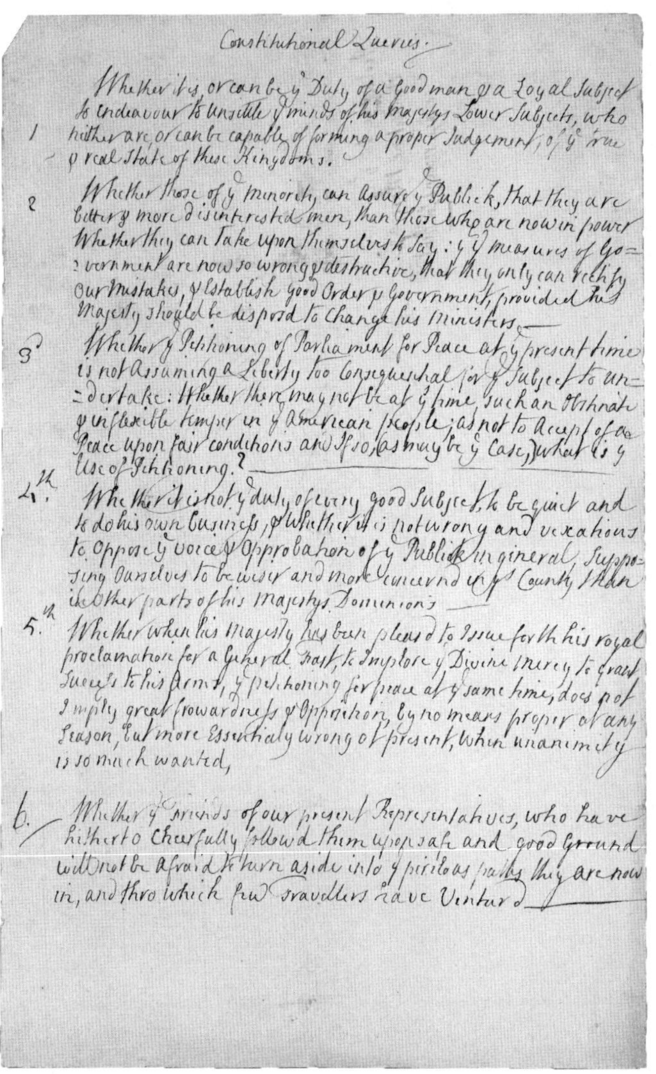

Constitutional Queries.

1 Whether it is, or can be ye Duty, of a Good man & a Loyal Subject to endeavour to unsettle ye minds of his Majestys Lower Subjects, who neither are, or can be capable of forming a proper Judgement, of ye true & real State of these Kingdoms.

2 Whether those of ye minority, can assure ye Publick, that they are better & more disinterested men, than those who are now in power Whether they can take upon themselves to say: y ye measures of Go=vernment are now so wrong & destructive, that they only can rectify our Mistakes, & Establish good Order & Government, provided his Majesty should be dispos'd to Change his Ministers.—

3d Whether ye Petitioning of Parliament for Peace at ye present time is not Assuming a Liberty too Consequential for ye Subject to un=dertake: Whether there may not be at ye time, such an Obstinate & inflexible temper in ye American People, as not to Accept of a Peace upon fair conditions and if so, (as may be ye Case,) what is ye Use of Petitioning?

4th Whether it is not ye duty of every good Subject, to be quiet and to do his own business, & Whether it is not wrong and vexatious to Oppose ye voice & Approbation of ye Publick in general, Suppo=sing Ourselves to be wiser and more concern'd in ys County, than in other parts of his Majestys Dominions —

5th Whether when his Majesty has been pleas'd to issue forth his royal proclamation for a General Fast, to Implore ye Divine Mercy to grant Success to his Arms, ye petitioning for peace at ye same time, does not Imply great frowardness & Opposition, by no means proper at any Season, but more Essentialy wrong at present, when unanimity is so much wanted,

6. Whether ye Friends of our present Representatives, who have hitherto Cheerfully follow'd them upon safe and good Ground will not be Afraid to turn aside into ye perilous paths they are now in, and thro which few travellers have Ventured —

Figure 11 *'Constitutional Queries'*

'Constitutional Queries'

NRO PRA 664/21

Date: Probably written between January and early February 1778. At this time, Thomas Coke (1754–1842), the current MP for Norfolk, and William Windham (1750–1810), the son of the recepient of Pratt's poem 'Grunnelia or the Sow in the Dumps', were canvassing for signatures for a petition to parliament opposing the raising of money and men for the war without parliamentary consent. They began their efforts after they disrupted a meeting held to raise funds for the American Revolutionary War at the Maid's Head Inn in Norwich in January 1778. Windham gave a vehement speech against the war at the meeting, thus launching his political career. See Kathleen Wilson, *The Sense of the People Politics, Culture and Imperialism in England* (Cambridge: Cambridge University Press, 1995), p. 419. The petition was presented to the House of Commons on 17 February 1778 and gained 5,400 signatures across Norfolk. See William Cobbett, *The Parliamentary History of England, From the Earliest Period to the Year 1803* (36 vols., London: T. C. Hansard, 1814–), 19:762. This would make the fast day that Pratt alludes to in the queries the one that was held on 27 February 1778. There is a note on the back of the manuscript sheet of paper reading 'Prologue to ye Clandestine Marriage college receipt for Rent'. This note seems to have been written about a year after the queries were drawn up, probably late 1778 to early 1779, when Pratt would have been at work on the 'Occasional Prologue to the Clandestine Marriage', performed on 22 March 1779.

Authorship: The text is in Pratt's hand and the implicit attack on the North Administration's handling of the American Revolutionary War is consistent with 'Political Duck-Hunting', published the same year. The 'Constitutional Queries' can confidently attributed to Pratt.

Physical Description: Questions handwritten in ink on one side of a single sheet of manuscript paper in Pratt's hand, measuring 20.5 cm by 32.5 cm.

[*f. 1r*]

Constitutional Queries.[1]

1 Whether it is, or can be ye Duty of a Good man & a Loyal Subject to endeavour to Unsettle ye minds of his Majestys Lower Subjects, who neither are, or can be capable of forming a proper Judgment, of ye true & real State of these Kingdoms.

2 Whether those of ye minority can Assure ye Publick, that they are better & more disiniterested men, than those who are now in power[.] Whether they can take upon themselves to Say: y^{t} ye measures of Government are now so wrong & destructive, that they only can rectify our Mistakes, & Establish good Order & Government, provided his Majesty should be disposd to Change his Ministers—

3^{d} Whether ye Petitioning of Parliament for Peace at ye present time is not Assuming a Liberty too Consequential for ye Subject to undertake: Whether there may not be at y^{s} time, such an Obstinate & inflexible temper in ye American people[2]; as not to Accept of a Peace upon fair conditions and If so, (as may be ye Case,) what is ye Use of Petitioning?[3]——————

4th. Whether it is not ye duty of every good Subject, to be quiet and to do his own business,[4] & whether it is not wrong and vexatious to Oppose ye voice & Opprobation of ye Publick in general, Supposing Ourselves to be wiser and more concernd in y^{s} County than in other parts of his Majestys Dominions——

5th. Whether when his Majesty has been pleasd to Issue forth his royal proclamation for a General Fast,[5] to Implore ye Divine mercy to grant

1 This text appears to be Pratt's original composition although its form is inspired by William Pitt's *Constitutional Queries, Earnestly Recommended to the Serious Consideration of every True Briton* (London, 1751) and *Constitutional Queries Humbly Addressed to the Admirers of a Late Minister* (London, 1761).

2 Reference to the American Revolutionary War (1775–1783).

3 For the history of petitions to the British Parliament during the American Revolutionary War see James E. Bradley, *Popular Politics and the American Revolution in England* (Macon, G.A.: Mercer University Press, 1986).

4 1 Thessalonians 4:11: 'And that ye study to be quiet, and to do your own business, and to work with your own hands, as we commanded you' (*Oxford KJB*).

5 Fast days, during which time Anglican priests like Pratt were expected to give sermons in support of the war divided the church. An occasional churchwarden, Richard Hayes, wrote in his diary on 27 February 1778 'A general Fast. But we now begin to find we must

Success to his Arms, ye petitioning for peace at ye same time, does not Imply great frowardness & Opposition, by no means proper at any Season, but more Essentialy wrong at present, when unamity is so much wanted,

6. Whether ye Friends of our present Representatives, who have hitherto Cheerfully followd them upon safe and good Ground will not be afraid to turn aside into ye perilous paths they are now in, and thro which few Travellers have Venturd———[6]

restore peace to the Americans. I was not at Church. I do not like this War.' Qtd. in Stephen Conway, *The British Isles and the War of American Independence* (Oxford: Oxford University Press, 2000), p. 144.

6 Over the page Pratt has written the note 'Prologue to y^e Clandestine Marriage college receipt for Rent'.

‘Thoughts on Repentance’
and
‘A Prayer to be Used any Time of the Day’

NRO PRA 664/20

Date: The date is difficult to ascertain, especially with the lack of an identifying watermark in the booklet. Pratt’s mention of the infirmities of age in ‘A Prayer to be Used any Time of the Day’ might be taken to suggest a later date of composition (perhaps in the 1780s) but we cannot be sure.

Authorship: ‘Thoughts on Repentance’ is written in Pratt’s hand and can be confidently attributed to him. ‘A Prayer to be Used any Time of the Day’ draws on different prayers in The Book of Common Prayer but also appears to be Pratt’s own composition and can be confidently attributed to him.

Physical description: Handwritten short moral essay and accompanying prayer handwritten in ink in a sewn booklet in Pratt’s hand, measuring 15 cm by 18.5 cm.

[*f. 1v*]

Thoughts on Repentance

Hon'd Sr.[1]

You desired my thoughts upon a very interesting Subject, "What kind of Repentance it is, that God requires from his Creatures, to Intitle them to a state of Salvation"[2]—I have sent you my thoughts upon ye Subject, and they are much at your Service; and I beseech God, to remove from your mind all doubts, and Scruples, all anxiety and dejection of Spirits, and safely Lead you thro' ys Vale of Misery to a state, where no Evil thoughts, or Disquietude, will molest you.

——Christian Repentance, as set forth in ye Gospel, implies a relinquishing those favourite sins yt do most Easily beset us; tis a resolute proceeding in all ye Virtues of a Godly Life as much as we are Able: it takes its rise, and beginning in our thoughts and resolutions; & is to be perfected afterwards; in our words and Actions—There were in ye first Ages of Christianity some unreasonable people, who Affirmed, that If any sinned presumptuously after their Baptism, there remained no more Sacrifice for Sin, for as ye death of Christ could not be repeated again; so they could not Obtain a farther Pardon: these men, mistaken some passages in St Paul's Epistle to the Hebrews took upon them to declare; that even Supposing [*f. 2r*] a Sinner should sincerely repent him of his Sins, committed after Baptism; yet nothing was to be expected for him, but ye wrath of God, and his condemnation.[3] ye Absurdity of ye Argument will appear to us, by considering yt neither our Saviour, or his Apostles, had any Such notions, of ye irremissibleness of Sins, committed after Baptism—In this case, ye Gospel of Christ would in vain profess to bring men to Salvation, If every Deviation

1 The recipient of 'Thoughts on Repentance' (if there was one) is unknown.

2 Pratt uses two sets of double quotation marks, one on top of the other, at the beginning and end of the quotation.

3 Paul's letter to Hebrews undertakes a detailed exposition of the relationship between the Old and the New Covenants. In this context it emphasizes the unique and unrepeatable nature of Christ's sacrifice and the forgiveness of sins it has offered to humanity: 'For if we sin wilfully after that we have received the knowledge of the truth, there remaineth no more sacrifice for sins,/ But a certain fearful looking for of judgment and fiery indignation, which shall devour the adversaries' (Hebrews 10:26–27: *Oxford KJB*); 'Now the just shall live by faith: but if any man draw back, my soul shall have no pleasure in him' (Hebrews 10:38: *Oxford KJB*). Pratt nevertheless argues that these verses are interpreted overly literally by some.

from ye rules of Virtue, were so unpardonable, as no Amendment would be sufficient, for past transgressions; as it is impossible to Live free from sin, If God pleased not, to Accept of repentance when we have offended him who is there that could be Saved? but ye absurdity of ye supposition will appear, from almost all ye parts in ye holy writings: God is represented as merciful and Gracious, abundant in goodness, forgiving Iniquities and transgressions; He himself has assured us, that he has no pleasure in ye death of ye wicked, but y^t ye Wicked turn from his ways, and Live[4]: he sent his son into ye World to bind up ye broken-Hearted,[5] & to Loose men from the burthen of their sins; He gave his Apostles commission to preach repentance amongst all nations, being Willing that none should perish, but that all might come to Repentance; So that it seems as plain [*f. 2v*] as words can make any thing, y^t no act of Sinning we can be Guilty off; in ye ordinary course of Sinning will deprive us of God's forgiveness; If we seriously return to him in time, with sorrowful and penitent Hearts and where there is nothing in a mans Life, that is different from ye common Life of Other men; nothing more particularly Sinful, than those common failings & imperfections, y^t do Arise from ye natural corruptions of his nature, Let him rest easy, and satisfied, y^t God will Open to him ye door of his mercy, & pardon all his Offences: for, it is as reasonable to infer, that as he, who once Lived well and righteously, and should afterwards grow wicked and profane, would never be ye better for his former Goodness, So he, who has been formerly wicked may afterwards by repentance, & proper Obedience blot out his transgressions, & be received to mercy and pardon[.]

As it is evident then both from reason & Scripture, that God will Accept of returning sinners, If they return to him in time and seek him diligently, so ought we to represent him to our thoughts as a God of mercy and forgiveness: Let not a man be disturbed that he feels within himself, such passions and Affections, such fears and Apprehensions, as fill him with terror and disquietude; these [*f. 3r*] are inherent in his nature, make part of himself and are inseparable from humanity: ye son of God himself had his hopes and fears, dejection of Spirits and heaviness of Soul as well as ourselves, with this only difference, y^t what are sometimes exorbitant in us, in him were free from all irregular Disquietude—The motions of our minds are very Little, If at all under our power and dominion: we

4 Ezekiel 33:11: 'Say unto them, As I live, saith the Lord God, I have no pleasure in the death of the wicked; but that the wicked turn from his way and live: turn ye, turn ye from your evil ways; for why will ye die, O house of Israel' (*Oxford KJB*).

5 Psalm 147:3: 'He healeth the broken in heart, and bindeth up their wounds' (*Oxford KJB*).

are not such Masters of ourselves as to be Able to stop them at first, they are often produced suddenly, that they take possession of ye mind before it is apprehensive of them: Our thoughts, tho they should sometimes be indecent & irregular, yet as they are often involuntarily Obtruded upon us, are to be Accounted for as ye infirmities of our nature, and cannot possibly be imputed to us as sins, which we cannot hinder: it is not Always in our power to suppress them, nor prevent impious fancies, or even blasphemous Suggestions, from arising within ourselves: they are frequently owing to indisposition of body, by which we sometimes Loose ye Government of our thoughts; from hence Strange terrors & frightful Imaginations will intrude upon us; and in such a Case, A man will be no more condemned for his thinking, than he who talks Treason in a fever, ought to be condemnd, for what he [*f. 3v*][6] could not possibly prevent——

Considering then, that man is of himself but a feeble and infirm Creature, and in continual want of something to Lean upon, and Support him it should teach him to turn his thoughts upon God, & make him ye Object of all his wishes: whatever it is you may suffer in Life it can be but Short, and y^{t} you are born for Everlasting Ages: No pain, or disquietude of soul cometh out of ye Dust, neither doth trouble spring out of ye ground: If your Cup be bitter it is ready mixed for you by ye hand of God, and he who knows what it is you Suffer, can make it up to you a thousand ways[.] Represent God to yourself, as a tender and compassionate Father, ready to forgive and to receive you; Represent him to yourself as a kind and Amiable Being, not pleased with ye wretchedness of his Creatures, but ever ready to Assist them; Consider as Seneca directs, how many there are behind thee, as well as those before you,[7] how many are in a worse condition than thyself, more exposed to temptations, & under worse pain and Afflictions: he says Solomon who Looses ye Management of himself and has not ye rule over his own Spirits [*f. 4r*] is Like a City that is broken down and without walls;[8] and as a City in this condition would be Liable to be ruined by an Enemy, so he who Looses ye management of himself will be exposed to

6 A second 'he' appears in the manuscript here, which we have omitted.

7 *DLCL*: Seneca, *Moral Essays*, 'Of Anger,' Book 3 (p. 331) 'Nulli ad aliena respicienti sua placent. Inde diis quoque irascimur, quod aliquis nos antecedat, obliti quantum sequatur a tergo ingentis invidiae.' 'No man when he views the lot of others is content with his own. This is why we grow angry even at the gods, because some person is ahead of us, forgetting how many men there are behind us, and how a huge mass of envy follows at the back of him that envies but a few.'

8 Proverbs 25:28: 'He that hath no rule over his own spirit is like a city that is broken down, and without walls' (*Oxford KJB*).

various Accidents and temptations: Consider too, in ye Extremities of Life, when ye faculties are disturbd & Injured, ye body weak and declining, it is as impossible in Age to Avoid fears and Apprehensions[,] distress, and disquietude, as it is to avoid dirt and rain in a Long Journey; And whilst you are Sojourning here below, you should put on a Travellers indifference to what you meet with, ready to go hence as a Traveller from a dirty Inn, where ye Ill Accommodation he meets with, makes his stay disagreeable to him & ye joy of Leaving it more welcome, ye Giving up a Life of sorrow, & disappointment, for a more desirable state, where neither pain, or Grief, Evil thoughts, or any kind of Disquietude will ever reach you.

[*f.* *4v*]

A prayer to be Used any time of ye Day.[9]

Merciful God, by whose Gift it cometh,[10] y^t^ we are able to look up to the throne of Mercy pitifully behold ye prayers and Supplications of thy Servant, here prostrate before thee, in great Weakness of body, confessing, and bewailing his Sins with the deepest sorrow, and Compunction of Spirit—If thou Oh!, Blessed Lord, art Extreme to mark what is done amiss in me; how shall I be able to Look up, & Implore thy pardon—But as thou art a God of mercy & pardon do not bring to thy remembrance ye many ways I have Offended thee, in thought, word, or Deed—make me O God, to condemn myself and my Sins, that I may not be condemnd at thy great tribunal;—Oh! Thou, who seekest out sinners to make them good, do not reject me when I fly unto thee for comfort and protection: Enlighten my mind, & Dispel those mists which overshadow it, put from me All Evil thoughts, All unnecessary fears and apprehensions, y^t^ do Assault my Soul, & put into my mind such good desires such peacible and Quiet thoughts, such [*f.* *5r*] comfortable feelings by thy Heavenly Assistance, that I may serve thee for ye time to come, with a Joyful & Quiet mind—Have mercy upon me O God, and for ye sake of thy beloved Son, forgive me All that is past[—]Oh, Forsake me not Utterly now in ye time of Old Age when my mind and bodily faculties are impair'd, When ye Vigour of my Days is past,

9 There appears to be no single prayer on which this prayer is based. Instead, the prayer seems to be a mélange of quotations from the Book of Common Prayer and common phrases from the sermons of this period.

10 The collect for the Thirteenth Sunday after Trinity in the Book of Common Prayer begins 'ALMIGHTY and merciful God, of whose only gift it cometh' (BCP, 352).

& my Evening Sun is near its Setting, when I am not able to compose my Shattered thoughts nor Approach thee as I ought to do, Lead me then I most humbly beseech thee by ye blessed conduct of thy Holy Spirit, thro' all ye dangers and difficulties of this mortal Life, thro all temptations, Ghostly and bodily; that when I am dissolved from y^s tabernacle of flesh, I may be received into thy Heavenly kingdom there, to remain with thee for ever and ever in perfect and Everlasting Happiness; Hear me O God for y^e sake of thy beloved son, my most Gracious Saviour and Redeemer——Amen.

Appendices

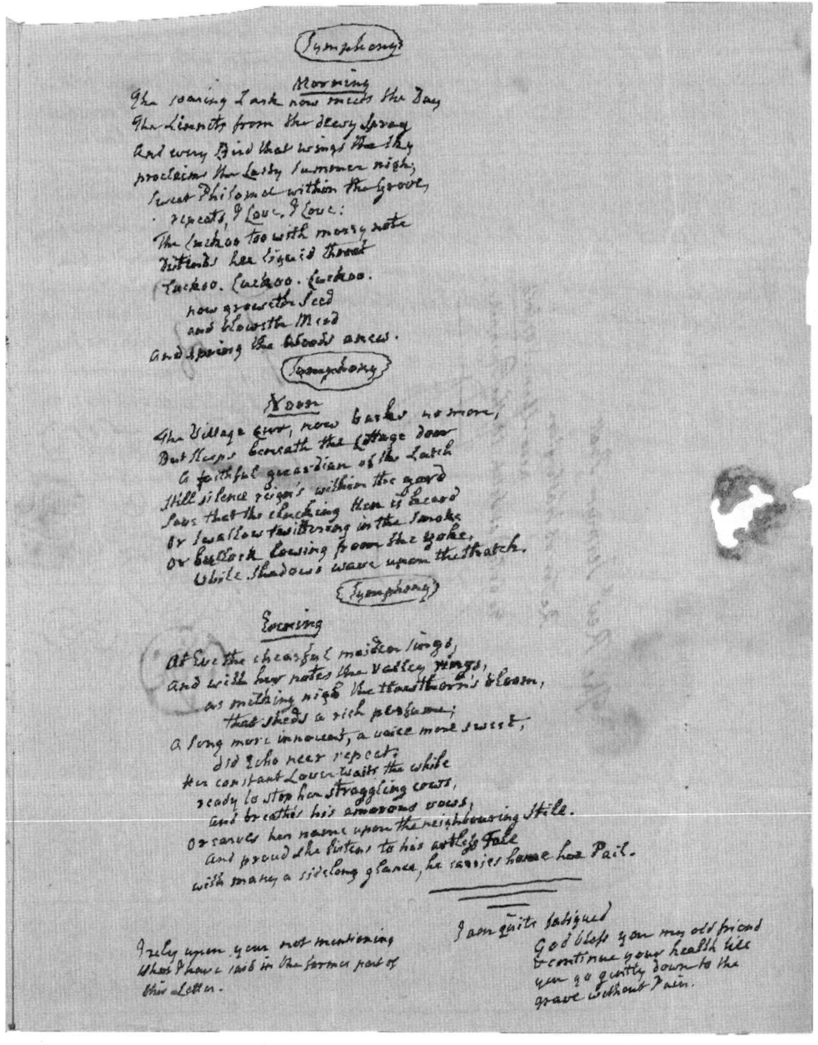

(Symphony)

Morning

The soaring Lark now meets the Day
The Linnets from the dewy Spray
And every Bird that wings the Sky
proclaims the Lusty Summer nigh;
Sweet Philomel within the Grove,
repeats, I Love, I Love:
The Cuckoo too with merry note
Distends her liquid throat
Cuckoo. Cuckoo. Cuckoo.
now groweth Seed
and bloweth Mead
and Spring the Woods anew.

(Symphony)

Noon

The Village Cur, now barks no more,
But sleeps beneath the Cottage door
a faithful guardian of the Latch
Still silence reigns within the yard
Save that the clucking Hen is heard
Or Swallow twittering in the Smoke
Or Bullock Lowing from the Yoke,
While Shadows wave upon the thatch.

(Symphony)

Evening

At Eve the chearful maiden sings,
and with her notes the Valley rings,
as milking nigh the Hawthorn's bloom,
that sheds a rich perfume;
a Song more innocent, a voice more sweet,
did Echo neer repeat;
Her constant Lover waits the while
ready to stop her straggling cows,
and breathes his amorous vows,
Or carves her name upon the neighbouring Stile.
and proud she listens to his artless Tale
with many a sidelong glance, he carries home her Pail.

I rely upon your not mentioning what I have said in the former part of this Letter.

I am quite fatigued
God bless you my old friend & continue your health till you go quietly down to the grave without Pain.

Figure 12 *Page from Letter from Charles Davy to Jermyn Pratt* [*f. 2r*]

Appendix 1: Two Replies to Pratt's Two Squibs on the Norfolk Election

***Norwich Mercury*, 16 January 1768, p. 3.** (Letter Responding to Pratt's Mock Newspaper Article on the 1768 Norfolk Election)

***Norwich Mercury*, 23 January 1768, p. 3.** ('To. Mr. Ranti-Puff')

Date: 18 January 1768 (Date of composition recorded in the poem itself)

Authorship: A handwritten note in one of the two copies of *The Contest* at the British Library (shelfmark 8135.bb.85.(5.), p. 68) records that both the replies are said to be by the Reverend Robert Potter. Potter (1721–1804) was a clergyman, translator, and writer, who published numerous poems, translations and sermons as well as political tracts, including on the 1768 election in Norfolk. He was the master of Scarning School in Dereham (*Oxford DNB*). Potter and Pratt overlapped at Cambridge and may well have known one another.

Physical Description: Newspaper letter measuring 7 cm by 7 cm (Letter Responding to Pratt's Mock Newspaper Article on the 1768 Norfolk Election) and newspaper poem measuring poem measuring 7 cm by 4 cm ('To. Mr. Ranti-Puff').

a) Letter Responding to Pratt's Mock Newspaper Article on the 1768 Norfolk Election[1]

[*p. 3*]

DOWNHAM, *January* 4, 1768.

Mr. CHASE,

SEEING an Advertisement inserted in Three Country News-Papers, respecting the Reception of the Members of this County in our Town, I could not readily determine which most to admire, the Falshood or the Folly of it; admitting a Majority in this, in favour of the Writer's Friends, if he had looked on Two Large Towns to the East and West of this Place, or even taken our whole Hundred of Clackclose at one View, the opponents would have found no cause of Triumph: but this Puff verifies the Proverb, *Sinking Men catch at a Straw*. Another Writer in your Paper of the 26th Ult. in an Essay signed a TRUE FRIEND, &c.[2] admits that he was surprised at seeing so many Gentlemen of Fortune (as 184) in a List published (as he acknowledges) to the Credit of our present worthy Members, let me tell that true Friend to the new Candidates, that he should advise his Patrons to drop their Weekly Assertion, that they were nominated by the Majority, or controvert that List, or otherwise it remains a sufficient Answer to all the Puffs that ever have been, or shall hereafter be made in favour of the new Interest.

Your's, &c. ANTI-PUFF

1 The response was printed in the *Norwich Mercury*, 9 January 1768, p. 3 and we believe the Reverend Robert Potter was the author.

2 For this essay see *Norwich Mercury*, 26 December 1768, p. 3.

b) 'To. Mr. RANTI-PUFF'

[*p. 3*]

DOWNHAM, *Jan.* 18, 1768.

The Man who lives in a House of Glass, should not be the first, to throw Stones.

To. Mr. RANTI-PUFF.

Dear Sir,

As you have chosen to transpose your Language to Versification, perhaps the History you gave us, of the Military March into this Town, may be found more harmonious in your own Ear, as well as more grateful to your Friends, in the following Cantata, in which you will find a respectable Notice taken of your sweet self, by one who was

A SPECTATOR.

To the Tune of the Dust Cart.[3]

RECITATIVE.

'Twas at the Goose-pye feast, for Downham won,
By Pretty Pratty,[4] Ruston's hopeful son,
His mob of bullies, shouting all around,
'Till dispark'd Stow,[5] re-eccho'd to the sound:
On joint-stool high advanc'd the hero stood,
And thus in soothing strains address'd the crowd.

AIR.

This is the great, th' important day,
To drive these Colonels far away,
However they may mutter:

3 For a version of the song's lyrics see *The Polite Songster: A Collection of Three Hundred of the Most Celebrated English and Scots Songs* (London: J. Ross, 1758), pp. 261–2.

4 i.e. Edward Pratt.

5 Stow Hall near Stow Bardolph, about 1 mile north east of Downham Market. To "dispark" is to convert a park to other uses such as agriculture etc: *OED*.

For if they come in their buff-jerkins,
They'll seize your bridge,[6] and strip your firkins,[7]
And take away your butter.

CHORUS.

Butter, butter, butter, butter
Butter is our staple trade;
If they take away our butter,
Downham Market soon must fade.

AIR.

Sir A————e[8] brings a General Warrant,
To seize you all; so pray take care on't;
You know I am no *Liar*
D— G——[9] hates freedom in his heart,
And always takes L—d T——n——d's[10] part;
So let them come no nigher,

RECITATIVE.

He spoke: Amazement seiz'd the trembling throng,
Till S——ry,[11] rough and ugly, rush'd along,
And cry'd, confound your nonsense, captain P——,
You speak much worse than Jacky B————n's[12] hat,
They seize our butter! Let them if they dare;
And what for General Warrants need we care?

6 Downham Market's butter market was held by a bridge by the Ouse.

7 Small caskets that could be used for storing butter; *OED*.

8 Sir Armine Wodehouse (1714–1777), MP for Norfolk and colonel of the East Norfolk Militia.

9 Thomas De Grey (1717–1781), MP for Norfolk and lieutenant-colonel of the West Norfolk Militia.

10 George Townshend (1724–1807), soldier and former MP for Norfolk.

11 An Edmund Savory of Downham Market voted for Sir Edward Astley and Wenman Coke in the 1768 election. See *The Poll of the Knights of the Shire for the County of Norfolk* (Norwich: W. Chase, 1768), p. 222.

12 John Buxton of Shadwell (1717–82). Buxton spoke on behalf of Wenman Coke and Sir Edward Astley in the nomination meeting held on 8 October 1767 and wrote a pamphlet on their behalf. See *Contest*, p. 3,

AIR.

Mean while the doleful tidings came,
The Colonels are enter'd the town;
O run, cries Et—n,[13] run, for shame,
My boys, pull the bell ropes all down,
No more for folks like these, I hope,
Shall Downham bells merrily ring;
And if they find and inch of rope,
To be sure they will make us all swing,
Now J————n P——, we look to you,
For you are both witty and wise:
In this distress what shall we do,
To save both ourselves and our pies?

RECITATIVE.

J———n P——, who had enough of frays before,
His plaister'd shins from hard-soal'd H—t—n[14] sore
His modest eyes first cast upon the ground,
Then rais'd his head, and leering look'd around:
He cough'd, he spit, and after much deep studying,
At length thus spoke the reverend Jack Pudding.

AIR.

Come pull up your breeches,
And make no more speeches,
Our trusty friend thus to dishearten;
For Moore of Moore-Hall,[15]
Will attend to our call,
And combat this dragon of Merton.[16]
Sir A————e, we're told,
Is now grown so old,

13 The Reverend Richard Eaton (1730–1779), rector of Downham Market: *CDB*.

14 i.e. 'Houghton'—referring to the seat of the Walpoles at Houghton Hall where George Walpole (1730–1781), 3rd Earl of Orford was resident.

15 George Hunt Holley (1724–1798) was the owner of Salle Moore Hall in Norfolk but was better known the owner of the nearby Blicking Hall.

16 i.e. Thomas De Grey, whose residence was at Merton Hall in Norfolk.

That his purse and his spirits are broke;
And St———[17] so true,
Without more ado,
Will hang him all up on an oak.
If all this should fail,
We know what will prevail;
Sir E———,[18] our glorious defender,
Will grant a press warrant,[19]
And will take care on't,
And send them abroad of a tender.

RECITATIVE.

M—e, valiant M—e,[20] they call, the air resounds;
The learned clerk was feeding of his hounds
St———n was digging pits beneath the snow,
To trap th'unweary traveller, friend or foe;
Glorious Sir E———d as the story goes,
Was holding hartshorn to his lady's nose.[21]

AIR.

But hark, the drum,
The colonels come,
And honour leads the train:
The P—tts, unable to conceal their pain,
Gaz'd on the pair
That caus'd their care,
And sigh'd and look'd, sigh'd and look'd,
Sigh'd and look'd, and sigh'd again.

---

17 Nicholas Styleman. See 'To N. S.' for more information on Styleman.

18 Sir Edward Hawke (1705–1781), First Lord of the Admiralty .

19 A press warrant provided a legal licence for press gangs to force those they found in the streets or in public houses to join the navy. Sir Edward Astley was accused of making 'improper use of a press warrant' as High Sheriff of Norfolk. See *Contest*, pp. 75, 100.

20 i.e. 'Moore'.

21 Dame Ann Astley, Sir Edward Astley's wife. On hartshorn see note 45 in *The Grange*.

But Billy A— —n,[22] hating strife,
Slipt away to kiss his wife:
And S—y,[23] behind broad shoulder'd P—tt,[24]
Tore half his cookade from his hat,
And silent let his Colonel pass,
Asham'd to shew his pyebald face.
When the danger was over, Bold Et—n stept forth,
And harangu'd them on C—, and on A—,[25] great worth,
Tho' an hermit at home, if you pay for his dinner,
He holds that a publican may be no sinner.
Would you taste the fine goose-pye,
To the Swan[26] with ardour fly;
Where C— and A—, hand in hand,
Will treat as long as we can stand.
Round the board the punch-bowl flows;
Shouting, hollowing, as it goes;
Fill it out, and as you drink,
Sweetly let your glasses clink,
When no more your heads can bear,
Rest repos'd in elbow chair;
Whilst in coaches all alone,
Knight and squire shall lay them down,
All alone; for at their cost,
Still we'll urge the circling toast;
'Till drunk or sober, they shall own,
Their goose-pye friends are friends alone.

---

22 A 'William Atkinson, Cl' voted for Wenman Coke and Sir Edward Astley in Downham Market in the 1768 election. See *The Poll of the Knights of the Shire for the County of* Norfolk, 221. This may be the same Atkinson who was admitted to Emmanuel College at Cambridge in 1764 and became Rector of Hillington in 1782. *AC.*

23 William Say (*d.* 1775). An epitaph to William Say in an unknown hand is included in the Pratt folder (NRO PRA 664/18). A 'Say' was a lieutenant-captain in the West Norfolk Militia. See Colonel Sir Charles Harvey (ed.), *The History of the 4th Battalion Norfolk Regiment (Late East Norfolk Militia)* (Jarrold & Sons: London, 1899), p. 27.

24 Presumably Edward Pratt rather than Jermyn Pratt.

25 Wenman Coke (1717–1776) and Sir Edward Astley (1729–1802), the challengers of De Grey and Wodehouse for the Norfolk county seat.

26 The White Swan tavern in Norwich. See note 14 to *Cinderetta*, p. 224 in our edition.

GRAND CHORUS.

Happy, happy, happy they,
None but their friends, none but their friends,
None but their friends shall taste the Pye.[27]

27 The original text has a comma here.

Appendix 2: Mr. and Mrs. Clagett's Epitaph (Manuscript Version)

NRO PRA 664/24

Date: After Mary Clagett's death on 24 July 1775.

Authorship: See the notes to the version of the epitaph included in Shorter Poems.

Physical Description: Epitaph handwritten in ink on one side of single piece of paper in Pratt's hand, measuring 16 cm by 20.5 cm.

[*f. 1r*]

——————M^{r} & Mrs Clagetts Epitaph——————

Stay moralist, and with one transient View
Read oe'r these Lines, which Friendly speak to you:
If through Lifes waves, thy Bark serenely Glides
Trust not too far, nor Dare the Adverse Tides—
Here rests a pair, to whom Indulgent Heav'n
Had every gift;[1] and every Virtue giv'n:
Blessings[2] like theirs, too exquisite to Last
In one sad Hour, received the fatal blast
So tender Plants[3] of most distinguishd worth
Shrink at ye Storm; & drop at once to Earth:
Such are thy ways, thou Providenc divine!
And blessed be, the unerring hand of thine

1 The inscription replaces 'gift' with 'Wish'.
2 The inscription replaces 'Blessings' with 'But Joys'.
3 The inscription replaces 'tender Plants' with 'the best Fruits'.

Appendix 3: An Occasional Prologue to *The Clandestine Marriage*

NRO PRA 664/7

Date: Late 1778 to early 1779. For a full explanation of the date see the headnotes to the version of 'An Occasional Prologue to *The Clandestine Marriage*' included in Dramatic Writings.

Authorship: See the notes to the version of 'An Occasional Prologue to *The Clandestine Marriage*' included in Dramatic Writings.

Physical Description: Draft Prologue written for a performance of *The Clandestine Marriage* handwritten in ink on a single page at the back of a sewn paper booklet with a marbled cover in Pratt's hand, measuring 20.5 cm by 32 cm.

Note: This manuscript text of 'An Occasional Prologue to *The Clandestine Marriage*' is included on the final page of the marbled sewn booklet that contains the manuscript of *The Grange*. We have chosen to reproduce the manuscript version of 'An Occasional Prologue' separately as a diplomatic transcription given the complexity of the revisions this working draft captures. 'An Occasional Prologue' clearly represents a significantly less polished stage of a draft than *The Grange* and Pratt seems to have used the last page of the booklet with *The Grange* manuscript, written down at an earlier date, for a working draft of 'An Occasional Prologue'.

[*f.* 29*v*]

Aw'd, to <u>Behold</u>

Prologue Awed

Surevey
Awe'd, to Behold, this radiant Circle round:
trod tread
Unsaught before ~~we~~ trembling touch ye ground
then
Traind to no Stage, to night we humbly Strive
To keep for once the Comic Muse a Live
Compassion gave those Hints we here pursue
And Let compassion plead our cause with you
We claim ye feeling not the Actors part
Our wish to please, our Aim to move ye Heart
mind
To ease y^e ~~Heart~~, to Stop the trickling tear
For we act for this you come to Hear
~~This is no Farce~~ there is no Acting Here:
however we please
~~Whateer~~ Our Fate, If rightly Understood
Tho bad ye Actor: yet, ye Motives good:
Brittanias
~~Your Honest~~ Tars so generous, bold & brave?
With Keppels[1] fire wave
~~Whi Whilst you set Warm~~ undaunted mount y^e
Climb ye high Decks, & Stand exposd to View
Thy Navy Act; and we will Act for you—
Browd[2] If some Proud Critic Here should lift ye Dead[3]
To strike at once, us half formed Actors; Head
Ladies from you, from you one Single Frown

---

1 Augustus Keppel, 1st Viscount Keppel (1725–1786), a prominent officer in the Royal Navy, who rose to the rank of an Admiral; he took part in naval battles during the War of the Austrian Succession, the Seven Years' War, and the American Revolutionary War: *Oxford DNB*. Keppel notably commanded the British fleet at the Battle of Ushant on 27 July 1778, which is satirized by Pratt in 'Political Duck-Hunting'.

2 'Browd' appears to be added in the left margin as an insertion intended as an alternative to 'Proud' in same line.

3 Pratt originally wrote 'Head' here—he probably meant to correct the 'Head' at the end of the following line to 'Dead'.

Will set all right, & beat the monster down:

such
O Heavn felt Joy to see ~~those~~ Laughing Eyes—

When you approve we feel our spirits rise
You make us Act;—I feel my Spirits rise
Beauty has this peculiar art to please

win much
You ~~give~~ us pleasure, & you kill with Ease

Appendix 4: 'Political Duck-Hunting' (Manuscript Version)

NRO PRA 664/6

Date: 1779. For a full explanation of the date, see the headnotes to the version of 'Political Duck-Hunting' included in Shorter Poems.

Authorship: The manuscript of the poem in Pratt's hand is included in the Pratt folder. We are very confident the poem is by him.

Physical description: Poem handwritten in ink on one side of a single sheet of manuscript paper, measuring 18.5 cm by 30.5 cm.

Note: Explanatory footnotes to this poem are included with the newspaper version in Shorter Poems.

[*f. 1r*]

Political Duck-Hunting

[*f. 1v*]

Political Duck-Hunting—

1

Once, on a Time, some Idle Folke's;
Who Lov'd to Laugh, & cut their Jokes
    (For Idle Folkes Love Fun)
Duck-Hunting went; their favourite Sport.
And If it suits the common Sort
    Why; Let their will<s> be Done.——

2

<There, on the> ^Down Severns^ Stream; they Did Discern
A Mallard Deck'd, from head to stern:
    A First Rate of his Line:
Tray, wagd his Tail; & Seem'd to Say
Whoof—we shall have fine sport to Day;
    That Mallard, shall be mine;

3

But, as in Merry Æsops Days
When Birds were wise, an^d^[1] <thousand> ^had sly^ Ways:
    So this Sagacious Fowle:
Knowing old Tray; was cursed Tough
And that he ne'er could Swim enough
    Calld in, Her Neighbour, Owle

4

Her Neighbour came with Solemn Pride:
<But slily crept> ^She dropt aster^[2] to ^th^ Mallards Side
    Now cheerd, and now Saluted:
Tray, thought it best; to Swim around
Was Sometimes Lost, & sometimes found
    Mal, Quack'd, & Madg'y, Hooted:

5

To Day they Sink; To Day alive:
Now Tray gets Hold, Now Mallard Dive
    Now running, Now pursuing:
The common people swore by G—d
They neer saw a sight so Odd:
    Such Fuss, and Nothing doing:

---

1 Rather than cross out 'an' and write 'and' above the line, Pratt has kept 'an' and written 'd' above the line to turn 'an' into 'and'. The original phrase read 'an thousand Ways' and the revisions turn the line to 'and had sly Ways'.

2 The 'n' is missing from 'astern'.

6

When Lo, three Sturdy Farmers Sons*
Came Down that way with Loaded guns
    And Swore they'd have no more:
Madge took the Hint; & sought her Nest
The Mallard wing'd his way for Brest
    And Tray; got safe to Shore—

* Russia, Prussia, & Holland.[3]

3 Pratt's note is written vertically into the right-hand margin.

Appendix 5: The Sunday Visit[1]

NRO PRA 664/19

Date: *c.* 21–25 February 1781, based on the dates given to the short diary. For a full explanation of the date, see the headnotes to the version of 'The Sunday Visit' included in Shorter Poems.

Authorship: The manuscript of the poem in Pratt's hand is included in the Pratt folder.

Physical description: Poem handwritten in ink on three sides of a single piece of paper, in Pratt's hand, measuring (in its folded state) 20 cm by 32.5 cm.

Note: We have left the numbers above the lines in as these seem to be there to help Pratt keep track of the meter—they give the sense of his working practices as a poet.

1 Explanatory notes for this poem are in the newspaper version in Shorter Poems.

[f. 1r]

The Sunday Visit in a Letter
From Brother William to Brother Gregory—

1 2 3 4 5 6
Brother, Greg you enjoind and I'm, proud, to,[2] Obey
1 tell 2 3 4 5
For, k to ~~send you~~ in verse how we spent y^{e}, Lords day
Good 2 3
My Wife, you well know, was ye Niece of a Priest
So she Loves to ride out, and partake of a feast
1 2 3 4 5
T'other night she began when we both were in bed
1 2 ~~my~~ now my dear
My Billy, (pray child take your hand from my, head
3 4 5
I should Like If you please, just by way of a change
X X X
To dine Sunday next at Old Guzzle-down grange X[3]
Cousin Hollocks oft says and I know he speaks true
M^{rs}. Hunter my Wife would be proud to see you
1 2 at ye time
So we rose ~~on ye morn~~ and I made ye Jade ready
1 2 up & 3 soon 4 dret
~~Little~~ Bet was soon^[4] drest, ~~& quite smart~~ was my Lady
1 packd 2
The ~~dear~~ child ~~rode~~ before & my Wife hung behind

2 This comma appears to mark the end of the fifth foot of the line. Commas that seem to be there solely to help Pratt keep track of the metrics recur throughout the manuscript of the poem and we have reproduced them as written. We have however omitted the numbers that appear haphazardly throughout the manuscript of the poem that also appear to be there to help Pratt keep track of the meter.

3 The 'X' marks here appear to indicate that the first two lines from the text written vertically in the left-hand margin of the manuscript should be inserted after the line beginning 'To dine, Sunday next.' The lines appear in this same place in the newspaper version of the poem and so we have inserted these lines in our edition of this poem (as lines 9–10).

4 This is Pratt's own insertion mark.

~~packd~~ prancd
And our Bobby ~~paced~~ by on a Hobby thats blind
X X X X[5]
So we trotted & chatted, & made our remarkd [*sic*]
Whilst our Bobby, was driving & chasing ye Larks

a
What a sweet pretty seat, what ~~a~~ pitty His Honor
1 2
Should Lay such a weight of, some thousands upon her
ye child
By Golds said ~~our Bet~~ I could wish from my soul,

2 our 3 4 4
That my nurse & Ned ~~Heaven~~, were possed of ye whole[6]
3 4
When we came to ye Grange, Cousin Hollocks comes out
1 2 3 4 5
And he, Cry~~d~~ what, a pox have ye all been, about
What ye took ye wrong turn, when ye came into Town
1 2 3 4
Then he kist Little Bet, as he took ye child down
2 2 3 5
And Bobby ~~he~~ said you'r, as fine as your Sister
Bob 2 3
But ~~ye Boy~~ lookd, confusd for hed rode up a blister
1 2 3
When we enter'd ye Grange, at the end of a fork
~~poor~~ bolts 2
The maid ~~runs~~ away with a Huge Leg of pork—
she /staring/
And ~~looking~~ at us, Lud it dropt from her hand

5 The 'X' marks appear to indicate that the first two lines from the text written vertically in the left-hand margin of the manuscript should be inserted after the line beginning 'To dine, Sunday next.' The lines appear in this same place in the newspaper version of the poem and so we have inserted these lines in our edition of this poem (as lines 15–16).

6 This lines and the three preceding lines are appended at the end of the poem on [*f. 2r*]. In the newspaper version they appear after the line: 'Whilst our Bobby was driving and chasing the Larks' and we have inserted them into our transcription accordingly.

                    2   3   4
So she rubd it, and blowd it & cleard it, of Sand
of a past^[7] Then we sat down to dine and we merrily drank
Mistress "M^{rs}. Hunter y^{r} Health, Im obliged to you Frank

                                     n
"Master Bobby is grow~~ing~~ a sweet Handsome fellow
And Miss, ~~Bet~~ never, Lookd, half so, well as in yellow
Nelly, pray Tuck a cloth round my dear Bobbys throat
                sweet Boy   3
For fear y^{e} ~~Dear Child~~ should <u>contamin</u> his Coat
Mistress, Hunter, my dear, now I beg you be free
Is ye goose to your mind, do our <u>Tatus</u> agree
Our Tradesmen dont send ye best things to ye Grange
But my Dear I Subsist, y^{t} you soon make a change

        bless my heart   carving
my dear, maister Hollocks, do let
why
you help ye dear Girel[8] to no more
than a bone———————[9]

[*f. 1v*]

  1   2
The dinner remov'd, you will think it a Sin
                                   3
That we walkd round ye Farm, with y^{e}, Bells ringing in,
By ye Lord said old Hol, tis a sad burning shame
That these, sweet fields of corn, should be ruind by game
They Subscribe & Protect, & their Tenants defend
                                         erve
Yes afaith so they will for to ~~Save~~ their own end
                    Brother Greg 3   4
Now Suppose ~~If you please~~, ye clock half after four

7 Pratt's own insertion mark although it is not clear where exactly in the poem he intended the phrase to go.

8 i.e. 'girl'.

9 This fragmentary piece of text is written perpendicular to the main text in the left-hand margin. We have not counted it as part of the lines to the poem proper.

our
Tea & Toast Swallow down & ~~the~~ Jade at ye door
Many ~~Fifty~~ Curtsies & bows, were returning & passing
With nodding and Squinting and curvetting and Ar——[10]

high
The Harkerchief Shakd, & held ~~up~~ in ye Air
Bye Bye; Little souls, O we wish~~d~~ ye Lived here

most
When we rode half a Mile unhappy to tell you
Little Bet found ye cheese curd besieging her belly
So I dropt ye Child down, and she ran to ye Hedge
And Laid a good heap on a bundle of Sedge
Misfortunes dear Greg are not oft unattended
For our Bob broke his Girth, yt was so lately mended

then He a
And turning ~~ye~~-Lane, the Lord Harry knows how

old
The old ~~This~~ saddle ~~came~~ round and he dropt in a Slough

out
~~Here~~ my molly she Shriekd, & she scolded & Grumbled
Her tooth was so bad & her child was so tumbled
Oh, If she came abroad it was always ye same
Willy, pray kick ye Jade, for the Devil is Lame

her
When I got to my home comes my Aunt with ~~a~~ bible
black
In ~~an old~~ tattered bonnet well whited with Crible

Heres your
So So,— She began, this is very fine doing—
No wonder say I yt some folks come to ruin

~~poor~~
dear My first Husband said & he always spoke true
If you slight ye Lords day, yt ye Lord will slight you
Not a soul could I get, not a man to my Aid
Theres your Ralph hobbled out with ye old parsons
maid,

10 i.e. 'arsing' (the newspaper version has 'a——g')

[*f.* 2*r*]

th
And ~~y^{e}~~ Boy watched ye all from ye cheese chamber, wicket
And, away ran ye rogue Like a devil to cricket
Poor Old Crumps in ye ditch, & so bruised her back
vow
That I ~~wow~~ it will turn to a mortifyd black
And ye sow thats shut up with her Tribe of fifteen
Has swallowd ye whole, not a pig to be seen
Here she stopt her Harrangue & I drove off ye Pillion
And found both my cheeks of a bblessed [*sic*] vermilion
O Greg without doubt these are sad Horrid times
When we Farmers ride out, in ye hearing of chimes
You remember ye time, when with family pride
How
~~When~~ We all ran to church, by ye Ministers side
good in
When we Joind in ye Psalms, thought ye sermon had
Tho we sometimes believd that it ruind ye Pudding
For ye terms of my Lease for my years still to come
I will neer on ye Sabbath be rambling from home
For as my Aunt says, we shall all find it true.
If ye; slight y^{e}, Lords day, y^{t} ye Lord will slight you.
84. Lines——

[*f.* 2*v*]

Fast day. 21. 1781[11]
Preach.^{d} Oonly [*sic*]
John Flat Buried
Matthew Barkers Wife Bu[12]

11 This diary entry is written on the back of the last page of the manuscript of 'A Sunday Visit'. 21 February 1781 was appointed to be one of three public fast days during the American Revolutionary War, the others being 13 December 1776 and 26 February 1778. See Paul Langford, 'The English Clergy and the American Revolution' in Eckhart Hellmuth, ed. *The Transformation of Political Culture in Britain and Germany in the Later Eighteenth Century* (Oxford: Oxford University Press, 1980), pp. 275–307.

12 i.e. 'buried'.

Feb.[y] 25—buried Harrisons
Child officiated myself
march. 4. did all y[e] duty

Rodewelle[13]

13 This word is written upside down on the page. Rodewell (Rothwell) was a hundred in the county of Northamptonshire and also a town in West Yorkshire. 'Rodewelle' could also be a person's last name. It is not clear why Pratt wrote this.

Appendix 6: Letter from Charles Davy to Jermyn Pratt

NRO PRA 664/3

Date: 6–8 January 1791 (the letter began to be written on 6 Jan 1791 and was sent on 8 January 1791).

Authorship: We identified Charles Davy[1] as the author from contextual evidence and his handwriting. We have checked samples of Davy's handwriting and from a note in a presentation copy of his *Letters Addressed Chiefly to a Young Gentleman* in the editors' possession.

Physical Description: Letter and accompanying poem handwritten in ink on a single piece of paper, folded once, in Charles Davy's hand, measuring (in its folded state) 23 cm by 18.5 cm.

[*f. 1r*]

[Stamped] STOW[2]

[Stamped] JA 8 91[3]

The Rev[d] Jermyn Pratt

Rector of Watlington

near Lynn Norfolk

To be left at Setch Hythe Turnpike[4]

1 For more information on Charles Davy (1720–1797), see our Introduction, pp. 5–6, 19, 29, and 46–7.

2 i.e. Stow Hundred.

3 i.e. 8 January 1791.

4 William Faden's 1797 map of Norfolk shows that there was a turnpike at Setchly (or Setchley), on the River Ouse. Setchly is about three miles walking distance from Watlington. A 'hythe' is a landing place on a river, as in Hythe Bridge in Downham Market.

[*f. 1r*]

My dear Jermyn

I am very sorry to hear you can laugh but on one side of your mouth. I was entirely a stranger to your ^having^ met with any affliction to interrupt your chearfulness since the loss of your good wife, my dear Friend, and impute what may have happend to you since to your excessive sorrow upon this account: Accept my thanks for your kind pressent which comes very opportunely to pay one of my curates who wants his money for a young Family, though advanced himself to an age when he might have had more prudence than to take a second wife, or beget sons & daughters; you may possibly know him, he married a sister of Professor Symonds;[5] and after dispensing a moderate independent fortune, he joined himself upon becoming a widower, to a tall thin genteel young woman, of the name of Chatter without any other position, or <illeg.> [?fortune] other besides what nature gave her.[6] You are just in the observation, that I scarce <illeg.> [?am] an Œconomist, & have beset myself by an imprudent easiness if you still will not allow it to a generosity of temper, I have labourd many years under distresses of the pecuniary Sort, and now when I most want the comforts of Life, with more of its conveniences I am incapable of being any thing to increase my income; yourself with some other of my friends have frequently been very kind to me, my annual expenses still rather exceed my rents of every kind; In one-year longer I hoped & trusted I should have been clear in the world, but I stood engaged for another parson; That debt is fallen upon me & I have fourscore pounds to pay wch I did not dream of: this will throw me into new difficulties, wch in my sixty ninth year my breath is almost too weak to ^struggle^ with: you will be so friendly as not to mention it, but I have a comfort in opening myself to an old friend & I trust that I shall yet have spirits to bear up under this unexpected burthen. In the greatest of my Sufferings I have maintained my accustomed cheerfulness, & can enjoy your unextinguished fund of humour, though I have none of my own. I shall be happy to see you, I have one of the best men in the world with me [*f. 1v*] whose second praise[7] it is to be one of the first Physicians in it, who

5 The Reverend John Symonds (1729–1807), Professor of Modern History at Cambridge University: *Oxford DNB*. Jermyn Pratt was related to John Symonds through Thomas Jermyn, 2nd Baron Jermyn and Mary Jermyn, née Merry: Pratt through their eldest daughter Mary and Symonds through their younger daughter Merelina.

6 Unfortunately, we have been unable to identify either the curate or his bride.

7 Common phrase in the period: someone's 'second praise' tended to be a skill in a vocation while the implied 'first praise' was goodness of character.

has resided with me now upwards of seven months, & another Gentleman with whom he traveld, very dear to me, as you are a reader you have met with the Doctors name wch is Goodwyn,[8] he has hitherto accepted no fees from any person rich or Poor: but done all the good in his power from a native benignity of Heart. He has had the humour of receiving the Gold medal for his treatise on Suffocation from the benevolent Society,[9] & is highly esteemd by all the professional men of Learning & medical Science in Europe. I shall only tell you one thing more of him, that he refused an appointment from the King of Spain wch would have produced him at least two thousand pounds a year, & yet this Gentleman was born in Suffolk. I am told you still continue to write & publish. I have learnd wit enough to know that what I am capable of writing is not of sufficient Importance to induce any persons to read what I can put together. I have no Invention left, if even I found any such power: yet I now & then amuse myself during my sleepless & often painful nights, with the Muses, if my silly rhymes will authorise my saying so much, I shall trust a specimen of my poor attempts to your candour. you <illeg.> advise me to scribble & I shall have no scruple to comply with your request, my last performance was a prosaic affair wch is of too serious dull a cast to afford you the least entertainment, & I will try to recal the translation of a Song written about the year 1450 wch was the scrambling performance of a night—the last Spring. but my hand and mind are tired & I will leave off till to morrow morning when I shall be recovered and my memory more active & perhaps somewhat else may present itself.

Thursday Jan 6th seven o'clock in the Evening

I have had but an uncomfortable night my dear Jermyn and awoke to new uneasiness & pain this morning: but here's the Sonnet of 1460

Summer is i cumen in
Lhude sings cuccu
Groweth Sed and blowth Med
And springeth the Wde nu:
Ewe bleteth after Lamb
Loueth after Calve Cu,
Bulluc sterteth

8 Edmund Goodwyn (1756–1829) physician, born in Framlingham in Suffolk: *Oxford DNB*.

9 Goodwyn's *The Connection of Life with Respiration* (London, 1788) was awarded the gold medal for the best treatise on human respiration by the Humane Society in the same year it was published.

Buck verteth
Merri sings cuccu
Ne swith thee never nu.[10]

The attempt
wch you will have the candour to overlook the faults of
is on the other side

[*f.* 2*r*]

Symphony

Morning

The soaring Lark now meets the Day
The Linnets from their dewy Spray
And every Bird that wings the Sky
Proclaims the Lusty Summer nigh;
Sweet Philomel within the Grove,
Repeats, I Love. I Love:
The Cuckoo too with merry note
Distends her Liquid throat
Cuckoo. Cuckoo. Cuckoo.
Now groweth Seed
    And bloweth Mead
And spring the Woods anew.

Symphony

Noon

The Village curr, now barks no more,
But sleeps beneath the cottage door
    A faithful guardian of the Latch
Still silence reign's within the yard
Save that the clucking Hen is heard

10 Davy's friend Charles Burney prints and discusses 'Sumer is Icumen in' in his *A General History of Music: From the Earliest Ages of the Present Period* (4 vols., London, 1776–89), ii, pp. 405–12. Vol. 2 appeared in 1782.

Or Swallow twittering in the smoke
Or bullock lowing from the yoke,
While shadows wave upon the thatch.

Symphony

Evening

At Eve the chearful maiden sings,
And with her notes the valley rings,
As milking nigh the Hawthorn's bloom,
That sheds a rich perfume;
A song more innocent, a voice more sweet,
Did Echo neer repeat:
The constant Lover waits the while
Ready to stop her straggling cows,
And breathes his amorous vows,
Or carves her name upon the neighbouring Stile.
And proud she listens to his artless Tale
With many a sidelong glance, he carries home her Pail.

———————————

—————

———

—

I am quite fatigued

I rely upon you not mentioning what I have said in the former part of this Letter.

God bless you my old friend & continue your health till you go gently down to the grave without Pain.

Appendix 7: Catalogue of Jermyn Pratt's Library

NRO PRA 664/1

Date: After 6 October 1791 (the date of Pratt's Death).

Authorship: We do not know who wrote the list. Some of the mistakes (e.g. 'Tingal' for James Macpherson's poem *Fingal*) suggest that whoever drew up the catalogue was working at speed or was not familiar with the titles.

Description: Catalogue written in ink, in an unknown hand, in a sewn paper booklet with a marbled cover, measuring 20 cm by 16 cm.

[*f. 1r*]

A Catalogue of the Books of the Rev[d]. Jermyn Pratt; A.M

Deceased At Wattlington, In Norfolk

[*f. 2r*]

Folio

1 Stapletons Juvenal neat[1] 1616
2 Hammond on the New Testament[2] 1702

In the notes that follow, an initial ? indicates we have been unable to find an exact match between an edition of a book with the entry as written in the catalogue. When we are unable to match a text to the entry our procedure is to give bibliographical information for the text that we believe most likely corresponds to the entry.

Folio

1 ? Juvenal, *The Satyrs of Juvenal*, trans. Rob[ert] Staplyton (London: Humphrey Mosey, 1646). *EEBO*.

2 H[enry] Hammond, *A Paraphrase, and Annotations Upon all the Books of The New Testament*, 7th ed. (London: John Nicholson, 1702). *ECCO*.

3	New Universal Dictionary of Arts And Sciences with Supplement 3 Vols[3]	1751
4	Newcomes Harmony of the Gospels boards[4]	1778
5	Clarendons History of the Rebellion[5]	1702
6	Stackhouses History of the Bible 2 Vol[6]	1742
7	———— Body of Divinity[7]	1743
8	Fennings Geography 2 Vol neat[8]	1764
9	History of the Old & New Testament 3 Vol[9]	1759
10	Josephus's Works of Maynard cuts[10]	
11	Scapulo Lexicon G[r] [11]	1600
12	Biblia Sacra——————Ham[12]	1624
13	Pearsons Prelectiones Theologiae Lond[13]	1661

3 E[phraim] Chambers, *Cyclopædia: or, An Universal Dictionary of Arts and Sciences*, 7th ed. (2 vols., London: W. Innys et al., 1751–52). *ECCO*.

4 William Newcome, *A Harmony of the Gospels* (Dublin: William Hallhead, 1778). BLPC.

5 Edward [Hyde], Earl of Clarendon, *The History of the Rebellion and Civil Wars in England, Begun in the Year 1641. Volume the First* (Oxford: No Publisher, 1702). *ECCO*. The second and third volumes appeared in 1703 and 1704 respectively.

6 Thomas Stackhouse. *A New History of the Holy Bible, From the Beginning of the World, to the Establishment of Christianity*, 2nd ed. (2 vols., London: Stephen Austen, 1742–44). *ECCO*.

7 Thomas Stackhouse, *A Compleat Body of Speculative and Practical Divinity*, 3rd ed. (London: T. Cox, 1743). *ECCO*.

8 Daniel Fenning et al., *A New System of Geography* (2 vols., London: S. Crowder, 1764–65). *ECCO*. Vol. 1 appeared in 1764 and vol. 2 in 1765.

9 Robert Clayton, *A Vindication of the Histories of the Old and New Testament* (Dublin and London: R. Baldwin, 1759). *ECCO*.

10 Josephus, *The Genuine and Complete Works of Flavius Josephus*, trans. George Henry Maynard (London: No publisher, *c*. 1790). *ECCO*. The title pages to the early printings do not give a year of publication and *ECCO* suggests it was produced between 1785 and 1792. The entry in the catalogue of Pratt's library should of course read 'Maynard's Works of Josephus'.

11 Joannis Scapulae, *Lexicon Græcolatinum Nouum* (London: Societatem Bibliopolarum, 1619). *EBBO*.

12 ? *Biblia Sacra Vulgatae Editionis* (Rome: A. Brugiotti, 1624). BLPC. The 'Ham' in the entry is puzzling: Jean Baptiste Du Hamel did edit editions of this bible. But he was born in 1624 and could not have been involved in the 1624 edition.

13 Rich[ard] Holdsworth, *Prælectiones Theologicæ*, ed. Richard Pearson (London: James Flesher, 1661). *EEBO*.

[*f.* 2*v*]

14	Thesarus Sacrarum Historicum Novi Testamentum Pr by Jode[14]	1585
15	Reynolds Works[15]	1658
16	Blount Censura Celebriorum Authorum Sive Tractatus Lond[16]	1690
17	A Miss in Divinity[17]	
18	Caves Lives of the Farthers cuts[18]	1677
19	Whitby on the New Testament, 2 Vol[19]	1706
20	Stebbings Polemical Tracts[20]	1727
21	Hoopers Works[21]	1662
22	Sidneys Discourse on Government[22]	1704
23	Guardens Sighs Tears & Complaints of the Church of England[23]	1659

[*f.* 3*r*]

24	Prynnes Life of Archbp Laud[24]	1644
25	-----------Canterburys Doom[25]	1646
26	Hammond on the Psalm[26]	1659
27	Nicholson on the Creed & Psalm[27]	1646

---

14 Gerard de Jode (ed.), *Thesaurus Sacrarum Historiaru Veteris Testamenti* (Antwerp: Gerard de Jode, 1585). BLPC.

15 Edward Reynolds. *The Works of Edw. Reynolds D.D.* (London: George Thomason, 1658). *EEBO.*

16 Thomas-Pope Blount, *Censura Celebriorum Authorum* (London: Richard Chiswell, 1690). *ECCO.*

17 i.e. 'MS'. It is not possible to identify this manuscript.

18 William Cave, *Antiquitates Apostolicæ*, 3rd ed. (London: R. Royston, 1677). *EEBO.*

19 Daniel Whitby, *A Paraphrase and Commentary on the New Testament*, 2nd ed. (2 vols., London: Awnsham and John Churchill, 1706). *ECCO.*

20 Henry Stebbing, *Polemical Tracts* (Cambridge: Cornelius Crownfield, 1727). TCDL.

21 ? George Hooper, *The Works of the Right Reverend Father in God, George Hooper, D.D.* (Oxford: J. Rivington and J. Fletcher, 1757). *ECCO.*

22 Algernon Sidney, *Discourses Concerning Government* (London: John Darby, 1704). *ECCO.*

23 John Gauden, *Hiera Dakrya, Ecclesiæ Anglicanæ Suspiria* (London: R. Royston, 1659). *EEBO.*

24 William Prynne, *A Breviate of the Life, of William Laud* (London: Michael Sparke, Senior, 1644). *EEBO.*

25 William Prynne, *Canterburies Doome* (London: Michael Sparke, Senior, 1646). *EEBO.*

26 H[enry] Hammond, *A Paraphrase and Annotations upon the Books of the Psalms* (London: Richard Davis, 1659). *EEBO.*

27 Two books are referred to: William Nicholson, *A Plain, but Full Exposition of the Catechisme of the Church of England* (London: Nathaniel Webb and William Grantham,

28	Pearson on the Creed[28]	1676
29	Book of Homilies rotten & Stained[29]	1683
30	Lowndes Parish Register[30]	1783
31	An Old Bible imperfect & stained[31]	1611

[*f. 4r*]

Quarto

1	Terentius notis Bentlies[1]	1726
2	Sparmans Voyage to Cape of Good Hope Cuts 2 Vol boards stained[2]	1785
3	Sherridans Course of Lictures on Elocution boards[3]	1762
4	Paybys Principles of Moral and Civil Philosophy boards[4]	1785
5	Dr. Hornes Commentary on the Book of Psalms 2 Vol boards[5]	1776

1655). *EEBO.* William Nicholson, *David's Harp Strung and Tuned* (W. Leake: London, 1662). *EEBO.*

28 John Pearson, *An Exposition of the Creed*, 4th ed. (John Williams: London, 1676). *EEBO.*

29 *Certain Sermons or Homilies Appointed to be Read in Churches* (London: Ann Mearn and Blanch Pawlet, 1683). *EEBO.* An edition printed in Oxford and sold by Moses Pitt also appeared in 1683. *EEBO.*

30 ? *Lowndes's Parish Registers for Banns of Marriage, Marriages, Births or Christenings, and Burials.* We have not found a surviving copy of this text but it is commonly mentioned in the advertisement for books printed at the end of books printed by W. Lowndes. See, e.g. Robert Brookes, *The Art of Angling* (London: W. Lowndes, 1790), 269. *ECCO. Lowndes's Parish Registers* was costed by the page, which suggests that Lowndes was printing material from parish registers as requested by patrons.

31 *The Holy Bible* (London: Robert Barker, 1611). *EEBO.* This is the first edition of the King James Bible.

Quarto

1 Terence, *Comoediae, Phaedri Fabulae Aesopiae, Publii Syri et Aliorum Veterum Sententiae* (Cambridge: Cornelium Crownfield, 1726). An edition of Terence and Phaedrus with textual notes by the Cambridge classicist and critic Richard Bentley. *ECCO.*

2 Anders Sparrman, *A Voyage to Cape of Good Hope* (2 vols., London: G. G. J. and J. Robinson, 1785). A Dublin edition also appeared the same year sold by Messrs. White, Cash, and Byrne. *ECCO.*

3 Thomas Sheridan, *A Course of Lectures on Elocution* (London: A. Millar, R. and J. Dodsley, T. Davies, C. Henderson, J. Wilkie, and E. Dilly, 1762). *ECCO.*

4 William Paley, *The Principles of Moral and Political Philosophy* (2 vols., London: R. Faulder, 1785). BLPC. There was also a Dublin edition published by Messrs. Exshaw et al. in 1785. *ECCO.*

5 George Horne, *A Commentary on the Book of Psalms* (2 vols., Oxford: John Rivington, T. Payne, T. Cadell, and G. Robinson, 1776). *ECCO.*

6	Lucians Works by Franklyn 2 Vol Boards[6]	1776
7	Burns Ecclesiastical Law 2 Vol boards[7]	1763
8	Juvenal and Persius Casambonus 2 Tom crit[8]	L Bat 1695

[*f.* 5*r*]

9	Milton Paradise Lost & Regained By Baskerville 2 Vol neat[9]	1759
10	Translation from the French by D: Y. boards[10]	1700
11	Pearces Communitaries on the Four Evangelists pub by Derby 2 Vol boards[11]	1777
12	Millars Historical View of the English Government boards[12]	1787
13	Reeves Poems much stained & creased[13]	1769
14	Michaeli's Lectures on the Sacred Books of the New Test. Sewed[14]	1761
15	Blackstones Tract relating to The Laws of England neat[15]	1771
16	Goldsmiths Dessrtied Village Fables Of Flora Goldsmiths Traveller a Poem half bound 1 Vol[16]	——

6 ? Lucian, *The Works of Lucian, from the Greek*, trans. Thomas Francklin (2 vols., London: T. Cadell, 1780). *ECCO*.

7 Richard Burn, *Ecclesiastical Law* (2 vols., H. Woodfall and W. Strahan: London, 1763). *ECCO*.

8 Juvenal and Persius et al., *D. Iunii Iuvenalis Aquinatis Satyræ*, ed. Isaac Casaubon (Leiden: Petrum Vander Aa, 1695). CUL. We are not sure what 'L Bat' refers to before the date.

9 John Milton, *Paradise Lost*, ed. Thomas Newton (Birmingham: J. and R. Tonson, 1759). *ECCO*.

10 D. Y. *Translations from the French* (King's Lynn: Printed for the Author by William Whittingham, 1770). *ECCO*. Pratt was a subscriber to this edition.

11 Zachary Pearce, *A Commentary, with Notes, on the Four Evangelists, and the Acts of the Apostles*, ed. John Derby (2 vols., London: T. Cadell, 1777). *ECCO*.

12 John Millar, *An Historical View of the English Government* (London: A. Strahan, T. Cadell, and J. Murray, 1787). *ECCO*.

13 Clara Reeve, *Original Poems on Several Occasions* (London: W. Harris, 1769). *ECCO*. Pratt was a subscriber to this edition.

14 Johann David Michaelis, *Introductory Lectures to the Sacred Books of the New Testament* (London: J. and R. Tonson, 1761). *ECCO*.

15 William Blackstone, *An Analysis of the Laws of England*, 6th ed. (Clarendon Press: Oxford, 1771). *ECCO*.

16 Pratt's copy of John Langhorne's *Fables of Flora* was probably bound together in a single volume with Goldsmith's poems *The Deserted Village* and *The Traveller*. It is impossible to tell what editions were bound together. Here is the bibliographical information on the first editions of each text. John Langhorne's *Fables of Flora* (J. Murray: London, 1771). *ECCO*. Oliver Goldsmith, *The Deserted Village* (W. Griffin: London, 1770). *ECCO*. Oliver Goldsmith, *The Traveller* (J. Newbery: London, 1764). *ECCO*.

[*f.* 6*r*]

17	Ades Walpolianae on a Discription of the Pictures at Houghton Hall[17]	175[2]
18	Middletons Free Inquiry into the Miraculous Powers neat[18]	1749
19	Apparatus Biblicus or an Introduction to the Holy Scripture cuts[19]	1723
20	Taylors Paraphrase on the Romans[20]	1754
21	Tingal an Ancient Epic Poem by Macpherson in boards[21]	1762
22	Littletons Latin & English Dict.[22]	1735
23	Holy Bible[23]	1743
24	Another Binding bad[24]	1697
25	A Volume of Tracts binding bad[25]	
26	Godwyns Civil & Ecclesiastical Rites[26]	1685

17 Horace Walpole, *Aedes Walpolinae*, 2nd ed. (No publisher: London, 1752). The last digit of the year is not legible in the manuscript of Pratt's library but this is the only edition published in the 1750s: the third edition was published in 1767. *ECCO.*

18 Conyers Middleton, *A Free Inquiry into the Miraculous Powers, which are Supposed to have Subsisted in the Christian Church, from the Earliest Ages through Several Successive Centuries* (R. Manby and H. S. Cox: London, 1749). A Dublin edition was published in the same year. *ECCO.*

19 Bernard Levy, *Apparatus Biblicus* (London: S. Palmer, 1723). The translator is unknown. *ECCO.*

20 John Taylor, *A Paraphrase with Notes on the Epistle to the Romans*, 3rd ed. (London: J. Waugh and W. Fenner, 1754). *ECCO.*

21 James Macpherson, *Fingal, An Ancient Epic Poem* (London: T. Becket and P. A. de Hondt, 1762). A second London edition also appeared in 1762. The misspelling 'Tingal' is in the original manuscript. *ECCO.*

22 Adam Littleton, *Dr. Adam Littleton's Latin Dictionary*, 6th ed. (London: J. Walthoe et al., 1735). *ECCO.*

23 ? *The Holy Bible* (Oxford: Printed by Thomas and Robert Baskett, 1743). *ECCO.* There was also a London edition, also printed by Thomas and Robert Baskett. Another possibility is *The Holy Bible* (Cambridge: Printed by Joseph Bentham, 1743). *ECCO.* An Edinburgh edition was also printed in 1743 by Richard Watkins. CUL.

24 *The Holy Bible* (Oxford: Printed by the University Printers, 1697). *EEBO.* Another possibility is *The Holy Bible* (London: Charles Bill and the Executrix of Thomas Newcomb deceas'd, 1697). *EEBO.*

25 It is impossible to know what these tracts are.

26 Thomas Godwyn, *Moses and Aaron: Civil and Ecclesiastical Rites, used by the Ancient Hebrews*, 12th ed. (London: R. Scot, T. Basset, J. Wright, R. Chiswel, B. Griffen, G. Connyers, and M. Wotton, 1685). *EEBO.*

[*f.* 7*r*]

27	Bp Patricke Comment on Genisis Exodus Leviticus Numbers Detronomy Joshua Judges Ruth Samuel & Kings 9 vols[27]	1685
28	Addingtons Penal Statues[28]	1775

Eighteen Vol. of Miscellaneous Sermons and Tracts[a]

[*f.* 8*r*]

Octavo

1	Tillotsons Sermons 12 Vol boards[1]	1743
2	Swifts Works containing Letters 3 Vol Sewed[2]	1766
3	Annual Register 1765 1766 1767 boards[3]	
4	The Same 1772 1773 1774 D° [4]	

27 ? Simon Patrick, *A Commentary upon the First book of Moses, called Genesis* (1695), *A Commentary upon the Second book of Moses, called Exodus* (1697), *A Commentary upon the Third Book of Moses, called Leviticus* (1698), *A Commentary upon the Fourth Book of Moses, called Numbers* (1699), *A Commentary upon the Fifth book of Moses, called Deuteronomy* (1700), *A Commentary upon the books of Joshua, Judges and Ruth* (1702), *A Commentary upon the Two Books of Samuel* (1703), *A Commentary upon the Two Books of Kings* (1705). All these books were published in London by Richard Chiswell. *ECCO.*

28 William Addington, *An Abridgement of Penal Statues* (London: W. Strahan and M. Woodfall; for P. Uriel; T. Cadell; E. and C. Dilly; and J. Robson, 1775). *ECCO.*

a It is impossible to know what these sermons and tracts are.

Octavo

1 John Tillotson, *The Works of the Most Reverend Dr. John Tillotson* (12 vols., London: R. Ware et al., 1742–44). *ECCO.*

2 Jonathan Swift, *Letters Written by the Late Jonathan Swift*, ed. John Hawkesworth (3 vols., London: T. Davies, R. Davis, L. Davis, C. Reymers, and J. Dodsley, 1766). *ECCO.* There was a twelve-volume set of Swift's complete works edited by Hawksworth published the same year, but the cataloguer of Pratt's library appears to refer to the separate 3 volumes of the letters.

3 All first editions of the volumes of *The Annual Register* for the years 1765, 1766, and 1767 were first published in London by James Dodsley. See William B. Todd, 'A Bibliographical Account of *The Annual Register*, 1758–1825', *The Library: The Transactions of the Bibliographical Society*, 16 (1961), 105 (104–20). As individual volumes of the *Annual Register* continued to be reprinted several years after the year to which they pertained, it is impossible to know for certain what years in which the editions of the *Annual Register* in Pratt's library were published.

4 All instalments of *The Annual Register* for the years 1772, 1773, and 1774 were

5 The Same 1784 1785 1786 1787 & 1788 &c° [5]
6 Davys Letters Addressed to Young Gentlemen 2 Vol versed[6] 1787
7 Priestleys History of Early Opinion of Jesus Christ 4 Vol boards[7] 1787
8 Smiths Tour in the United States of America 2 Vol boards[8] 1784
9 Hunters Moral Discourses on Providence 2 Vol boards[9] 1774
10 Fergusons Easy Introduction to Astronomy for
Young Gentlemen & Ladies boards[10] 1769
11 Nautical Almanac for 1774 boards[11]

[*f.* 9*r*]

12 Historical View of the Controversy of an Intermediate State boards[12]
13 Martines Philosophia Brittania cuts 3 Vol neat[13]
14 Mosheims Ecclesiastical History 1771
and Ancient and Modern by Maclaine 5 Vol neat[14] 1757

---

published in London by James Dodsley. See the explanatory note above for the first batch of annual registers in Pratt's library.

5 All instalments of *The Annual Register* for the years 1784, 1785, 1786, 1787, and 1788 were published in London by James Dodsley. See the explanatory note above for the first batch of annual registers in Pratt's library.

6 Charles Davy, *Letters, Addressed Chiefly to a Young Gentleman, Upon Subjects of Literature* (2 vols., Bury St Edmunds: Messrs. Payne and Son, T. and J. Merrill, R. Beatniffe, and R. Cruttwell, 1787). *ECCO*. For Pratt's relationship with Charles Davy see our Introduction (pp. 5–6, 19, 29, and 46–7) and the letter from Davy to Pratt in Appendix 6.

7 ? Joseph Priestley, *An History of Early Opinions Concerning Jesus Christ Compiled from Original Writers; Proving that the Christian Church was at First Unitarian* (4 vols., Birmingham: J. Johnson, 1786). *ECCO*.

8 J[ohn] F[erdinand] D[alziel] Smyth, *A Tour in the United States of America* (2 vols., London: G. Robinson; J. Robson; and J. Sewell, 1784). BLPC. A Dublin edition printed by G. Perrin also appeared in 1784. *ECCO*.

9 Thomas Hunter, *Moral Discourses on Providence and other Important Subjects* (Warrington: William Eyers, 1774). *ECCO*. A London second edition printed for the author and T. Cadell was also published in 1774. *ECCO*.

10 James Ferguson, *An Easy Introduction to Astronomy, for Young Gentlemen and Ladies*, 2nd ed. (London, Printed for T. Cadell, 1769). *ECCO*.

11 Great Britain. Commissioners of Longitude, *The Nautical Almanac and Astronomical Ephemeris, for the Year 1774* (London: J. Nourse, and Mess. Mount and Page, 1772). *ECCO*.

12 Francis Blackburne. *A Short Historical View of the Controversy Concerning an Intermediate State* (London: Mr. Walter, Mr. Henderson, and Messrs. Todd and Southeran, 1765). *ECCO*.

13 Benjamin Martin, *Philosophia Britannica*, 3rd ed. (3 vols., London: W. Strahan et al., 1771). *ECCO*

14 ? John Laurence Mosheim [Johann Lorenz von Mosheim], *An Ecclesiastical History, Antient and Modern, from the Birth of Christ, to the Beginning of the Present Century*, trans. Archibald Maclaine, new ed. (5 vols., London: T. Cadell, 1767). *ECCO*. There was also a

15	Edisards Translation of the Psalms[15]	1755
16	Dodd on the Miricles and Parables of our Saviour 4 Vol neat[16]	1757
17	Newton on the Prophecies 3 Vol neat[17]	1766
18	Quesnels New Testament with Moral Reflections upon every Verse pub by Russel 4 Vol neat[18]	1719
19	Priestley Disquisitions Relating to Matter & Spirit 2 Vol neat[19]	1777
20	Gastrells Christian Institutes[20]	1709
21	Juvenall & Persius translated by Madden 2 Vol neat[21]	1789

[*f. 10r*]

22	Popes Works by Warburton 9 Vol large Octavo neat[22]	1759
23	Abernethys Sermons on Various Subjects 4 Vol[23]	1762
24	Shakespeare Works 6 Vol[24]	1745
25	Bakers Beautifull & Instructive Passages of the Roman Poet 2 Vol neat[25]	

---

two-volume quarto edition printed in London and published by A. Millar in 1765 *ECCO*. and a four-volume octavo edition printed in Dublin and published by Ann Leathley in 1767. *ECCO*.

15 Thomas Edwards, *A New English Translation of the Psalms from the Original Hebrew Reduced to Metre by the Late Bishop Hare* (Cambridge: B. Dod, 1755). *ECCO*.

16 William Dodd, *Discourses on the Miracles and Parables of our Blessed Lord and Saviour Jesus Christ* (4 vols., London, T. Waller, W. Faden, and E. Dilly, 1757–8). *ECCO*.

17 Thomas Newton, *Dissertations on the Prophecies, which have Remarkably been Fulfilled, and at this Time are Fulfilling in the World*, 3rd ed. (3 vols., London: J. and R. Tonson, 1766). *ECCO*.

18 [Pasquier Quesnel], *The New Testament, with Moral Reflections upon Every Verse*, trans. Richard Russell (4 vols., London: Printed by J. R. for R. Bonwick, T. Goodwin, J. Walthoe, J. Wotton, S. Manship, Wilkin, B. Tooke, R. Smith, and T. Ward, 1719–25). *ECCO*.

19 Joseph Priestley, *Disquisitions Relating to Matter and Spirit* (London: J. Johnson, 1777). *ECCO*. This is a one-volume book, so Pratt may have had two copies in his library.

20 Francis Gastrell, *The Christian Institutes, or, the Sincere Word of God*, 2nd ed. (London: Henry Clements, 1709). *ECCO*.

21 Juvenal and Persius, *A New and Literal Translation of Juvenal and Persius*, trans. and ed. M. Madan [Martin Madan] (2 vols., London: Printed for the Editor, 1789). *ECCO*.

22 Alexander Pope, *The Works of Alexander Pope Esq*. ed. Thomas Warburton (9 vols., London: A. Millar et al., 1760). *ECCO*.

23 John Abernethy, *Sermons on Various Subjects*, 3rd ed. (2 vols., London: D. Browne, T. Osborne, and A. Millar, 1762). *ECCO*.

24 William Shakespeare, *The Works of Shakespear*, ed. Sir Thomas Hanmer (London: J. and P. Knapton et al., 1745). *ECCO*.

25 Henry Baker, *Medulla Poetarum Romanorum: or, the Most Beautiful and Instructive Passages of the Roman Poets* (2 vols., London: D. Midwinter et al., 1737). *ECCO*.

26	Lucretius of the Nature of Thinges cuts by Guineir 2 Vol neat[26]	1725
27	Fables of the Bees 2 Vol neat[27]	1725
28	South Sermons 6 Vol[28]	1737
29	Seeds Sermons 2 Vol[29]	1745
30	Smiths Preservative against Quakerism[30]	1732
31	Warners System of Divinity 4 Vol[31]	1767
32	Middletons Life of Cicero 3 Vol[32]	1742
33	Colemans Terences Comediae 2 Vol[33]	1768
34	Mandevilles Journey from Aleppo to Jerusalem cuts neat[34]	1749

[*f. 11r*]

35	Fleetwoods Sermons on Relative Duties[35]	1739
36	Stahhopes Epictetius Morals[36]	1721

26 ? T Carus Lucretius, *Of the Nature of Things, in Six Books. Illustrated with Proper and Useful Notes, Adorned with Copper-Plates, Curiously Engraved by Guernier, and Others* (2 vols., London: Daniel Browne, 1743). *ECCO*

27 [Bernard Mandeville], *The Fable of the Bees: or, Private Vices, Publick Benefits. with an Essay on Charity and Charity-Schools*, 4th ed. (London: J. Tonson, 1725). *ECCO*. This was a one-volume edition.

28 Robert South, *Sermons Preached upon Several Occasions* (6 vols., London: H. Lintot, 1737). *ECCO*. The cataloguer misnumbered this book as '29'.

29 Jeremiah Seed, *Discourses on Several Important Subjects*, 2nd ed. (2 vols., London: R. Manby and H. S. Cox, 1745). *ECCO*. The cataloguer misnumbered this book as '28'.

30 Patrick Smith, *A Preservative against Quakerism, or, a Complication of Deism, Enthusiasm, and Divers other Ancient and Modern Dangerous Errors and Heresies* (London: C. Rivington, 1732). *ECCO*.

31 Ferdinardo Warner, *A System of Divinity and Morality; in a Series of Discourses on all the Essential Parts of Natural and Revealed Religion*, 3rd ed. (3 vols., London: Printed for R. Baldwin, L. Hawes, W. Clarke and R. Collins, 1767). *ECCO*.

32 Conyers Middleton, *The History of the Life of Marcus Tullius Cicero*, 3rd ed. (3 vols., London: W. Innys and R. Manby, 1742). *ECCO*.

33 Terence, *The Comedies of Terence, Translated into Familiar Blank Verse*, trans. George Colman, 2nd ed. (2 vols., London: T. Becket, P. A. de Hondt, R. Baldwin, 1768). *ECCO*.

34 Henry Maundrell, *A Journey from Aleppo to Jerusalem; at Easter, A.D. 1697*, 7th ed. (Oxford: W. Meadows 1749). *ECCO*. A Dublin printing of the sixth edition sold by J. Leathley and others appeared in the same year. *ECCO*.

35 ? William Fleetwood, *The Relative Duties of Parents and Children, Husbands and Wives, Masters and Servants*, 4th ed. (London: J. and J. Knapton et al., 1732). *ECCO*. Fleetwood was a former Bishop of Ely.

36 Epictetus, *Epictetus his Morals, with Simplicius his Comment*, 4th ed. (London: Richard Sare, 1721). *ECCO*.

37	Fothergilles Sermons on Several Subjects 2 Vol[37]	1765
38	Bakers Reflections on Learning[38]	1727
39	Burke on the Revolution in France[39]	1790
40	Holdens Paraphrase on the Book of Isaiah 2 Vol boards[40]	1776
41	Dodingtons Diary in boards[41]	1784
42	Friendly Vindication of the Sacred Books Josephus in boards Glass[42]	1770
43	Whites Sermons in boards[43]	1785
44	Memoirs of Richard Gardiner Esqr boards[44]	1782
45	Bourrits Journey to the Glaciers by Davy 2 Copies 1 of them stained sewed[45]	1775

37 George Fothergill, *Sermons on Several Subjects and Occasions* (2 vols., Oxford: Daniel Prince et al., 1765). *ECCO.*

38 Thomas Baker, *Reflections upon Learning*, 6th ed. (London: James and John Knapton and Richard Wilkin, 1727). *ECCO.*

39 Edmund Burke, *Reflections on the Revolution in France* (London: J. Dodsley, 1790). *ECCO.* Burke's *Reflections* went through seven editions in 1790. See James K. Bracken and Joel Silver, *Dictionary of Literary Biography, Volume One Hundred Fifty-Four: The British Literary Book Trade, 1700–1820* (Detroit: Gale Research, Inc., 1995), 119. A Dublin printing of the *Reflections* sold by J. Sheppard and another sold by W. Watson and twenty-five others also appeared in 1790. *ECCO.*

40 Lawrence Holden, *A Paraphrase on the Book of Isaiah* (2 vols., Chelmsford: Printed for the Author, 1776). *ECCO.*

41 George Bubb Dodington, *The Diary of the Late George Bubb Dodington, Baron of Melcombe Regis Diary*, ed. Henry Penruddocke Wyndham (Salisbury: E. Easton and G. and T. Wilkie, 1784). *ECCO.* A Dublin edition was published by Messr. Price et al. the same year. *ECCO.*

42 Robert Findlay, *A Vindication of the Sacred Books and of Josephus, Especially the Former, from the Various Misrepresentations and Cavils of the Celebrated M. De Voltaire* (Glasgow: Robert and Andrew Foulis, 1770). *ECCO.*

43 Joseph White, *Sermons Preached before the University of Oxford, in the year 1784*, 2nd ed. (London: G. G. J. and J. Robinson, 1785). *ECCO.* There was also a Dublin edition claiming to be a printing of the third edition sold by John Exshaw and Luke White the same year. *ECCO.*

44 *Memoirs of the Life and Writings (Prose and Verse) of R-ch--d G-rd-n-r, Esq., Alias Dick Merry-Fellow, Of Serious and Facetious Memory!* (London: G. Kearsly and M. Booth, 1782). *ECCO.* For information on Pratt's association with Gardiner see our Introduction, pp. 23–5.

45 M[arc]-T[héodore] Bourrit, *A Relation of a Journey to the Glaciers, in the Dutchy of Savoy*, trans. C[harles] and F[rederick] Davy (Norwich: Richard Beatniffe, 1775). *ECCO.* Pratt was a subscriber to this edition. Charles and Frederick were brothers.

46 Memories of the Life & Writings of the late Rev. Thos Baker boards[46] 1784
47 Trial of Count Struensee sewed[47] 1776

[*f. 12r*]

48 Defence of Lord Shelburne sewed[48] 1783
49 Dawson on the Confesional sewed[49] 1769
50 Laws Earnest address to the Clergy sewed[50] 1761
51 View of Real Grivences sewed[51] 1772
52 Essay on the Immateriality and Immortality of the Soul boards[52] 1778
53 Answer to Sir H. Clintons Narrative[53] 1783

---

46 Robert Masters, *Memoirs of the Life and Writings of the Late Rev. Thomas Baker, B.D. of St John's College in Cambridge, from the Papers of Dr. Zachary Grey* (Cambridge: J. and J. Merill and J. Deighton, 1784). *ECCO*. Pratt owned a copy of Baker's *Reflections on Learning* (no.38 in the list of octavos).

47 Johann Friedrich Struensee, *The Trial of Count Struensee, Late Prime Minister to the King of Denmark, before the Royal Commission of Inquisition, at Copenhagen*, 2nd ed. (London: J. Whitaker, J. Fox, and T. Waters, 1776). *NLS*.

48 [Dennis O'Brien], *A Defence of the Right Honorable the Earl of Shelburne*, 5th ed. (London: J. Stockdale, 1783). *ECCO*. The sixth, seventh, eighth, and ninth editions also appeared in 1783, all sold by J. Stockdale. *ECCO*. There were also three Dublin printings in 1783, one by W. Wilson, one by R. Moncrieffe, J. Exshaw, and P. Byrne, and one by J. Exshaw and P. Byrne. *ECCO*.

49 Benjamin Dawson, *An Answer to Letters Concerning Established Confessions of Faith* (London: F. Newbery, Johnson and Payne, and E. and C. Dilly, 1769). *ECCO*.

50 William Law, *An Humble, Earnest, and Affectionate Address to the Clergy* (London: J. Richardson, 1761). *ECCO*.

51 [John Powell], *A View of Real Grievances, with Remedies Proposed for Redressing Them* (London: Messrs. Dodsley, Millan, Baldwin, and the Booksellers of York, Bristol, Exeter, Norwich, Lynn, &c., 1772). *ECCO*.

52 [Benjamin Caulfield], *An Essay on the Immateriality and Immortality of the Soul, and its Instinctive Sense of Good and Evil* (London: J. Dodsley, 1778). *ECCO*. This book included a response to Joseph Priestley's theories as presented in his introductory essays to his 1774 abridgement of David Hartley's *Observations on Man* (1749).

53 It is not clear whether the cataloguer means Lord Cornwallis's reply to Sir Henry Clinton's narrative or Clinton's answer to Cornwallis (the syntax of the entry suggests that Lord Cornwallis's book is meant but only Clinton's book uses the word 'answer' in the title). Therefore we give details on both books. Earl [Charles] Cornwallis, *An Answer to that Part of the Narrative of Lieutenant-General Sir Henry Clinton, K.B. which relates to the Conduct of Lieutenant-General Earl Cornwallis* (London: J. Debrett, 1783). *ECCO*. Sir Henry Clinton, *Observations on Some Parts of the Answer of Earl Cornwallis to Sir Henry Clinton's Narrative* (London: J. Debrett, 1783). *ECCO*.

54	Hurds 12 Sermons on the Prophecies sewed[54]	1772
55	Lardners Case of the Demoniacs in the New Testament boards[55]	1758
56	Consideration on the German War sewed[56]	1761
57	Hills Funeral of the Mass boards[57]	
58	Pointers Miscellanea in usum Academicae in boards[58]	1718
59	Ogdens Sermons 3 Vol small Octavo boards[59]	1780
60	Essay on Old Maids 3 Vol sewed[60]	1785
61	Collection of Funeral Sermons 2 Vol boards[61]	
62	Readings 116 Sermons for all Sundays in the Year 4 Vol neat[62]	1755

[*f. 13r*]

63	Carrs Sermons 2 Vol neat[63]	1784
64	Pyles Sermons 2 Vol neat[64]	1773
65	Ashtons Sermons on several Occasions[65]	1770

---

54 Richard Hurd, *An Introduction to the Study of the Prophecies Concerning the Christian Church*, 3rd ed. (London: for T. Cadell, 1772). *ECCO.*

55 Nathaniel Lardner, *The Case of the Demoniacs Mentioned in the New Testament* (London: C. Henderson and J. Buckland, 1758). *ECCO.*

56 [Israel Mauduit], *Considerations on the Present German War*, 4th ed. (London: John Wilkie, 1761). *ECCO.* In 1761 were also a fifth and sixth editions printed in London, both published by John Wilkie. The sixth edition is attested on *ECCO* and the *ESTC* notes the existence of a fifth edition. There was Dublin printing of this book in 1761 that was sold by George Faulkner *ECCO.* There was also a 'Part II' of this book printed in 1761 and sold by M. Thrush. *ECCO.*

57 [Daniel] Derodon, *The Funeral of the Mass*, ed. and trans. Richard Hill (London: Printed for the Author, 1716). *ECCO.*

58 John Pointer, *Miscellanea in usum Juventutis Academicæ* (Oxford: Ant. Peisley, Ja. Knapton, Hen. Clements, Will. Taylor, and Will. Meadows, 1718). *ECCO.*

59 Samuel Ogden, *Sermons*, 2nd ed. (2 vols., Cambridge: D. Prince, J. Cooke, J. F. & C. Rivington, T. Cadell, and T. Beecroft, 1780). *ECCO.*

60 [William Hayley], *A Philosophical, Historical, and Moral Essay on Old Maids* (3 vols., London: T. Cadell, 1785). *ECCO.*

61 ? The editors have not identified a book by this title—possibly the catalogue entry refers to a collection of separately printed funeral sermons bound together.

62 William Reading, *One Hundred and Sixteen Sermons*, 3rd ed. (4 vols., London: James Hodges, 1755). *ECCO.*

63 George Carr, *Sermons*, 5th ed. (2 vols, Edinburgh: Charles Elliot and Thomas Cadell, London, 1784). *ECCO.*

64 Thomas Pyle, *Sixty Sermons on Plain and Practical Subjects* (2 vols., Norwich: R. Beatniffe, 1773). *ECCO.* Pyle was the vicar of King's Lynn All Saints between 1719 and 1754 and died in 1754: *CDB.*

65 Thomas Ashton, *Sermons on Several Occasions* (London: J. Whiston, 1770). *ECCO.*

66	Clagets Sermons 4 Vol[66]	1689
67	South Sermons Vol 7,8,9,10,11,--5Vol[67]	1744
68	A Volume of Sermons by Biscoe & c.[68]	1717
69	Blairs Sermons[69]	1779
70	Letsomes Preachers Assistant[70]	1759
71	Guyves Sermons on Various Subjects[71]	1754
72	Hoadbys Sermons[72]	1734
73	Nichols's Conference with a Theist 2 Vol[73]	1723
74	Cunninghams Laws of Tythes[74]	1766
75	Hingestons Discourse on the Divine Covenants[75]	1771
76	Brydones Tour through Sicily and Malta 2 Vol neat[76]	1774

---

66 ? William Claggett, *Seventeen Sermons Preach'd upon Several Occasions*, 2nd ed. (London: William Rogers, 1694). *ECCO.*

67 Robert South, *Five Additional Volumes of Sermons Preached upon Several Occasions* (5 vols., London: Charles Bathurst, 1744). *ECCO.*

68 ? Edmund Calamy, *The Principles and Practice of Moderate Nonconformists with respect to Ordination, Exemplify'd: in a Sermon preach'd at the Ordination of Mr. John Munckley, January the 19th. 1717. And A Charge given to Mr. James Read, Mr. Henry Read, Mr. Richard Biscoe, Mr. George Smyth, and Mr. S. Chandler, after their being Ordain'd* (London: Printed for John Clark, at the Bible and Crown in the Poultry, near Cheapside, 1717). *ECCO.* A second edition was also printed in 1717, also sold by John Clark. This volume does not contain sermons by Richard Biscoe, although his name does appear on the title page along with other ordained ministers. 2nd ed. *ECCO.*

69 Hugh Blair, *Sermons*, 7th ed. (London: W. Strahan, T. Cadell, and W. Creech, 1779). *ECCO.* There was also a Dublin printing of the seventh edition sold by William Hallhead in 1779. *ECCO.*

70 ? Sampson Letsome, *The Preacher's Assistant* (London: Messrs. Birt, Williams, Fletcher, and Thurlbourn, 1753). *ECCO.*

71 ? John Guyse, *A Collection of Seventeen Practical Sermons on Various and Important Subjects* (London: Edward Dilly, 1756). *ECCO.*

72 Benjamin Hoadly, *Several Discourses Concerning the Terms of Acceptance with God*, 4th ed. (London: James, John and Paul Knapton, 1734). *ECCO.*

73 William Nichols, *A Conference with a Theist* (2 vols., London: J. Holland, J. Bowyer, A. Bettesworth, J. Batley; F. Clay; and J. Walthoe, Junr., 1723). *IA.*

74 Timothy Cunningham, *A New Treatise on the Laws Concerning Tithes*, 2nd ed. (London: W. Griffin, 1766). *ECCO.*

75 James Hingeston, *Discourses upon the Divine Covenants* (London: M. Hingeston, T. Cadell, T. Payne, and E. Johnson, 1771). *IA.* The title page describes this book as 'Part I' but we have not been able to find any continuation. Hingeston was the vicar of Raydon in Suffolk.

76 P[atrick] Brydone, *A Tour Through Sicily and Malta*, 2nd ed. (2 vols., W. Strahan and T. Cadell, 1774). There was also a third edition printed in London and sold by W. Strahan and T. Cadell in 1774. There was also a Dublin printing of the first edition sold by

77 Montagues Reflections on the Rise and Fall of the Ancient Republics[77] 1760

[*f. 14r*]

78 Bolingbrokes Letters on the Spirit of Patriotism neat[78] 1749
79 Hays Religio Philosophis neat[79] 1771
80 Burns Justice 3 Vol[80] 1757
81 Rayners Case of Tythes 3 Vol[81] 1783
82 Glanvil on Witches[82] 1726
83 Buchans Domestic Medicine[83] 1774
84 Salmons Geographical Grammar[84]
85 Brookes General Gazetter[85] 1762
86 Guthries Geographical Grammer[86] 1771

W. Wilson and another Dublin printing of the second edition sold by J. Potts, J. Williams, R. Moncrieffe, and T. Walker. *ECCO*.

77 Edward Wortley Montagu, *Reflections on the Rise and Fall of the Ancient Republicks*, 2nd ed. (London; A. Millar, 1760). *ECCO*.

78 Henry St John, First Viscount Bolingbroke, *Letters, on the Spirit of Patriotism: on the Idea of a Patriot King: and on the State of Parties, at the Accession of King George the First* (London: A. Millar, 1749). *ECCO*. There was also a Dublin printing sold by G. Faulkner in 1749. *ECCO*.

79 William Hay, *Religio Philosophi*, 4th ed. (London: J. Dodsley, 1771). *ECCO*.

80 Richard Burn, *The Justice of the Peace, and Parish Officer* (3 vols., London: A. Millar, 1757). *ECCO*.

81 John Rayner, *Cases at Large Concerning Tithes* (3 vols., London: Richardson and Urquhart, 1783). *ECCO*.

82 Joseph Glanvill, *Sadducismus Triumphatus: or, A Full and Plain Evidence, Concerning Witches and Apparitions* (London: A. Bettesworth, J. Batley, W. Mears, and J. Hooke, 1726). *ECCO*.

83 William Buchan, *Domestic Medicine*, 3rd ed. (London: W. Strahan; T. Cadell, J. Balfour, and W. Creech, 1774). *ECCO*. There was also a Dublin printing of the third edition sold by H. Saunders in 1774. BLPC.

84 [Thomas] Salmon, *A New Geographical and Historical Grammar* (London: William Johnston, 1749). *ECCO*. The thirteenth edition, entitled Salmon's *Geographical and Astronomical Grammar*, was published by C. Bathurst and others in 1785. *ECCO*. By this time the text had been thoroughly revised and a whole section on astronomy added. Pratt may have had any of the various geographical books published under Salmon's name that were printed under between these dates.

85 ? Richard Brookes, *The General Gazetter*, 2nd ed (London: J. Newbery, R. Baldwin, W. Johnston, S. Crowder, B. Law, J. Coote, Becket, De Hondt, and B. Collins, 1766). *ECCO*.

86 William Guthrie, *A New Geographical, Historical, and Commercial Grammar*, 2nd ed. (London: J. Knox, 1771). *ECCO*. There also a third edition printed in London, also sold by J. Knox, and a Dublin second edition sold by H. Saunders and J. Potts in 1771. *ECCO*.

87	Baileys English Dictionary bind & bad[87]	1740
88	Nelsons Companion for the Festivals And Feasts of the Ch of England[88]	1722
89	Walls Geography of the Old & New Testament 4 Vol neat[89]	1721
90	Derehams Phisico Theology[90]	1739
91	----- Another ----[91]	1732
92	Another Theology[92]	1715

[*f.* 15*r*]

93	Drelincourt on Death[93]	1762
94	Jonkens Reasonableness & Certainty Of the Christian Religion 2 Vol[94]	1708
95	Potters Antig. Greece 2 Vol[95]	1704
96	Chamberlaynes State of Great Britain[96]	1755
97	Quinceys Dispensatory neat[97]	1742

87 N[athan] Bailey, *An Universal Etymological English Dictionary* (London: D. Midwinter et al., 1740). BLPC.

88 Rob[ert] Nelson, *A Companion for the Festivals and Fasts of the Church of England*, 12th ed. (London: R. Bonwicke, J. Walthoe, B. and S. Tooke, R. Wilkin, and T. Ward, 1722). *ECCO*. There was also a Dublin printing of this book sold by A. Rhames, for J. Hyde, R. Gunne, R. Owen, and E. Dobson in 1722. TCDL.

89 Edward Wells, *An Historical Geography of the Old Testament*, 2nd ed. (4 vols., London: James Knapton, 1721). *ECCO*.

90 ? W[illiam] Derham, *Physico-theology*, 10th ed. (London: W. Innys and R. Manby, 1737). BLPC.

91 W[illiam] Derham, *Physico-theology*, 8th ed. (London: W. Innys and R. Manby, 1732). *ECCO*.

92 ? We cannot locate a 1715 printing of *Physico-Theology*. However the third edition of *Physico-Theology* was printed for W. Innys, at the Prince's-Arms in St Paul's Church-Yard in London in 1714 and the fourth edition was also printed for W. Innys in 1716. *ECCO*.

93 Charl[es] Drelincourt, *The Christian's Defence against the Fears of Death*, 19th ed. trans. Marius D'Assigny (London: J. Knapton et. al. 1762. *ECCO*.

94 Robert Jenkin, *The Reasonableness and Certainty of the Christian Religion*, 3rd ed. (2 vols., London: Richard Sare, 1708). *ECCO*.

95 John Potter, *Archæologia Græca: or, the Antiquities of Greece*, 2nd ed. (London: S. and J. Sprint, John Nicholson, and Timothy Child, 1706). *ECCO*.

96 John Chamberlayne, *Magnæ Britanniæ Notitia: or, the Present State of Great-Britain* (London: S. Birt et al., 1755). *ECCO*.

97 John Quincy, *Pharmacopœia Officinalis & Extemporanea. or, a Complete English Dispensatory*, 12th ed. (London: Thomas Longman, 1742). *ECCO*.

98	Barclays Apology for the Quakers[98]	1736
99	Tissots advice to the people in General with Regard to health[99]	1765
100	Pyle on the Revelations[100]	1735
101	Trial of the Witnesses of the Jesus Christ[101]	1729
102	Laws Serious call to a Devout and Holy Life[102]	1729
103	Holy Bible by Questions and Answers[103]	1748
104	Present State of Great Britain Imperfect[104]	
105	Smiths Complete Housewife[105]	1759
106	Bennetts Confutation of Quakerism[106]	1705

[*f. 16r*]

107	Gibsons Ferriers New Guide[107]	1731
108	Wright on the Religious Observations of the Lords Day[108]	1726

---

98 Robert Barclay, *An Apology for the True Christian Divinity*, 6th ed. (London: T. Sowle Raylton and Luke Hinde, 1736). *ECCO*.

99 [Samuel-Auguste] Tissot, *Advice to the People in General, with Regard to their Health*, trans. J[ames] Kirkpatrick (London: T. Becket and P. A. de Hondt, 1765). *ECCO*.

100 Thomas Pyle, *A Paraphrase with Notes on the Revelation of St John* (London: J. Noon, 1735). *ECCO*. For Pyle's Norfolk connections, see Octavo 64 above.

101 [Thomas Sherlock], *The Tryal of the Witnesses of the Resurrection of Jesus* (London: J. Roberts, 1729). There were second, third, fourth, and fifth editions printed the same year, all sold by J. Roberts. *ECCO*.

102 William Law, *A Serious Call to a Devout and Holy Life* (London: William Innys, 1729). *ECCO*

103 *The Holy Bible, or, the Old and New Testament, Explained by Question and Answer* (London: S. Austen, 1748). *ECCO*.

104 We have found two books that correspond to this title: *The Present State of Great Britain* (London: J. H. Nicholson, A. Bell, R. Smith, and J. Round, 1707). *ECCO*. *An Account of the Constitution and Present State of Great Britain, Together with a View of its Trade, Policy, and Interest, Respecting other Nations, & of the Principal Curiosities of Great Britain and Ireland* (London: Printed for J. Newbery, 1759). *ECCO*.

105 ? E[liza] Smith, *The Compleat Housewife, or, Accomplish'd Gentlewoman's Companion*, 16th ed. (London: C. Hitch et al., 1758). *IA*.

106 Thomas Bennet, *A Confutation of Quakerism; or A Plain proof of the Falshood of what the principal Quaker Writers (Especially Mr. R. Barclay in his Apology and other Works) do Teach* (Cambridge: Edmund Jeffery and James Knapton, London, 1705). *ECCO*.

107 W[illiam] Gibson, *The Farrier's New Guide*, 7th ed. (London: J. Osborn and T. Longman, 1731). *ECCO*.

108 S[amuel] Wright, *A Treatise on the Religious Observation of the Lord's Day, According to the Express Words of the Fourth Commandment*, 3rd ed. (London: J. Clark, R. Hett, and E Matthews, 1726). *ECCO*.

109	Stebbing on Prayer[109]	1739
110	Dr. Eachards Works bad Copy[110]	1705
111	Bennett on the Common Prayer[111]	1709
112	T a Kempis Christian Pattern[112]	1732
113	Grays Memoria Teachnica[113]	1737
114	Leslies Snake in the Grass[114]	1697
115	Veneer on 39 Articles[115]	1725
116	Causes of the Decay of Christian Piety[116]	1671
117	Kilburns Office of a Justice[117]	1715
118	Government of the Tongue[118]	1774
119	The Principles of the Christian Religion explained[119]	1708
120	Defence of a Book intituled The Snake in the Grass[120]	1700

109 Henry Stebbing, *A Brief Account of Prayer, and the Sacrament of the Lord's Supper; and other Religious Duties Appertaining to the Christian Worship* (London: Fletcher Gyles, 1739). *ECCO.*

110 John Eachard, *Dr. Eachard's Works*, 11th ed. (London: J. Phillips, H. Rhodes, and J. Taylor, 1705). *ECCO.*

111 Thomas Bennet, *A Paraphrase with Annotations upon the Book of Common Prayer*, 2nd ed. (London: Edmund Jeffery, 1709). *ECCO.*

112 ? Thomas à Kempis, *The Christian's Pattern: or, A Treatise of the Imitation of Jesus Christ*, trans. George Stanhope, 12th ed. (London: J. J. and P. Knapton et al., 1733). *ECCO.* The *ESTC* notes that the title page's attribution to à Kempis is now disputed.

113 Richard Grey, *Memoria Technica: or, a New Method of Artificial Memory, Applied to, and Exemplified in Chronology, History, Geography, Astronomy*, 3rd ed. (London: A. Bettesworth, C. Hitch, F. Clay, and D. Brown, 1737). *ECCO.*

114 Charles Leslie, *The Snake in the Grass: or, Satan Transform'd into an Angel of Light*, 2nd ed. (London: Charles Brome, 1697). *EEBO.*

115 John Verneer, *An Exposition on the Thirty-Nine Articles of the Church of England* (London: C. Rivington, 1725). *ECCO.*

116 [Richard Allestree], *The Causes of the Decay of Christian Piety. Or an Impartial Survey of the Ruines of Christian Religion, Undermin'd by Unchristian Practice* (London: M. Garthwait, 1671. *EBBO.*

117 Richard Kilburn, *Choice Precedents upon all Acts of Parliament, Relating to the office and Duty of a Justice of Peace*, 8th ed. (London: Jacob Tonson, 1715). *ECCO.*

118 ? [Richard Allstree], *The Government of the Tongue* (Oxford: At the Theater in Oxford, 1674). *EBBO.*

119 William Wake, *The Principles of the Christian Religion Explained: In a Brief Commentary upon the Church-Catechism*, 3rd ed. (London: Richard Sare, 1708). *ECCO.*

120 [Charles Leslie], *A Defence of a Book Intituled, The Snake in the Grass* (London: C. Brome, W. Keblewhite, and Geo. Strahan, 1700). *ECCO.*

[f. 17r]

121	Rowes Callepoedia or the Art to have handsome Children[121]	1710
122	Bennetts of Rome bad Copy[122]	1719
123	Patrick's Witness to Christianity[123]	1695
124	The Christian Sacrifice[124]	1671
125	Introduction to the Knowledge of the most Eminent Painters[125]	1778
126	Dialogue betwixt two Protestants in Answer to a Popish Catechism[126]	1686
127	Animadversions upon a Book Intitled Fanaticism[127]	1674
128	Orrerys Remarks on the Life and Writings of Dr. Swift[128]	1752
129	Millers Gardners Kalender[129]	1751
130	Bennetts Answer to the Dissenters Plea[130]	1711
131	Youngs Love of Fame[131]	1741
132	Falkners Christian Loyalty[132]	1679

121 ? [Claude] Quillet, *Callipædia; or, an Art how to have Handsome Children*, trans. Nicholas Rowe (London: Edmund Curll, 1712). There was a previous edition by the same title with a translation by William Oldisworth published by John Morphew in 1710.

122 ? Benjamin Bennet, *The Persecution and Cruelty of the Church of Rome* (Glasgow, 1746). *ECCO*.

123 ? Simon Patrick, *The Witnesses to Christianity; or, The Certainty of our Faith and Hope* (London: R. Royston, 1675). *EEBO*.

124 [Simon Patrick], *The Christian Sacrifice* (London: R. Royston, 1671). *EEBO*.

125 [Matthew Pilkington], *A Concise Introduction to the Knowledge of the Most Eminent Painters* (London, T. Cadell, 1778). *IA*.

126 *A Dialogue Betwixt Two Protestants, (In Answer to a Popish Catechism, Called A Short Catechism Against all Secretaries)*, 2nd ed. (London: Samuell Tidmarsh, 1686). *EEBO*.

127 [Edward Hyde], *Animadversions upon a Book, Intituled Fantaticism Imputed to the Catholic Church, by Dr. Stillingfleet* (London: R. Boyston, 1674). *EEBO*.

128 [John Boyle] Earl of Orrery, *Remarks on the Life and Writings of Dr. Jonathan Swift* (London: A. Millar, 1752). *ECCO*. There was also a Dublin edition sold by J. Cooper printed in 1752.

129 Philip Miller, *The Gardeners Kalendar*, 9th ed. (London: John and James Rivington, 1751). *ECCO*.

130 ? Tho[mas] Bennet, *A Discourse of Schism … An Answer to a Book Intituled, Thomas Against Bennet: or, The Protestant Dissenters Vindicated from the Charge of Schism*, 3rd ed. (Cambridge: Edmund Jeffery, and James Knapton, London, 1704).

131 Edward Young, *Love of Fame, the Universal Passion*, 4th ed. (London: J. and R. Tonson, 1741). *ECCO*.

132 William Falkner, *Christian Loyalty: or, A Discourse wherein is Asserted that just Royal Authority and Eminency, which in this Church and Realm of England is Yielded to the King* (London: Walter Kettilby, 1679). *EEBO*.

[*f. 18r*]

133	Fullers Commentary on Ruth[133]	1654
134	Norris's Philosophical Discourse on the Immortality of the Soul[134]	1732
135	Causes of the Decay of Christian Piety[135]	1674
136	Offices of the Church 2 Copies bad cond[136]	
	52 Odd Monthly & Critical Reviews	
137	Book of Common Prayer blue Turkey[137]	
138	Another cuts bad Condition untitled[138]	
	Two Parcels of Quarto and Octavo Pamphlets[b]	

[*f. 19r*]

Latin Octavo

139	Schrevilis Lexicon G^{r} a Lat[139]	1738
140	Horatii Opera Delph[140]	1727
141	Davidsons Horace Lat & Eng 2 Vol[141]	1743
142	Homeri Ilias G^{r} & Lat Clarke 2 Vol[142]	1735
143	Dionysiii Longinui Gr & Lat[143]	1762

133 Thomas Fuller, *A Comment on Ruth* (London: G. and H. Eversden, 1654). *EEBO.*

134 John Norris, *A Philosophical Discourse Concerning the Natural Immortality of the Soul*, 5th ed. (London: Edmund Parker, 1732). *ECCO.*

135 [Richard Allestree], *The Causes of the Decay of Christian Piety. Or an Impartial Survey of the Ruines of Christian Religion, Undermin'd by Unchristian Practice* (London: Robert Pawlett, 1674). *EEBO.*

136 *The Offices, According to the Use of the Church of England* (Cambridge: Joseph Bentham and Charles Bathurst, 1751). It is not possible to know what edition or editions of *The Offices* these are.

137 The Book of Common Prayer was first published in 1549. It is not possible to tell what edition this particular Book of Common Prayer is.

138 It is not possible to tell what edition this particular Book of Common Prayer is.

b It is not possible to tell what pamphlets these are.

139 Cornelisa Schrevel and Joseph Hill, *Lexicon Manuale Græco-Latinum & Latino-Græcum*, ed. Joseph Hill, 11th ed. (London: D. Midwinter et al., 1738). CUL.

140 Horace, *Quinti Horatii Flacci Opera*, 8th ed. (London: J. Knapton et al., 1727). *ECCO.*

141 Horace, *The Satires, Epistles, and Art of Poetry of Horace Translated into English Prose* (London: Joseph Davidson, 1743). *ECCO.* The translator is unknown.

142 Homer, *Ilias Græce et Latine*, ed. Samuel Clarke, 2nd ed. (2 vols., London: Jacobi, Johannis, and Pauli Knapton, 1735). *ECCO.*

143 Longinus, *Peri Hypsous. De Sublimitate*, ed. Zacharias Pearce (London: J. and R. Tonson, 1762). *HT.*

144	M. Minucii Felicis Octavius[144]	1672
145	Sydenham Opera Universia[145]	1685
146	Ciceronis Orationes Delph[146]	1714
147	----- de Officiis a Tooly[147]	1729
148	Templer Idea Theologiae Leviathenis[148]	1673
149	Whitbys Ethices Compendeum[149]	1713
150	Pufendorifii de Office iuxta Johnson[150]	1737
151	Holmes Greek Grammar[151]	1735
152	Summa Conciliorum a Carangar[152]	1697

[*f.* 20*r*]

Twelves

1	Knox Moral Essays 2 Vol sewed[1]	1782
2	-- on Liberal Education sewed[2]	1788

---

144 M[arcus] Minucius Felix, *Octavius*, ed. Jacques Oisel (Leiden: Ex Officia Hackiana, 1672). *IA*

145 Thomas Sydenham, *Opera Universa* (London: Walter Kettilby, 1685). *EEBO.*

146 Cicero, *M. T. Ciceronis Orationes quædam Selectæ: Cum Interpretatione & Notis quas in usum Serenissimi*, ed. P. Carolus Meroüville [Charles Mérouville] (London: J. Nicholson, J. and B. Sprint, B. Tooke, R. Wilkin, D. Midwinter, B. Cowse, & W. Innys, 1714). *ECCO.*

147 Cicero, *M. T. Ciceronis de Officiis Libri Tres, Cato Major, Lælius, Paradoxa, Somnium Scipionis*, ed. Tho[mas] Tooly (Oxford: Sam. Wilmot, 1729). *ECCO.*

148 John Templer, *Idea Theologiæ Leviathanis* (London: G. Morden, 1673). *EBBO.*

149 Daniele [Daniel] Whitby, *Ethices Compendium, in usum Academicæ Juventutis* (London: Gul. Innys, 1713). *ECCO.*

150 Samuel Freiherr von Pufendorf, *S. Pufendorfii De Officio hominis & Civis juxta Legem Naturalem Libri Duo*, ed. Tho[mas] Johnson, 2nd ed. (London: Impensis Gul. Thurlbourn, Prostant apud Knapton, Innys, Vaillant, Rivington, Birt, Fletcher, and Clements, Oxonii, 1737). *ECCO.*

151 John Holmes, *The Greek Grammar; or, A Short, Plain, Critical, and Comprehensive Method of Teaching and Learning the Greek Tongue* (London: A. Bettesworth, C. Hitch, and A. Feazer, 1735). *ECCO.*

152 ? Bartholomæum Caranza [Bartholomaeus Carranza], *Summa Conciliorum* (Lovanni [Leuven]: Typis Hieronymi Nempæ, 1681). *HT.*

Twelves

1 Vicesimus Knox, *Essays Moral and Literary*, new ed. (2 vols, London: Charles Dilly, 1782). *ECCO.*

2 Vicesimus Knox, *Liberal Education: or, A Practical Treatise on the Methods of Acquiring Useful and Polite Learning*, 9th ed. (2 vols., London: Charles Dilly, 1788). UM.

3	Francis Sermons 2 Vol sewed[3]	1773
4	Peregrinations of the Mind sewed[4]	1700
5	Beauties of Sterne versed wants title[5]	
6	British Legacy or Fountain of Knowledge sewed[6]	1754
7	Remarks of Johnsons Life of Milton sewed[7]	1714
8	Davies on the Immortality of the Soul sewed[8]	1714
9	Norfolk tour sewed[9]	1772
10	Fentons Death of the Righteous 2 Vol[10]	1725
11	Scotch Preachers Vol 1.2.3[11]	1789
12	Attempt to Explain the Word Reason de of the Catholic Church Subscription[12]	1766

3 John Francis, *Sermons Preached on Several Occasions, at the Cathedral in Norwich, and at the Parish Churches of St. Peter's, Mancroft, and St. John's, Maddermarket, in the Said City* (2 vols., London: Benjamin White and Stanley Crowder, 1773). In addition to St Peter's, Mancroft and St John's, Maddermarket, Francis was also rector of Morley in Norfolk. *ECCO.* John Francis's son, also John Francis, served Jermyn friend Charles Davy as the curate of Topcroft.

4 ? The Rationalist [William Baker], *Peregrinations of the Mind through the most General and Interesting Subjects, which are usually Agitated in Life* (London: G. Pearch, 1770). *ECCO.*

5 There were 11 London editions published during Pratt's lifetime (between 1782–1790) of Laurence Sterne, *The Beauties of Sterne.* The first edition was printed in London and sold by G. Kearsle in 1782. *ECCO.* The last London printing in Pratt's lifetime was in 1790, also sold by G. Kearsle. *ECCO.*

6 Edward Knight *The British Legacy: or, Fountain of Knowledge* (London: Thomas Chandler, 1754). *ECCO.*

7 ? [Francis Blackburn], *Remarks on Johnson's Life of Milton* (London, No Bookseller, 1780). *ECCO.* The date given of '1714' in the catalogue is an obvious error.

8 John Davies, *The Original, Nature, and Immortality of the Soul* (London: Hammond Banks, 1714). *ECCO.*

9 Richard Beatniffe, *The Norfolk Tour: or, Traveller's Pocket Companion* (London: G. Robinson and R. Beatniffe, 1772). *ECCO.*

10 Jean La Placette, *The Death of the Righteous: A Treatise, Consisting of Discourses, Meditations, and Prayers, Conducive towards Dying Well,* ed. Thomas Fenton (2 vols., London: Bernard Lintot, 1725). UA.

11 *The Scotch Preacher: or, A Collection of Sermons, by Some of the Most Eminent Clergymen of the Church of Scotland,* 2nd ed. (4 vols., Edinburgh: J. Dickson and T Cadell, 1776–1789). *ECCO.* The first volume bears no date, the second volume is dated '1776' and the third and fourth volumes are dated '1789'. Pratt evidently only had the first, second, and third volumes.

12 William Robertson, *An Attempt to Explain the Words Reason, Substance, Person, Creeds, Orthodoxy, Catholic-Church, Subscription, and Index Expurgatorius* (London: W. Johnston, 1766). *ECCO.* There was also a Dublin 're-printed' edition sold by Thomas Ewing that appeared the same year. *ECCO.*

13	Maws Gardner[13]	1769
14	Cottons Poetical Works[14]	1734
15	Youngs Night Thoughts[15]	1755

[*f. 21r*]

16	Dictionary of the Bible[16]	1766
17	Wards Seasonable Advice to those in health[17]	
18	Great Importance of a Religeous Life	1790[18]
19	Several Orations of Demosthenes	1702[19]
20	Instructions of a Minister to his Parishoners[20]	
21	Gullivers travels edin	1752[21]
22	Eachards Contempt of the Clergy[22]	1670
23	Patrickes Devout Christian[23]	1711

---

13 Thomas Mawe [and John Abercrombie], *Every Man his own Gardener*, 3rd ed. (London: W. Griffin, 1769). There was also a fourth London edition printed in the same year, alsos sold by W. Griffin. *ECCO.*

14 Charles Cotton, *The Genuine Poetical Works of Charles Cotton, Esq*, 3rd ed. (London: J. Walthoe, R. Wilkin, J. and J. Bonwicke, S. Birt, T. Ward and E. Wicksteed, 1734). *ECCO.*

15 Edward Young, *The Complaint: or, Night-Thoughts on Life, Death, and Immortality*, new ed. (London: A. Millar, and R. and J. Dodsley, 1755). There was another edition printed in 1755 that does not list either the place of publication or give any information on the printer or bookseller. *ECCO.*

16 [Alexander MacBean], *A Dictionary of the Bible; or, An Explanation of the Proper Names and Difficult Words in the Old and New Testament* (London: J. Newbery, 1766). *ECCO.*

17 John Ward, *Seasonable Advice to those who are in Strength and Health, Frequently to Think upon Death and Judgment* (London: Freeman Collins, 1701). *ECCO.*

18 William Melmoth, *The Great Importance of a Religious Life Considered*, 28th ed. (London: J. F. and C. Rivington, et al., 1790). *ECCO.*

19 Demosthenes, *Several Orations of Demosthenes, to Encourage the Athenians to Oppose the Exorbitant Power of Philip of Macedon* (London: Jacob Tonson, 1702). *ECCO.*

20 Henry Stebbing, *The Instructions of a Parish Minister to his Parishioners, on the Subject of Popery* (2 vols., London: C. Davis, 1753). *ECCO.*

21 Lemuel Gulliver [Jonathan Swift], *Travels into Several Remote Nations of the World* (Edinburgh: W. Gray junior, 1752). *ECCO.*

22 [John Eachard], *The Grounds & Occasions of the Contempt of the Clergy and Religion Enquired Into* (London: N. Brooke, 1670). *ECCO.*

23 Sy. [Simon] Patrick, *The Devout Christian Instructed how to Pray and Give Thanks to God: or, A Book of Devotions for Families, and for Particular Persons, in Most of the Concerns of Humane Life* (London: B. Aylmer, R. Bonwicke, W. Rogers, C. Brome, J. Nicholson, J. and B. Sprine, T. Chapman, M. Atkins, and W. Carter, 1711). *ECCO.*

24 The Fort-Royal of the Scriptures or a Vade Mecum Concordance edin[24] 1732
25 Mortons Threefold State of Man[25] 1629
26 Book of Common Prayer[26] 1743
27 Priors Poem's 3 Vol[27] 1733
28 Thos Bankers Sure Guide[28] 1768
29 Comes Commercii or Traders Companion[29] 1766
30 Tablet of Memory excised[30] 1783

[*f.* *22r*]

31 Spectators 8 Vol[31] 1744
32 Tatler 4 Vol[32] 1749
33 Guardian 2 Vol[33] 1745
34 Francis Horace 4 Vol[34] 1750
35 Fordyces Sermons to Young Women 2 Vol[35] 1767

---

24 John Hart, *The Fort-Royal of the Scriptures; or, A Vade-Mecum Concordance*, 3rd ed. (Edinburgh: J. Trail, W. Millar, and Al. Millar, 1732). *ECCO*.

25 Tho[mas] Morton, *A Treatise of the Three-Fold State of Man. Or, An Anatomie of the Soule* London: Rob: Davvlman, 1629). *EEBO*.

26 Church of England, *The Book of Common Prayer, and Administration of the Sacraments, and other Rites and Ceremonies of the Church, According to the Use of the Church of England* (Cambridge: Joseph Bentham and Charles Bathurst, 1743). *ECCO*. In 1743 there was also an Oxford edition printed by Thomas and Robert Baskett. *ECCO*.

27 ? Matthew Prior, *Poems on Several Occasions*, 3rd ed. (3 vols., London: S. Birt and W. Feales, 1734). *ECCO*.

28 S. Thomas, *The Banker's Sure Guide: or, Monied Man's Assistant*, 2nd ed. (London: G. Robinson, J. Roberts, and T. Slack in Newcastle, 1768). *ECCO*.

29 Edward Hatton, *Comes Commercii, or, The Trader's Companion*, 12th ed. (London: H. Woodfall et al., 1766). *ECCO*.

30 [Philip Luckhome], *The Tablet of Memory, Shewing every Memorable Event in History, from the Earliest Period to the Year 1783*, 5th ed. (London: G. Robinson, 1783) *ECCO*.

31 [Joseph Addison and Richard Steele], *The Spectator*, 8 vols (London: J. and R. Tonson, 1744). *ECCO*.

32 [Joseph Addison and Richard Steele], *The Tatler or The Lucubrations of Isaac Bickerstaff, Esq* (London: H. Lintot et al., 1749). *ECCO*.

33 [Joseph Addison and Richard Steele], *The Guardian* (2 vols., London: J. and R. Tonson and S. Draper, 1745). *ECCO*.

34 Horace, *A Poetical Translation of the Works of Horace*, trans. Philip Francis, 4th ed. (4 vols., London: A. Millar, 1750) *ECCO*.

35 James Fordyce, *Sermons to Young Women*, 4th ed. (2 vols., London: A. Millar, T. Cadell, J. Dodsley, J. Payne, 1767). *ECCO*. There were also Dublin printings advertised as sixth and seventh editions, both sold by J. Williams. *ECCO*.

36	Hamway on the Lords Supper[36]	1782
37	Goldsmiths Essays[37]	1765
38	Webb on Poetry & Painting[38]	
39	Grove on the Lords Supper[39]	1741
40	Tibullus translated by Grainger 2 Vol[40]	1789
41	Salmons English Peerage[41]	1758
42	Rochefoucalts Moral Maxims[42]	1749
43	Labbe Eruditu Pronuntiationes Catholica Indices neat[43]	1751
44	Malhams Schoolmasters Companion[44]	1783
45	Perrys English Dictionary[45]	1778
46	Thoughts on the Manners of the Great Sewed[46]	1788

36 *The New Week's Preparation for a Worthy Receiving of the Lord's Supper, as Recommended and Appointed by the Church of England With Forms of Examination*, 37th ed. (London: Printed from the edition of the late Edwd. Wicksteed, 1782). *ECCO*. It is not clear why 'Hamway' appears in the catalogue.

37 [Oliver] Goldsmith, *Essays* (London: W. Griffin, 1765). *ECCO*.

38 Daniel Webb, *Observations on the Correspondence between Poetry and Music* (Dublin: Printed for James Williams, at No. 5, in Skinner-Row, 1769). *ECCO*. A London edition printed for J. Dodsley appeared in 1769 but this was an octavo so Pratt likely had the Dublin duodecimo edition. *ECCO*.

39 Henry Grove, *A Discourse Concerning the Nature and Design of the Lord's Supper* (London: John Wilson, 1741). *ECCO*.

40 ? Tibullus, *A Poetical Translation of the Elegies of Tibullus; and of the Poems of Sulpicia*, trans. James Grainger (2 vols., London: A. Millar, 1759). *ECCO*.

41 Nathaniel Salmon, *A Short View of the Families of the Present English Nobility*, 2nd ed. (London: William Owen, 1758). *ECCO*.

42 [François de] La Rochefoucault, *Moral Maxims* (London: A. Millar, 1749). BLPC.

43 Philippe Labbe, *Eruditæ Pronuntiationis Catholici Indices*, ed. Edward Leeds (London: Impensis J. & J. Rivington, 1751). *ECCO*.

44 ? D[aniel] Fenning, *The Schoolmaster's Most Useful Companion, and Scholar's Best Instructor in the Knowledge of Arithmetic* (London: S. Crowder, 1765). There was a second London edition printed in 1768 and a third London edition printed in 1775, also sold by S. Crowder. *ECCO*. We could not find a *Schoolmaster's Companion* authored by a Malham.

45 William Perry, *The Royal Standard English Dictionary*, 2nd ed. (Edinburgh: Printed by and for the Author, and sold at his Printing Office there; also by J. Wilkie, T. Evans, C. Elliot, W. Charnley, and C. Etherington, 1778). UCL.

46 [Hannah More], *Thoughts on the Importance of the Manners of the Great to General Society*, 2nd ed. (Dublin: P. Byrne, 1788). *ECCO*. There was also a third, fourth, and fifth Dublin duodecimo editions all sold by P. Byrne. There were second, third, and fourth London editions printed in 1788 and all sold by T. Cadell but these were octavos, so Pratt likely had a Dublin edition.

Select Bibliography

MANUSCRIPT SOURCES

Cambridge University Libraries

Cambridge University Library, MS Add. 9457, William Manning, Journal of Tours, England, 1744–45

Gonville and Caius College, GOV/02/01/02, Pandectae, 1658–1821

King's Lynn Borough Archives

King's Lynn, Court Record of 9 October 1773, KL/C20/3 (Microfilm in the Norfolk Record Office)

The National Archives

PROB 11/1213/231 Last Will and Testament of the Reverend Jermyn Pratt

Norfolk Record Office (NRO)

ANF 12/15/145 Marriage licence bond: Thurlow Stafford and Henrietta Pratt, 18 September 1752

ANW 24/47/170 Marriage license bond: William Clagett and Mary Stanforth, 5 January 1773

BUL 8/10, 614X8 Tenant receipt and expenditure accounts of Jermyn Pratt for estates in Denver, Roydon, Fordham etc., 1739–79

DN/VIS 27a/8 Visitation Questions: Fincham 1777

DN/VIS 30/3 Visitation Questions: Fincham 1784

PD 66/3 Parish Records of St Michael at Plea, Norwich: Baptisms and Burials 1743–1811

PD 464/1 Parish Records of Ryston with Roxham: Baptisms and Marriages 1687–1776

PRA 328-329, 378X9 Lease and release. Roger Pratt of Ryston, Esq., to Jermyn Pratt of Stoke Ferry, clerk, his son, for life, 1758

PRA 519-520, 381X7 Marriage articles of Revd Jermyn Pratt of Downham Market, clerk, and Anne eldest daughter of Mary Stanforth of Salthouse, widow, 3 July 1753

PRA 664 Folder of papers of Revd Jermyn Pratt, 1684–1795

WKC 7/56/7, 404X3 Miscellaneous letters to William Windham and papers relating to him, 1717–61

PRINTED PRIMARY SOURCES

Bury and Norwich Post
Cambridge Chronicle
Ipswich Journal
Norfolk Chronicle
Norwich Mercury

Memoirs of the Life and Writings of R-ch--d G-rd-nr, Esq. (London & Norwich, 1782)

The Contest, or, A Collection of the Most Material Papers, in Prose and Verse, Published during the Controverted Election for the County of Norfolk in 1768 (London, 1768)

L. Bagot, *A Charge Delivered to the Clergy at the Primary Visitation of Lewis, Lord Bishop of Norfolk 1784* (Norwich, 1784)

Gentleman of the Inner-Temple, and a Native of the Diocese of Norwich, *A Description of the Diocese of Norwich: or, The Present State of Norfolk and Suffolk* (London, 1785)

F. de La Rochefoucauld, *A Frenchman's Year in Suffolk*, ed. and trans. Norman Scarfe (Woodbridge, 1784)

[J. Pratt], *The Inundation, or The Life of a Fen-Man* (King's Lynn, 1771)

[J. Pratt], *The Coal-Heavers, A Mock Heroic Poem* (King's Lynn, 1774)

[J. Pratt], *September, a Rural Poem* (King's Lynn, 1780)

H. Repton and M. Armstrong, *The History and Antiquities of the County of Norfolk* (10 vols. Norwich, 1781)

C. Smart, *The Poetical Works of Christopher Smart*, ed. K. Williamson et al. (6 vols. Oxford, 1980–96)

C. Smart, *The Annotated Letters of Christopher Smart*, eds B. Rizzo and R. Mahony (Carbondale, 1991)

J. Woodforde, *The Diary of a Country Parson*, ed. J. Beresford (5 vols. Oxford, 1924–31)

P. Yonge, *The Charge of the Reverend Father in God, Philip, Bishop of Norwich, Delivered to the Clergy of his Diocese, at his Primary Visitation, A.D. 1763* (Norwich, 1763)

SECONDARY WORKS

D. Alff, *The Wreckage of Intentions: Projects in British Culture, 1660–1730* (Philadelphia, 2017)

E. H. Ash, *The Draining of the Fens: Projectors, Popular Politics, and State Building in Early Modern England* (Baltimore, 2017)

G. Barnes and T. Williamson, *Rethinking Ancient Woodland: The Archaeology and History of Woods in Norfolk* (Hatfield, 2015)

M. and C. Blackwell, *Norwich Theatre Royal: The First 250 Years* (Norwich, 2007)

J. E. Bradley, *Popular Politics and the American Revolution in England* (Macon G.A., 1986)

S. Conway, *The British Isles and the War of American Independence* (Oxford, 2000)

P. J. Corfield, *Towns, Trade, Religion, and Radicalism: The Norwich Perspective on English History* (Norwich, 1980)

M. J. Ezell, *Social Authorship and the Advent of Print* (Baltimore, 1999)

J. F. Fone, 'The Stoke Ferry Turnpike', *Norfolk Archaeology* 38 (1981), pp. 195–202

R. Forby, *The Vocabulary of East Anglia* (2 vols. London, 1830)

J. Gascoigne, *Cambridge in the Age of the Enlightenment* (Cambridge, 1989)

R. T. Gunther, ed., *The Architecture of Sir Roger Pratt, Charles II's Commissioner for the Rebuilding of London After the Great Fire: Now Printed for the First Time from His Note-books* (Oxford, 1928)

C. Harvey, *The History of the 4th Battalion Norfolk Regiment (Late East Norfolk Militia)* (London, 1899)

W. M. Jacob, 'A Practice of a Very Hurtful Tendency', in Derek Baker, ed., *The Church in Town and Countryside* (Oxford, 1979), pp. 316–26

W. M. Jacob, *The Clerical Profession in the Long Eighteenth Century 1680–1840* (Oxford, 2007)

E. C. Le Grice, *New Theatre Royal Norwich: Its Past History and Present Story* (Norwich, 1947)

M. McCormack, *Embodying the Militia in Georgian England* (Oxford, 2015)

R. Maguire, *Africans in East Anglia, 1467–1833* (Woodbridge, 2021)

V. Morgan, *A History of the University of Cambridge, Volume II: 1546–1750* (Cambridge, 2004)

C. Mounsey, *Christopher Smart: Clown of God* (Lewisburg, 2001)

N. Riches, *The Agricultural Revolution in Norfolk* (2nd edn. London, 1967)

N. Rogers, *Whigs and Cities: Popular Politics in the Age of Walpole and Pitt* (Oxford, 1989)

G. Rudé, *Wilkes and Liberty: A Social Study of 1763 to 1774* (Oxford, 1962)

H. G. Sampson, *The Anglican Tradition in Eighteenth-Century Verse* (The Hague, 1971)

A. Santesso, 'Poetry and the Public School', *Eighteenth-Century Life*, 32 (2008), pp. 57–80

B. A. Schellenberg, *Literary Coteries and the Making of Modern Print Culture: 1740–1790* (Cambridge, 2016)

J. Sorensen, *Strange Vernaculars: How Eighteenth-Century Slang, Cant, Provincial Languages, and Nautical Jargon Became English* (Princeton, 2017)

J. Stobart, 'Genteel or Respectable? The Material Culture of Rural Clergy in Late Georgian England', in J. Eales and B. Tjerngren, eds. (Cardiff, 2021)

N. Sykes, *Church and State in England in the 18th Century* (Cambridge, 1934)

P. Virgin, *The Church in an Age of Negligence: Ecclesiastical Structure and Problems of Church Reform 1700–1840* (Cambridge, 1989)

J. R. Western, *The English Militia in the Eighteenth Century: The Story of a Political Issue 1660–1802* (London, 1965)

C. Wigston Smith, *Women Work and Clothes in the Eighteenth-Century Novel* (Cambridge, 2013)

K. Wilson, *The Sense of the People: Politics, Culture and Imperialism in England, 1715–1785* (Cambridge, 1995)

F. Wood, 'Fuelling the Local Economy: The Fenland Coal Trade, 1760–1850', in K. Bruland and P. O'Brien, eds., *From Family Firms to Corporate Capitalism: Essays in Business and Industrial History* (Oxford, 1998), pp. 199–215

C. Wordsworth, *Social Life at the Universities in the Eighteenth Century* (Cambridge, 2009, rpt. from 1874)

UNPUBLISHED THESES

J. M. Barney, 'The Merchants and Maritime Trade of King's Lynn in the Eighteenth Century' (University of East Anglia, PhD thesis, 1997)

B. D. Hayes, 'Politics in Norfolk, 1750–1832' (University of Cambridge, PhD thesis, 1958)

W. M. Jacob, 'Clergy and Society in Norfolk 1707–1806' (University of Exeter, PhD thesis, 1982)

Index